HOW TO PRINT

THE ULTIMATE GUIDE TO ACHIEVING THE PERFECT PHOTOGRAPHIC PRINT

GLYN DEWIS

HOW TO PRINT

THE ULTIMATE GUIDE TO ACHIEVING THE PERFECT PHOTOGRAPHIC PRINT

Glyn Dewis
glyndewis.com

Editor: Jocelyn Howell
Project manager: Lisa Brazieal
Marketing manager: Koryn Olage
Interior design, layout, and type: Anthony Paular Design
Cover design: Dave Clayton

ISBN: 979-888814-419-0
1st Edition (1st printing)
© 2026 Glyn Dewis
All images © Glyn Dewis

Rocky Nook Inc.
1010 B Street, Suite 350
San Rafael, CA 94901
USA
www.rockynook.com
info@rockynook.com
(415) 747-8756

Represented in the E.U. by:
Rheinwerk Verlag GmbH
Rheinwerkallee 4
53227 Bonn
Germany
service@rheinwerk-verlag.de

Distributed in the UK and Europe by Publishers Group UK
Distributed in the U.S. and all other territories by Publishers Group West

Library of Congress Control Number: 2025936872

This book is printed on acid-free paper.
Printed in United Arab Emirates

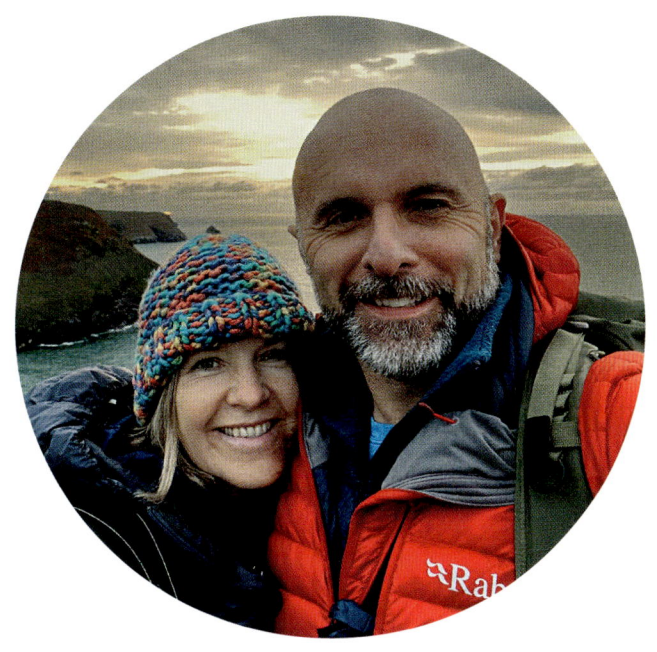

For Anne

Thank you for believing in me, always and without question. x

ACKNOWLEDGMENTS

Putting together this book and the video course that it originates from has been one heck of an adventure, and like most good adventures, I haven't done it alone.

Along the way, I've been lucky to have the support of some truly wonderful people who offered encouragement and unwavering support, listened patiently, and made me laugh when I needed it most.

To everyone who's helped in big ways or small, whether through advice, friendship, honest feedback, or just being there with a coffee and a good chat … thank you. Your support has kept me moving forward, and I'm incredibly grateful to have had you in my corner as this project came to life.

My Wife, Anne: Thank you for your love, patience, and encouragement through every step of this journey. Your belief in me means everything.

Anthony Crothers: Thank you for your friendship, sharp eye, and honest advice. Always ready to lend a hand, your support has meant a great deal throughout this process; 'bout time for another Road Trip, I reckon!

Ian Munro, Anthony Crothers, Brian Dukes, Gerwyn "Gez" Williams, and Simon "Foxy" Fowler: You guys are the BEST! What we have is something very special and unique. It's more than friendship, it's family. No matter the time, no matter the place … if you needed me, I'd be there!

Steve Healy: Proud to have you as a friend. I love our chats and I'm always looking forward to our next outing, but if memory serves me correctly … breakfast is on you next, right?

Dave Clayton: The Design-meister Strikes Again! A new book just wouldn't be the same without some of that Clayton Magic. We don't get to hang out as often these days, but when we do it's like it was only yesterday. Bring on the next time!

Krishen "Krish" Nagar: You're a Top Man and a treasured friend. Always good to spend time with you. Can't thank you enough for the support.

Brian Matiash: Truly one of life's good people! Blessed to have you as a friend. Your high standards and product knowledge is nothing short of inspiring. I so look forward to some quality time hanging out.

Mark Baber: I've said it before, but the more time goes on, the longer we're friends, the more we work together … the more it's reinforced. You set the standard, in both work life and in personal life. Blessed to have you as a friend.

Lee Churchill: So glad we're getting to know each other more because it's so clear to see the great person that you are. You've a big heart and admirable values and those lucky enough to know you are truly blessed.

Calvin Hollywood: You the man! This industry introduced us and made us friends and now all these years later I'm more excited than ever with what we're working on. Can't thank you enough for your advice, wisdom, and friendship. Great times ahead!

Scott Kelby: Guv'nor ... I'll never forget the trust you had in me all those years ago. One phone call that put me on a path and changed everything. I'll be forever thankful.

Dave Cross: There are certain people without whom I wouldn't be doing and loving what I do each and every day, and be able to live the life I do. You are one of those people and I'll never be able to thank you enough.

Joel and Amy Grimes: I/we treasure your friendship. Two of the most genuine, good-hearted people that we are so grateful to have in our lives. Thank you for the constant support, inspiration, and encouragement.

Katrin Eismann: Learning from you when I first started out and getting to know and work with you over the years still feels a little surreal. I think I'll always feel that way, but please know that I am so incredibly grateful for the help you give and for you being "in my corner."

Dr. Chris Bai (BenQ): I'm so incredibly thankful to you for your willingness to share your knowledge and educate me in the world of color and color management. This book simply wouldn't have been possible without your support.

Vicente Lochschmidt (BenQ): It's a pleasure to know you and to work with you. Your tireless support and trust means so much. I can't thank you enough and neither can I thank the team at BenQ enough for reaching out and enabling me to do what I do because of such wonderful technology.

Brandon Heiss (FJ Westcott): Thank you for everything you do that makes it possible for me to do what I do. The best of products and the best of people!

Stewart Wood: Each and every one of us has "things" to deal with on a day-to-day basis, some more debilitating than others, but seeing you face things head on and push through is inspiring! I'm super proud to see how far you've come and am so excited for what's in store.

Scott Cowlin, Ted Waitt, and all at Rocky Nook: You guys are the BEST! There's no one else I would want to write a book with, because that's exactly how it feels ... "with." Can't wait to hang out again!

Jocelyn Howell (my editor at Rocky Nook): You deserve a medal for sifting through the words I write and making this, and my other books, a reality. Thank you so much.

PermaJet: Great people and a great product that makes the final step of the creative process such a thrill. Always enjoy working with you.

Dominic Gurney (Epson UK): Your advice, knowledge, and support have played such a big part in bringing this book and video course together. Thank you so much.

Trevor Williams (West Street Picture Framing, Axminster): Thank you so much for giving up your time to help and contribute to this book. It's VERY much appreciated.

Digitalab: The BEST printing lab and the BEST people in the industry! Says it all.

Town Mill Bakery, Lyme Regis: How could I not mention Town Mill Bakery??? My second office and the BEST place to grab coffee, breakfast, and lunch in Lyme Regis. Great people. Great food. Great place. Thank you Sarah, Jeremy, Charlie, and all.

CONTENTS

FOREWORD   X

INTRODUCTION   XIII

CHAPTER 1
HARDWARE   1

Choosing a Printer 2

Why You Should Avoid AirPrint for Serious Photo Printing on a Mac 4

OEM vs. Third-Party Inks: What You Need to Know 6

Choosing the Right Display for Photography and Printing 8

CHAPTER 2
DISPLAY CALIBRATION   17

The Real Issue Behind Dark Prints 17

Hardware You'll Need to Calibrate Your Display 18

My Calibration Setup 19

Calibrating the BenQ SW272U: My Display Settings for Photography
and Everyday Use 19

Software Calibration with Calibrite Profiler 31

Final Notes on Calibration and Everyday Use 36

CHAPTER 3
PRINTER QUALITY / HEALTH CHECK   39

Evaluation/Test Prints: Canon and Epson 40

Confirming Printer Accuracy and Why ICC Profiles Still Matter 46

Print an Image on Canon Using Luster Paper 47

The Final Print and a Word About Paper 51

Turning Off Color Management in the Printer Driver 52

CHAPTER 4
PRINTING A BLACK-AND-WHITE IMAGE   57

Printer Settings 59

Layout Settings 64

Color Settings 65

Black Point Compensation and Rendering Intent 66

Final Print Result 67

CHAPTER 5
PRINTING A COLOR IMAGE 69

Choosing Paper and Printer Settings 70

Using an ICC Profile 71

What Are ICC Profiles? 72

Printing with ICC Profiles in Lightroom (on macOS) 74

Printing Onto Third-Party Papers 76

Creating Custom ICC Profiles with PermaJet 80

Creating Your Own ICC Profiles 83

Installing ICC Profiles 88

Understanding Rendering Intent 89

Black Point Compensation (BPC) 91

Compatibility with Rendering Intent 93

CHAPTER 6
COLOR SPACE 95

Common Color Spaces 95

A Conversation with a Color Scientist Dr. Chris Bai 101

My Preferred Color Space Preferences and Workflow 103

CHAPTER 7
RESOLUTION AND RESIZING 107

Pixels, Dots, and Print Quality 107

Native Printer Resolution 108

Matching Image and Printer Resolutions 108

Determining Maximum Print Size from Image Resolution 109

How Image Size Affects Resolution 112

Maintaining Resolution When Resizing 114

Choosing the Right Resampling Method 114

Cropping Images Without Losing Control Over Quality 118

Enlarging Images for Print 123

CHAPTER 8

SHARPENING   131

Sharpening for Print: What, When, and How 131

What Sharpening Actually Is. 133

Real-World Example: A Portrait of Nathan 134

A Note on Paper and Printer Settings. 138

Why I Recommend Sharpening After Resizing 138

Final Thoughts on Sharpening Workflow. 139

CHAPTER 9

SOFT PROOFING   141

Simulate Paper and Ink: Useful or Gimmick?. 142

Printing as a Creative Process 142

Case Study 1: Soft Proofing and Printing a Portrait. 143

Case Study 2: Soft Proofing and Printing a High-Contrast Black-and-White Image . .148

Case Study 3: Soft Proofing and Printing with Photoshop 154

Final Thoughts on Simulate Paper and Ink 162

CHAPTER 10

PAPER   165

Paper Terminology Explained. 166

Matching Paper to Image: A Conversation on Print Choice with Colin Hulley. 167

When and Why to Use Protective Print Sprays on Matte Papers. 174

How Paper Choice Influences the Final Print 175

CHAPTER 11

PRINTING SOFTWARE   179

Printing a Color Image from Photoshop. 180

Printing a Black-and-White Image from Photoshop 183

Printing a Color Image from Lightroom Classic. 184

Printing a Black-and-White Image from Lightroom Classic 189

Printing a Color Image with Epson Print Layout 192

Printing a Black-and-White Image with Epson Print Layout. 194

Printing a Color Image with Canon Professional Print & Layout. 198

Printing a Black-and-White Image with Canon Professional Print & Layout 202

Printing with Qimage One: A Powerful, Cross-Platform Solution 204

Black-and-White Printing with Qimage One. 208

Printing with ON1 Photo RAW: A First-Time Experience 210

Black-and-White Printing with ON1 Photo RAW. 213

CHAPTER 12

COMPLETE PRINTING WORKFLOW 217

Downloading ICC Profiles. 219

Installing ICC Profiles. 220

Preparing the Black-and-White Image in Lightroom. 220

Printing with Epson Print Layout 226

Preparing the Color Portrait in Lightroom 228

Printing with Canon Professional Print Software. 232

CHAPTER 13

USING A PRINTING LAB 235

Understanding Color Space: Why Labs Ask for sRGB 236

Preparing an Image for Printing at a Lab 237

CHAPTER 14

EXTRA LEARNING 247

Dominic Gurney—Epson UK. 247

CHAPTER 15

MOUNTING & PRESENTING PRINTS 261

Mounting a Print to a Backing Board 262

Confidence and Care in the Mounting Process. 265

Using a Bevel Mount and Choosing the Right Presentation. 265

Common Framing Challenges and Best Practices 267

INDEX 270

FOREWORD

Photographers constantly move between their response to the physical world and their interpretation of how it appears in a photograph. Every time we use our camera, we make numerous technical decisions that affect the final interpretation of the image. When pressing the shutter, we decide whether to show critical sharpness or softness of focus. Do we freeze motion or use long exposures to blur the image? Is a telephoto or a wide-angle lens the better tool? These choices reveal how engaged we are in capturing fleeting moments of discovery, light, and wonder.

In composing a scene, we are saying, "What is inside the frame is more important than what is outside the frame." We may use formal "rules of composition" or a casual snapshot approach, but the image will not only reveal what we are experiencing and seeing, but also how we feel about the subject. Seeing is a primal recognition of the here and now, and most importantly, of oneself. We photograph to explore not only what is outside but also what is within us. We photograph to understand ourselves and the world around us. We choose to share our images with family, friends, and often in public forums with people we will never meet.

Photography challenges us to be aware and make critical decisions about the subject and environment, as well as the optics and light, and position and composition. For some, it's a profession, and for many, it's a rewarding hobby that draws us out of bed in the pre-dawn hours to explore new techniques, travel to distant lands, or experience new cultures. Even before we return, it's impossible to put off scrolling through the images, downloading them, and dedicating care and time to editing the very best ones. But just as the glimmer of the screen draws us in, the image remains tangibly just out of our reach, with nothing to hold.

Before the advent of digital technology, photographers devoted a considerable amount of time to the darkroom. Making a print was a mysterious dance, involving exposure, filtration, paper grades, chemicals, dodging, and burning, among other techniques. This was a physical and hands-on process of handling paper, focusing the enlarger, and adjusting the paper easel to determine the final crop. Then, moving from the dry side of the darkroom to the wet side, the greatest reward was, under a dim red light, seeing the latent image slowly appear in the gently rocked developer tray. The traditional process required many hours of concentrated attention to create the final photographic print.

Today, working on a computer or phone with your favorite imaging software can be just as magical as it was in the darkroom, with the added advantage that cleanup is so much easier. Viewing a work print that you made from your file is your moment to hold a tangible object and carefully consider the image, from shutter to edit to print. Make notes on this work print, circling areas you would like to improve; perhaps you need to remove dust or distractions, darken the edges, color correct the midtones, or add a bit of contrast. Make bold edit moves and then make another print to hold and study. The truth of an image is ultimately revealed when it is printed.

The following chapters will guide you through the equipment, techniques, and refined editing process of making digital photographic fine-art prints. Rather than being alone in a dimly lit darkroom, allow my friend Glyn Dewis to be your guide to complete the circle from the intangible to the tangible—from fleeting photons to an object that will be enjoyed, admired, held in your hand, viewed framed on a wall, or presented in a custom portfolio box.

I can think of no one more dedicated, generous, and talented than Glyn to be your guide on this journey of "How to Print." Allow the prints you make to speak to you; tape them onto a wall you pass by each day. Experiment with the sequence or scale of the prints to see how stories and relationships change. Living with your work will teach you about your photography, and learning from Glyn will teach you how to be a better artist.

Katrin Eismann
Artist & Educator
Adobe Lightroom, Senior Product Manager for Learning & Inspiration

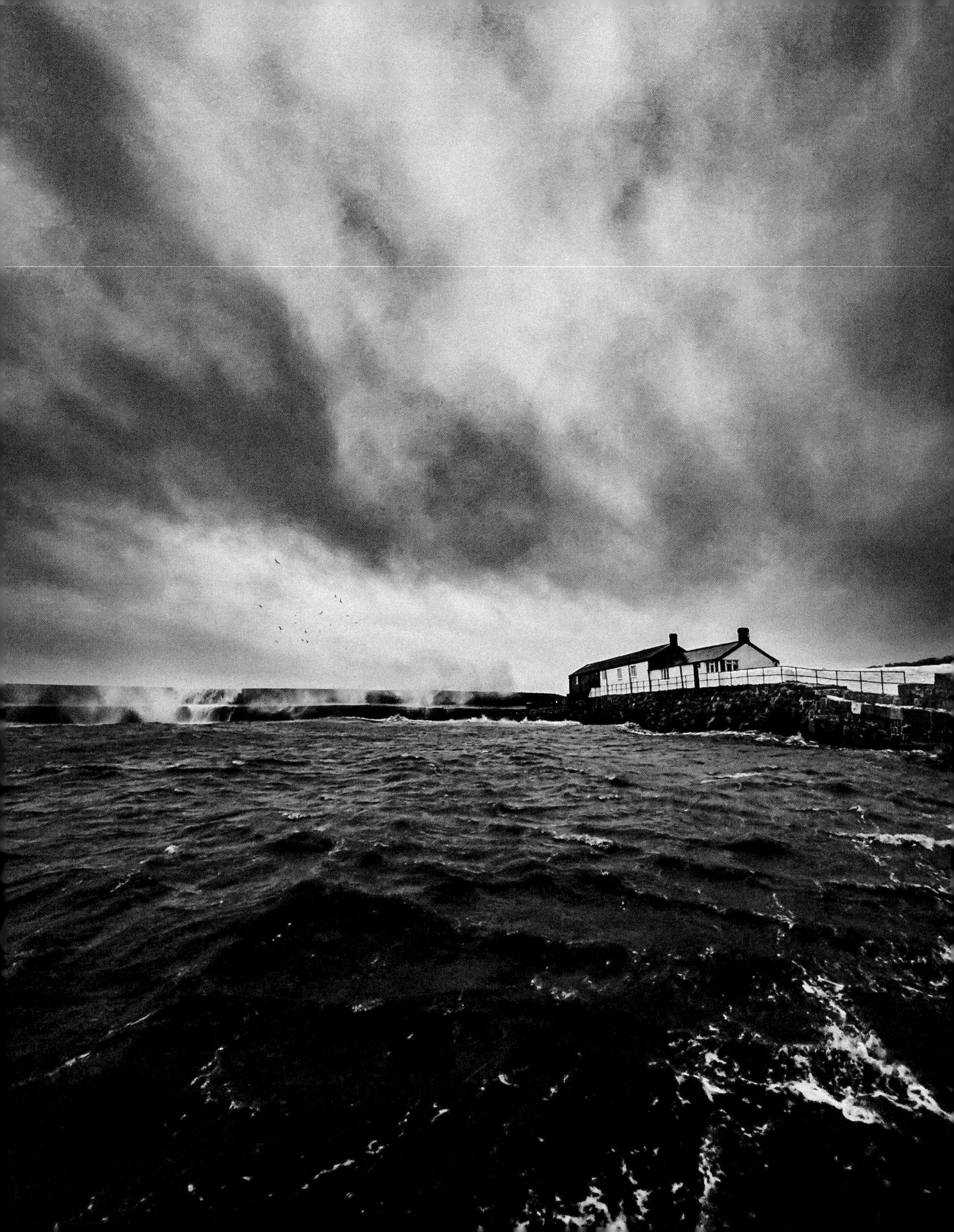

INTRODUCTION

There's something magical about holding a photograph in your hands, something that no digital screen, no matter how advanced, can replicate. Yet for years I avoided printing altogether, frustrated by the disconnect between what I saw on my monitor and what emerged from my printer. Every print felt like a gamble, and more often than not, I lost.

Like many photographers, I eventually gave up. I retreated to the safety of digital displays and outsourced my printing to labs. However, I always felt like something was missing. I wasn't seeing the process through from start to finish. The final step, the moment when light becomes tangible, was happening without me.

Years later, I returned to printing with fresh determination. I studied color management and slowly began to understand the alchemy that transforms pixels into prints. The breakthrough came gradually, then all at once. Suddenly, I could press "print" with confidence, knowing that what would emerge from my printer would be what I wanted and expected … not an unwelcome surprise.

This mastery changed everything. Printing didn't just complete my photographs, it completed me as a photographer. It slowed me down in the best possible way, forcing me to be more deliberate with my captures and more thoughtful in my editing. Each image had to earn its place on paper, and this higher bar elevated my entire body of work.

More than that, dare I say, printing made me feel like an artist, seeing through the full creative journey from concept through capture, edit, and finally to print. I was no longer just taking pictures; I was creating something tangible.

There's an intimacy to printed photographs that screens simply cannot match. Watch someone receive a print of themselves or a moment they treasure: They don't just look at it, they experience it. They hold it close to study the details, then at arm's length to take in the whole. They turn it toward the light, show it to others, carry it with them. It becomes an object with weight, texture, and presence.

Digital images, for all their convenience and brilliance, remain ephemeral. They flicker on screens and disappear with the swipe of a finger, but a print endures. It occupies space. It demands attention. It creates connection.

This is why I believe every photographer, whether professional or passionate amateur, should embrace printing. It's not just about having physical copies of your work; it's about completing the creative process, understanding your craft more deeply, and creating something genuinely meaningful in an increasingly digital world ... which I have to add, I love and fully embrace.

Printing has fundamentally changed me as a photographer. It has taught me patience, attention to detail, and the value of slowing down in our increasingly fast-paced digital world. The process of moving from capture through post-processing to physical print has deepened my appreciation for every aspect of photography. When you hold a print of your own work, one that matches your vision perfectly, you'll understand what I mean. There's something profound about transforming light and pixels into a tangible object that can be held, shared, and preserved. This transformation doesn't just complete the photographic process; it completes the photographer.

Printing forces you to be more deliberate with your captures, more thoughtful in your editing, and more intentional with your creative choices. It raises the bar for your entire body of work because not every image deserves the investment of ink and paper.

Ultimately, printing elevates your photography because, as my friend Katrin Eismann says, *"The truth is revealed when the ink hits the paper."*

The journey from monitor to print doesn't have to be the frustrating experience I once knew. With the right knowledge and approach, it becomes one of the most rewarding aspects of photography, and this book will guide you through that journey, ensuring that your first print and every one after matches your vision perfectly.

In the end, photography isn't just about capturing light; it's about giving that light physical form, creating something that can be held, treasured, and passed on. And nothing in the digital realm comes close to that feeling.

THE *HOW TO PRINT* BOOK AND HOW TO USE IT

Thank you for purchasing this book, a book that represents not just my own evolution as a photographer, but the collective wisdom of countless photographers who shared their questions, challenges, and aspirations along the way.

What you have in your hands is just the beginning, because this book is designed to grow with you and the ever-evolving world of photographic printing through the accompanying website **www.thehowtoprintbook.com**, where you'll find resources and videos that will be updated over time when necessary to cover new techniques and emerging technologies.

While I work primarily on Mac systems, I understand that photographers use diverse setups. Throughout this book, you'll find dedicated sections showing Windows-specific workflows wherever possible. This isn't just a Mac book or a PC book, it's a Photographer's book, regardless of your chosen platform.

Similarly, I've incorporated both Canon and Epson printer systems, giving you exposure to the two most popular professional printing platforms. You'll see me navigate both software environments, helping you understand the nuances and capabilities of each system. This dual approach ensures that whether you're starting fresh or working with existing equipment, you'll find relevant, actionable guidance.

You'll notice that my printing workflow is deliberately systematic and methodical. This isn't by accident; it's the result of years of learning that when it comes to printing, leaving anything to chance can be costly. Every sheet of paper and every drop of ink represents both financial investment and creative opportunity.

The methodical approach I'll share with you eliminates guesswork and reduces waste while maximizing your chances of achieving exactly what you want.

However, this doesn't mean you need to replicate my workflow exactly. As you progress through the book, you'll naturally develop your own rhythm and preferences. The key is understanding the essential steps that cannot be skipped, the foundational elements that separate successful prints from expensive mistakes.

This book exists for one reason: to help you achieve consistently excellent prints that match your creative vision. Every lesson, every technique, and every troubleshooting tip has been included because it serves that fundamental goal.

I encourage you to engage with the material actively. Take notes, experiment with the techniques, and don't hesitate to reach out with questions or suggestions for future content.

The world of printing can seem complex and intimidating at first, but I promise you this: With the right knowledge and approach, it becomes one of the most rewarding aspects of photography. You're about to discover that the magic of seeing your vision come to life on paper is worth every moment invested in learning to do it right.

Enjoy the Process!
Glyn

glyndewis.com
youtube.com/glyndewis
photography-community.com
thehowtoprintbook.com

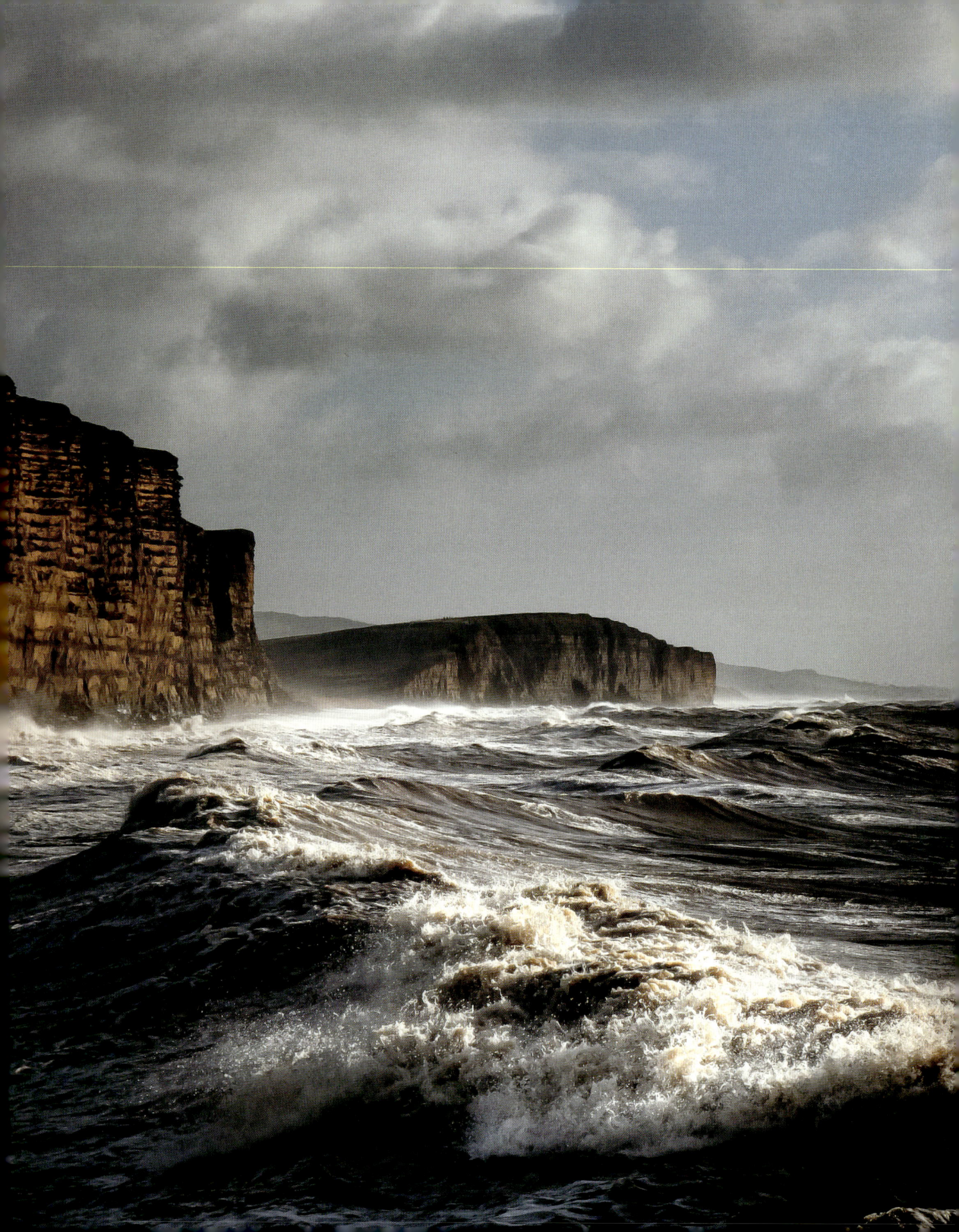

CHAPTER 1
HARDWARE

Before we dive into the process of printing our images, I thought it would be best to talk about hardware. By that I mean not only printers and monitors/displays, but also ink and HOW we connect our devices so that information is passed correctly between them. If that's not right, then no matter how methodical we are in terms of putting the ticks in all the right boxes, our prints won't turn out as we would hope.

To help with this, I spoke with a number of industry experts who have also contributed elsewhere throughout this book. For this chapter in particular, I have to thank Colin Hulley **(Figure 1.1)** from PermaJet (the brand of paper that I use most frequently and that you will see me using in this book), who has over forty years experience within the printing, paper, and ink industry, and Dr. Chris Bai **(Figure 1.2)**, Senior Color Expert at BenQ and Vice Chair of the ICC (International Color Consortium).

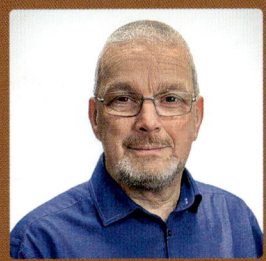

FIGURE 1.1: Colin Hulley

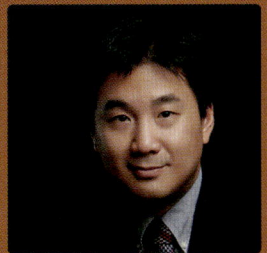

FIGURE 1.2: Dr. Chris Bai

CHOOSING A PRINTER

What follows is a summary of the conversation I had with Colin Hulley concerning printer choice. Although he talks mainly about Canon printers, what he says is also relevant to Epson and other brands who offer comparable printer models.

CHOOSING THE RIGHT PRINTER FOR HIGH-QUALITY PRINTS

When someone new to printing approaches me and says they want to start making high-quality prints, there are several key considerations I would walk them through before they buy a printer. It's not just about choosing a brand, it's about matching the printer to your needs, space, and goals.

1. BUDGET: THE STARTING POINT

The first and most important question is: **What's your budget?** This will immediately narrow down your options.

For example, in the Canon range:

- **Pro-200S:** Starts at around $500
- **Pro-310:** Around $900
- **Pro-1100:** Around $1,350
- **Canon PIXMA 8700 series:** Entry-level options like the 8720 can go as low as $220

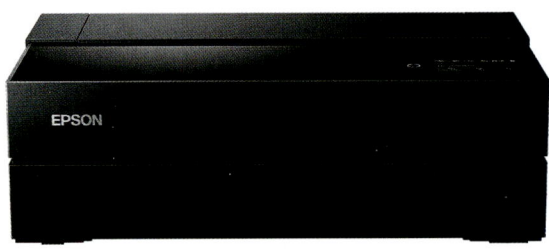

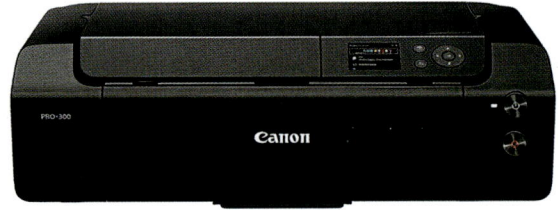

FIGURE 1.3: Epson SureColor SC-P900   **FIGURE 1.4:** Canon imagePROGRAF Pro-300

Keep in mind that while this list is Canon-specific, Epson and other brands offer comparable models in similar price ranges.

2. INTENDED USE: COLOR VERSUS BLACK AND WHITE

Next, it's important to consider the type of work you'll be doing. Are you printing mostly color images or black-and-white?

Lower-end printers typically have four to six ink cartridges. These may struggle to produce high-quality black-and-white images due to color casts. For consistent, neutral monochrome results, I recommend looking at printers with eight or more ink colors.

3. PHYSICAL SPACE: WILL IT FIT?

It might seem obvious, but space is often overlooked. Ask yourself: Where will you put the printer?

Some higher-end models are physically large, especially A2 printers like the Canon Pro-1100 or the Epson SC-P900. With a mount and frame, an A2 print becomes a substantial piece of wall art, and so does the machine that produces it.

For many people, an A3+ printer offers a good balance between size and capability: still capable of professional results, but more manageable in a home or studio.

4. SELLING YOUR WORK: PIGMENT VERSUS DYE-BASED INKS

Another major consideration is whether you plan to sell your prints. If so, I highly recommend a printer that uses pigment-based inks. These offer significantly better longevity compared to dye-based inks, which fade faster over time. With pigment inks, you can assure your buyers that your prints will last forty to fifty years or more, which is important for archival quality.

5. PRINT SIZE: A3+ OR A2?

Your desired maximum print size also plays a role. If you're planning to exhibit or sell larger prints, an A2 printer like the Canon Pro-1100 might be worth the investment. If you're focused on smaller fine art prints, an A3+ printer is often sufficient.

6. OPERATING COSTS: THE HIDDEN INVESTMENT

Finally, you need to consider the cost of ink and maintenance. Surprisingly, higher-end printers tend to have lower long-term costs.

Even though higher-end printers have larger cartridges and higher initial costs, they offer better value per milliliter and require fewer cartridge replacements. If you're doing regular printing, this can dramatically affect your return on investment.

For instance, if you buy a Pro-310 and add two full sets of ink, you've already spent nearly as much as a Pro-1100, but the Pro-1100 still has a lot more ink left to use. This illustrates how spending more upfront can actually save money over time.

SUMMARY: QUESTIONS TO ASK BEFORE YOU BUY

When helping someone choose a printer, I always guide them through the following questions:

1. What's your budget?

2. Are you printing in color, black-and-white, or both?

3. How much physical space do you have for the printer?

4. Are you planning to sell your prints?

5. What's the maximum print size you need?

6. How often will you print, and what are you willing to spend on ink over time?

These considerations help ensure that you choose the right printer for your goals, whether you're a hobbyist, professional photographer, or fine art printmaker.

Now let's talk about how to connect your printer to your computer, which is relevant for both Windows and Mac users, but Mac users have something else to be aware of …

WHY YOU SHOULD AVOID AIRPRINT FOR SERIOUS PHOTO PRINTING ON A MAC

When it comes to photo printing from a Mac, one of the most common and overlooked issues is the use of Apple's AirPrint driver, especially when connecting a printer via Wi-Fi. While convenient, AirPrint often limits the full functionality of professional photo printers, leading to subpar results and frustrating limitations. It's really more suited to printing documents, not photographs.

THE PROBLEM WITH AIRPRINT

By default, macOS prefers users to connect to printers wirelessly with AirPrint, a simplified driver intended for casual home printing. The issue is that this driver strips out many of the advanced features needed for high-quality photo output, resulting in reduced functionality.

AirPrint often:

- Offers only basic media options, such as "photo paper" or "plain paper," and removes access to important media types like Platinum Glossy, Semi-Gloss, Heavyweight Fine Art, etc.

- Can result in inaccurate color reproduction. Colors can appear in blocky or unsegregated form, a clear sign that the full printer driver isn't being used.

- Lacks detailed control over settings, which is essential for professionals aiming for consistency and archival-grade output.

THE SOLUTION: USE A WIRED CONNECTION

To unlock your printer's full potential on a Mac, our strong recommendation is to connect it via a USB or Ethernet cable.

Doing so allows you to:

- Use the manufacturer's dedicated driver, rather than AirPrint.
- Gain access to full media and print quality settings.
- Benefit from faster, more stable data transfer.
- Avoid common Wi-Fi issues like printer pauses and bandwidth bottlenecks.

REAL-WORLD EXAMPLE: THE DRYING LINE ISSUE

One major issue we've observed with wireless printing is what we call a drying line or dry down differential, a visible artifact that occurs when the printer pauses mid-job waiting for data to arrive over Wi-Fi **(Figure 1.5)**.

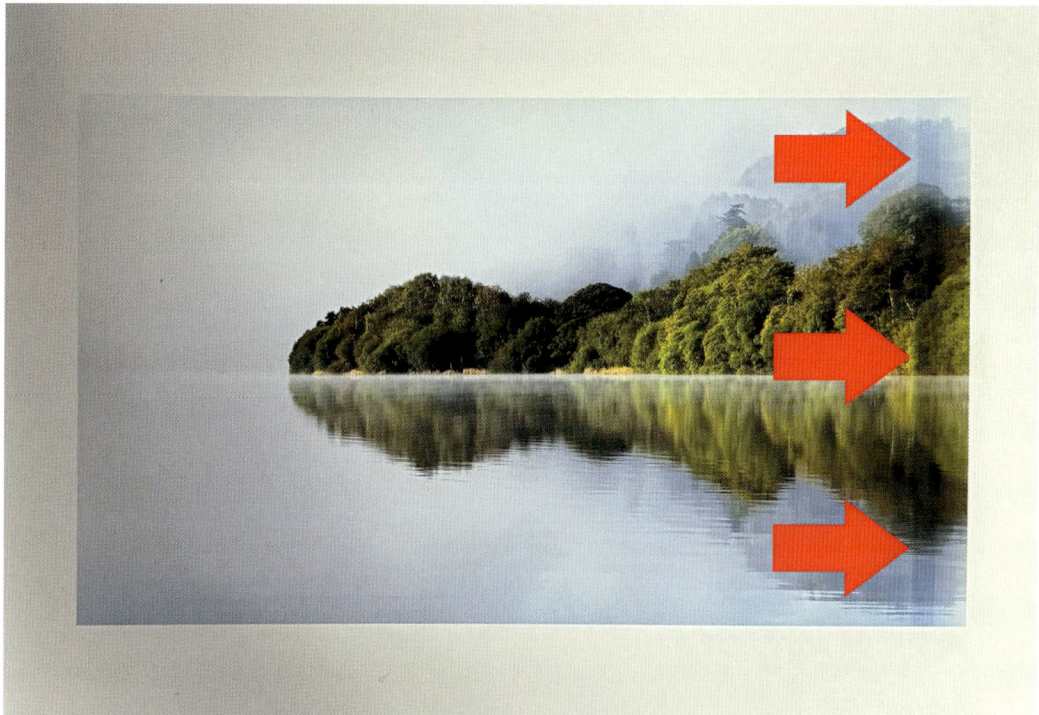

FIGURE 1.5

This type of error is almost entirely avoidable when using a wired connection. The steadier data stream prevents the printer from stalling or segmenting the job, especially on matte papers, which are more susceptible to uneven ink settling.

FINAL ADVICE: TWO ESSENTIAL TIPS FOR MAC USERS

If you're using a Mac and you care about quality printing, here are two non-negotiable tips:

1. Always use a wired connection (USB or Ethernet) to your printer, especially for professional or high-resolution work.

2. Avoid AirPrint when installing or configuring your printer. Take the extra steps to ensure the full manufacturer driver is used.

All this being said, if you do connect your printer wirelessly and find that you have no issues whatsoever, then stick with it if that's what you prefer. However, be aware that depending on the image you're printing, there could be potential to experience the drying line issue.

OEM VS. THIRD-PARTY INKS: WHAT YOU NEED TO KNOW

When it comes to ink, there's an old saying I like to use: **Buy cheap, buy twice.**

It perfectly captures the dilemma many photographers face: You spend good money on a quality camera and expensive paper to produce the best possible prints, but then try to cut corners with cheaper inks.

It might feel economical in the short-term, but the trade-offs can be significant.

THE TWO TYPES OF INK

There are two broad categories of ink you can use in desktop photo printers:

- **OEM (Original Equipment Manufacturer)** inks, made by the printer's brand (e.g., Canon, Epson, HP)

- **Third-party** or **compatible** inks, produced by independent companies

Each has its pros and cons, and choosing between them depends largely on your priorities and budget.

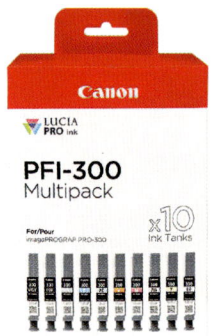

FIGURE 1.6: Canon OEM Ink

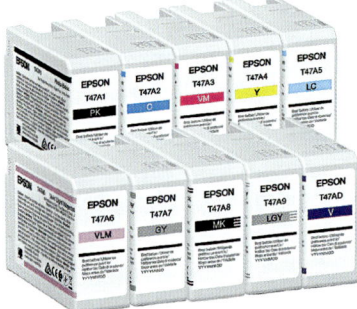

FIGURE 1.7: Epson OEM Ink

THE CASE FOR OEM INKS

If color accuracy and print quality are critical, or if you're printing professionally, then the safest option is to stick with OEM inks.

Here's why:

• OEM inks are guaranteed to work with your printer's hardware and firmware.

• They offer consistent quality and batch-to-batch reliability.

• OEM inks are covered under manufacturer warranties, which is especially important if your printer is still under warranty.

• Color profiles are optimized for OEM inks, so you'll get predictable, accurate color results without having to constantly recalibrate.

If budget isn't a constraint and you're striving for the best possible output, then OEM is the way to go.

WHEN THIRD-PARTY INKS MAKE SENSE

There can be significant cost savings when switching to third-party inks. If you're not printing for professional display, resale, or archival purposes, and if color precision isn't your top priority, third-party inks can be a viable option.

However, there are important guidelines to follow:

1. STICK WITH ONE BRAND

Switching between multiple third-party ink brands can introduce color inconsistency. That's because not all magentas, yellows, or blacks are created equal. Even small differences can throw off your color profiles and create visible shifts in tone.

"We've seen people mix cartridges from different suppliers, and suddenly the magenta is darker than expected. That's a recipe for mismatched prints," says Colin Hulley.

To avoid this, choose one reliable third-party brand and stick with it. Consistency is key.

2. EXPECT TO RE-PROFILE

If you switch to third-party ink, even from just one brand, you may need to create new printer profiles.

Color profiles made for OEM inks don't always transfer perfectly to third-party ink sets, especially if the dyes or pigments have subtle differences.

This means more time spent profiling, testing, and adjusting, which can eat into the cost savings.

3. DON'T USE THIRD-PARTY INKS DURING WARRANTY PERIOD

While many third-party inks are compatible, using them during your printer's warranty period can void your warranty if something goes wrong. Always use OEM inks while your printer is still covered, just to be safe.

FINAL THOUGHTS: BALANCING QUALITY AND COST

We understand that printing, especially at high volumes, can be expensive. Both ink and paper add up quickly, and it's only natural that people look for ways to save. That's why we don't dismiss third-party inks entirely. But we do urge users to be cautious and informed. To simplify:

- If quality and color accuracy are your top priorities, stick with OEM.

- If cost is the priority and you're printing casually, choose a trusted third-party brand and profile accordingly.

Ultimately, it's a balance, and each photographer needs to decide what trade-offs they're willing to make.

CHOOSING THE RIGHT DISPLAY FOR PHOTOGRAPHY AND PRINTING

Your display is the cornerstone of your digital photography and printing workflow. It influences everything, from retouching accuracy to color management and final print quality. Yet it's often overlooked in favor of more obvious investments like cameras, lenses, printers, or paper.

If you're serious about your images, then investing in a high-quality display is not optional; after all, if you're viewing your work on an uncalibrated, inaccurate screen, you won't be seeing things as they really are, no matter how expensive your camera or printer is.

THE ROLE OF ADOBE RGB

A critical feature to look for in any display used for photography is Adobe RGB color space coverage. In display specifications, you'll often see claims such as:

- 100% sRGB coverage

- 99% Adobe RGB coverage

You want a display that covers Adobe RGB as fully as possible, because that's the color space many printers and professional workflows rely on. Full sRGB coverage is fine for web use, but for accurate print soft proofing and tonal control, Adobe RGB is essential.

WHY NOT 100% ADOBE RGB?

Some displays, such as those from BenQ **(Figure 1.8)** state 99% Adobe RGB rather than 100%. This isn't a flaw, it's an intentional and ethical marketing choice.

"We could technically produce units that achieve 100%, but not all mass-produced units will meet that standard. So, we list 99% to avoid overpromising," says Dr. Chris Bai.

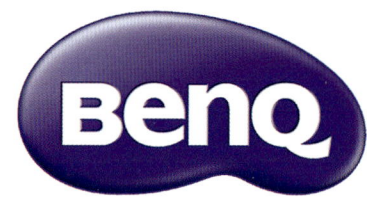

FIGURE 1.8

BenQ's stance is one of realistic transparency: They may exceed 99% in individual units, but they won't guarantee 100% coverage unless every single monitor can consistently achieve it.

DISPLAY SIZE: WHAT'S IDEAL?

Having used 24-inch, 27-inch, and 32-inch displays, I've found 27 inches to be the sweet spot. It's large enough to work comfortably with images and editing tools, yet not so big that it overwhelms a desk or strains the eyes.

My primary display is the BenQ SW272U **(Figure 1.9)**, a 4K monitor with Adobe RGB support. For those looking for a slightly more affordable alternative, the SW272Q is identical in design but offers a 2K resolution, which still provides excellent detail and usability.

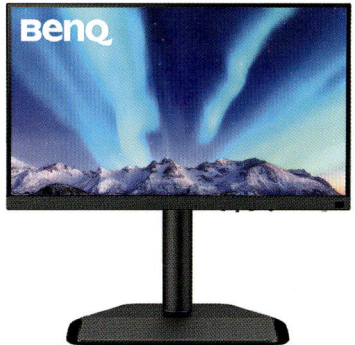

FIGURE 1.9: BenQ SW272U

SHADING HOODS AND ANTI-REFLECTION COATINGS

A quality display should come with or support a shading hood, which helps block ambient light from spilling onto the screen. This is critical for accurate image assessment.

The BenQ SW272U comes supplied with a shading hood **(Figure 1.10)** and also includes a special anti-reflective coating, reducing glare even in brighter rooms. Together with the shading hood, this ensures unobstructed viewing of fine tonal detail, which is especially useful when soft proofing for print.

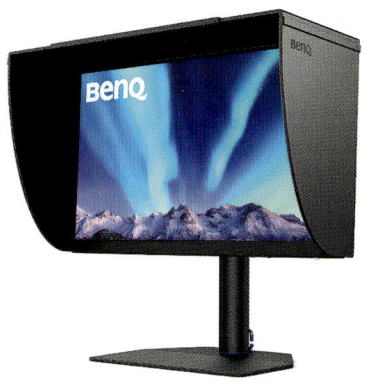

FIGURE 1.10: BenQ SW272U Shading Hood

THE POWER OF HARDWARE CALIBRATION

One of the key features to look for is hardware calibration. Unlike software calibration, which stores the ICC profile within the operating system, hardware-calibrated displays store the calibration directly in the monitor's internal chip.

BENEFITS OF HARDWARE CALIBRATION:
- Not affected by OS updates or driver issues.
- Multiple calibration modes (e.g., photo editing, video editing, print proofing).
- Easier to share displays between different machines.
- Reliable, consistent color across sessions.

This means I can unplug my calibrated display from my main editing computer and plug it into another, and it will still show the correct color. No need to recalibrate every time.

This level of flexibility and accuracy is something software-calibrated displays simply can't match.

SECONDARY DISPLAYS AND THE PD SERIES

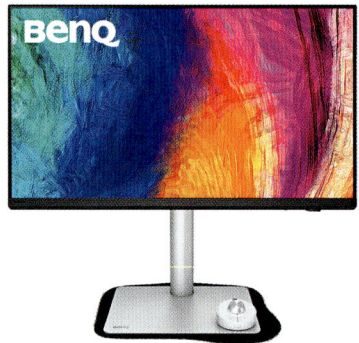

I also use a BenQ PD-series ultrawide display as a second monitor (**Figure 1.11**). While it's a more budget-friendly option and excellent for general computing, video editing, and graphic design, it doesn't support Adobe RGB; instead, it supports the DCI-P3 color space.

Bottom line, if your primary use case is photography and printing, you want a monitor with the Adobe RGB color space (**Figure 1.12**).

FIGURE 1.11: BenQ PD-Series Ultra-wide Display

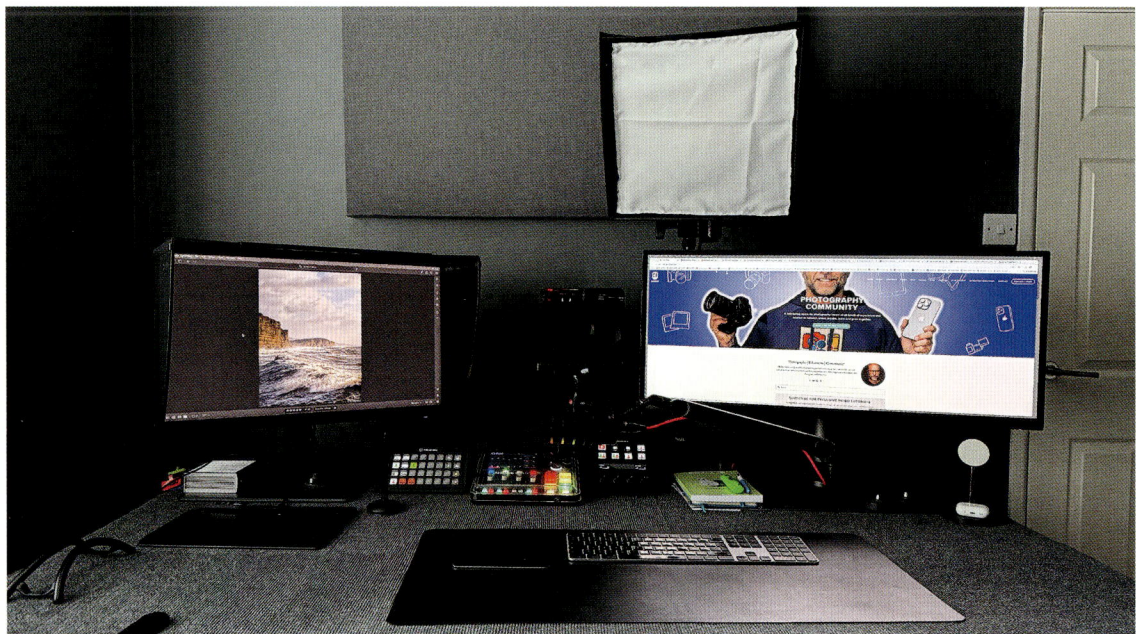

FIGURE 1.12: My Current Workspace

FINAL TIPS AND RECOMMENDATIONS

To summarize, here are the key things to look for when choosing a display for photography and print work:

1. Look for Adobe RGB color space support; 99% is realistic and sufficient.

2. Choose the right size; 27 inches is a comfortable middle ground.

3. Use a display with a shading hood and anti-reflective coating.

4. Invest in a hardware-calibrated display for long-term consistency.

5. Avoid displays that only support sRGB or DCI-P3, unless you're working only in web or video.

Also, make sure your display is properly calibrated (which I'll be going over in Chapter 2) and positioned to avoid ambient light interference. That way, you'll be seeing your images as they are meant to be seen, and your prints will reflect the precision of your screen.

> **BONUS TIP:** *If you're considering a BenQ display and would like a discount, feel free to reach out; I may be able to help you reduce the cost of your investment.*

WHY HDMI COULD BE UNDERMINING YOUR DISPLAY CALIBRATION

When it comes to photography and printing, ensuring that you're viewing images accurately on your display is essential, and that means using a proper display, and also connecting it to your computer the right way, which is a detail that even many experienced creatives overlook.

I learned something surprising in a conversation with Dr. Chris Bai from BenQ **(Figure 1.13),** something that changed the way I connect my displays forever. It turns out that how you connect your display matters just as much as what display you use.

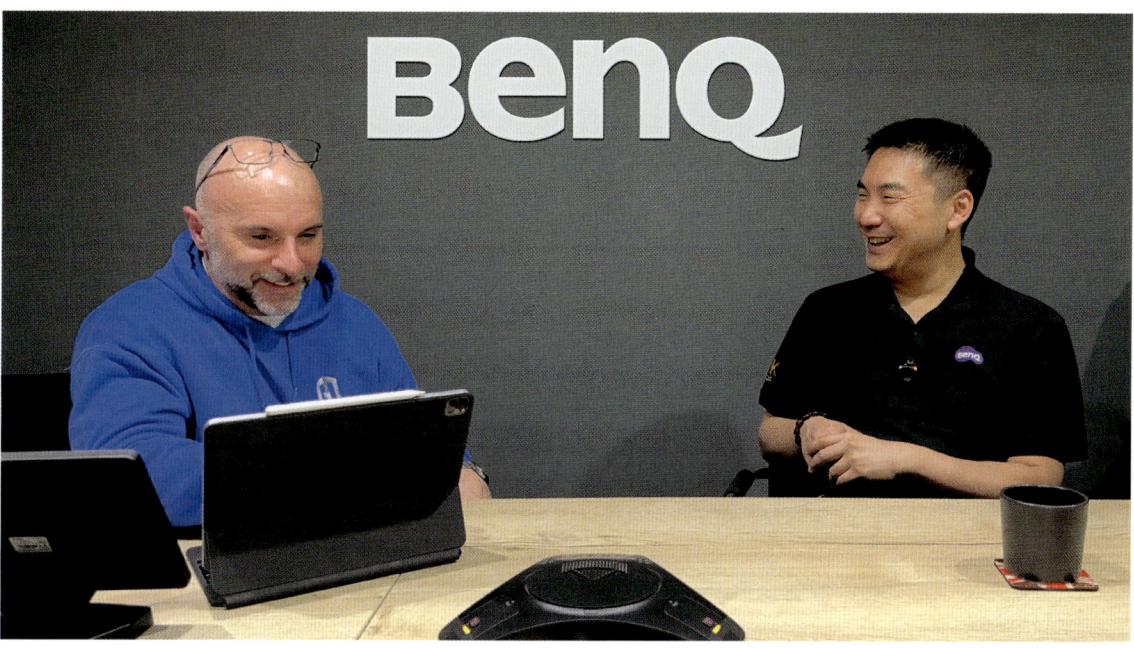

FIGURE 1.13

THE HDMI TRAP: WHY IT'S NOT IDEAL FOR COLOR-ACCURATE WORK

Most people naturally use an HDMI cable to connect their display to their computer. It's common, convenient, and included with most monitors. But there's a hidden issue that can sabotage your calibration efforts: HDMI defaults to a limited RGB range, not full RGB.

FULL VS. LIMITED RGB RANGE

Dr. Chris Bai explains it this way:

- **Full RGB Range:** 0–255 (what we want for photography, design, and printing workflows)
- **Limited RGB Range:** 16–235 (designed for older television systems to save bandwidth)

In limited RGB, you're missing the critical values at both ends of the scale; the deepest blacks and the brightest whites. This compresses your tonal range, leading to:

- Washed-out highlights
- Muted shadows
- Poor contrast accuracy
- Calibration errors

HDMI was originally designed for televisions, not for color-accurate displays. The limited range is ideal for video content, where high contrast and saturated colors "look better," but for photography, it creates a false representation of your image.

WHY CALIBRATION FAILS WITH HDMI

If your computer is outputting limited RGB, but your calibration software assumes full RGB, your monitor ends up being calibrated against the wrong baseline.

As a result:

- Your calibration report may fail **(Figure 1.14)**.
- Your grayscale or gamma may appear off.
- You'll never achieve an accurate print-to-screen match.

And the real culprit? Often it's just the HDMI connection.

Users frequently blame the monitor or calibration device, unaware that HDMI is quietly corrupting their color workflow.

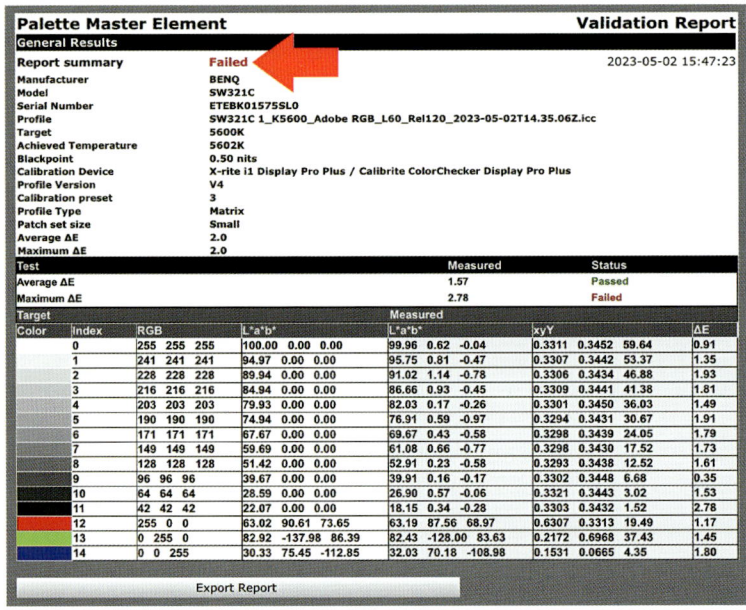

FIGURE 1.14

WHAT'S THE BEST WAY TO CONNECT YOUR DISPLAY?

According to Dr. Chris, the two best connection types for color-critical work are **(Figure 1.15)**:

• USB-C

• DisplayPort (DP)

Both support full RGB range by default and are designed with professional workflows in mind. They allow accurate transmission of color data and are fully compatible with hardware calibration processes.

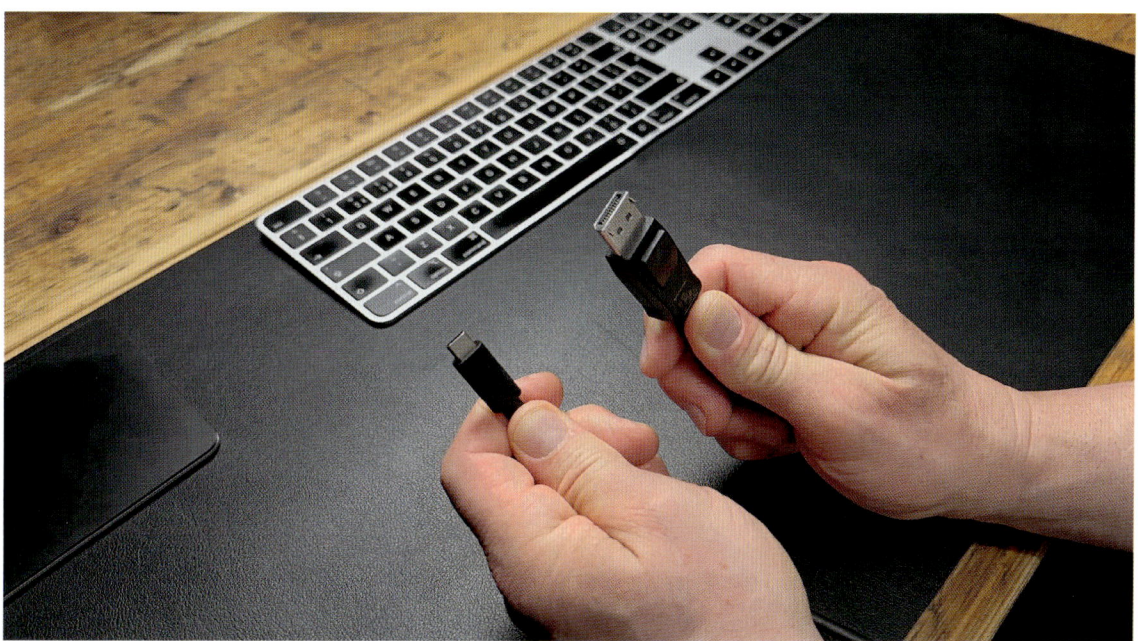

FIGURE 1.15: USB-C and DisplayPort (DP) Connection

According to Dr. Chris Bai, "With DisplayPort or USB-C, you get clean, uncompromised signal transmission; ideal for calibration and consistent performance."

CAN YOU FIX HDMI ON WINDOWS?

If you're using HDMI on a Windows machine, there's some good news: You can often manually switch your color range from limited to full. How you do this is dependent on the operating system, but it is a very simple process to check if you are using limited or full, and to change the setting if needed.

WHAT ABOUT HDMI ON MACOS?

Unfortunately, on a Mac, it's a different story. MacOS does **not** allow manual override of the HDMI output range. The RGB range is automatically determined based on the type of connection.

Here's an example:

- Using HDMI on a BenQ SW272U, the input defaults to Limited RGB.

- Using USB-C or DisplayPort, the display switches to Full RGB.

You can confirm this by accessing the monitor's info settings:

1. Press the center button on the BenQ Hotkey Puck **(Figure 1.16)**.

2. Navigate to the Display section.

3. Scroll to Information.

4. Check the RGB Range. If it's "Limited," switch to USB-C or DisplayPort **(Figure 1.17)**.

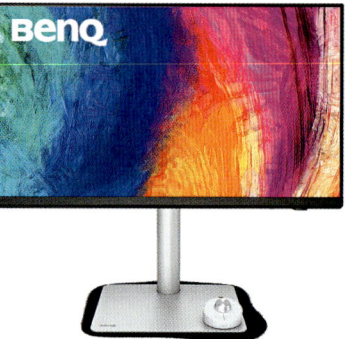

FIGURE 1.16: BenQ Hotkey Puck

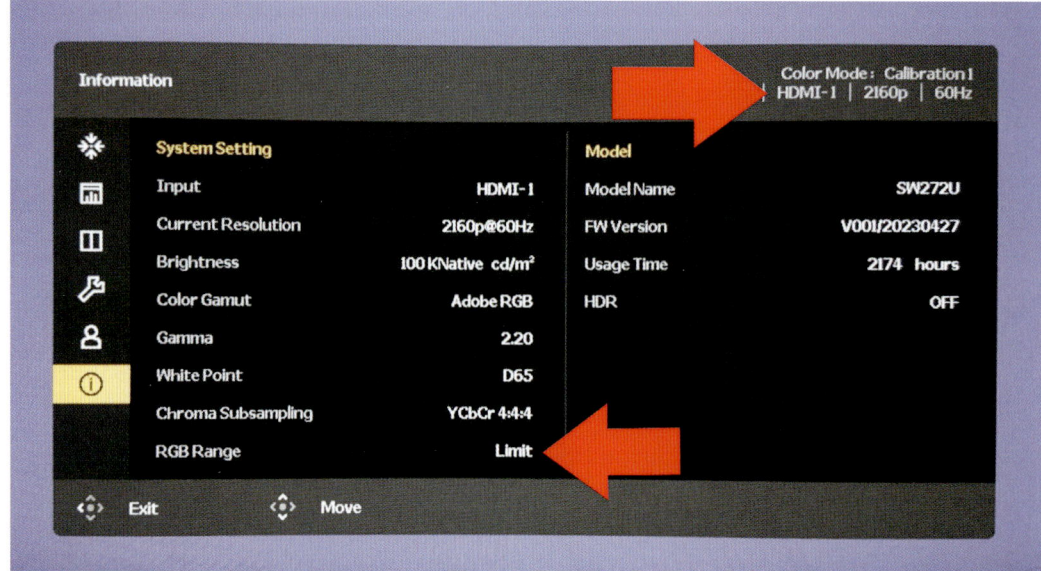

FIGURE 1.17

FINAL RECOMMENDATION

If you're using your display for photography, retouching, or printing:

• Avoid HDMI unless you can verify full RGB range is being used.

• Use USB-C or DisplayPort for accurate, full-range color transmission.

• If you're stuck with HDMI on Windows, change the RGB setting manually.

• On a Mac, use USB-C or DisplayPort to guarantee full range output.

"You can invest in the best display and best calibration tools, but if your connection is wrong, the results will never be right," says Dr. Chris Bai.

This small adjustment in how you connect your monitor can have a huge impact on your workflow and final output.

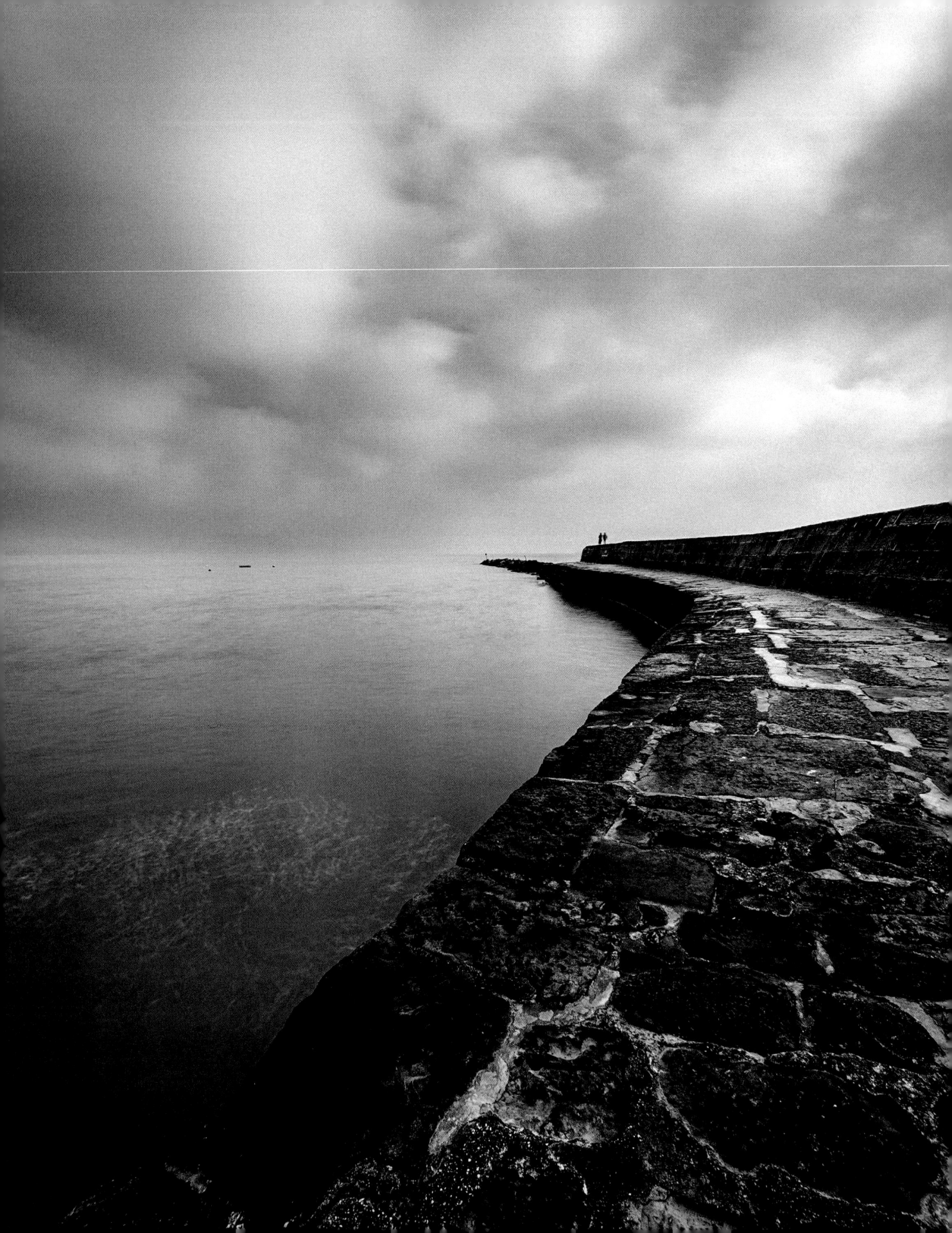

CHAPTER 2
DISPLAY CALIBRATION

THE REAL ISSUE BEHIND DARK PRINTS

Now we're going to go through how to correctly calibrate your display, which in my opinion is the key to getting the best possible prints out of your printer and the best possible screen-to-print match.

So often I hear that people struggle with getting their prints to match what they see on their display. But it's important to understand we will never get a perfect match. Our screens are illuminated; they're effectively a light source, and paper can never match this.

In the section on paper, you'll see how the paper you choose to print your images on can have a big impact on the final print; for example, it may make the image appear warmer or reduce the overall contrast.

However, the biggest complaint of all, without a doubt, isn't about colors being off; it's about prints coming out way too dark. And from my experience doing a lot of printing and a lot of testing, this comes down to not having your display calibrated correctly.

This is because display or screen calibration isn't given the importance that it should be.

If you've retouched your images so that they have adequate tonal range and the histogram looks good, but your prints are coming out too dark, then the screen you're working on is too bright. That's it. No ifs, no buts.

If this sounds familiar to you, don't blame yourself. I've seen it written down and I've heard it said so many times to calibrate your display brightness between 80 and 120 candela, and everything will be fine. But for me, it never was; I always ended up with prints that were too dark. And the more this happened, the more I followed the generic advice, the more I started to think that the problem was me.

But it wasn't me, and it isn't you either.

So in this chapter, we're going to fix this. I'm going to show you how to correctly calibrate your display for your workspace. I'll go through both hardware calibration and software calibration, but first, we'll kick things off by looking at some hardware.

HARDWARE YOU'LL NEED TO CALIBRATE YOUR DISPLAY

If we're going to calibrate our displays, we of course need hardware that enables us to do that, hardware that can measure the color, brightness, and contrast levels of our displays.

There are lots of choices out there, such as the original X-Rite i1 devices, the new Calibrite devices, and the popular Spyder devices by Datacolor. In the past, I have always used X-Rite devices, such as the i1 Display and the i1 Studio, and have never had an issue. They would and still do exactly what they're made to do. But very recently I've upgraded my display to the BenQ SW272U with its updated screen technology **(Figure 2.1)**, so with that, I've also upgraded my calibration devices and now have the new Calibrite Display Pro HL **(Figure 2.2)** with its updated sensor.

If you still have something like the X-Rite i1 Display, you're absolutely fine. I can't speak for the Datacolor Spyder devices, as I've never used them, but I do have lots of friends and colleagues who have them, and they seem happy enough.

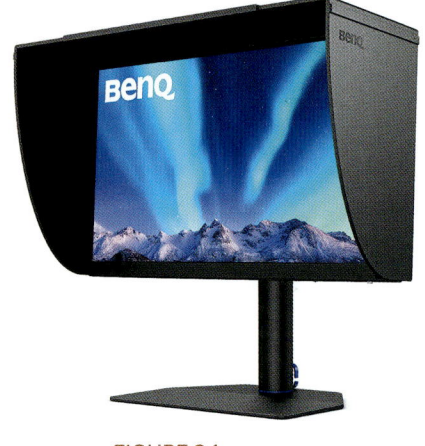

FIGURE 2.1

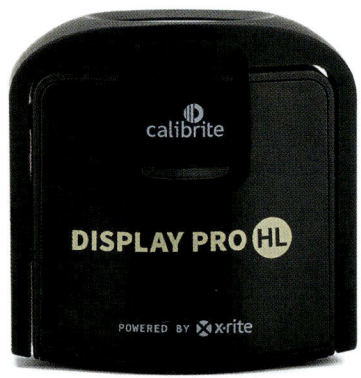

FIGURE 2.2

MY CALIBRATION SETUP

First, I'm going to show you how I calibrate my main display that I use for retouching my images and for printing, my BenQ SW272U. As I mentioned in the section about choosing a display, this piece of equipment is hardware calibrated.

The great thing about this display is that it can hold up to three different calibration settings. I have two calibration settings to choose from, depending on what I'm doing: one for retouching and printing, and the other for general day-to-day computing, like emails, watching YouTube videos, Netflix, writing, and so on.

I'll show you the settings I use for both, and also how I switch between them.

PRE-CALIBRATION CHECKLIST

Before we go through the process of calibrating our display, whether it's hardware or software calibrated, there's a checklist we need to go through to make sure everything is set correctly:

1. **Warm up the display**
    Don't calibrate your display until it has been turned on for a minimum of thirty minutes, preferably sixty minutes. This gives the display time to settle down and ensures everything is working as it should.

2. **Turn off screen mirroring**
    If you're using more than one display and you have screen mirroring turned on, turn it off for the purpose of calibrating your display.

    Once you've completed the calibration, you can turn it back on. But having it on can cause the calibration device and software to become confused about which screen it's supposed to be working on. In fact, most calibration software won't even continue until you've turned mirroring off.

3. **Check HDMI settings**
    If you're using HDMI to connect your display to your computer, then make sure you have it set to full range Adobe RGB.

    If you don't know how to check that or change it, make sure to watch the video on HDMI in the Color Management section.

CALIBRATING THE BENQ SW272U: MY DISPLAY SETTINGS FOR PHOTOGRAPHY AND EVERYDAY USE

Now I'll go through how I calibrate my BenQ SW272U display, which, as I've said, is capable of being hardware calibrated.

I'll start with the calibration I use when retouching and printing my images, and then cover the calibration settings I use for day-to-day use of my computer (but not for retouching or printing).

This second calibration is for daily tasks like checking email, browsing the internet, watching YouTube videos, and so on. The settings are different, as you'll see, because this calibration is designed for the best viewing experience: a nice bright display, plenty of contrast, and deep blacks.

CALIBRATION SOFTWARE AND DEVICE SETUP

For both of these calibrations, I'll be using BenQ's software Palette Master Ultimate, but the settings I use will transfer to whatever you're using.

First, I have my Calibrite Display Pro HL connected to my computer. This device is USB-C, but it comes with a USB adapter so I can choose how to connect it. I could plug it directly into my computer, but for no particular reason, I choose to plug it into the USB port built into my display.

This works the same way, but you need to ensure you're using the correct power setting for that USB port. On my BenQ display, I go into the menu by pressing the center button on the hotkey puck, scroll down to the system menu, press the center button again, and then scroll to USB configuration. I have it set to 60 Hertz **(Figure 2.3)**. If it were set to 30 Hertz, it wouldn't work.

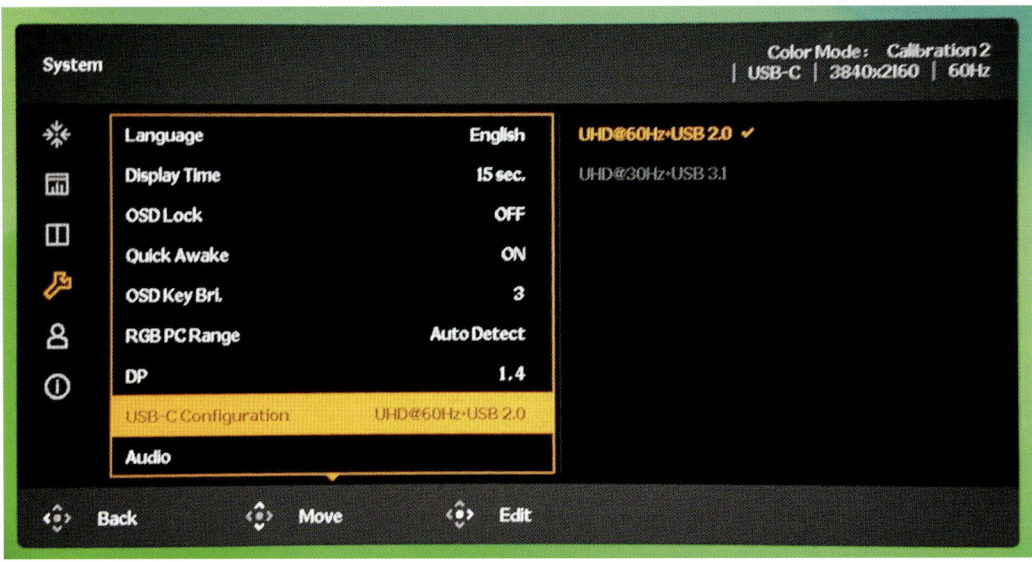

FIGURE 2.3

LAUNCHING THE CALIBRATION PROCESS

Next I open the Palette Master Ultimate software **(Figure 2.4)**.

1. Open the Model Name drop-down menu and choose the name of your display.

2. Under Calibrator, select Calibrite Display Pro HL. After a brief moment, the software recognizes the device.

3. In the box on the right side of the dialog, choose from:

    • Color Calibration

    • Advanced Color Adjust

    • Validation

I chose Color Calibration.

4. Click Start.

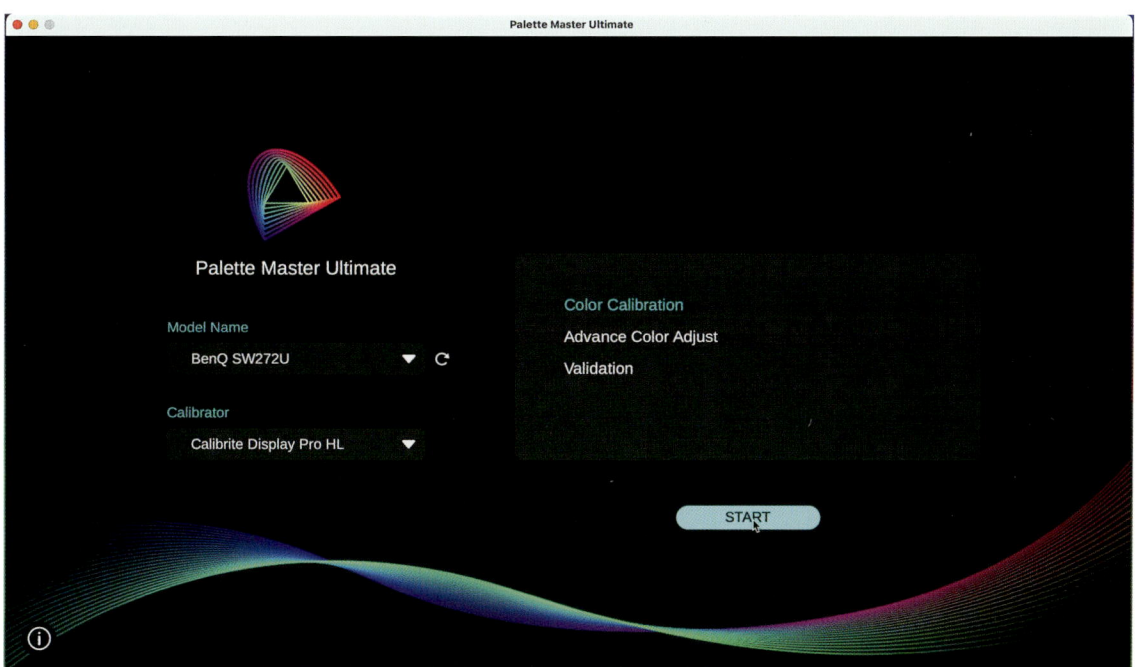

FIGURE 2.4

CREATING A CUSTOM CALIBRATION TARGET

The next screen summarizes what I'm doing and what I'm using **(Figure 2.5)**:

• Color calibration

• Model of the display

• Model of the calibration device

At the top, there's a Calibration Target menu, which includes presets for different tasks like Photography, Web Design, and Video Editing.

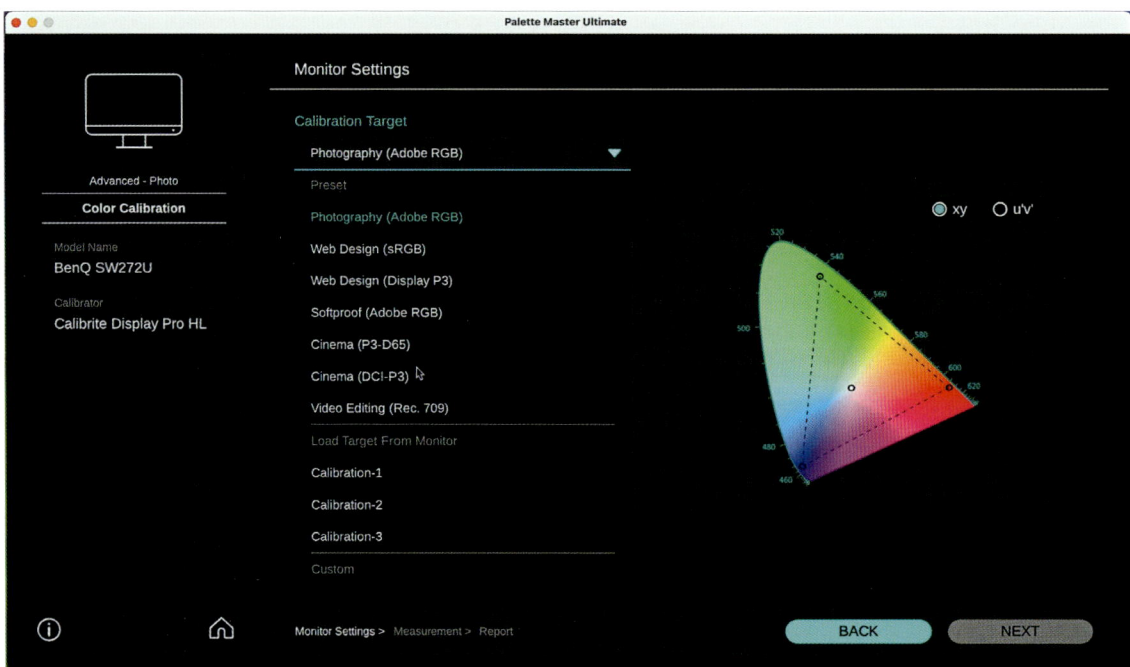

FIGURE 2.5

By default, Photography is selected and you can see the target settings it would calibrate to, but these aren't what I want. In my experience, the default settings make the display too bright, the temperature too cool, and the image too contrasty, with blacks that have no detail.

So, I choose Edit Target **(Figure 2.6)**, but before that, I choose where to store this calibration: Calibration 1, 2, or 3, each of which corresponds to a button on the BenQ Hot Key puck **(Figure 2.7)**.

I use Calibration 1 and then click Edit Target.

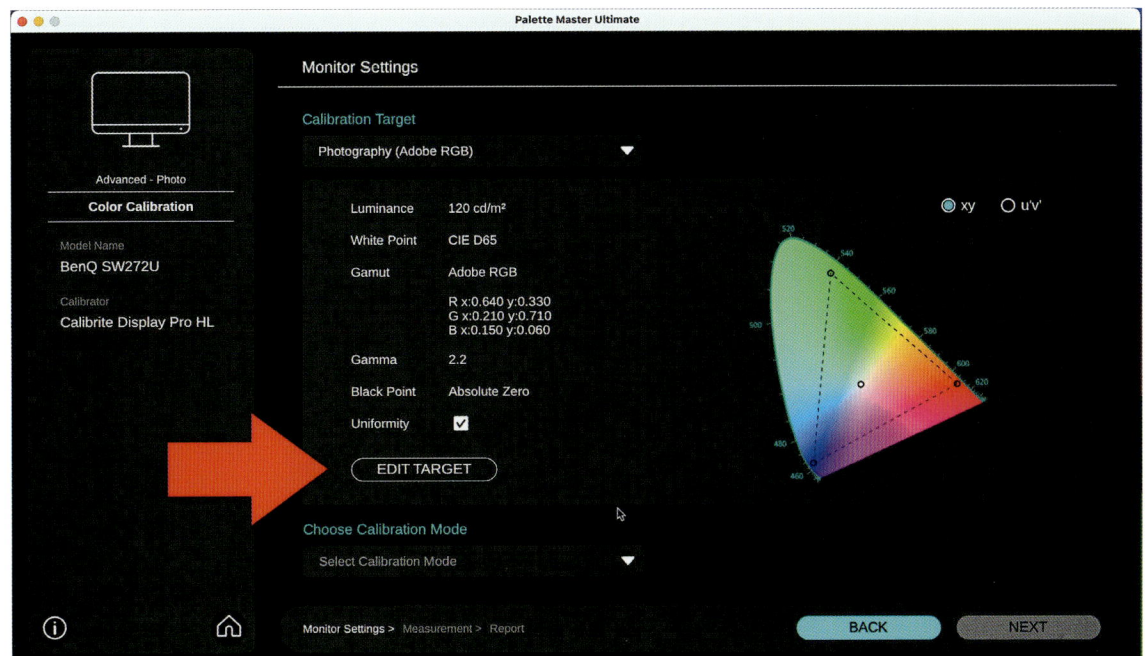

FIGURE 2.6

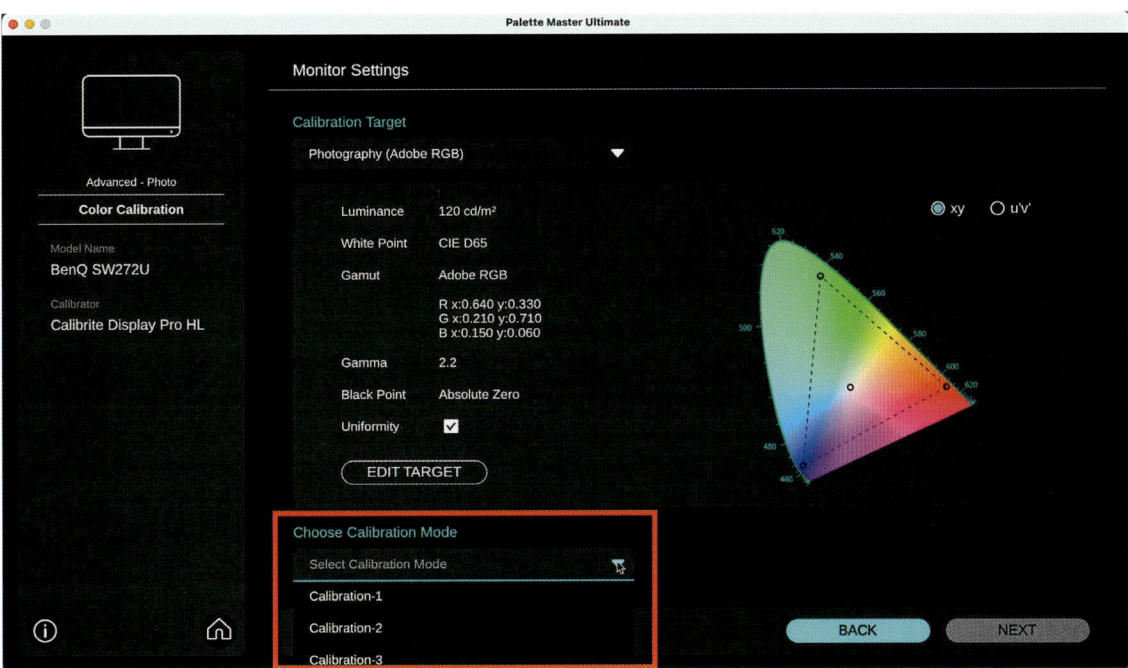

FIGURE 2.7

MY CUSTOM CALIBRATION SETTINGS FOR PHOTOGRAPHY

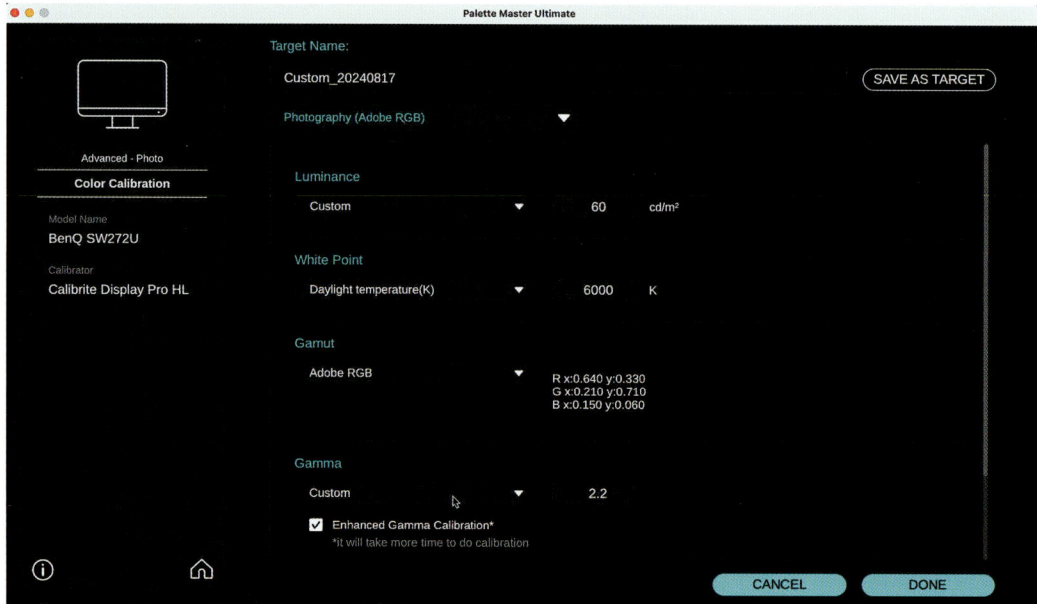

FIGURE 2.8

LUMINANCE (BRIGHTNESS)

Luminance, or brightness, is measured in candelas per square meter. The default is 120, and common advice is to calibrate between 80 and 120 candelas. But for my workspace, this is too bright.

I've tested several values and the one that works best is 60 candelas. I open the menu, choose Custom, and type in 60 **(Figure 2.8)**.

Many calibration devices can measure the ambient brightness of the room. But no matter where I was, the reading was always 80 candelas, which is still too high for me, so I stopped using it.

WHITE POINT

In past videos, I've recommended various settings: 5000K, 5600K, etc. I now use 6000 Kelvin to match the lighting in my room, which consists of an overhead LED, front light, and viewing lamp.

I input this by choosing Daylight Temperature and changing it to 6000.

COLOR SPACE

I use Adobe RGB.

GAMMA

I set this to 2.2. Palette Master Ultimate also offers Enhanced Gamma Calibration, which is good for black-and-white printing. Since I enjoy black-and-white printing, I use this, and doing so doesn't negatively affect color images.

BLACK POINT

By default, Black Point is set to Absolute Zero, which gives you very deep blacks, but no detail. That's great for watching videos, but not for retouching. Even the darkest areas should have a hint of detail, so I set this to 0.5 candelas by selecting Custom and entering 0.5 **(Figure 2.9)**.

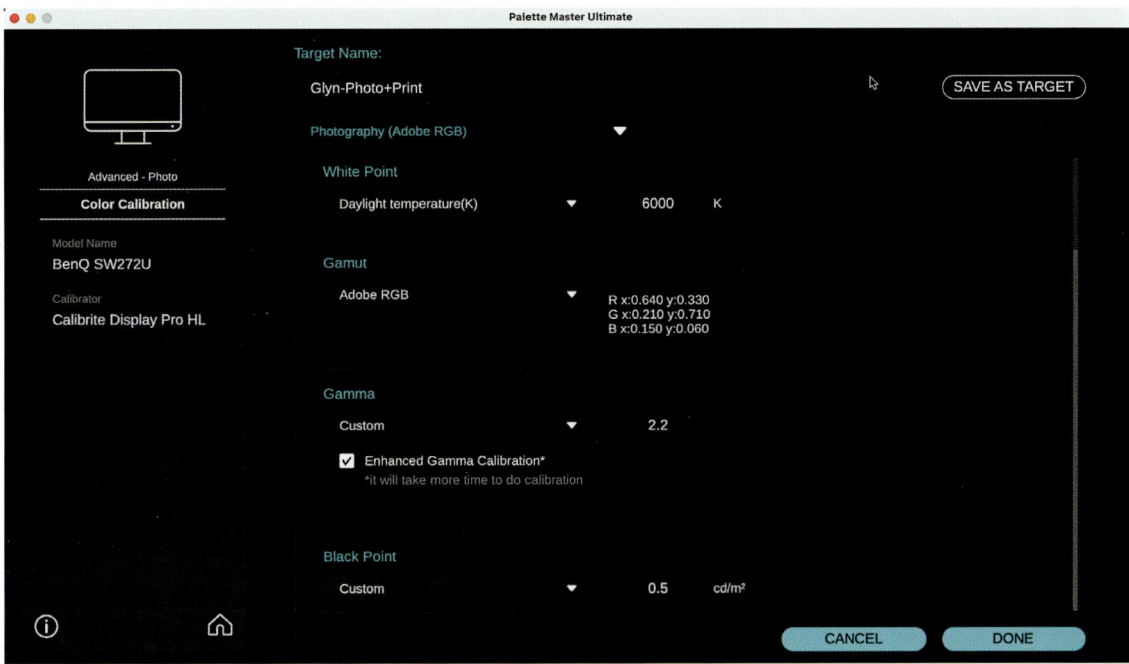

FIGURE 2.9

SAVING AND STARTING THE CALIBRATION

I save these settings as a preset so I don't have to re-enter them each time. Under Target Name, I name this preset "Glyn-Photo+Print," and then click Save as Target. I could have selected this from the Calibration Target menu in the beginning if it were already saved.

Click Next.

Now I see a summary of the settings I've chosen **(Figure 2.10)**, and I click Next again.

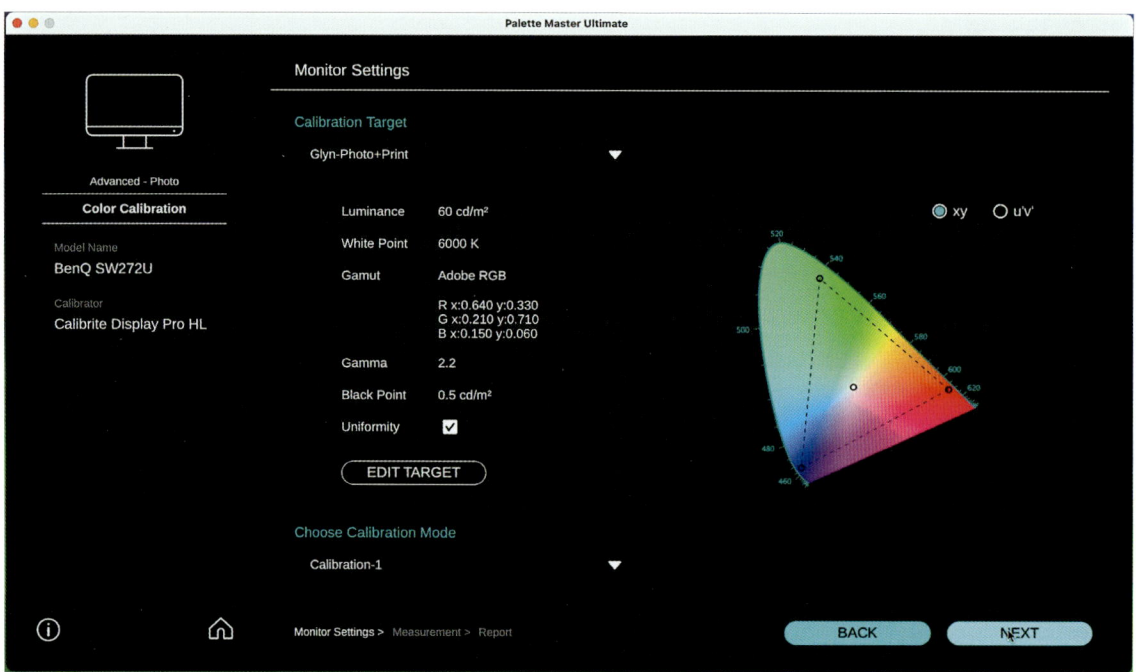

FIGURE 2.10

PRE-CALIBRATION CHECKLIST AND ICC SETTINGS

Here, the software reminds me of the pre-calibration checklist with one extra step to turn off any screensaver, in case it activates during calibration.

At the bottom, I choose ICC version 4 (unless I'm using very old software), and the profile name consisting of the target values and current date are all displayed **(Figure 2.11)**.

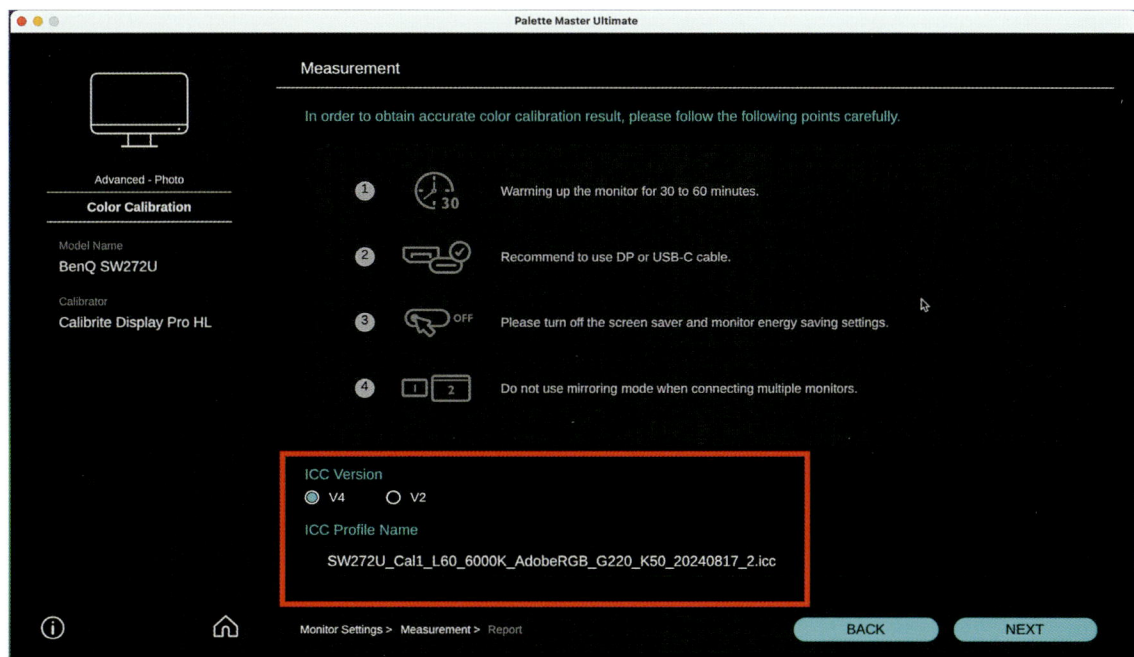

FIGURE 2.11

RUNNING THE CALIBRATION

I'm now instructed to rotate the sensor cover on the Calibrite Display Pro HL, and then I place it on the center of the screen. The software tells me to tilt the screen back slightly to help the sensor sit flat.

I feed the cable through the opening in the hood, use the weight on the cable to balance it, and close the cover gently to hold it in place **(Figure 2.12)**.

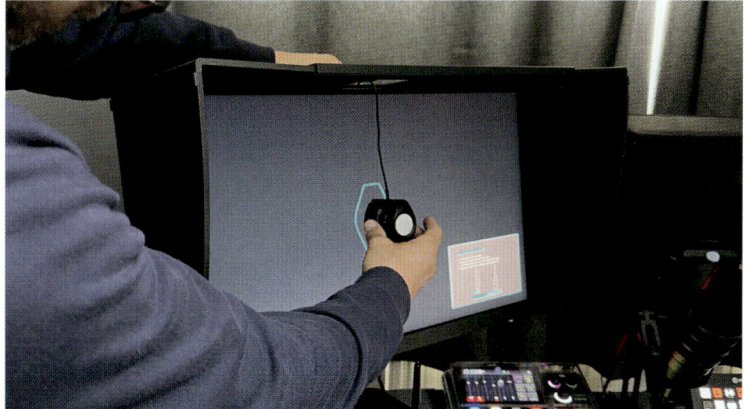

FIGURE 2.12

Click Next, then Start, and the calibration begins. This takes about 7 minutes, including the validation.

REVIEWING CALIBRATION RESULTS

Once calibration is complete, I click Check Report.

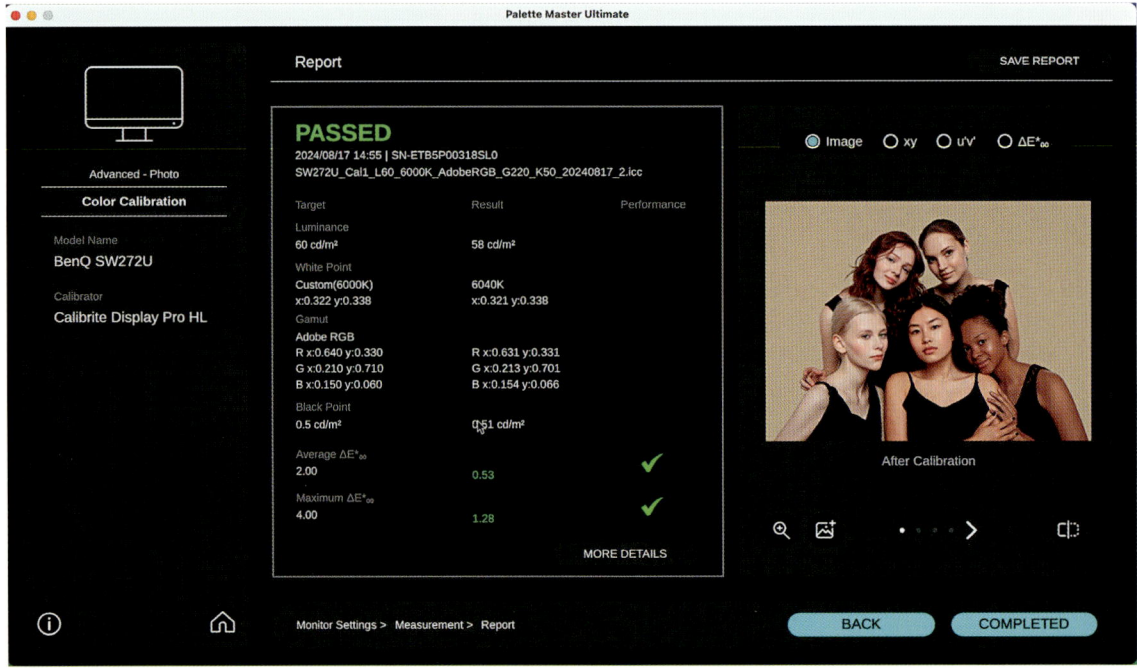

FIGURE 2.13

Here I can see **(Figure 2.13)**:

- **Target Luminance:** 60 ➜ Result: 58

- **Target White Point:** 6000 ➜ Result: 6040

- **Target Black Point:** 0.5 ➜ Result: 0.51

These results are more than acceptable.

DELTA E

At the bottom of the dialog, you'll see the Delta E measurements in green. This is key, as it measures display accuracy. A value of 4 or below is very good. Below 2 is superb.

This calibration achieved:

- **Average Delta E:** 0.53

- **Maximum Delta E:** 1.28

I'm very happy with this.

Over time, Delta E increases, so tracking it helps you know when a display may need replacement. To do this, you can save a copy of the report by clicking on Save Report in the top-right corner of the dialog. Once done, click Completed.

EVERYDAY DISPLAY CALIBRATION: SETTINGS FOR GENERAL USE

Now I want to show you the settings I use for the everyday use of my computer. These settings give me a great viewing experience for watching YouTube and Netflix, going through emails, writing, and so on.

USING THE PHOTOGRAPHY PRESET FOR DAY-TO-DAY USE

So, back in the Palette Master Ultimate software, the very first screen we come to once we've chosen our display and connected the calibration device is the screen shown in **Figure 2.14**.

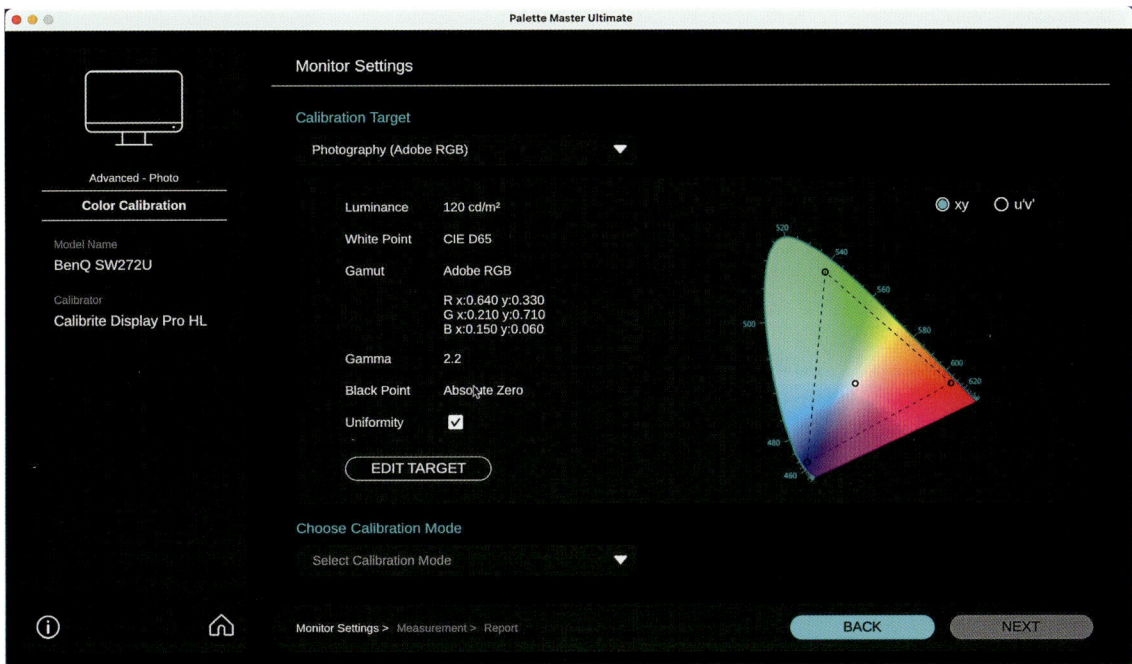

FIGURE 2.14

You'll remember I mentioned the available presets, and how I said that the Photography preset is not suitable for actual photography. However, it's perfect for everyday use. The luminance is bright. The white point is set to D65, which is the industry standard for televisions, iPads, smartphones, and so on. The black point is set to absolute zero, which gives a nice contrasty display with deep blacks. So I just use these default settings.

I'll assign these settings to Calibration 2, and then click through the process, again using ICC version 4, correctly positioning the calibration device on the screen, and then going through the measurement process.

And that's it.

STORED CALIBRATION SETTINGS AND THE BENQ HOTKEY PUCK

When I assigned a certain calibration to a specific calibration preset (1, 2, or 3), these relate to the Calibration Preset buttons 1, 2, and 3 on the Hotkey Puck **(Figure 2.15)**.

However, you might find they haven't been assigned by default. To assign them is a very simple process **(Figure 2.16)**.

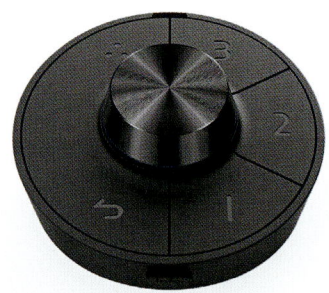

1. Press down on the center dial on the Hotkey Puck. This brings up the menu on the display.

2. Rotate the dial to go to the Custom Menu, then press down on the center dial again to access the options.

FIGURE 2.15

3. Scroll down to Shortcut 1, 2, 3, then press the center dial to select it.

4. Choose Color Mode, press the center dial, and then select from the Calibration options to assign the appropriate preset.

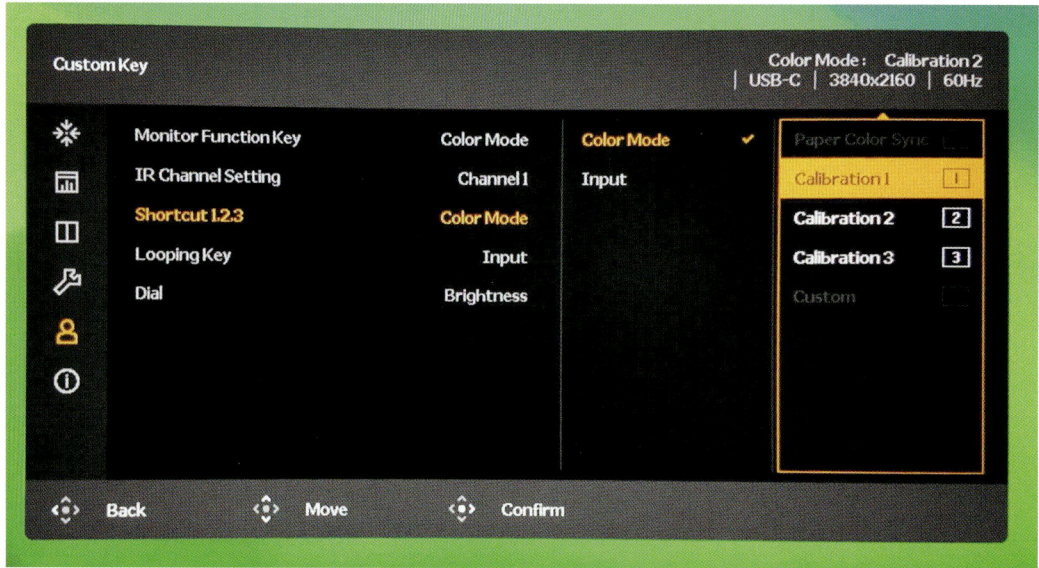

FIGURE 2.16

Now, when using my display, if I'm working on images or printing, I press button 1 on the Hotkey Puck, and if I'm doing general day-to-day tasks, I press button 2 for a brighter, more contrasty viewing experience.

SOFTWARE CALIBRATION WITH CALIBRITE PROFILER

Now I want to take you through a software calibration using the Calibrite Profiler software. This isn't software you would use if you have a BenQ, Eizo, or any other brand of display that supports hardware calibration. For those, you would use software specifically designed for that display.

That said, the settings I'll be going through are identical. The only difference is that this is a software calibration. So, what we set the display to now is what it will look like until you physically change it by adjusting the brightness or contrast (if your display allows that).

With software calibration, you don't have the advantage of switching between calibrations depending on what you're doing.

SETTING UP CALIBRITE PROFILER

Figure 2.17 shows the opening dialog for the Calibrite Profiler software. At the top section, I choose which device I want to calibrate. I'm going to calibrate my BenQ display, just pretending it's a software-calibrated display.

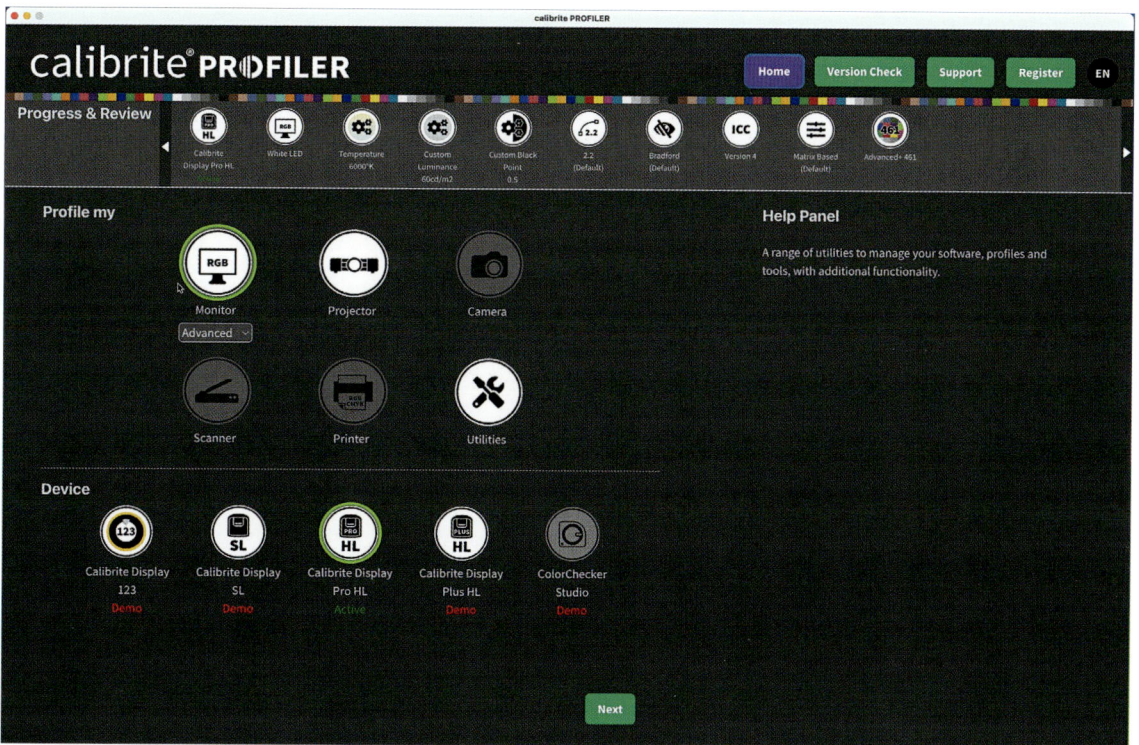

FIGURE 2.17

So, I choose the first option here: RGB Monitor.

I have a choice between Advanced and Basic. I want total control over the settings and to get my money's worth, so I'm choosing Advanced.

Below, in the Device section, the Display Pro HL is listed as Active (since it's plugged in). I click Next.

CHOOSING THE DISPLAY AND SKIPPING PRESETS

On the next screen, both of my BenQ displays are listed. The one with the green circle is the one I'll be calibrating **(Figure 2.18)**.

Below that, just like in the BenQ Palette Master Ultimate software, there are presets, but we won't be using those.

Instead, all the settings we want are found in the progress bar at the top, going from left to right:

- Calibration device
- Display type (correctly showing as White LED)
- White point

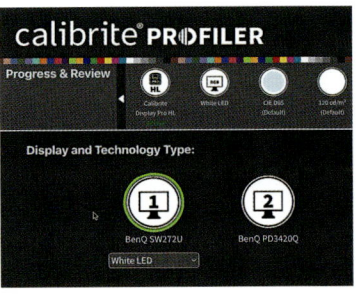

FIGURE 2.18

WHITE POINT

The white point is currently set to D65. As you'll remember, my preferred white point for photo retouching and printing is 6000 Kelvin, so I click on that, then on Custom:

1. Use the slider (or up/down arrows) to bring the white point down to 6000 **(Figure 2.19)**.

2. Click Save.

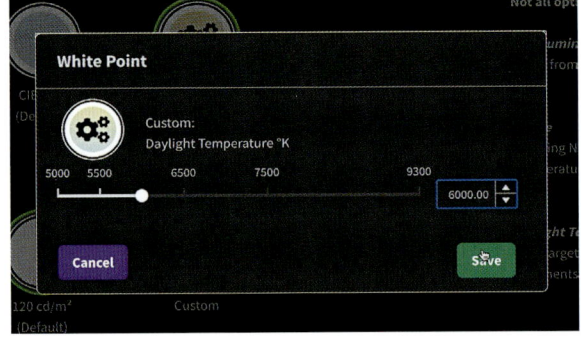

FIGURE 2.19

SETTING THE LUMINANCE

The luminance (brightness) is currently set to 120 candela. I lower this to 60 candela by clicking Custom and then entering 60 **(Figure 2.20)**.

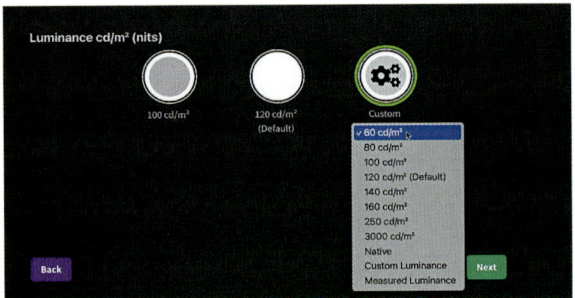

FIGURE 2.20

SETTING THE CONTRAST RATIO (BLACK POINT)

Now we set the black point **(Figure 2.21)**.

1. Click Custom, then Custom Black Point.

2. Type in 0.5.

3. Click Save.

The Gamma is set to the default 2.2, which is great.

Click Next.

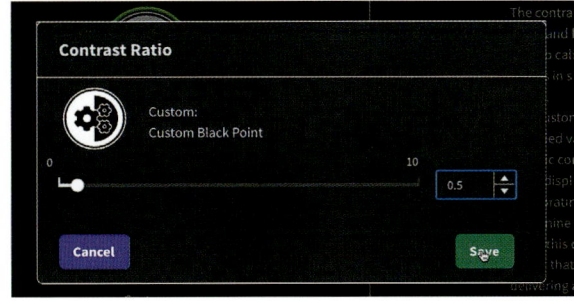

FIGURE 2.21

ADVANCED PROFILE OPTIONS

Now we reach the Advanced Profile Options screen **(Figure 2.22)**.

Here we see:

- Ambient Light Auto Adjust

- Flare Correct

These may sound useful, but we're not using them. Why? Because you should control the lighting in your workspace using bulbs, curtains, etc.

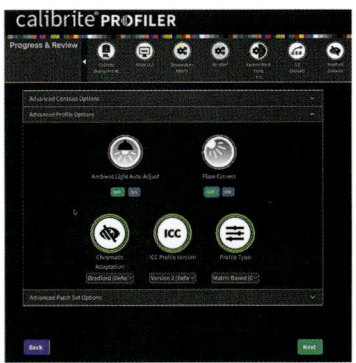

FIGURE 2.22

These features require you to leave the calibration device plugged in to constantly measure ambient light and adjust your screen accordingly, which leads to inconsistency, so we turn them off.

- **Chromatic Adaptation:** Leave it on Bradford

- **ICC Profile Version:** Use Version 4

- **Profile Type:** Use Matrix

Click Next.

CHOOSING PATCH COUNT AND STARTING MEASUREMENT

This next screen asks how many color patches you want the device and software to measure from **(Figure 2.23)**.

The more patches, the longer it takes, but the more accurate the profile. My advice: Go for it. You're calibrating anyway, so a few extra minutes are worth it. I choose 461 patches, then click Next.

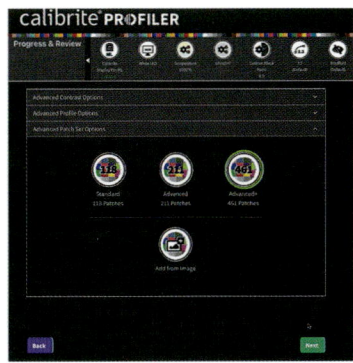

FIGURE 2.23

SAVING PRESET AND STARTING MEASUREMENT

At this point, I can save the settings as a preset so I can quickly reuse them later. Then I click Start Measurement.

Next, I select which controls I have available on my display **(Figure 2.24)**:

- Brightness
- RGB
- Contrast

I only check the ones that are available, then click Continue.

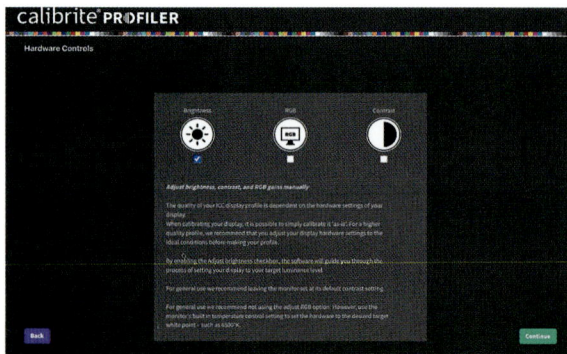

FIGURE 2.24

POSITIONING THE CALIBRATION DEVICE

Now I'm instructed to:

- Rotate the cover on the calibration device to reveal the sensor.
- Place the device on the screen.

The next screen allows me to use my display's brightness controls to get the Target White Luminance (green marker) and Measured White Luminance (red triangle) to match as closely as possible by moving the red arrow to align with the green square **(Figure 2.25)**.

Once matched, I click Next.

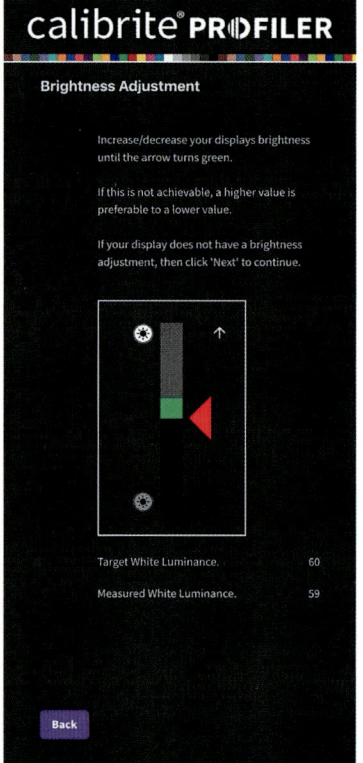

FIGURE 2.25

MEASUREMENT AND PROFILE CREATION

Now we're ready to start the measurement process. As the software works through the 461 color patches, you'll see progress in the bottom left, and a colored bar across the bottom. When it's done, click Next.

You'll then see all 461 color patches, showing the Target Colors versus the Achieved Colors **(Figure 2.26)**.

Click Next again. Save the ICC profile and choose to set a calibration reminder (though I don't use this feature).

Click Save.

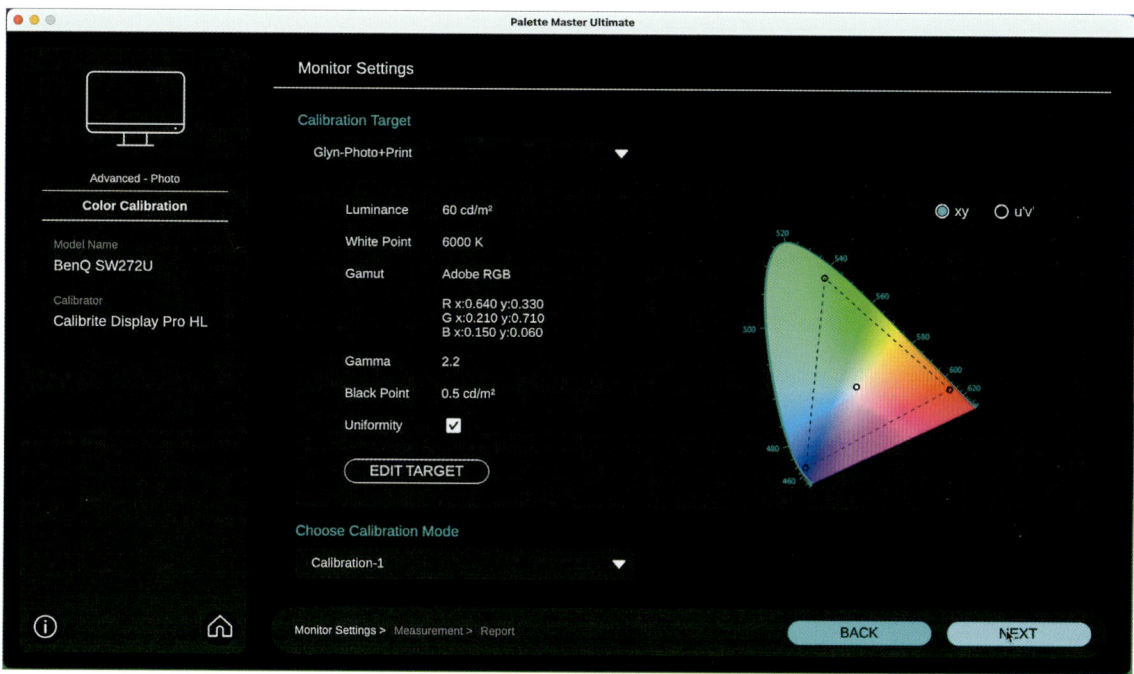

FIGURE 2.26

VALIDATION AND DELTA E RESULTS

At the bottom, you'll see the option to go through the validation process. Click Next, leave the settings at default, then click Next again.

Follow the instructions to place the calibration device back on the screen, and the software will run a shorter measurement process.

When finished, you'll see whether the calibration passed or failed; this one passed **(Figure 2.27)**.

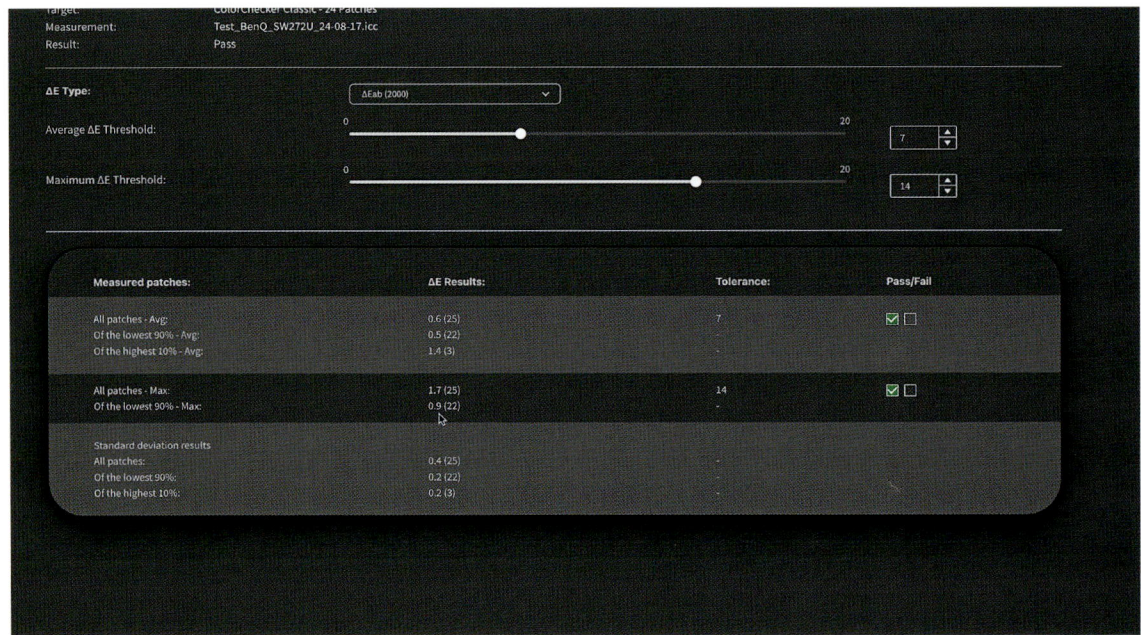

FIGURE 2.27

You'll also see the Delta E Results:

- Delta E of **4** and below = Very good

- Delta E below **2** = Superb

In this case, the calibration achieved very low Delta E numbers, so this is a great result.

You can also save the report to monitor these values over time and keep an eye on how your display is performing over weeks, months, or years.

FINAL NOTES ON CALIBRATION AND EVERYDAY USE

So that's how I calibrate my display, whether it be a hardware-calibrated display like my BenQ SW272U or a software-calibrated display. To finish off there are just a few extra things I want to mention.

HOW OFTEN I CALIBRATE MY DISPLAY

First, how often do I calibrate my display?

Well, I don't set any reminders. I don't do it every week or every two weeks or follow any kind of schedule. I generally calibrate when I think about it and when I know I'm going to be doing some printing.

Because I have two calibration settings saved, I never manually adjust the brightness of my display. That means there's no chance of it drifting out of calibration. I just switch between the two preset calibrations, depending on what I'm doing.

A WORKAROUND FOR SOFTWARE-CALIBRATED DISPLAYS

Obviously, as you've seen with a hardware-calibrated display like those made by BenQ, you can switch between different calibrations. But here's a possible workaround if you're using software calibration:

- Once you've calibrated your display for working on your photographs, tap the brightness controls to see how many markers appear for that particular brightness level.
- If you want it brighter for another activity, simply tap to increase the brightness.
- As long as you remember the original brightness position used for photo editing, you can reset it back to that later.

ADJUSTING TO LOWER LUMINANCE

Finally, a note about luminance: If you lower your display like I have to around 60 candelas, this will initially feel like a big difference compared to what you're used to, but you will adjust to it. It will begin to appear normal after a short while.

My only advice if you're using a hardware-calibrated display is to not switch calibration modes and immediately resume working. Instead, give your eyes a bit of time to adjust before continuing to work on your images.

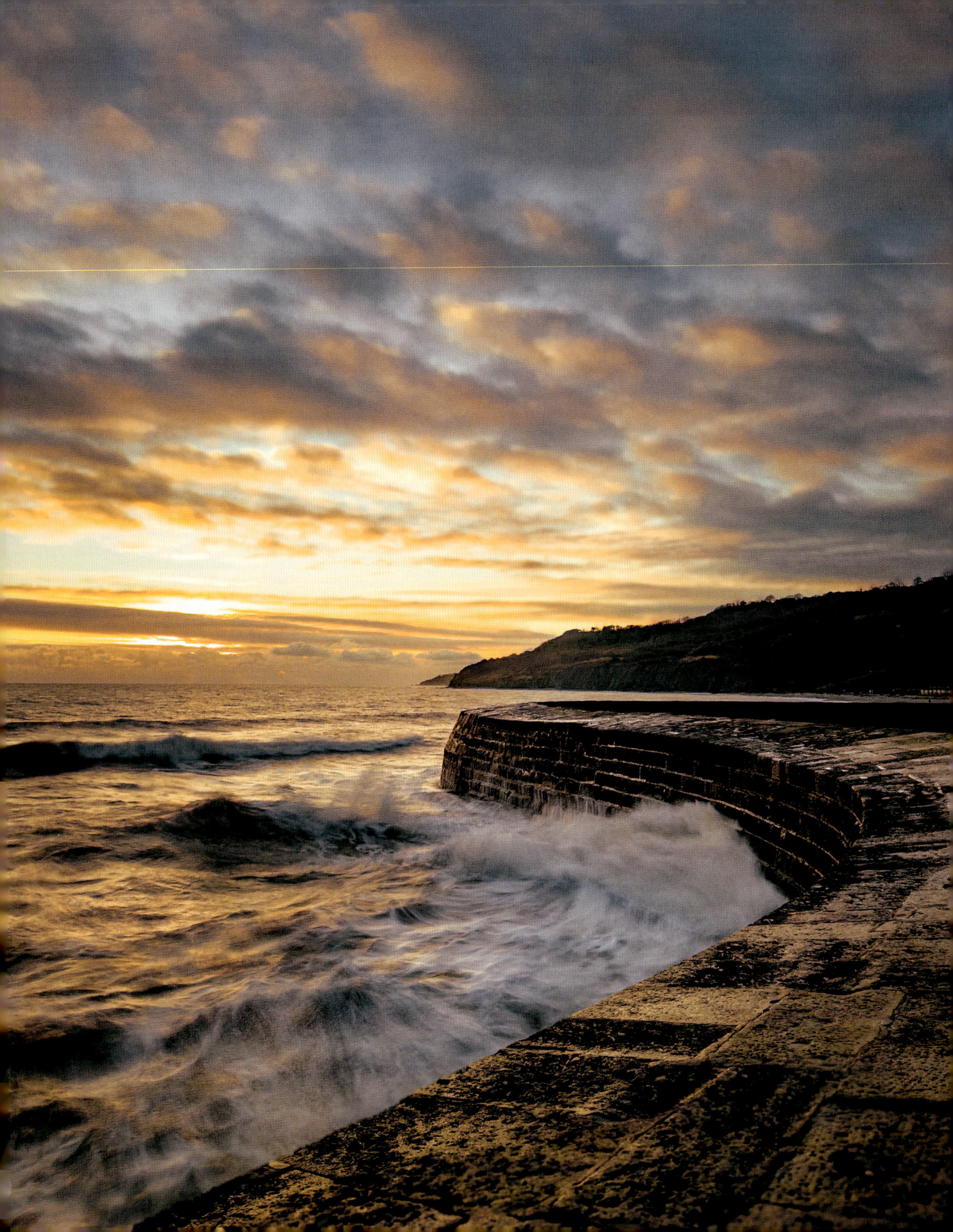

CHAPTER 3
PRINTER QUALITY /
HEALTH CHECK

Now that we've correctly calibrated our display, and before we dive into printing and start using ICC profiles and experimenting with different papers, we need to check that our printer is actually performing as it should. You should do this both when you first get your printer and if you're having any problems getting prints to look right, even after following all the steps in this book.

Sometimes, no matter what we do, there could still be something affecting the final print. You'll see later in this book how even just the printing software you use can cause variations in your prints.

But before all of that, let's make sure the printer is working correctly.

EVALUATION/TEST PRINTS: CANON AND EPSON

We'll go through this process with both Canon and Epson printers. I'm going to print out what's called an Evaluation Print or Test Print, which can be seen in **Figure 3.1.** As you can see, this file contains a wide variety of imagery that will allow us to evaluate:

- Gradients
- Skin tones
- Colored squares
- Grayscale
- Vibrant colors, and more

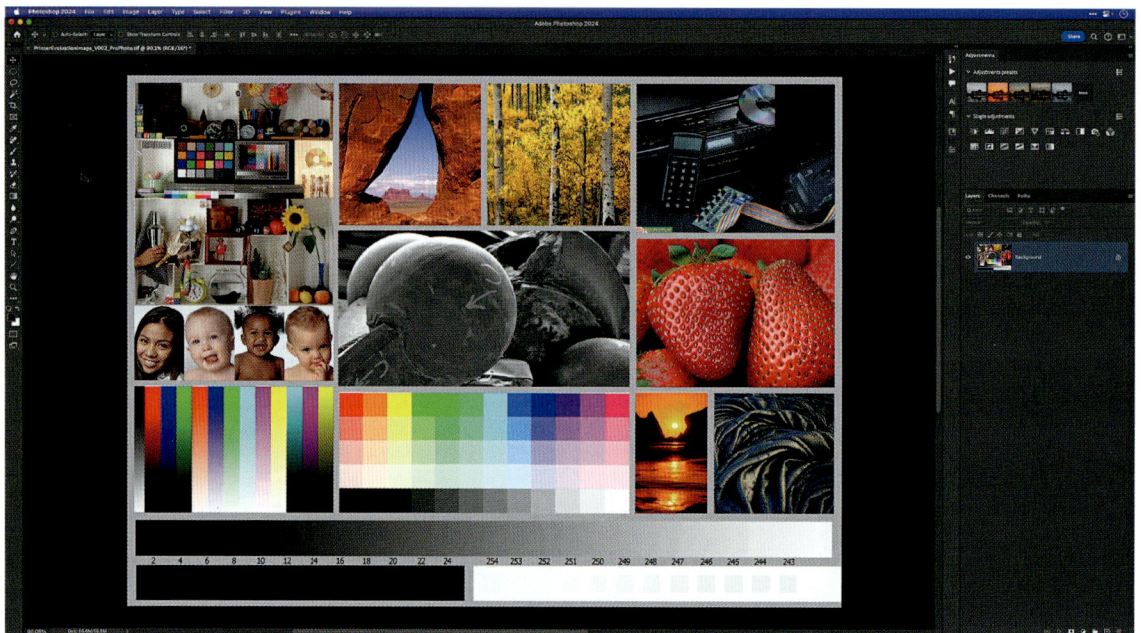

FIGURE 3.1

Download a copy of the Evaluation / Test Print file from www.thehowtoprintbook.com.

I'll start by running this through the Canon printer and my Apple (Mac) computer.

OPENING THE EVALUATION FILE

The Evaluation Print file is a TIFF file in the ProPhoto RGB color space. I already have this file open in Photoshop **(Figure 3.2)**, and you'll notice there's an asterisk at the end of the file name and zoom percentage.

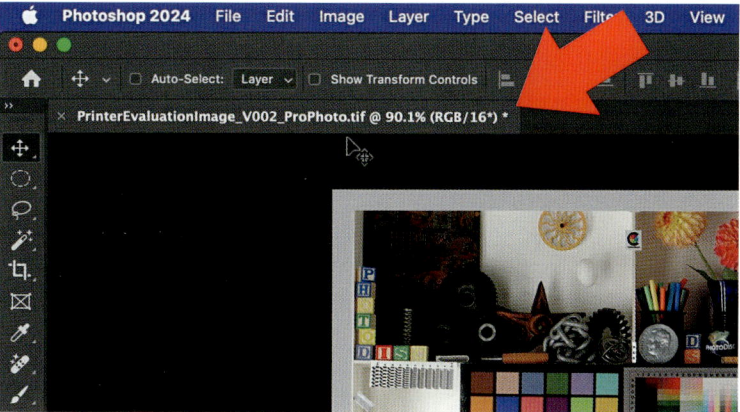

FIGURE 3.2

This means there's a color space mismatch (i.e., the working color space in Photoshop is different from the embedded color space of the image).

If I go to **Edit** > **Color Settings**, you'll see that my working space is currently set to Adobe RGB **(Figure 3.3)**, and that's why we're seeing the asterisk. (You might already have yours set to ProPhoto RGB, in which case you wouldn't see the asterisk.)

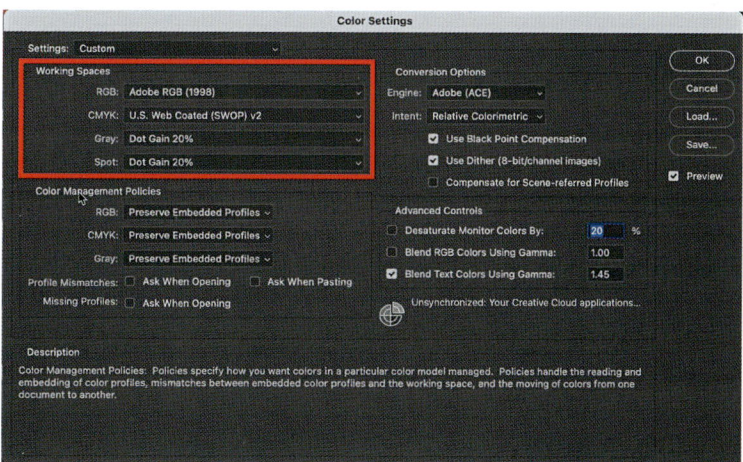

FIGURE 3.3

IMPORTANT: *Do not convert the embedded color space of the image. Leave it as it is. If you get a warning dialog box, **do not** choose the option to convert the image.*

PRINTING THE FILE: CANON PRO-300 ON MAC

Now, let's go to **File** > **Print (Figure 3.4)**.

1. Select the correct printer, which in this case is the Canon Pro-300 **(Figure 3.5)**.

2. In the Color Handling menu under Color Management, select Printer Manages Colors. This means all color management is handled by the printer and its driver.

3. Leave the Rendering Intent at Perceptual, then click Print Settings at the top of the dialog to access the printer driver.

> **NOTE:** *Because we're letting the Canon printer handle color, you must use Canon ink and Canon paper. If you're using third-party inks or papers, you need to manage color using ICC profiles, which we'll cover later.*

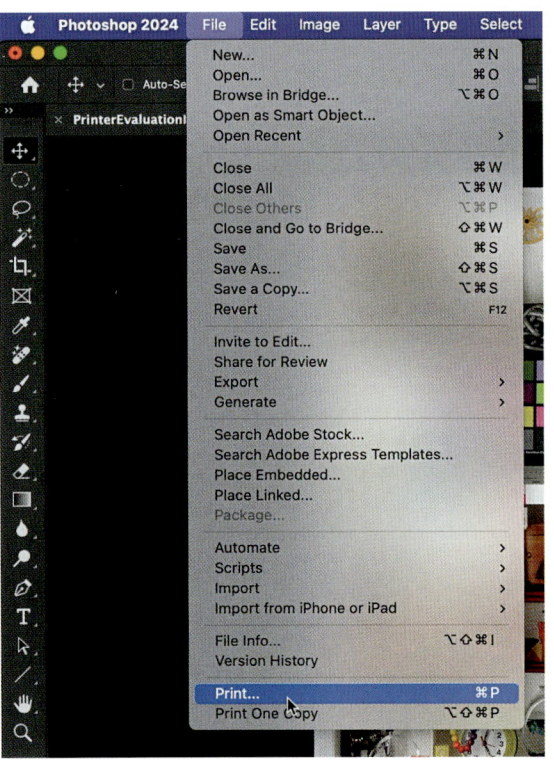

FIGURE 3.4

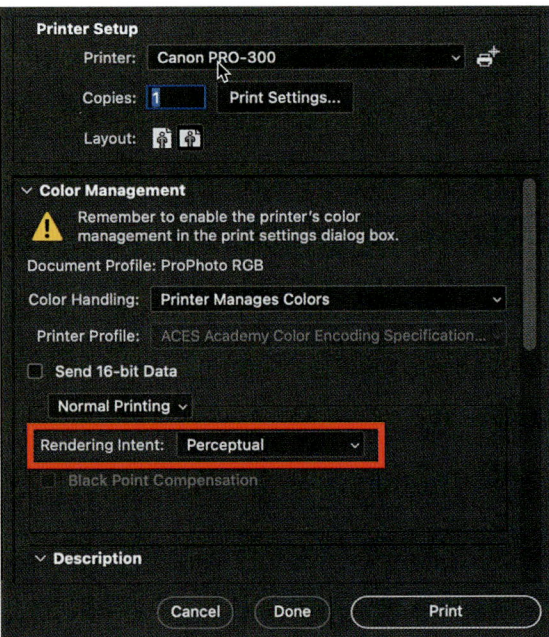

FIGURE 3.5

PRINTER DRIVER SETTINGS—CANON PRO-300

In the print driver settings, here are the options I go with:

- **Paper Size:** A4.

- **Color Matching:** The system uses Canon Color Matching, which is exactly what we want.

- **Quality & Media:** This is where you select which Canon paper you're using. This tells the printer how thick the paper is (to adjust printhead height), how much ink to use, and which black ink to use (photo or matte), if your printer has both. It also selects the correct Canon ICC profile installed with the printer driver. I'm

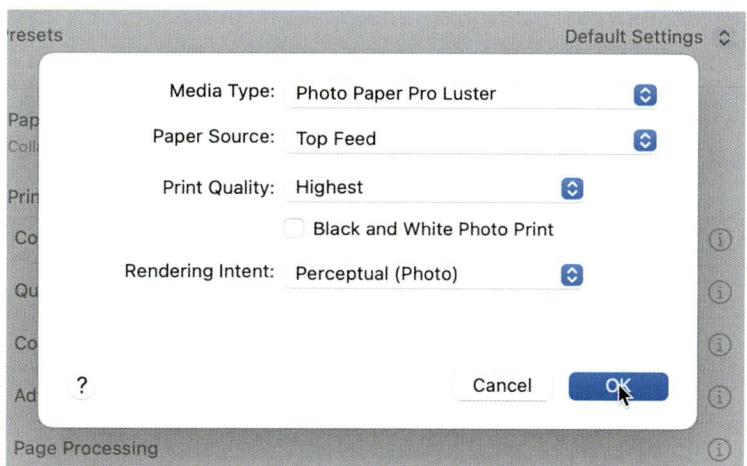

FIGURE 3.6

going to use Canon Photo Paper Pro Luster, so I choose that under Media Type, and I set the Print Quality to Highest and the Rendering Intent to Perceptual **(Figure 3.6)**.

Click OK, then Save, and finally Print**.**

PRINTING THE FILE: EPSON P900 ON WINDOWS

Now I'll print out the same Evaluation Print file on the Epson P900, this time from Photoshop on a Windows computer.

Just like before, I have the evaluation image open in Photoshop, and once again, we see the asterisk next to the file name. The reason for this is that there is a color space mismatch **(Figure 3.7)**.

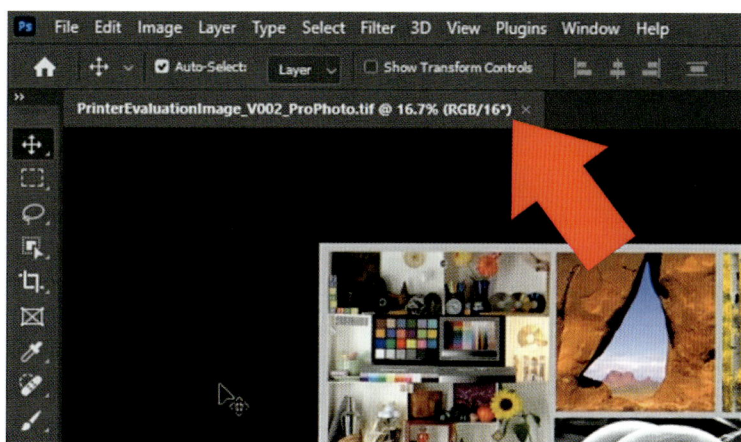

FIGURE 3.7

This is nothing to worry about. It just means that my chosen working color space in Photoshop is Adobe RGB, whereas the Evaluation Print file has an embedded color space of ProPhoto RGB.

PRINTING FROM PHOTOSHOP: KEY SETTINGS

Go to **File** > **Print**.

1. Select the printer, which in this case is the Epson SC-P900 Series **(Figure 3.8)**.

2. In the Color Handling menu under Color Management, choose Printer Manages Colors. This means all color management is handled by the printer and its driver.

3. For the Rendering Intent, this time choose Relative Colorimetric.

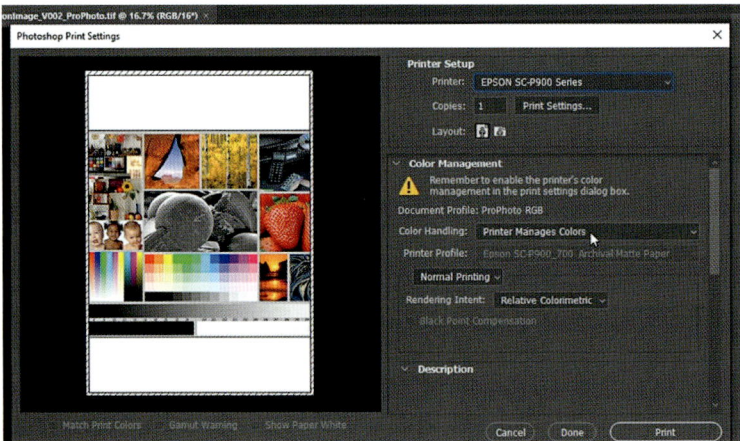

FIGURE 3.8

If the orientation of the image is incorrect, you can adjust it by clicking the icons next to Layout near the top of the dialog.

PRINTER DRIVER SETTINGS—EPSON P900

Now let's dive into the printer driver by clicking on Print Settings. Here are the options I select (**Figure 3.9**):

- **Paper Type:** I'm using Epson Premium Luster Photo Paper, so I select that.

- **Print Mode:** Color.

- **Quality Level:** High Quality.

- I untick the **Black Enhance Overcoat** checkbox because I don't want anything extra added to this print. This is purely to test that it's printing as it should.

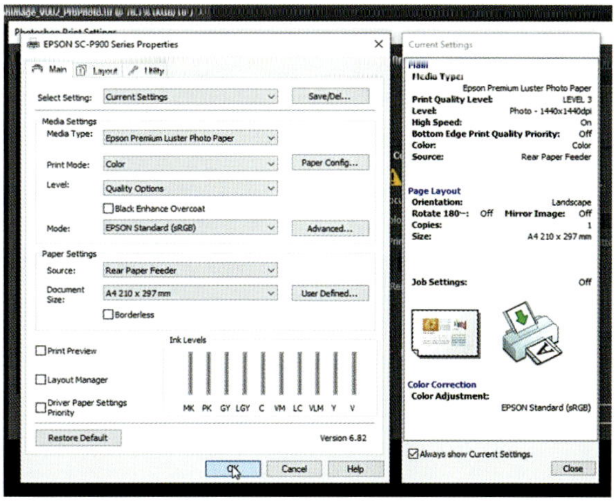

COLOR MODE AND OUTPUT SETTINGS

For the Mode, we have the following options:

- **Epson Standard**

- **sRGB**

- **ICM**

I choose Epson Standard.

The ICM option would make the driver automatically select the profile settings for this Epson paper and printer.

I choose the following under Paper Settings:

- **Source:** Rear Paper Feeder

- **Document Size:** A4

Click OK.

FIGURE 3.9

CONFIRMING PRINTER ACCURACY AND WHY ICC PROFILES STILL MATTER

The two printouts of the Evaluation Print file, one from the Canon printer and one from the Epson, look pretty much identical **(Figure 3.10)**. They've both printed beautifully.

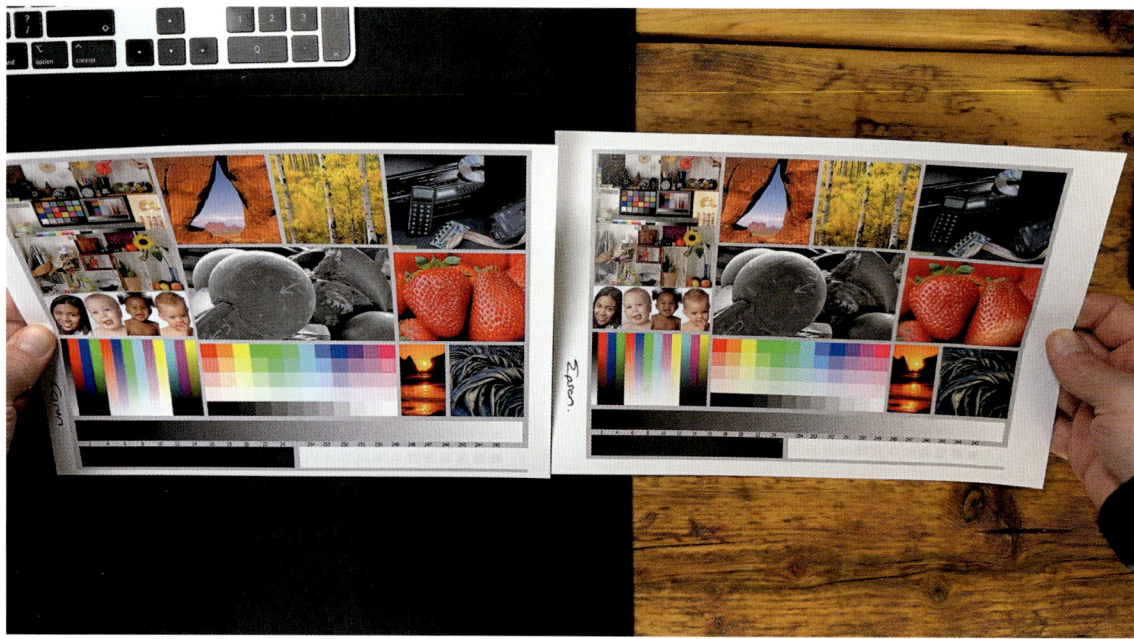

FIGURE 3.10

The black-to-white gradient is nice and smooth. The dark tones from 24 down to 2 are all visible when I view them under the daylight-balanced light in my office. The lighter patches, from 243 to 254, are also clearly visible.

The grayscale image looks great. The skin tones appear exactly as they should.

The saturated colors in the landscape areas are vibrant and true to life, and the strawberries look good enough to eat.

So yes, this 100 percent confirms that both printers are performing exactly as they should.

But if the prints look great already ... why ICC profiles?

Well, yes, you *can* get near-perfect prints this way, but that's only true when you're using the printer brand's paper and ink.

- For Canon, that means Canon paper and Canon ink.

- For Epson, that means Epson paper and Epson ink.

As soon as you want to use another manufacturer's paper, that approach no longer works reliably. That's where ICC profiles become absolutely essential.

PRINT AN IMAGE ON CANON USING LUSTER PAPER

Let's now actually print an image and see how it turns out.

I'll print the image shown in **Figure 3.11** using Photoshop on my Mac, and I'll do that on the Canon printer, again using Canon Luster paper and Canon ink.

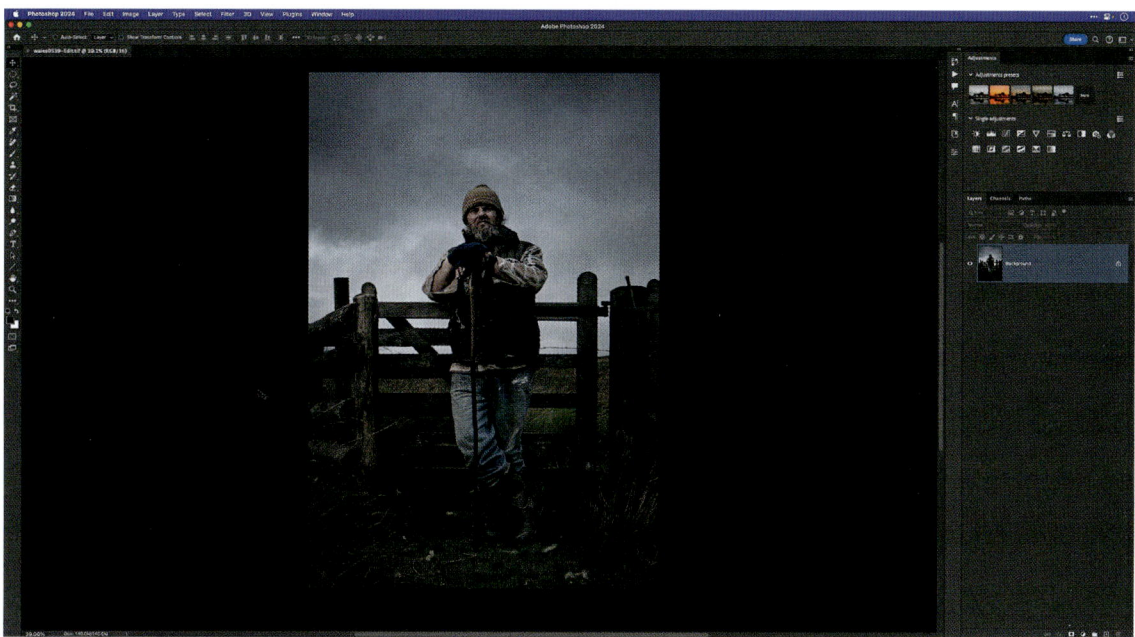

FIGURE 3.11

You'll notice that with this image open, there's no asterisk at the far right of the tab that contains the file name **(Figure 3.12)**. This means the working color space in Photoshop is the same as the embedded color space of the image.

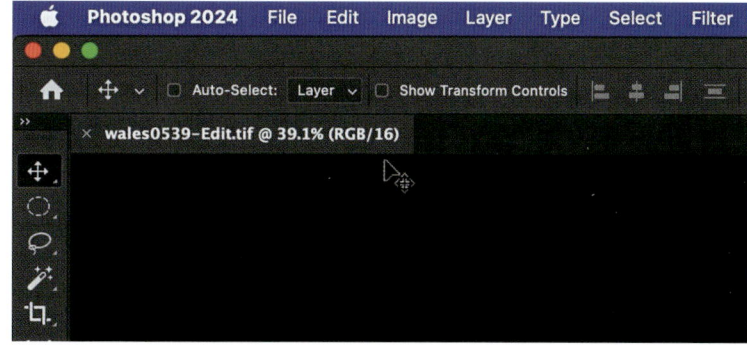

FIGURE 3.12

If I go to **Edit** > **Color Settings**, you'll see that my working color space is Adobe RGB **(Figure 3.13)**.

If I now go to **Edit** > **Convert to Profile (Figure 3.14)**, you'll see at the top that the source profile (that is, the image's embedded profile) is also Adobe RGB **(Figure 3.15)**.

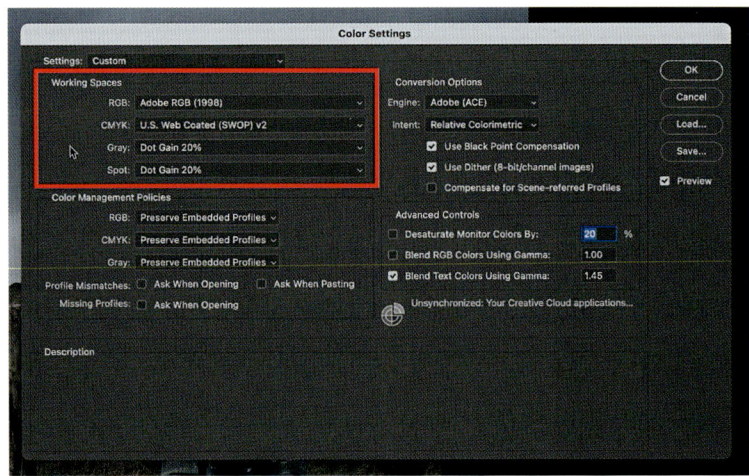

FIGURE 3.13

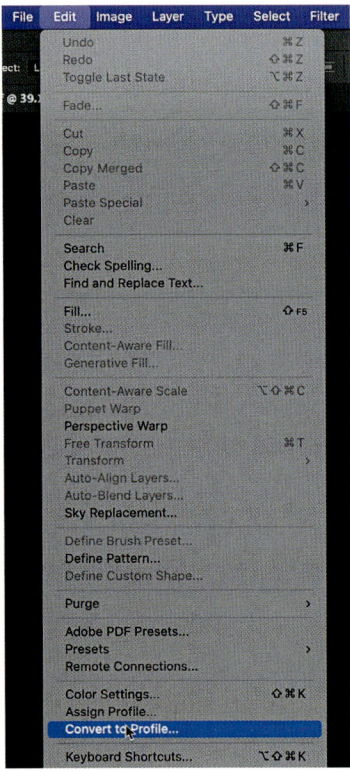

FIGURE 3.14

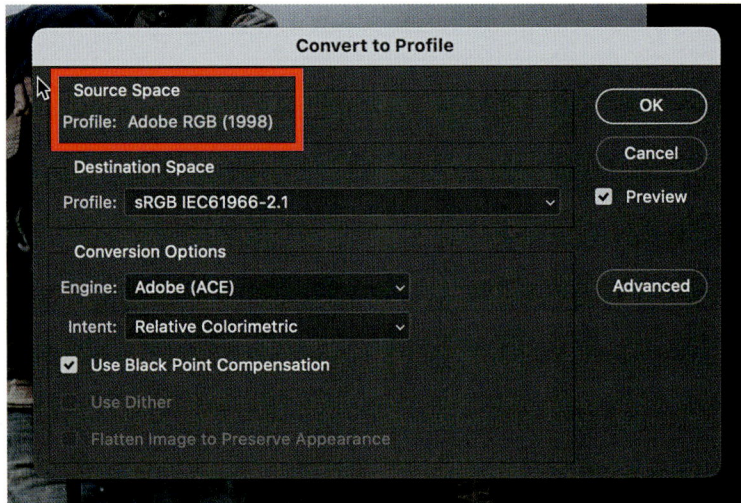

FIGURE 3.15

Next, I'll resize the image to fit on an A4 sheet of Luster paper by going to **Image** > **Image Size** and changing dimensions to inches. For the Height, I enter 10, and for Resample, I choose Bicubic Sharper (reduction) rather than leaving it set to Automatic **(Figure 3.16)**.

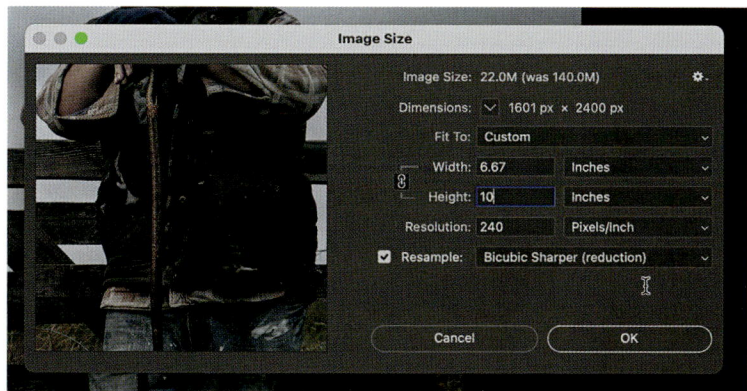

FIGURE 3.16

Choosing the appropriate resample method, like Bicubic Sharper for reduction or Preserve Details for enlargement, will give you better print results.

Click OK and that's done.

PRINTING FROM PHOTOSHOP WITH CANON

Now I go to **File** > **Print**.

I'll choose the Canon printer, and under Color Handling, select Printer Manages Colors **(Figure 3.17)**.

This time, I'll also tick the box for Send 16-Bit Data, since it's a 16-bit file. We probably won't see any visual difference, but there's no harm in enabling it.

I'll leave Rendering Intent set to Perceptual.

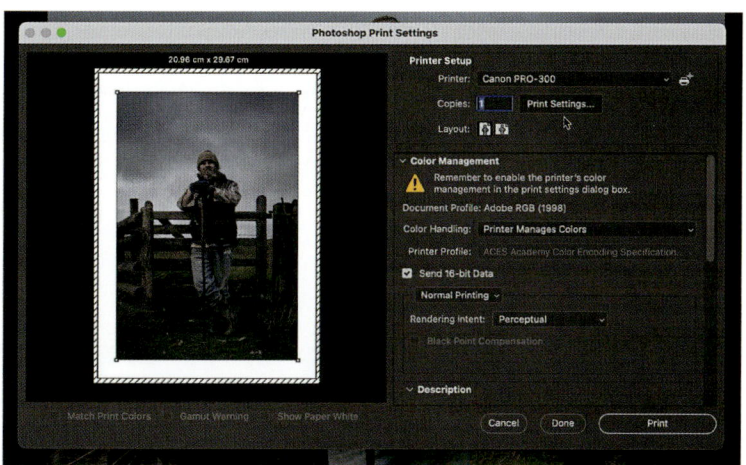

FIGURE 3.17

NOTE: *I go over the differences in Rendering Intent more thoroughly later on.*

Under Color Management, you'll also see a reminder to enable the printer's color management in the Print Settings dialog.

Now I click Print Settings up near the top of the dialog.

CANON PRINTER DRIVER CONFIGURATION

Here are the options I go with in the Print Settings **(Figure 3.18)**:

- **Paper Size:** A4.
- **Printer Options** > **Color Matching:** Confirm that Canon Color Matching is selected.
- **Quality & Media:**
  - **Media Type:** Pro Luster (the paper I'm using)
  - **Paper Source:** Top Feed
  - **Print Quality**: Highest
  - **Rendering Intent:** Perceptual

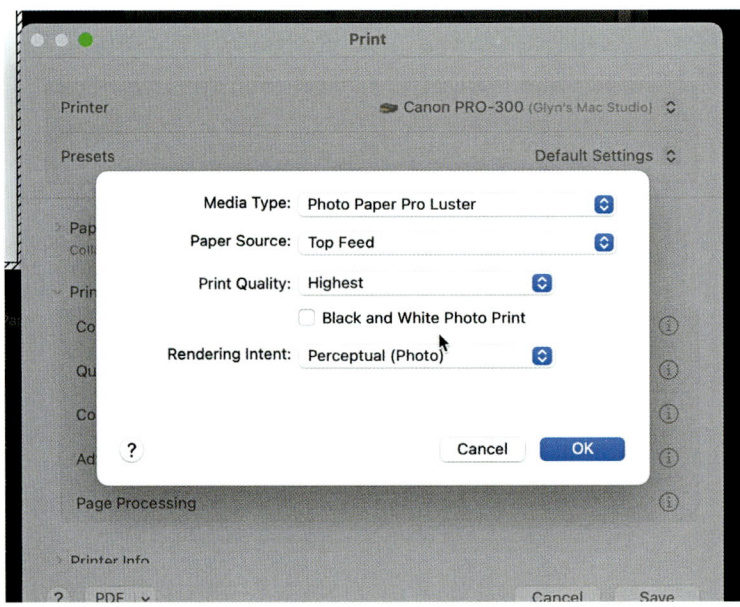

FIGURE 3.18

Click OK, then Save, and finally Print.

THE FINAL PRINT AND A WORD ABOUT PAPER

The final print looks brilliant **(Figure 3.19)**. I'm very happy with it.

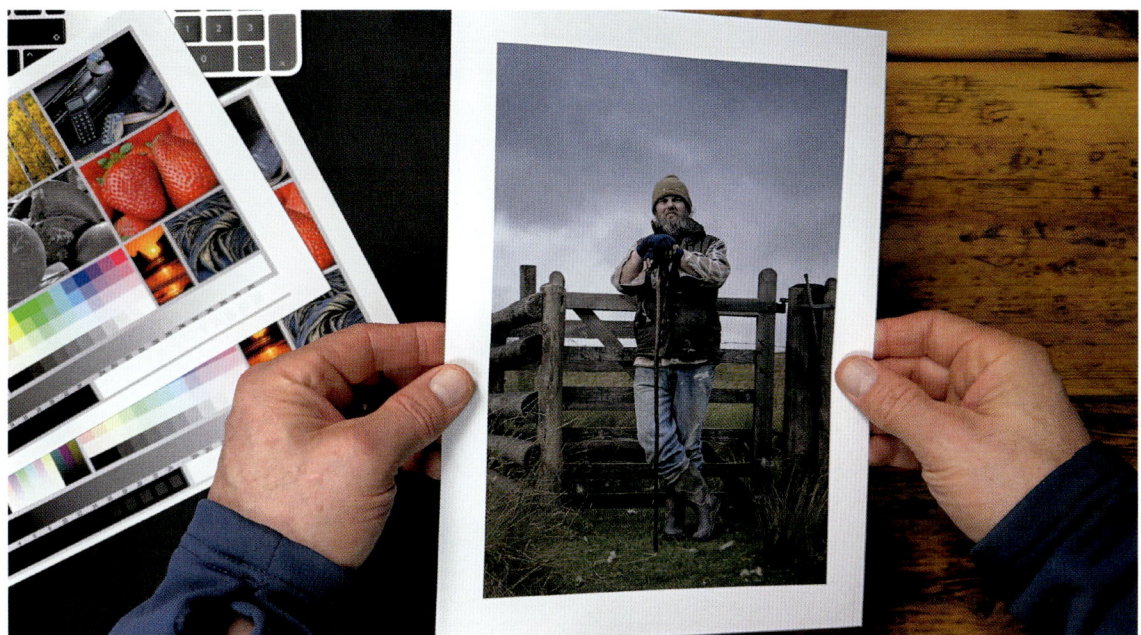

FIGURE 3.19

But to be honest, Luster paper isn't the kind of paper I'd really want to print this image on. Sure, it looks great, but it's amazing how the right paper can really bring a picture to life.

What I'd want instead is something with a different feel, with different characteristics, and that would likely be from another paper manufacturer.

To use that kind of paper properly, I would need to use a specific ICC profile for that paper on that printer, with Canon ink.

I'm going to go through exactly how to do that, but before we get there, there are a few other things I need to mention.

TURNING OFF COLOR MANAGEMENT IN THE PRINTER DRIVER

When we're using ICC profiles, it's vitally important that we leave the color handling to the printing software and the ICC profile for the specific paper we're using. What we don't want is any kind of confusion within the computer about what's managing color, so we need to turn off color management in the printer driver.

How you do this depends on:

- The operating system you're using (Mac or Windows)

- The brand of printer you're using (Canon or Epson)

ON A MAC

When using a Mac and printing with an ICC profile, color management is automatically turned off in the printer driver. You can see this when you go to **Printer Driver** > **Printer Options** > **Color Matching**. The Color Matching options will be grayed out **(Figure 3.20)**. This means color management is disabled in the driver, which is exactly what we want.

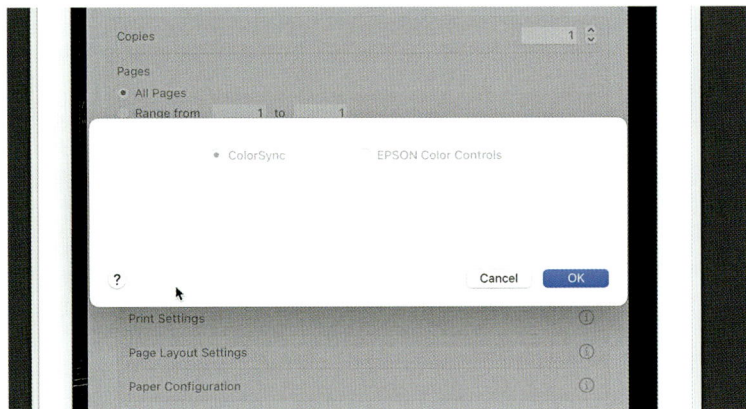

FIGURE 3.20

ON WINDOWS: CANON

When using Windows with a Canon printer, it's a bit different **(Figure 3.21)**.

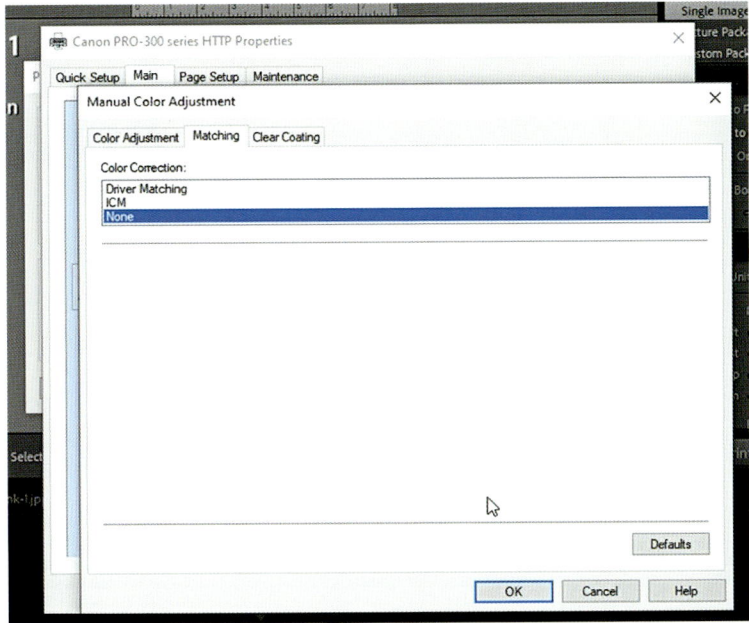

FIGURE 3.21

Here's what to do:

1. Go to Properties.

2. Click on Main.

3. Under Color/Intensity, choose Manual, then click on Set.

4. In the next screen, go to Matching and choose None.

5. Click OK.

This ensures the printer driver doesn't interfere with the ICC profile being used in Photoshop or your chosen printing software.

ON WINDOWS: EPSON

When using Windows with an Epson printer on Windows, follow these steps **(Figure 3.22)**:

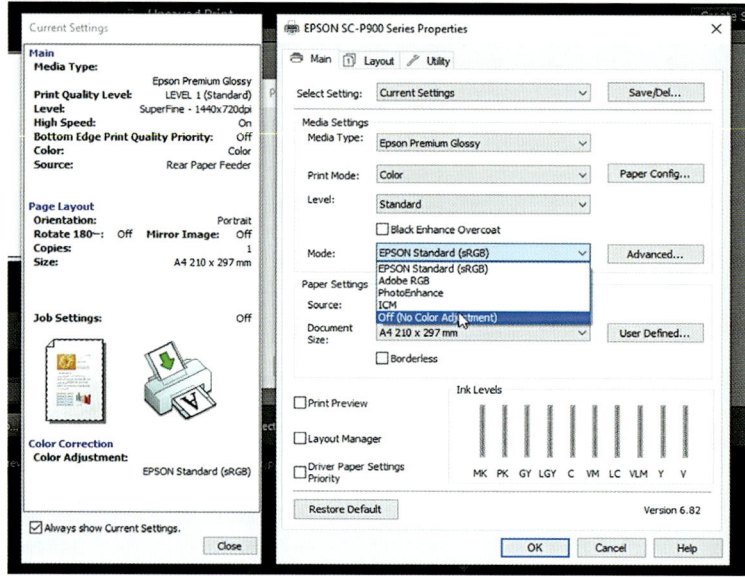

FIGURE 3.22

1. Go to Properties.

2. In the Main section, find the Mode drop-down menu and choose Off (No Color Adjustment).

3. Click OK.

This disables Epson's internal color management, letting the ICC profile and software take full control.

ALWAYS DOUBLE-CHECK

Always go back in and double-check your settings to ensure that color management is turned off in the printer driver. This is something you should check every single time you print, even if you think it's already set, even if you just printed five minutes ago. It's a small step that avoids big problems with color inconsistency and ultimately helps you to avoid wasting money on ink and paper.

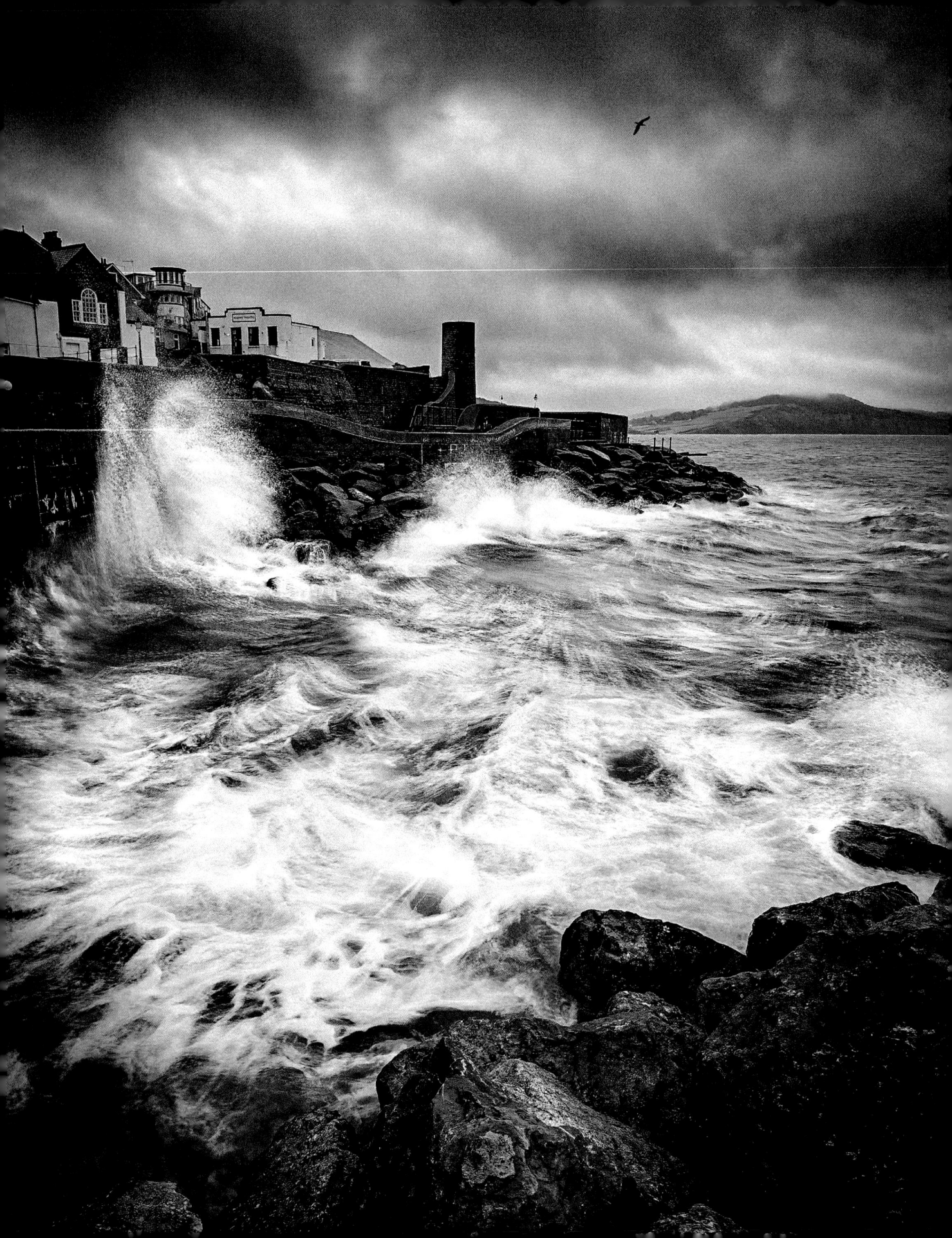

CHAPTER 4
PRINTING A
BLACK-AND-WHITE IMAGE

In this chapter I'll take you through the process of printing a black-and-white image. My aim here is to give you an overview of some of the common controls and settings you'll encounter. Regardless of the software you choose to print from, whether you're using Photoshop, Lightroom Classic, Canon software (if you're using a Canon printer), or Epson software (as I will be for this example), the settings covered here will be relevant.

Later in the book, you'll find sections that cover the complete workflow from start to finish, including guidance on retouching, resizing, sharpening, soft proofing, exporting, and more. However, this chapter serves as a good introduction to foundational printing knowledge.

For this example, the print will be made using the Epson P900, and I'll be working within the Epson Print Layout software **(Figure 4.1)**.

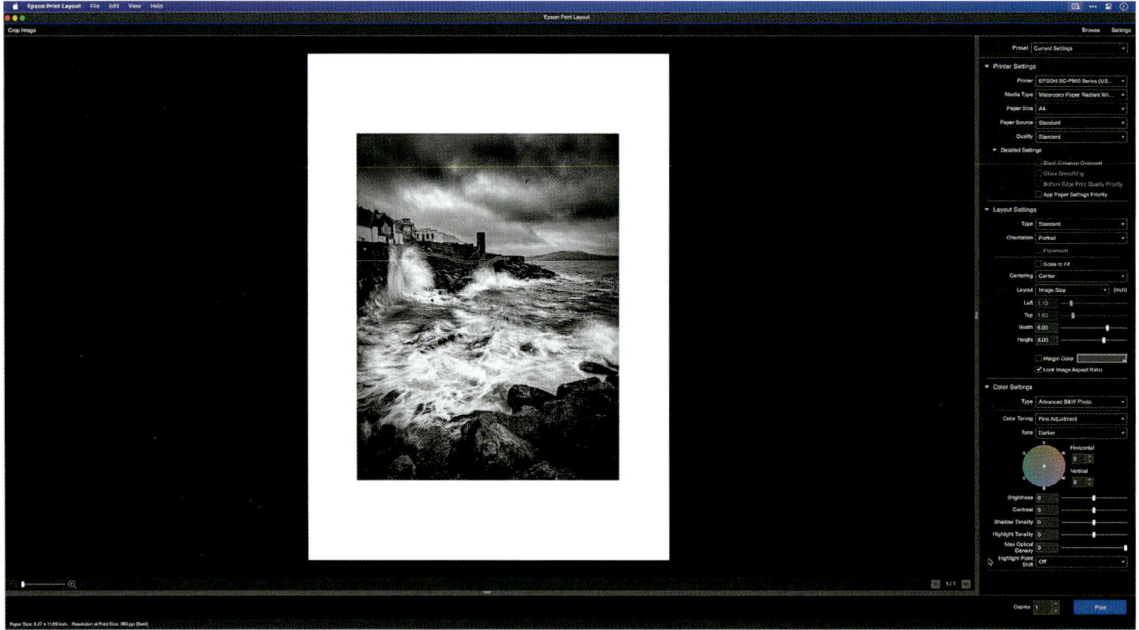

FIGURE 4.1

The image has already undergone retouching, resizing, sharpening, and soft proofing, and is now imported into the software, ready to print. I'm going to print on matte paper, which is my preferred paper type, specifically Smooth Rag, produced by PermaJet **(Figure 4.2)**. This paper is part of their Heritage Range and it has a lovely smooth texture, a good weight and thickness, and is capable of producing rich colors and deep blacks.

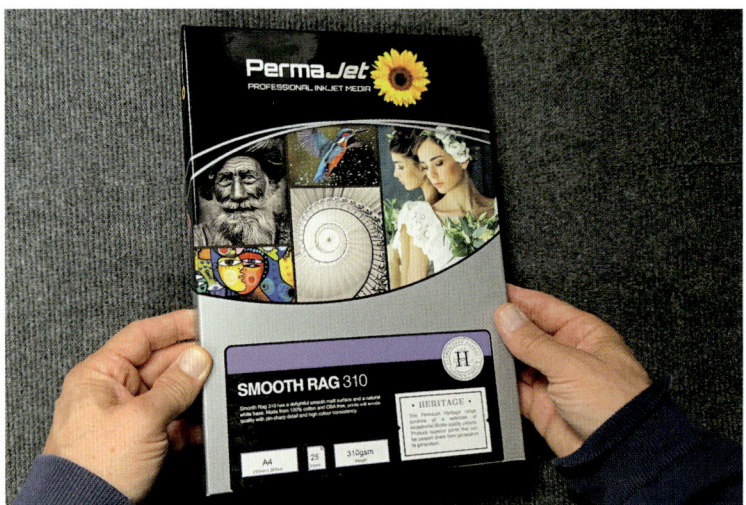

FIGURE 4.2

PRINTER SETTINGS

At the top of the Epson Print Layout application, you can see that the Epson P900 is selected as the active printer, and it is connected to my computer via USB **(Figure 4.3)**.

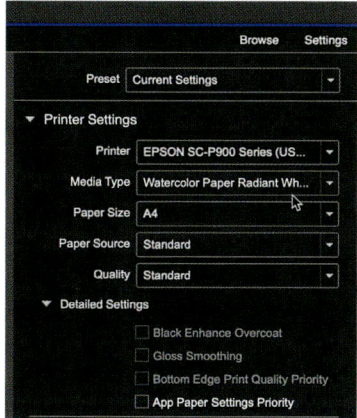

FIGURE 4.3

MEDIA TYPE

Next, we have the Media Type, which, as you'll see throughout this book, is a very important setting **(Figure 4.4)**. The media type basically tells the printer how to handle the paper that you're printing on. In the Media Type menu, there are a number of different options, and these are all installed when the driver for the Epson printer is installed **(Figure 4.5)**. All of the papers listed here are Epson papers that have different finishes and characteristics, and it's these finishes and characteristics that the printer responds to when we choose the Media Type.

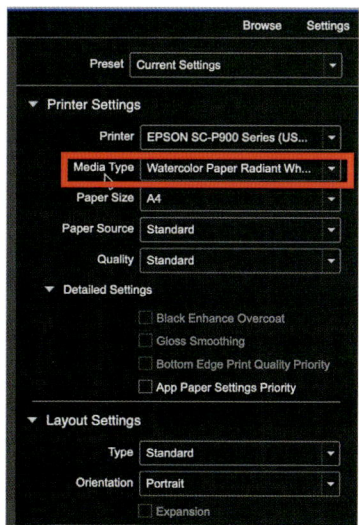

FIGURE 4.4

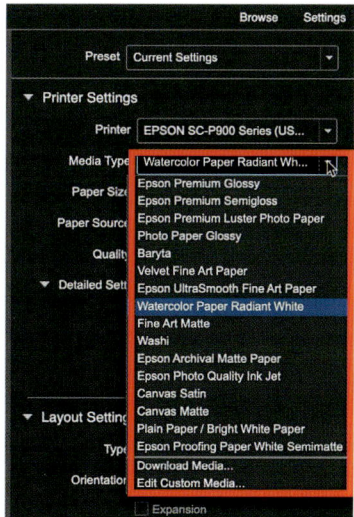

FIGURE 4.5

WHY MEDIA TYPE MATTERS

The Media Type gives the printer certain instructions, such as how high or low to lift the printhead. If the printhead is too low when using a thicker paper, you could potentially get what is called a printhead strike, which is where the printhead strikes each side of the paper as it goes back and forth. This will cause ink marks on the paper each time it hits it. More importantly, this can lead to damage to the printhead, which we obviously don't want. Selecting the appropriate media type prevents this from happening **(Figure 4.6)**.

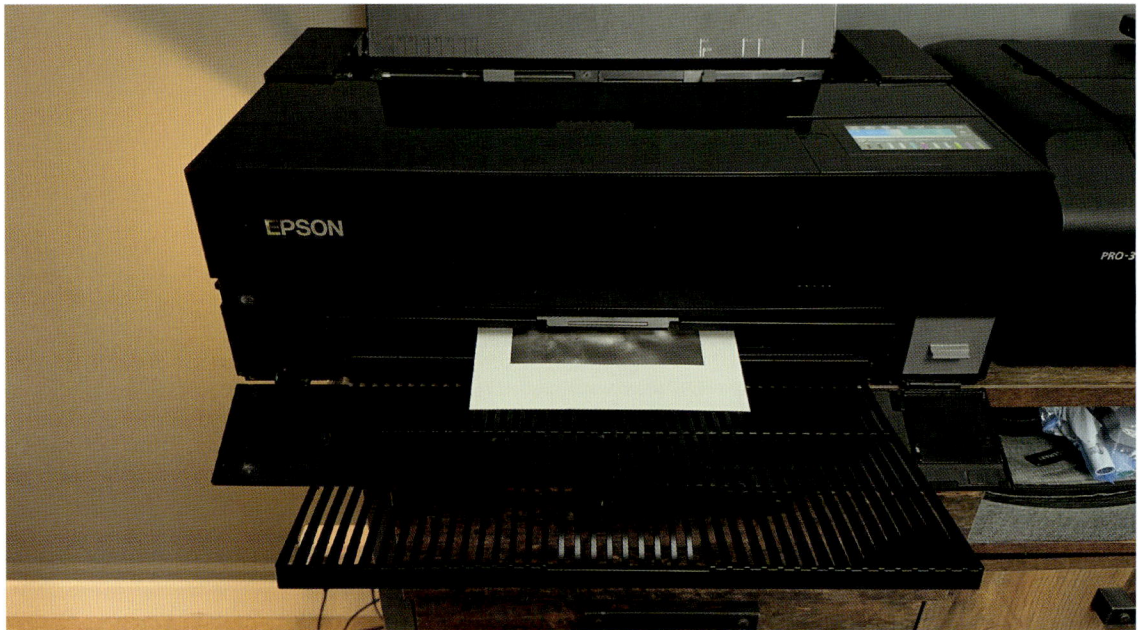

FIGURE 4.6

With regard to feeding the paper through the printer, the Media Type can also include such information as to how the printer brings the paper through, how hard the rollers should press against it, how many rollers to use, and so on. If you are using a fine art paper with a textured surface and the paper is gripped too hard, it could potentially leave marks on the paper. You can see an example of this in **Figure 4.7**.

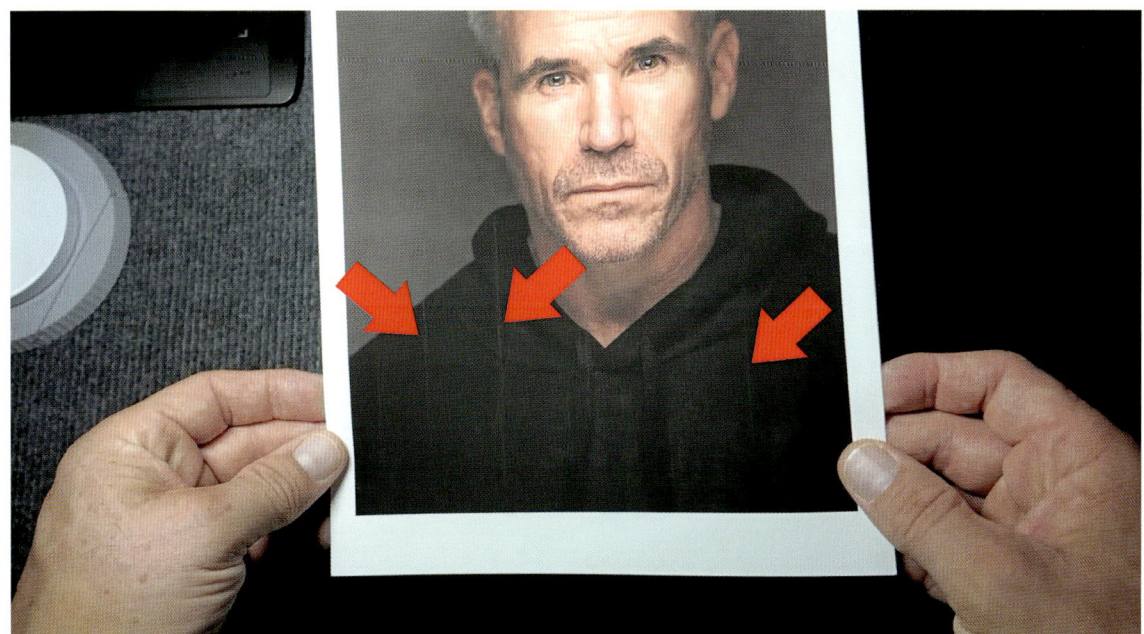

FIGURE 4.7

The Media Type also tells the printer which black ink to use **(Figure 4.8)**. In most photo printers, there will be two types of black ink: photo black and matte black.

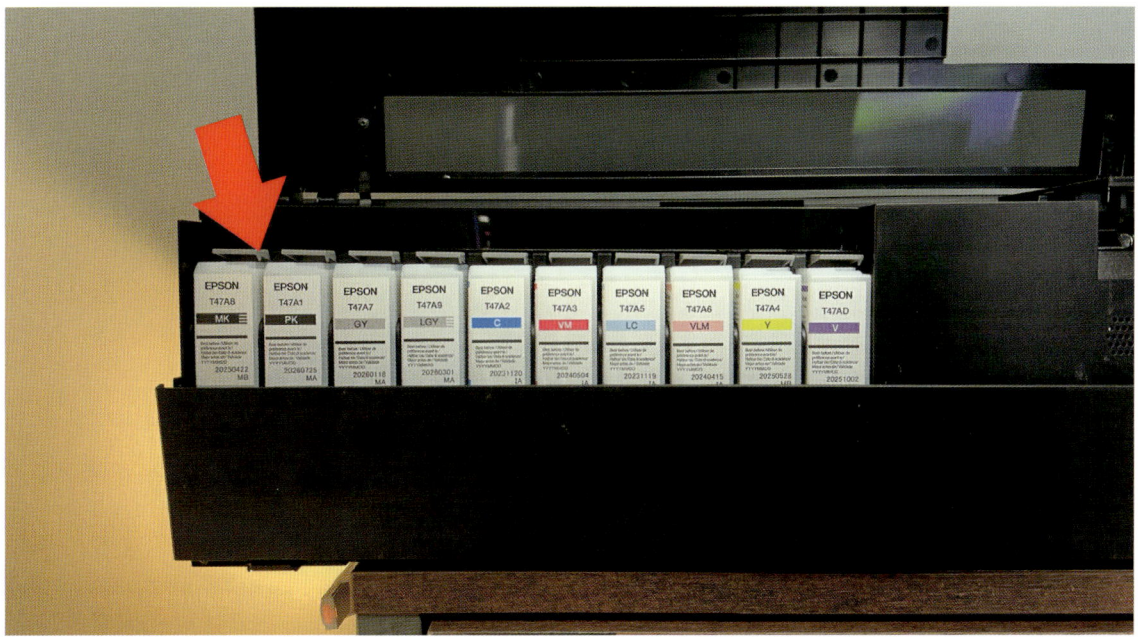

FIGURE 4.8

- If you are using a coated paper or anything other than a matte surface, generally a gloss or a baryta paper, the printer will use the photo black ink.

- If you are using a matte paper, or a fine art paper, the printer will use a matte black ink.

> **NOTE:** *The Media Type is different from an ICC profile, which I'll explain in chapter 5.*

HOW TO CHOOSE THE RIGHT MEDIA TYPE

As for which Media Type to use, if you are printing on an Epson paper, you can simply select that from the Media Type menu. However, for different brands of paper, you will find that the paper manufacturer will advise you on which Media Type to use so that the printer behaves correctly. PermaJet, for example, lists this information on a sheet of A4 provided with their paper, as well as on their website **(Figure 4.9)**.

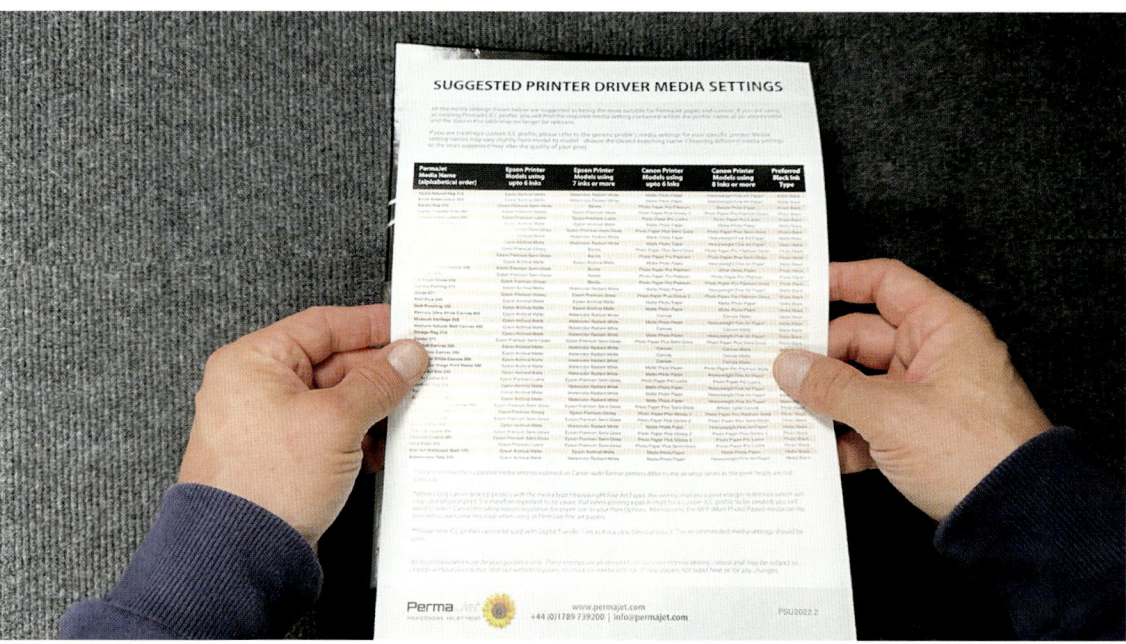

FIGURE 4.9

So for the example I'm using here, I'll find the Smooth Rag paper on the information sheet, and then look across for the appropriate printer, which in this case is my Epson P900, and that has more than seven inks. The recommended Media Type is Epson Watercolor Radiant White, which is the one I have chosen.

PAPER SIZE

For this example, I'm printing onto an A4 sheet of paper.

PAPER SOURCE

Paper Source refers to how the paper is fed into the printer. In this case, it's set to Standard, which corresponds to the regular method of feeding paper from the top.

Depending on the paper type, its thickness, or whether it comes on a roll (which this printer supports), you may need to change the feed method. For the Smooth Rag paper, however, I'll be sticking with the standard top feed **(Figure 4.10)**.

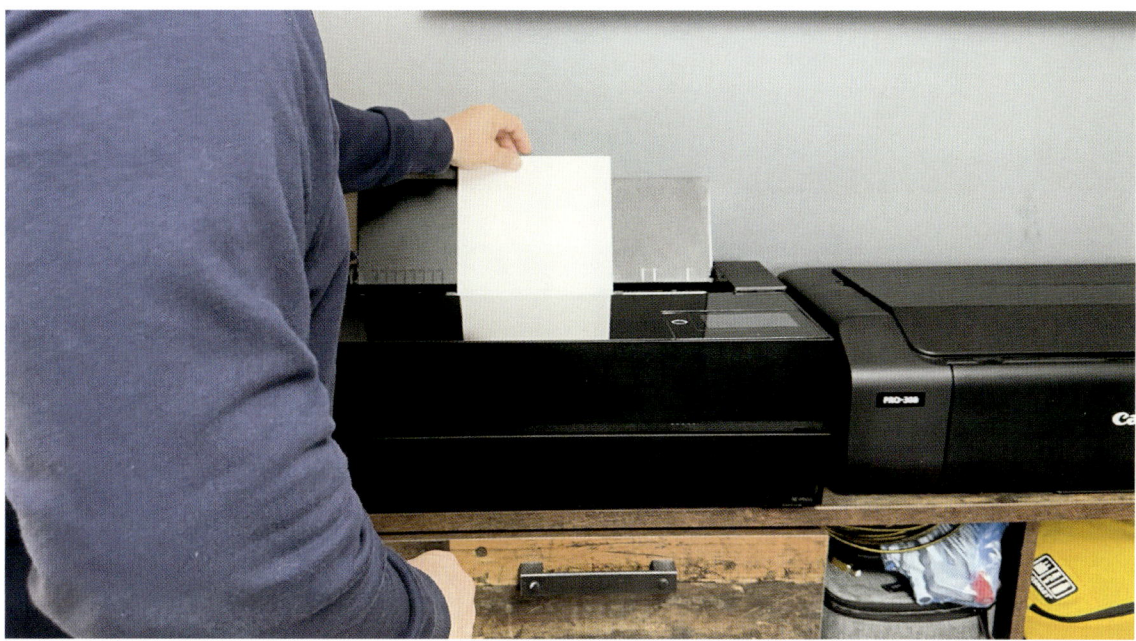

FIGURE 4.10

PRINT QUALITY

The Quality setting refers to print resolution; that is, how many dots of ink the printer will place on the paper per inch. This used to be represented numerically, such as 720 DPI or 1440 DPI, but that has changed. You'll understand why in the interview with Dominic Gurney from Epson, included in chapter 14.

For this particular Media Type, the available options are Max Quality or Standard. I usually stick with the default that the software chooses **(Figure 4.11)**.

If I were using a different paper, such as baryta paper, more options would become available **(Figure 4.12)**. This reflects how differently such paper handles ink, including the size of the color gamut that can be reproduced.

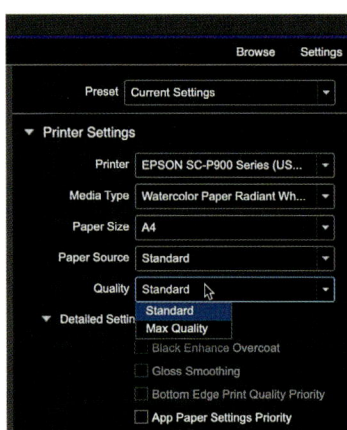

FIGURE 4.11

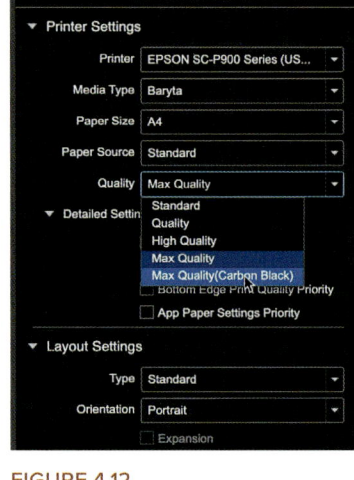

FIGURE 4.12

LAYOUT SETTINGS

Next are the Layout Settings:

- **Type:** This refers to the kind of print being made, such as a regular print, panorama, or gallery wrap. Here, I'm doing a standard print, so that's what I'll leave it set to **(Figure 4.13)**.

- **Orientation:** I've set this to Portrait.

- **Positioning and Size:** The image has already been sized to 6 inches by 8 inches, and I've chosen to center it on the A4 sheet of paper.

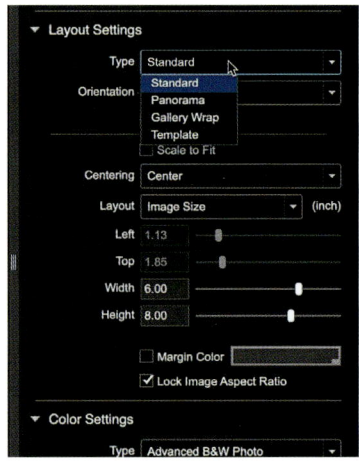

FIGURE 4.13

COLOR SETTINGS

In the Color Settings section of the print software, because I'm printing a black-and-white image, I won't be using an ICC profile. Instead, I'll be using the black-and-white mode specific to the printer:

• In the Epson software, this setting is called Advanced B&W Photo **(Figure 4.14)**.

• In the Canon software (such as when using the Canon Pro 300), it's called Black and White Photo **(Figure 4.15)**.

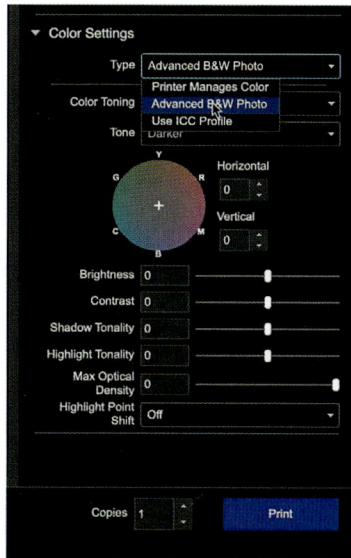

FIGURE 4.14

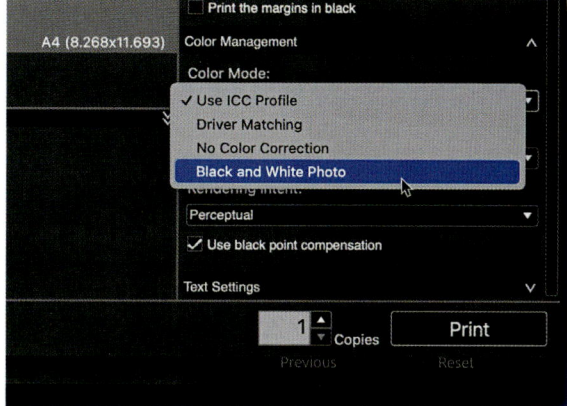

FIGURE 4.15

There are several reasons for this, but the main one is that the black-and-white mode guarantees a neutral print. In contrast, if I used an ICC profile, I couldn't guarantee that same neutrality. Sometimes, using an ICC profile may result in a black-and-white image that has a slight magenta or greenish tint. This does not happen when using the printer's black-and-white mode.

TONING CONTROLS

In the Epson software, there are additional controls available to fine-tune the final appearance of the print.

COLOR TONING

Color Toning allows you to add an intentional tone to the image, such as Cool, Warm, or Sepia. Once a tone is selected, it appears in the preview area. You can click and drag the plus icon to fine-tune the color toning. For even more precision, use the arrow keys to incrementally move the toning vertically and horizontally.

I'm sticking with Neutral, but the flexibility is there for anyone wanting more customization **(Figure 4.16)**.

TONE ADJUSTMENT

Another control I like is the Tone setting, which adjusts the overall brightness or darkness of the print. Options include:

- Lighter

- Normal

- Dark

- Darker

- Darkest

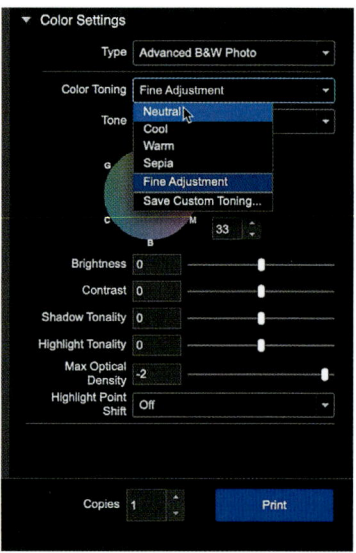

FIGURE 4.16

I'll set it back to Normal, which looks good. Trying Dark also gives a pleasing result. Darker is a bit too intense for this image, so I'll stick with Dark.

Finally, I simply press Print.

BLACK POINT COMPENSATION AND RENDERING INTENT

While the print is being made, it's worth noting that:

- In the Epson software, there is no option to turn Black Point Compensation on or off in Advanced B&W Photo, as it is enabled by default.

- In the Canon software, Black Point Compensation is shown, but again, it is enabled by default and cannot be changed.

- If you print from Lightroom, it is also on by default with no option to change it.

- You'll also notice there is no mention of Rendering Intent within the Epson software.

Both Black Point Compensation and Rendering Intent play a significant role in how the final image appears in print. These settings are covered in more depth in the next chapter, which deals with printing color images.

FINAL PRINT RESULT

Now that the print is complete, I'm able to review it under my viewing lamp and the result looks fantastic **(Figure 4.17)**. Lots of detail, neutral tones (so no color cast), perfect brightness, and rich blacks.

Yes … very happy!

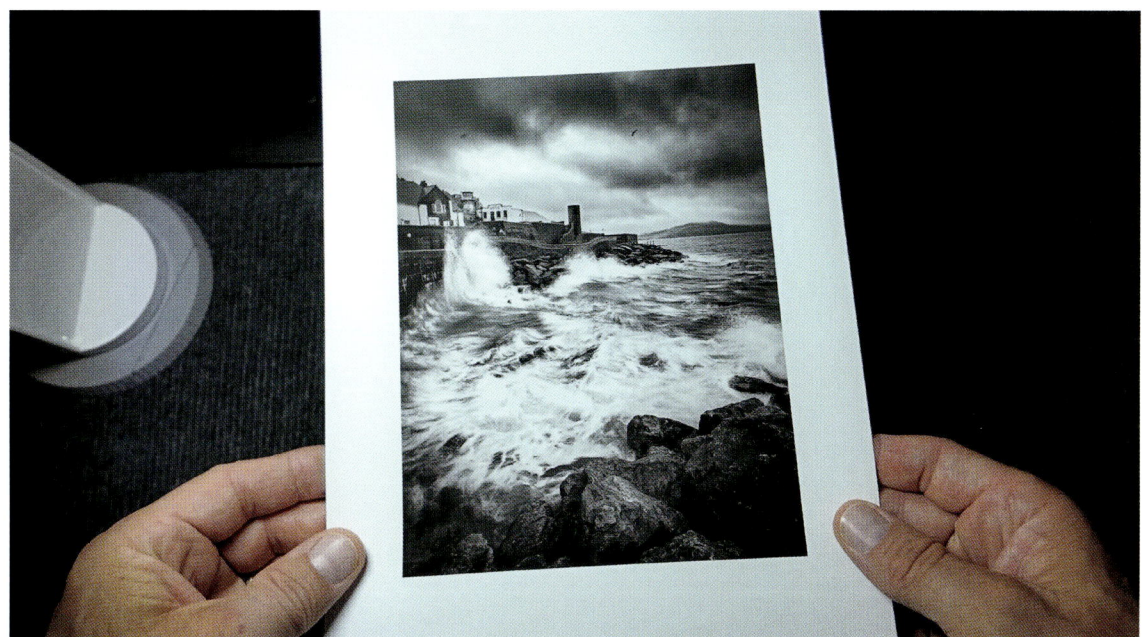

FIGURE 4.17

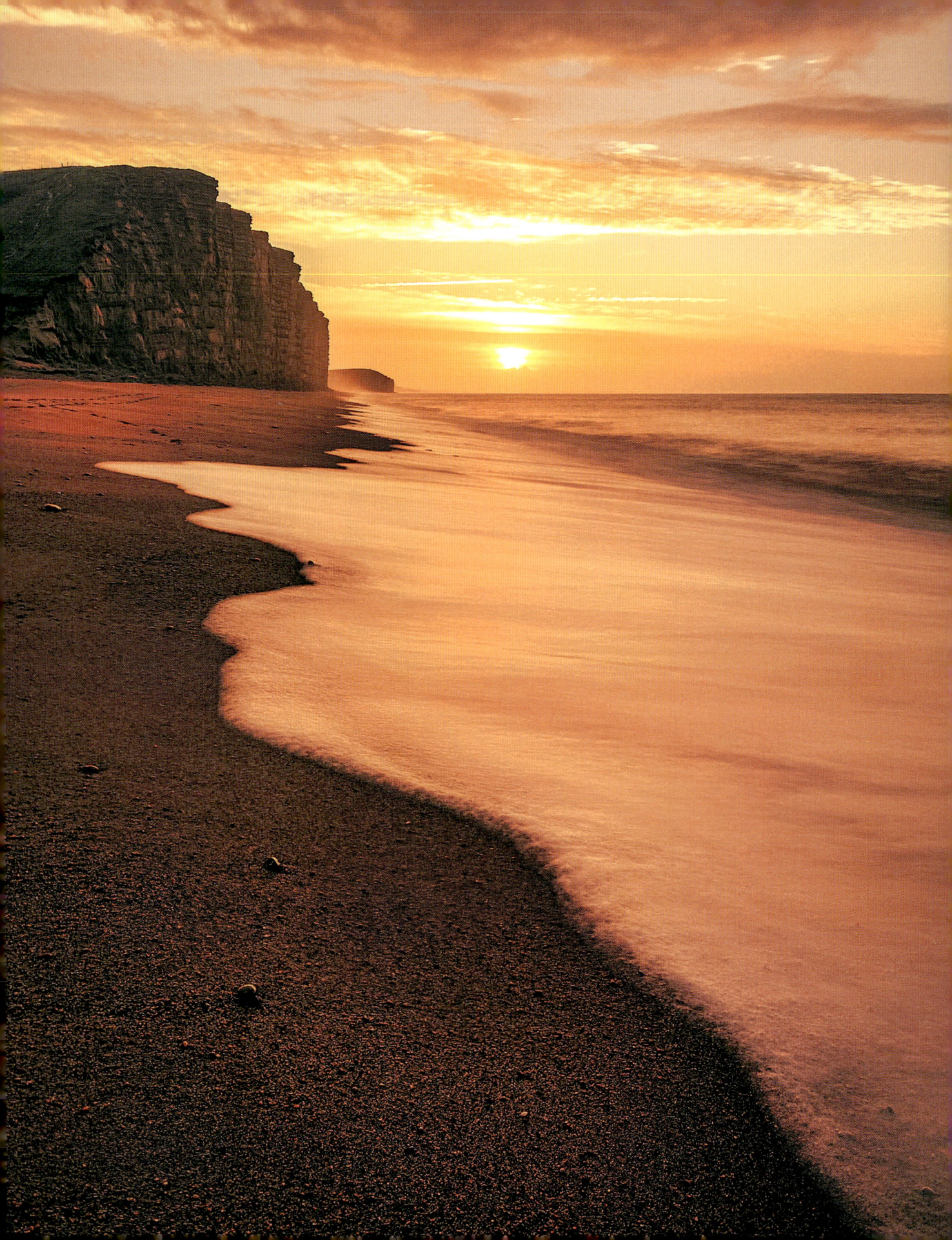

CHAPTER 5
PRINTING A COLOR IMAGE

In this section, I'm going to take you through the process of printing a color image. The goal here isn't to go over every step from start to finish, as those are covered in detail in the complete workflow later on, but rather to show the common settings you'll encounter in different printing software, and to explain them clearly.

For this print, I'm using the Epson P900 printer and the Epson Print Layout software.

The image you see here has already gone through all the necessary preparation steps: It's been resized, sharpened, and soft-proofed. It's now ready to print **(Figure 5.1)**.

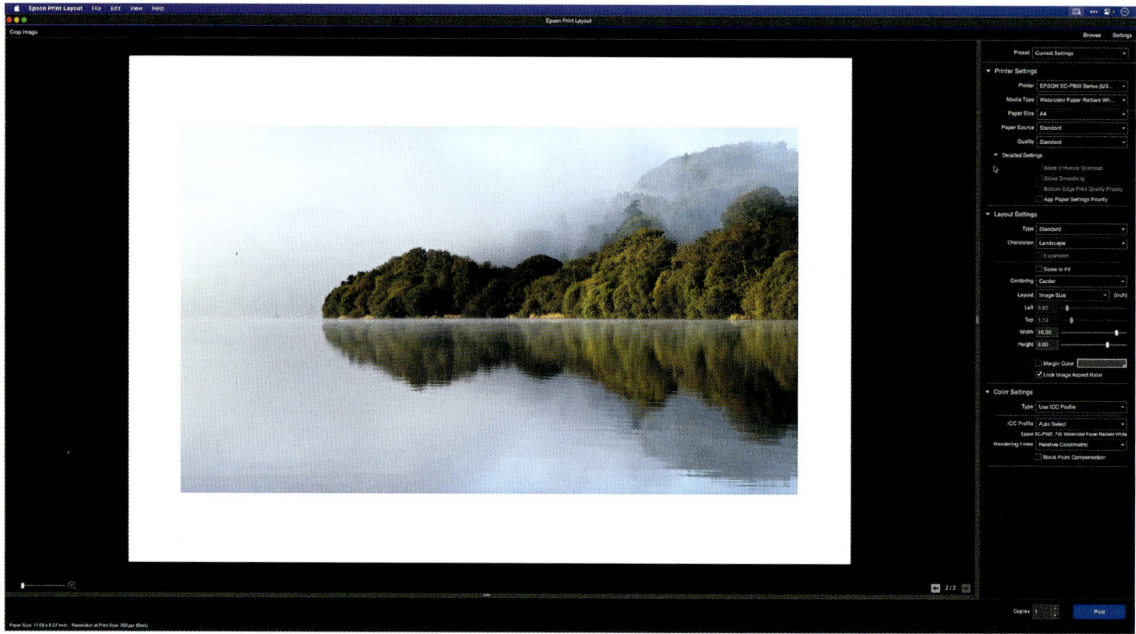

FIGURE 5.1

CHOOSING PAPER AND PRINTER SETTINGS

For this particular print, I'm using Smooth Rag paper from PermaJet.

Because of that, the Media Type is set to Epson Watercolor Paper Radiant White. This is a recommended match for Smooth Rag, as indicated by PermaJet.

Here's a quick overview of the key settings **(Figure 5.2)**:

- **Paper Size:** A4
- **Paper Source:** Standard top feed
- **Quality:** Standard (chosen by default by the software)
- **Type:** Standard print (not a panorama or gallery wrap)
- **Orientation:** Landscape
- **Image Size:** 10 inches by 6 inches

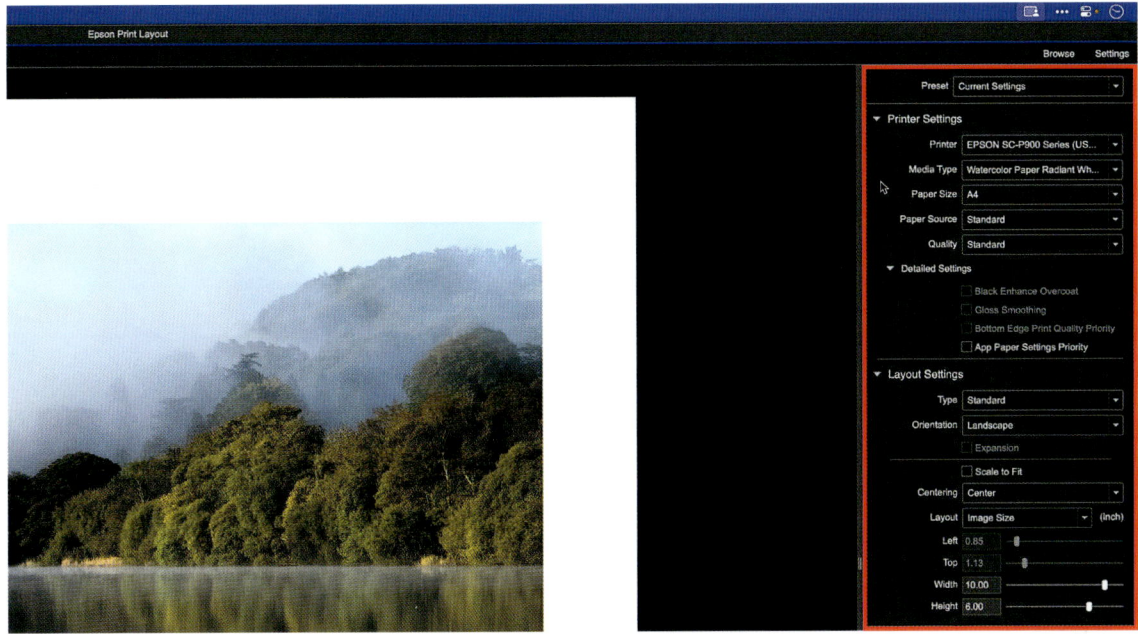

FIGURE 5.2

Everything here is identical to the black-and-white print example from the previous chapter except for the color management settings, which we'll go into next.

USING AN ICC PROFILE

Now, because this is a color print, the color settings need to be handled differently. In this case, I'm not letting the printer manage colors; instead, I'm using an ICC profile.

By default, the Epson software will automatically select an ICC profile based on the Media Type setting. In this case, it selects the Epson Watercolor Paper Radiant White ICC profile, which is appropriate for Epson paper on the P900 or P700 **(Figure 5.3)**.

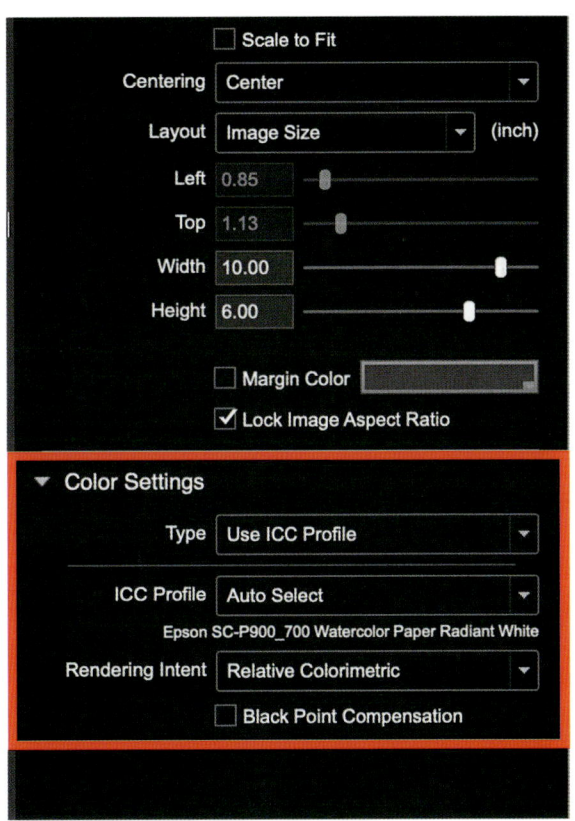

FIGURE 5.3

However, I'm not using Epson paper, I'm using third-party paper from PermaJet, so I need to manually select the correct ICC profile for this paper. I've already downloaded the appropriate profile from the PermaJet website, and now I'll go into the ICC Profile menu in the Epson software and select it from the list **(Figure 5.4)**.

At this point, the ICC profile is applied, and everything is set up for printing, so this is a good opportunity to pause and cover a few important things about ICC profiles, such as what they are, where to get them, how to install them, and even how to create your own.

WHAT ARE ICC PROFILES?

One of the most crucial aspects of achieving color accuracy and consistency in printing is the use of ICC profiles, also known as *paper profiles*. The acronym ICC stands for *International Color Consortium*, a global standard for color management. While this may seem like a complex topic, the principle is actually quite straightforward.

An ICC profile is a computer-generated file that tells your printer how to reproduce colors correctly when printing an image using a specific combination of ink and paper. Think of it like a paint recipe. Just as an artist mixes different colors to match a desired hue, an ICC profile instructs your printer on how much of each ink to use to closely match what you see on your calibrated display.

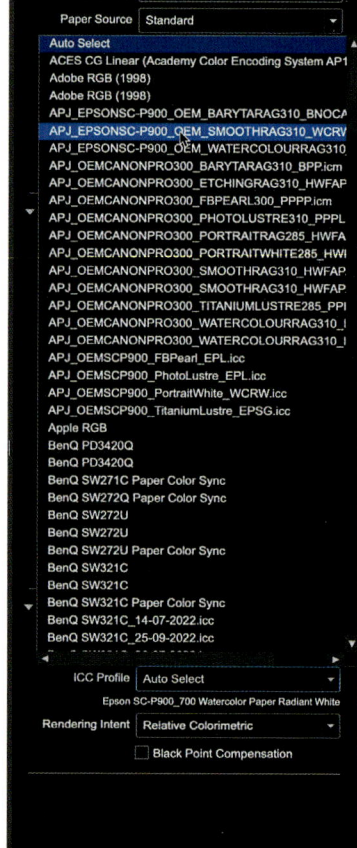

FIGURE 5.4

Crucially, ICC profiles are *printer* and *paper specific*. For instance, an ICC profile created for the Canon Pro-300 using PermaJet FB Gold Silk paper cannot be used on a Canon Pro-1000 with PermaJet Lustre paper, or with any other combination. Attempting to do so won't yield accurate prints and may result in wasted paper and ink.

TYPES OF ICC PROFILES

There are two main categories of ICC profiles:

1. **Generic Profiles:** These are created by paper manufacturers and are usually available for free download from their websites. They provide excellent results for most users.

   Generic Profiles are also supplied by printer manufacturers like Canon and Epson, and these are automatically installed alongside the printer driver. They support the manufacturer's own branded papers and ink.

2. **Bespoke (Custom) Profiles:** These are made specifically for your printer, using your inks and paper. They ensure the most accurate color reproduction and are ideal for professionals seeking maximum consistency.

When I first installed the Canon Pro-300 driver, it came bundled with ICC profiles for all of Canon's standard photo papers **(Figure 5.5)**.

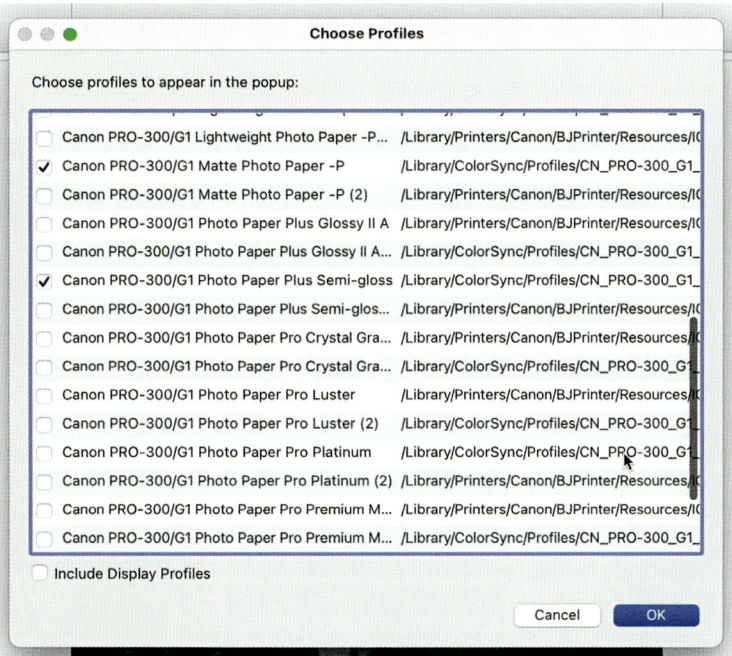

FIGURE 5.5

These Canon profiles are created by Canon using the same printer model, measuring printed color charts to produce accurate mappings, and they do produce great prints … when printing an image on Canon paper and using Canon (OEM) ink.

> **OEM** *stands for Original Equipment Manufacturer. This is ink made by the printer manufacturers (Canon, Epson, etc.) to the highest level of precision and quality for getting the very best, predictable results.*

WHY NOT JUST STICK WITH GENERIC ICC PROFILES?

You might wonder: If the included profiles produce good results, why bother with custom ones?

The answer lies in variability. No two printers, even of the same model, are exactly alike. Differences in manufacturing, quality control, and even age or usage patterns mean that your specific printer might not behave exactly like the one used to create the generic profile.

A bespoke profile ensures the highest fidelity by accounting for these unique characteristics.

PRINTING WITH ICC PROFILES IN LIGHTROOM (ON MACOS)

Let's walk through the process of printing an image using a generic Canon ICC profile in Lightroom Classic on a Mac. For this example, I'll use my Canon Pro-300 printer, Canon's Matte Photo Paper, and Canon OEM ink.

1. **Image Setup**

    Start by selecting your image. I'll be using a photo that I've already retouched and soft-proofed **(Figure 5.6)**.

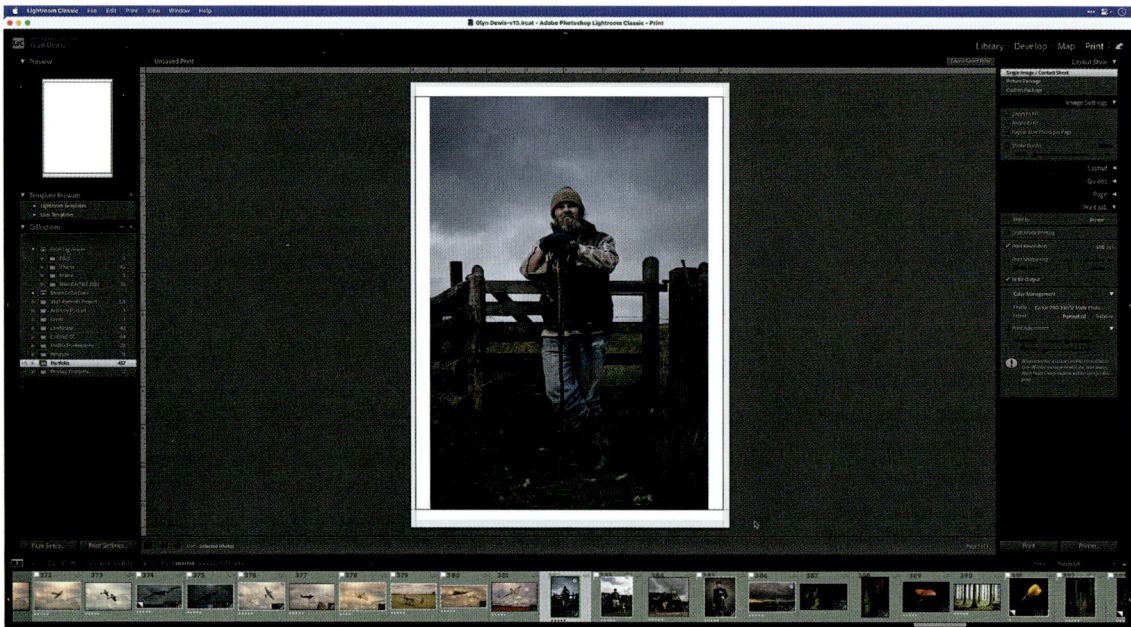

FIGURE 5.6

2. **Color Management Settings**

    Scroll to the Print Job section in Lightroom Classic and locate the Color Management area. Click on Profile, and select the ICC profile for Canon Matte Photo Paper **(Figure 5.7)**.

    Set the Rendering Intent to Perceptual (explained a little later).

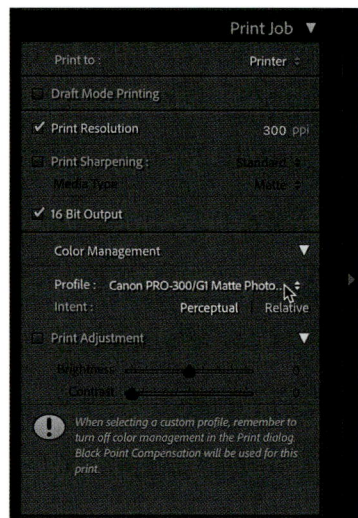

FIGURE 5.7

3. **Printer Settings**

Click Printer. Since I'm using a Mac, the color management is automatically disabled. You'll see that the Color Matching settings are grayed out, which is exactly what we want **(Figure 5.8)**.

> **NOTE:** *Windows users can refer to chapter 3 for information on how to turn off color management.*

4. **Quality and Media Selection**

In the Quality & Media section, for Media Type, select the appropriate Canon paper type, which in this case is Matte Photo Paper. This setting also tells the printer how to handle the paper physically, such as how high to lift the printhead and whether to use Photo Black or Matte Black ink **(Figure 5.9)**.

5. **Final Print Settings**

Set the Paper Source (Top Feed in this example) and ensure the Print Quality is set to Highest.

6. **Print**

With everything set, click Print. The printer will now use the ICC profile to render your image as accurately as possible using Canon ink and Canon paper.

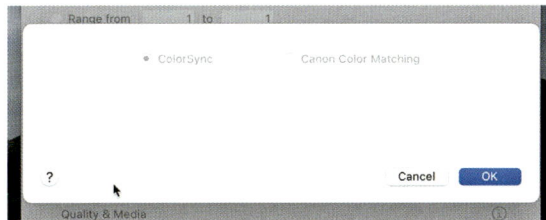

FIGURE 5.8

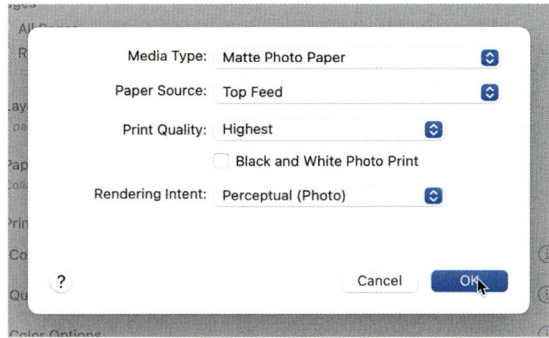

FIGURE 5.9

RESULTS AND SUMMARY

The final print looks great, with rich tones and accurate colors; exactly what I'd expect when using matched OEM ink, paper, and profiles **(Figure 5.10)**.

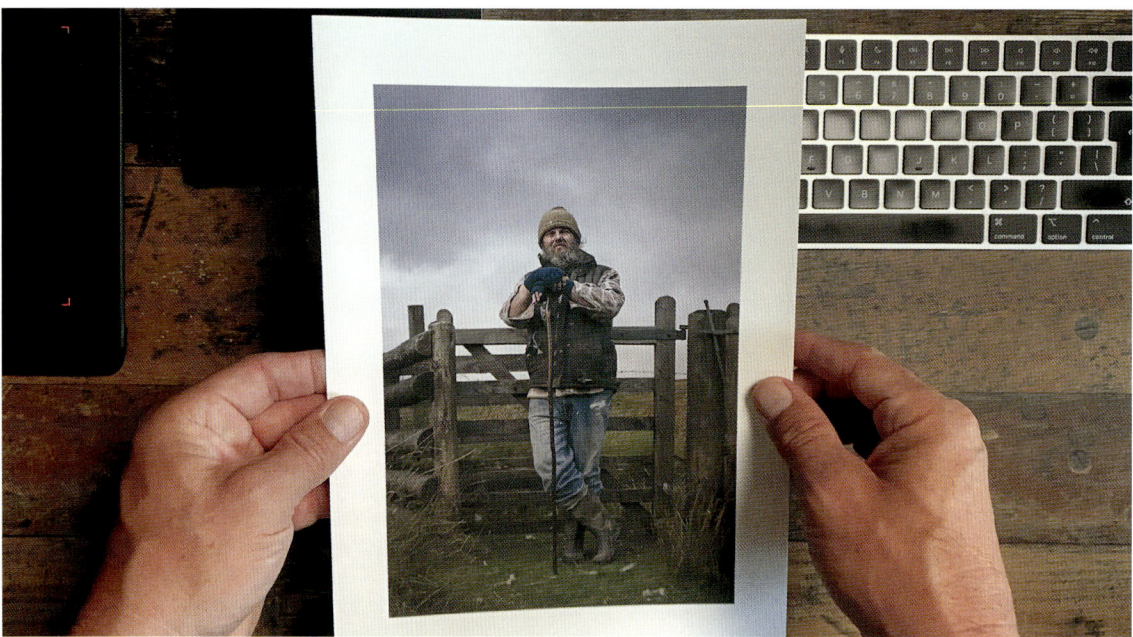

FIGURE 5.10

However, if you plan to use third-party paper or ink brands, generic ICC profiles from those manufacturers or, even better, bespoke profiles become essential.

PRINTING ONTO THIRD-PARTY PAPERS

Now we'll step away from using Canon paper with a Canon printer and instead explore printing with a different brand of paper, PermaJet, a paper manufacturer I use most frequently **(Figure 5.11)**.

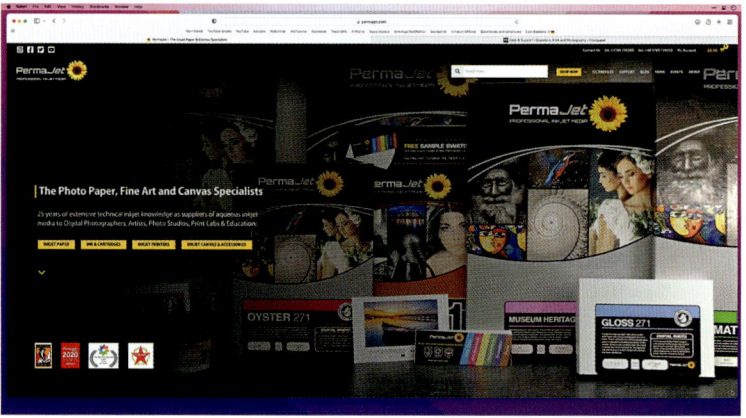

FIGURE 5.11

Since PermaJet is a third-party brand, using their paper with a Canon printer requires an ICC profile to ensure accurate color reproduction.

To achieve this, you can use any of the following:

• A generic ICC profile provided by PermaJet

• A bespoke (custom) ICC profile made specifically for your printer, paper, and ink combination

• An ICC profile you've created using specialist hardware

> **NOTE:** *PermaJet offers free custom profiles for their own paper and charges a small fee for profiles for other paper brands.*

SELECTING THE PAPER: PERMAJET WATERCOLOUR RAG 310

The paper used in this example is Watercolour Rag 310 from PermaJet's Heritage Range **(Figure 5.12)**. It features a beautiful textured surface with a natural white tone reminiscent of an artist's canvas. This texture, along with the paper's weight and finish, makes it ideal for fine art–style prints.

FIGURE 5.12

DOWNLOADING THE GENERIC ICC PROFILE

To get started:

1. Visit the PermaJet website and log in to your account (you need one to download the ICC profiles).

2. Navigate to the ICC Profiles section.

3. From the drop-down menu, select your printer model.

4. Choose OEM ink, assuming you're using the printer manufacturer's official ink.

5. Select the paper type; in this case, Watercolour Rag 310.

6. Click Submit, then download and install the ICC profile.

I'll show how to install ICC profiles in more detail a little later (page 88).

PRINTING WITH A GENERIC ICC PROFILE IN LIGHTROOM CLASSIC

Now let's walk through printing the image in Lightroom Classic using the generic ICC profile.

1. Open the Print Module and choose the image you want to print.

2. Assign the ICC Profile:

   • Navigate to the Color Management section (bottom-right).

   • Click on Profile, and from the drop-down, choose the PermaJet Watercolour Rag 310 profile you installed **(Figure 5.13)**.

3. Click Printer to enter the printer dialog box, and here are the key settings:

Color Matching: Ensure this is grayed out (Mac), meaning Lightroom Classic is controlling the color management (as it should when using ICC profiles) **(Figure 5.14)**.

Quality & Media: Use the recommended Media Type for the paper. For PermaJet Watercolour Rag 310 on the Canon Pro-300 (10-ink printer), use Heavyweight Fine Art Paper. You can double-check this recommendation on the information sheet included with each box of

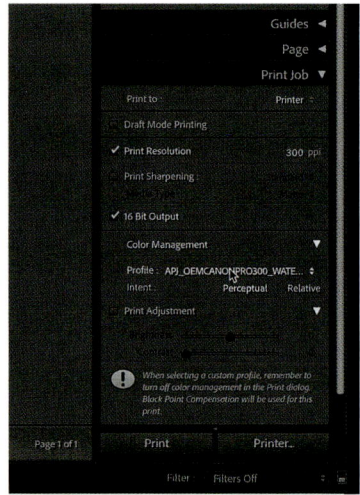

FIGURE 5.13

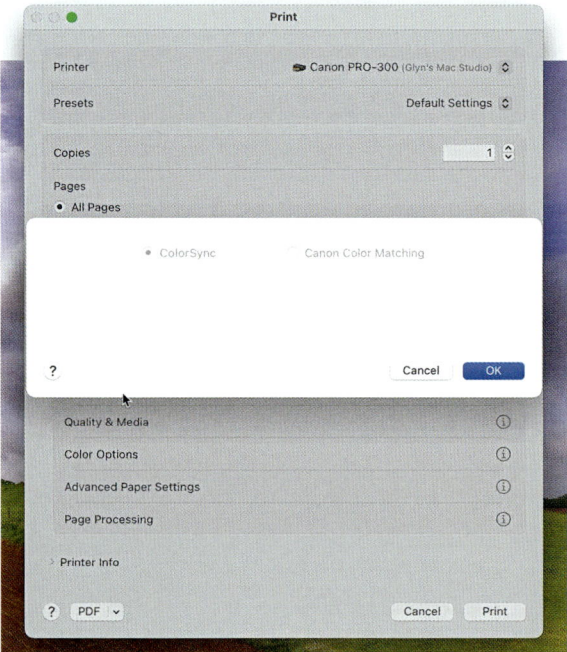

FIGURE 5.14

PermaJet paper **(Figure 5.15)**, on the PermaJet website, or, most reliably, in the ICC profile file name, look for something like HWFA (Heavyweight Fine Art) **(Figure 5.16)**.

- **Paper Source:** Top Feed
- **Print Quality:** Highest Available

4. Once all settings are confirmed, click Print.

The final print using PermaJet's generic ICC profile delivers excellent results. The color reproduction is rich and vibrant, while the paper's texture gives it a painterly, fine-art feel **(Figure 5.17)**.

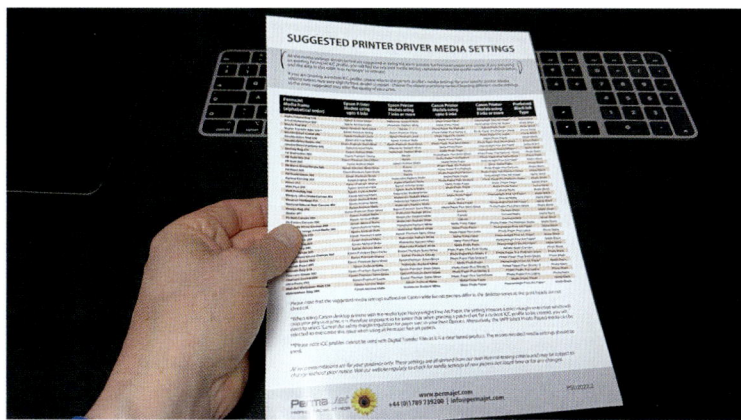

FIGURE 5.15

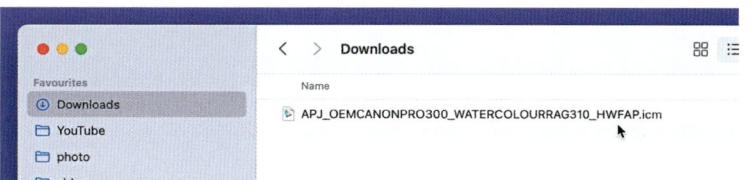

FIGURE 5.16

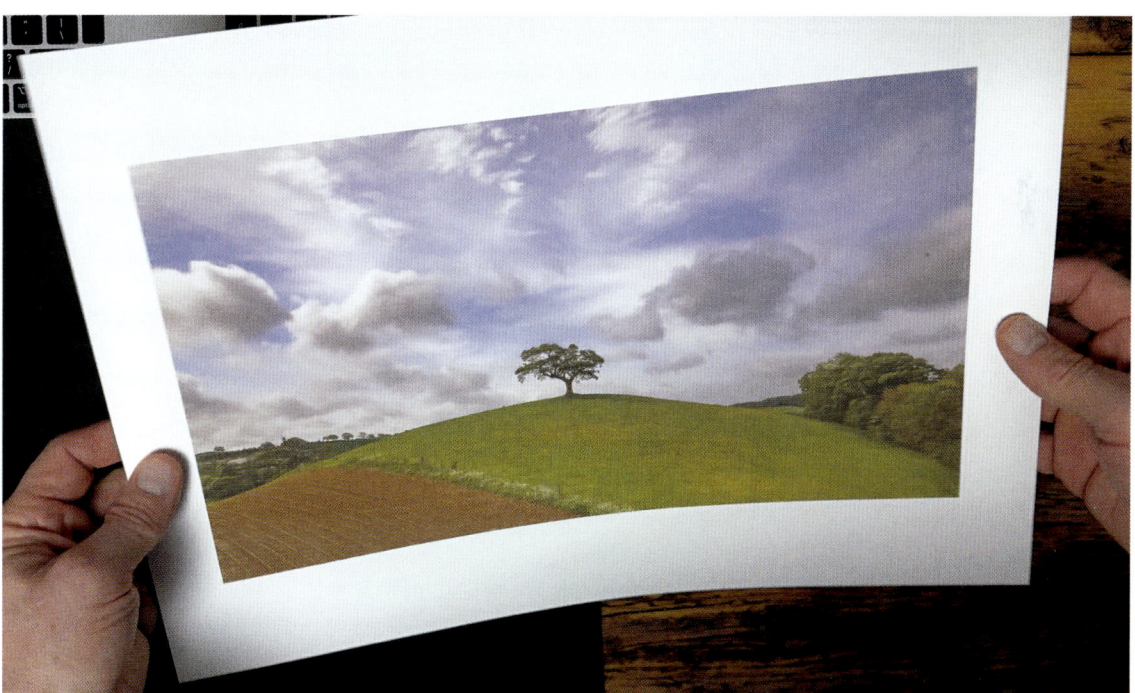

FIGURE 5.17

So now that you've seen how to use generic ICC profiles successfully, the next step is learning how to create your own bespoke ICC profiles that are completely customized to your specific printer, paper, and ink combination.

CREATING CUSTOM ICC PROFILES WITH PERMAJET

WHY CHOOSE CUSTOM ICC PROFILES?

While generic ICC profiles can deliver excellent print results, custom or bespoke ICC profiles provide a more precise match between your printer, ink, and paper combination.

The reason for this is simple: Every printer has slight variances, even within the same model range. A profile custom-made for your specific printer ensures the most accurate color reproduction possible.

There are two main ways to obtain custom profiles:

1. Have a professional company create them for you.

2. Create them yourself using specialized hardware.

USING PERMAJET'S FREE CUSTOM ICC PROFILE SERVICE

Since I frequently use PermaJet paper, I'll walk you through their custom ICC profiling service. PermaJet offers this service free of charge when you're using their papers. If you're using a third-party paper, they can still create a profile for you, typically for a small fee.

To get a free custom ICC profile from PermaJet, you'll need to download the Profile Pack from PermaJet's website. You can find this by going to the ICC Profiles tab and selecting the Free Custom Profiles option. This contains essential tools, including the Adobe Color Print Utility (ACPU) and a test chart to be printed.

If you're a Windows user, once you've downloaded the pack, you can simply navigate to where you downloaded it and click to open the Adobe Color Print Utility software.

However, If you're using a Mac you'll need to open the Adobe Color Print Utility by double-clicking the icon. You may encounter a security warning because macOS doesn't recognize the developer **(Figure 5.18)**. To bypass this, click Cancel on the warning, and then go to **System Preferences** > **Security & Privacy**. Click the lock icon to unlock the settings and click Open Anyway to allow the app to launch **(Figure 5.19)**.

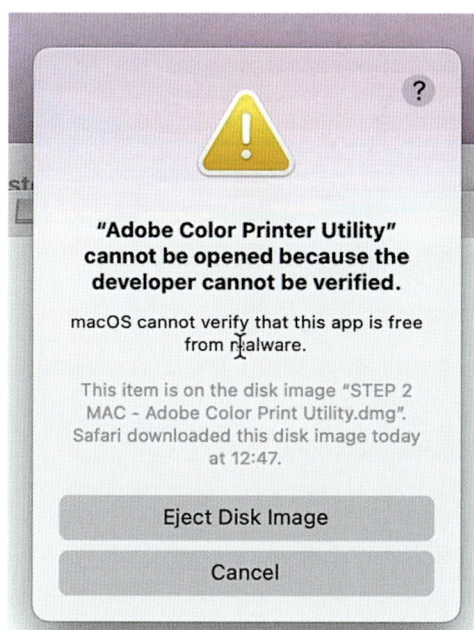

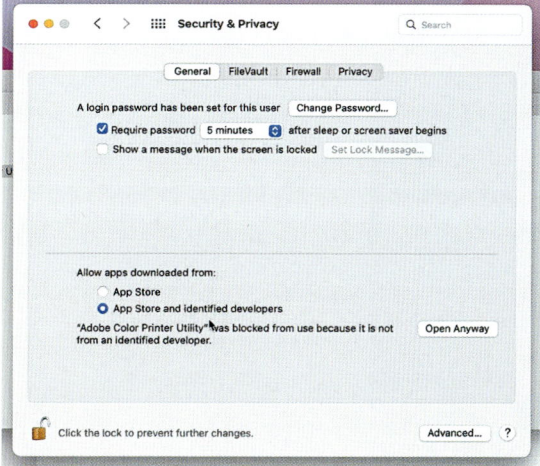

FIGURE 5.19

FIGURE 5.18

The utility will then automatically display the profiling chart **(Figure 5.20)**.

Ensure that the Page Setup is set to A4, as the chart must be printed at 100% size. It's really important that you don't scale the file because the printed chart will later be scanned by PermaJet using a precise measuring device that only accepts A4-sized charts.

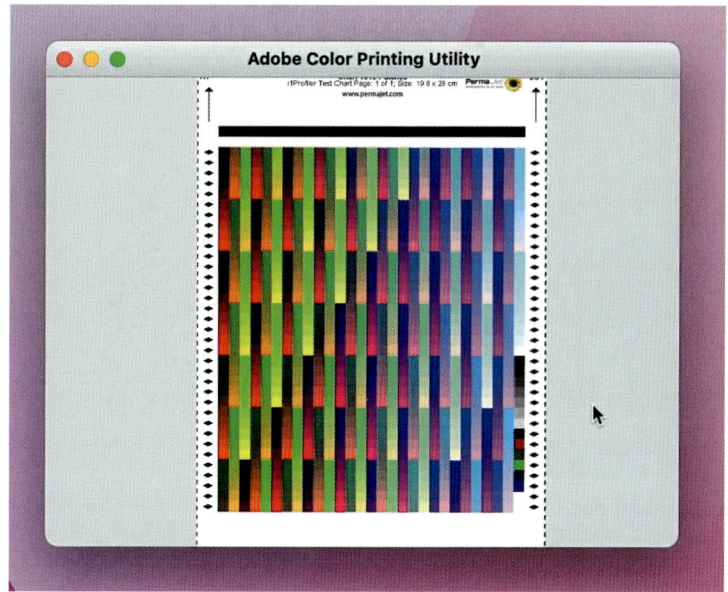

FIGURE 5.20

CONFIGURING THE PRINTER SETTINGS

Before printing, adjust your printer settings carefully.

1. Turn off color management.

   - On a Mac, color management is automatically disabled when printing from the Adobe Color Print Utility.

   - On Windows, you'll need to manually turn it off (refer to chapter 3, page 53).

2. Select the correct Media Type.

   - PermaJet provides a media recommendation chart (both in the paper box and on their website). This chart tells you:

     - Whether the printer should use Photo Black or Matte Black ink.

     - How much ink density to apply.

     - How high or low to set the printhead (to avoid printhead strikes).

Selecting the correct Media Type is crucial to avoid ink pooling, smudging, or damage to the printhead.

FINAL STEPS

Once you've chosen your media type, click Print to produce the color chart. The chart should appear vibrant and accurate, showing clear separation between colored swatches **(Figure 5.21)**.

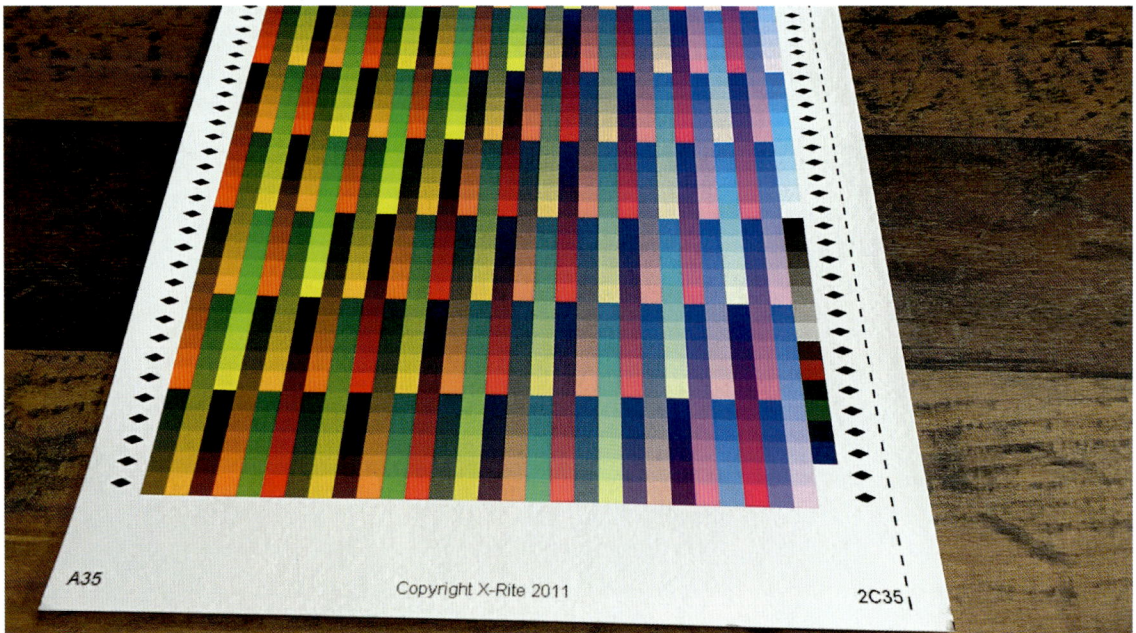

FIGURE 5.21

Before sending it to PermaJet, let the chart dry for at least thirty minutes and inspect it carefully to ensure that no areas are smudged or missing.

Now with your printed chart ready, you'll be instructed (typically via PermaJet's provided instructions) to mail it back to them. They will then scan it and return a custom ICC profile made just for your printer, ink, and paper combination.

A NOTE ON AIRPRINT (MAC USERS)

AirPrint, Apple's wireless printing system, is not suitable for printing profiling charts. Always use a USB or wired connection to ensure accurate data transmission. Printing via AirPrint can result in altered color output, which defeats the purpose of generating a custom ICC profile.

You can see in **Figure 5.22** the difference between a print generated via the printer driver (left) and one printed with AirPrint (right). Notice how the squares patches aren't clear and defined in the AirPrint version.

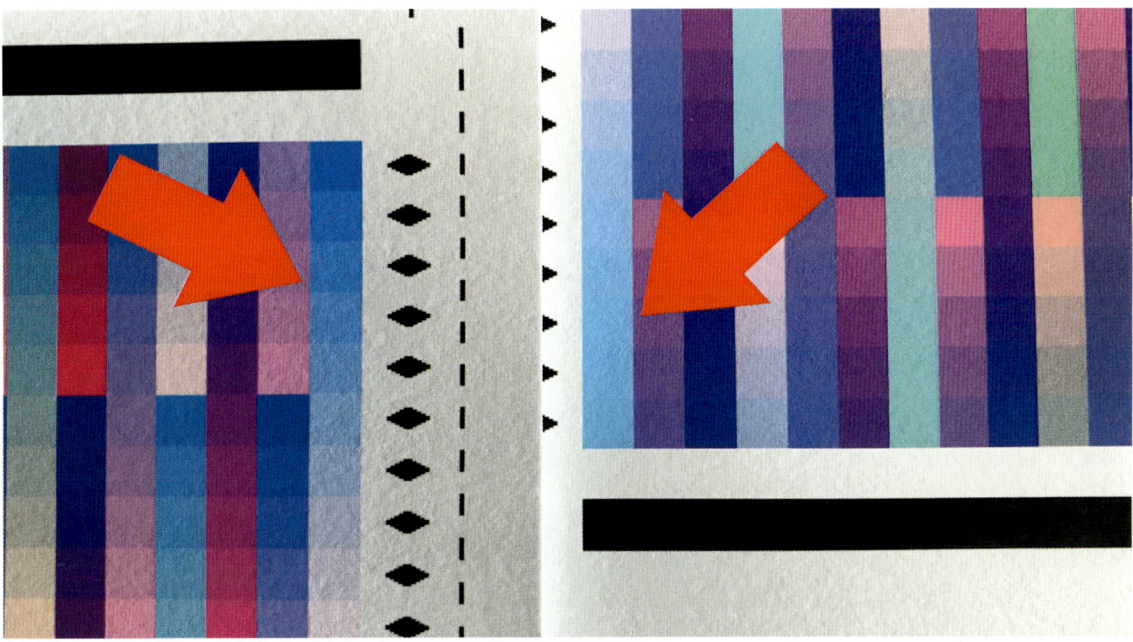

FIGURE 5.22

CREATING YOUR OWN ICC PROFILES

Until now, we've covered how to acquire ICC profiles by downloading generic ones from a paper manufacturer's website or having a custom profile created for you. But what if you want complete control and the ability to start using a profile immediately, no waiting, no outsourcing?

Creating your own ICC profiles has some major advantages. Not only can you bypass the wait time for a bespoke profile, but you also get the flexibility to build color profiles for any paper you choose. The trade-off, however, is the initial investment in profiling hardware.

THE TOOLS YOU'LL NEED

For my setup, I use the Calibrite ColorChecker Studio **(Figure 5.23)**. This tool isn't just for scanning profiling targets; it also supports monitor calibration, projector profiling, scanner profiling, and video display calibration. It's a powerful all-in-one solution. At the time of writing, it retails for around $569 USD or £522 GBP.

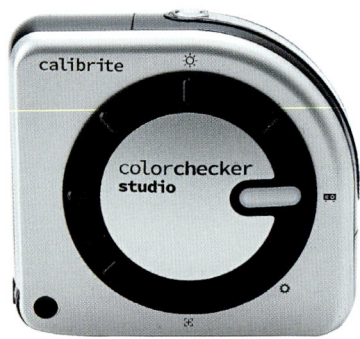

FIGURE 5.23

DOWNLOADING AND INSTALLING THE SOFTWARE

To get started, you'll need to download the appropriate software.

1. Visit the Calibrite website.

2. Navigate to the Products tab and select Software Downloads.

3. Locate the software for the ColorChecker Studio and choose the appropriate version for Mac or Windows.

Once installed, connect your ColorChecker Studio device to your computer using the provided USB cable, then launch the software.

SETTING UP FOR PROFILING

When the software opens, you'll see the ColorChecker Studio selected (indicated by an orange highlight around its icon) **(Figure 5.24)**.

In the menu on the left side of the dialog, select Color Print under the Printer Calibration section.

> **NOTE:** *There is an option for Black/White Print, but I don't use ICC profiles for black-and-white work. Instead, I rely on the printer's own black-and-white mode.*

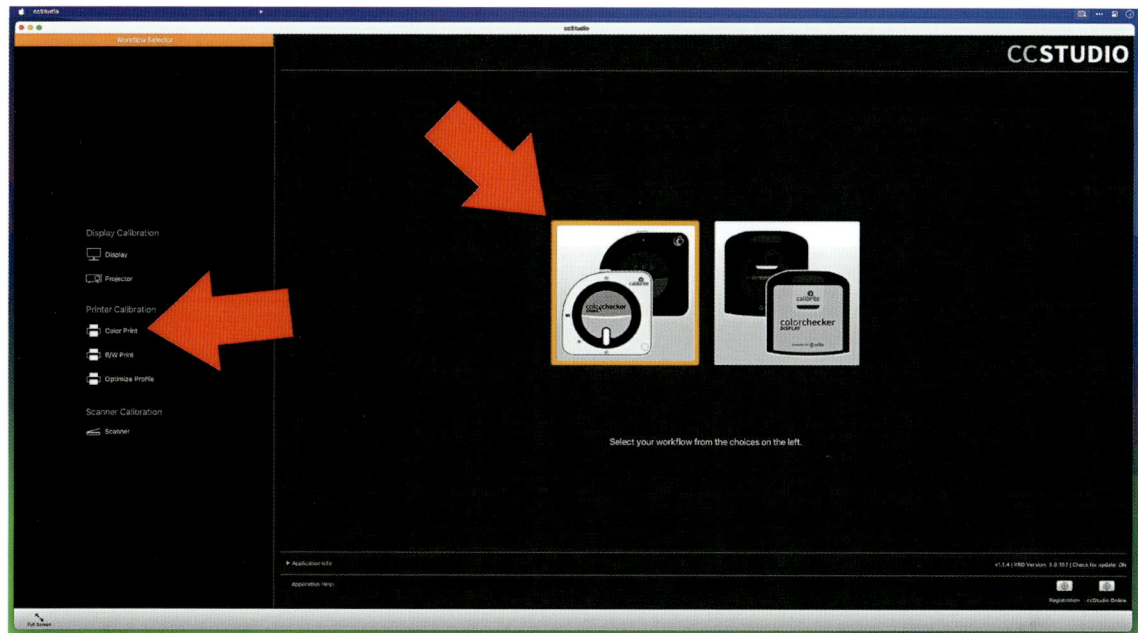

FIGURE 5.24

Next:

1. Choose your printer. I selected the Canon Pro-300.

2. Set the Paper Size to A4.

3. Leave the Units in millimeters (mm).

4. In the Paper Description field, enter a name for the paper; in my case, PJSmoothRag (for PermaJet Smooth Rag 310) **(Figure 5.25)**. You'll see this name appear on the profiling chart.

Click Print to send the first target chart to your printer.

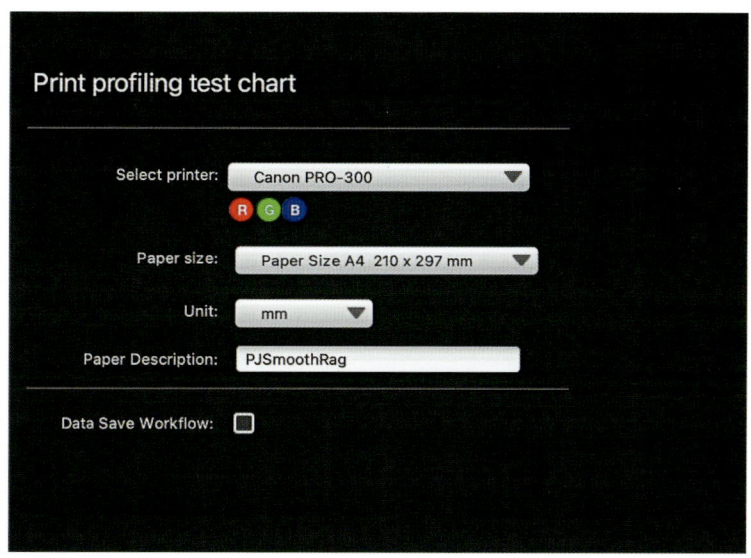

FIGURE 5.25

CONFIGURING THE PRINTER SETTINGS

In the printer driver:

1. Choose the correct printer (Canon Pro-300).

2. Set the Paper Size to A4 and the Orientation to Portrait.

3. Go to the Color Matching tab and ensure color management is turned off.

4. Navigate to Quality and Media and choose the recommended Media Type. For PermaJet Smooth Rag 310, this is Heavyweight Fine Art Paper.

5. Click OK, then Print.

Allow the printed chart to dry for at least thirty minutes before proceeding **(Figure 5.26)**. Then follow the onscreen instructions for how to use the Calibrite ColorChecker Studio to scan the patches **(Figure 5.26)**.

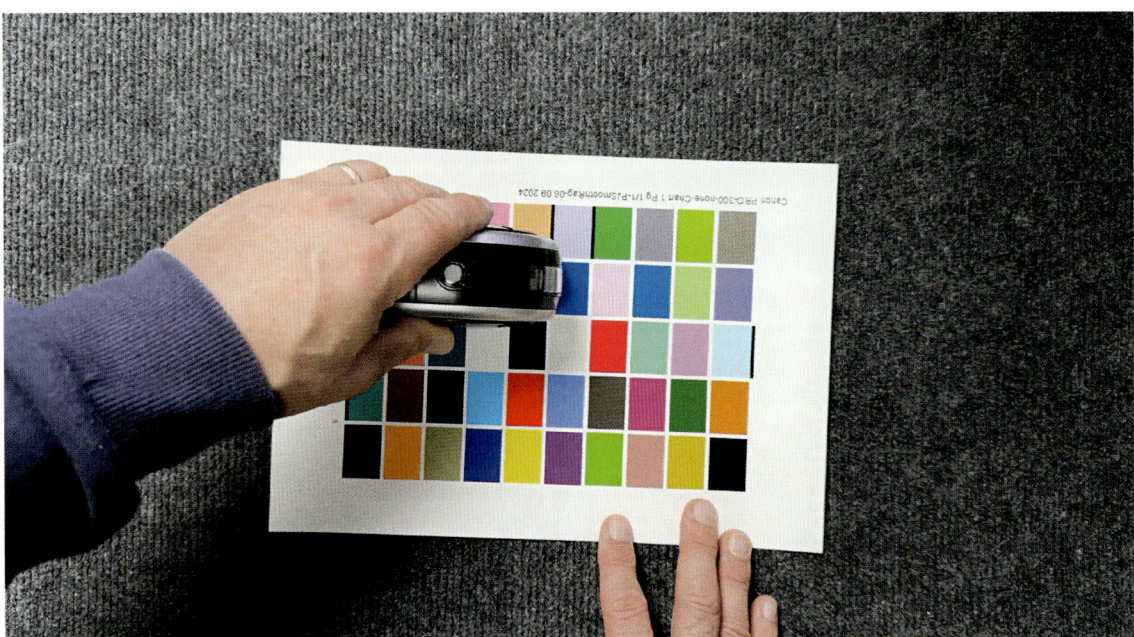

FIGURE 5.26

This process will take you through two separate scans, at the end of which you'll name your new ICC profile. Then, in the ccStudio software, choose Version 4 for the ICC Profile Version and click Save Profile **(Figure 5.27)**.

The ICC profile is now created and automatically saved into the correct system folder, ready for use.

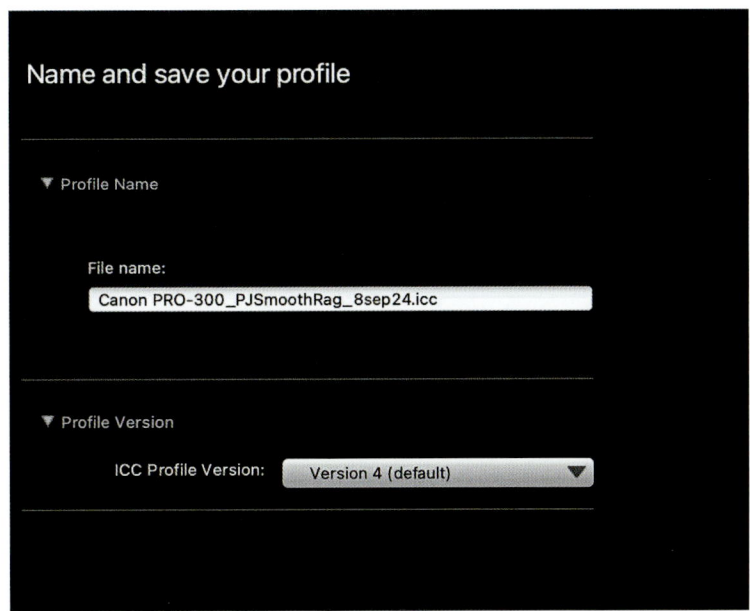

FIGURE 5.27

COMPARING THE RESULTS

With both prints side by side, I found the results impressively similar, virtually indistinguishable to the eye. So, while some images may reveal subtle differences between a self-made and a generic profile, in this case, both delivered exceptional quality **(Figure 5.28)**.

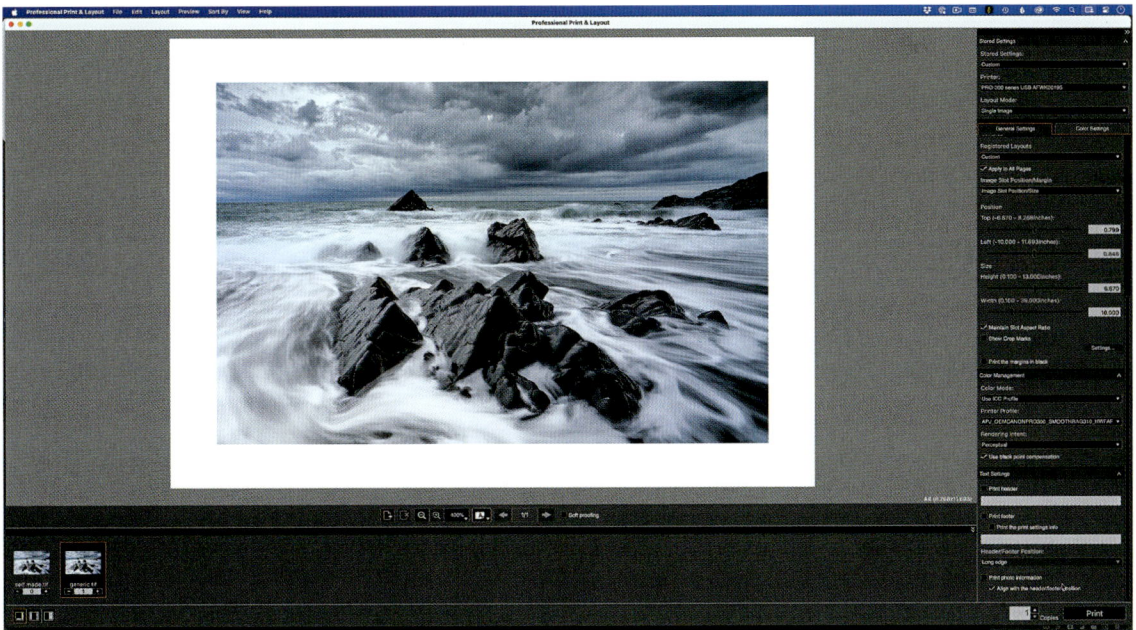

FIGURE 5.28

INSTALLING ICC PROFILES

Now that we've covered what an ICC profile is, and the different types available (custom/bespoke, generic, and self-made), let's take a look at how to install them so you can use them in your printing software of choice.

INSTALLING ON WINDOWS

This part is incredibly simple. All you need to do is right-click on the ICC profile file and choose "Install Profile."

That's it … you're done!

INSTALLING ON MAC

For Mac users, the process is slightly different. Start by opening the Go menu at the top of the screen, then select: **Computer** > **Your Hard Drive** > **Library** > **ColorSync** > **Profiles**.

Once you're in the Profiles folder, simply drag and drop the ICC profile into that location.

AFTER INSTALLATION

Depending on the printing software you're using, if it was open at the time you installed the ICC profile, you might find that it doesn't appear right away. If that happens, simply close the software and reopen it. After that, the ICC profile should be available and ready to use.

ENABLING ICC PROFILES IN LIGHTROOM CLASSIC

If you're using Lightroom Classic, once you've installed the ICC profile, go to the Profile section and then click on Other. Find the ICC profile you're after, tick the checkbox beside it, and click OK **(Figure 5.29)**.

You'll then see the profile listed and ready to use in the Profile section.

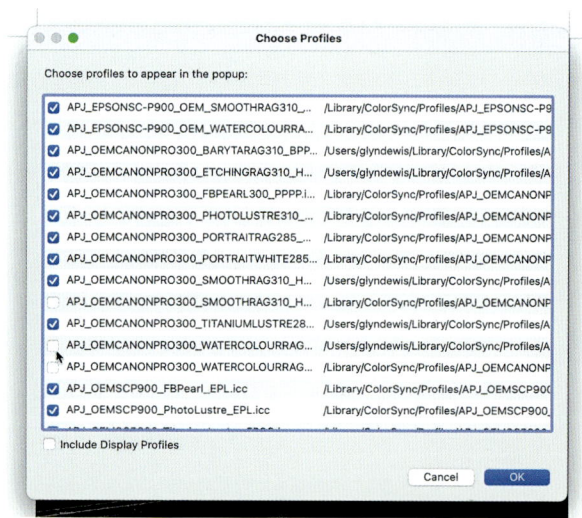

FIGURE 5.29

UNDERSTANDING RENDERING INTENT

Now carrying on with the color print, in the settings we come to Rendering Intent, and in here we have a choice of Perceptual or Relative Colorimetric. But what is Rendering Intent?

When preparing images for print, one of the most critical aspects of color management involves handling out-of-gamut colors, those colors that fall outside the reproducible range of your printer and paper combination. These colors can't be printed exactly as seen on your display, so we must decide how best to translate them using what's known as a *rendering intent*.

WHAT ARE RENDERING INTENTS?

Rendering intents are methods your software uses to deal with colors that your printer and paper cannot reproduce. These are available in all major printing applications, such as Photoshop, Lightroom Classic, and dedicated print layout software.

You'll commonly encounter two rendering intents:

- Perceptual
- Relative Colorimetric (often shortened to *Relative*)

While software like Photoshop offers additional options (Saturation and Absolute Colorimetric) for photographic printing, you only really need to concern yourself with Perceptual and Relative.

PERCEPTUAL VS. RELATIVE COLORIMETRIC

Both rendering intents manage out-of-gamut colors, but they do so differently:

- **Perceptual** adjusts *all* colors in the image slightly, preserving the visual relationships between colors. It's as if every color in the image moves a little to make room for those that are outside the printable gamut.
- **Relative Colorimetric**, on the other hand, only alters the colors that are outside the printable range. Everything else remains unchanged.

To illustrate this, imagine a crowded room:

- In the **Perceptual** approach, everyone shifts a bit to make room for new arrivals.
- With **Relative**, only the new people (out-of-gamut colors) squeeze in, and everyone else stays put.

VISUALIZING GAMUT WARNINGS IN LIGHTROOM

To see out-of-gamut colors in action, you can use the Soft Proofing feature in Lightroom Classic.

1. Open the Develop module and enable Soft Proofing **(Figure 5.30)**.

2. The histogram now displays additional indicators:

• Monitor Gamut Warning (blue overlay): Colors your monitor cannot display **(Figure 5.31)**.

• Destination Gamut Warning (red overlay): Colors your printer and paper cannot reproduce **(Figure 5.32)**.

By toggling between rendering intents (Intent) under the Soft Proofing controls, you'll notice how the tones in the histogram, and the image itself, shift subtly.

Changing the ICC profile (for example, switching from matte paper to a high-gamut luster paper) can reduce the red overlay, demonstrating that different paper and printer combinations offer varying color gamuts **(Figure 5.33)**.

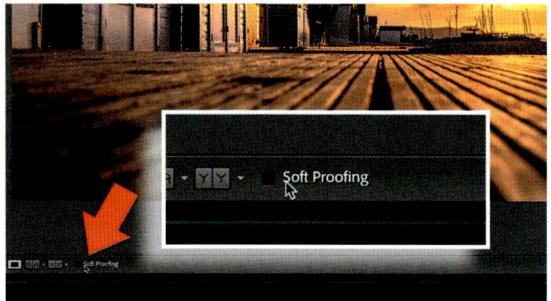

FIGURE 5.30

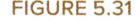

FIGURE 5.31

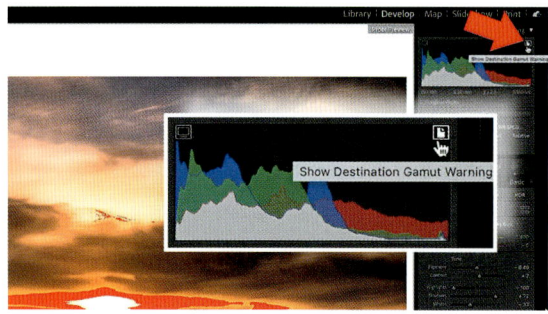

FIGURE 5.32

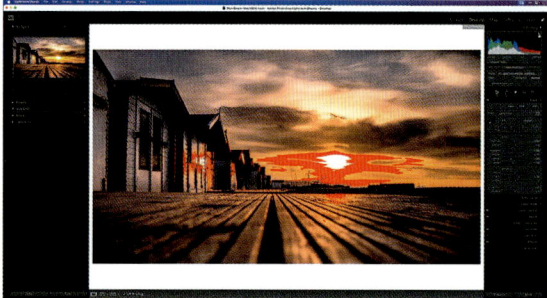

FIGURE 5.33

WHICH RENDERING INTENT SHOULD YOU USE?

Despite what you might have heard, there's no one-size-fits-all answer. Which rendering intent you choose depends on image content and what looks best to you. Here are some basic guidelines:

• **Use Relative Colorimetric** when accurate skin tones are essential. Skin tones are typically within gamut, so Relative keeps them unchanged.

• **Use Perceptual** for images with wide color variation or strong color gradients, where maintaining overall harmony is more important than exact color fidelity.

TEST, EVALUATE, DECIDE

The choice of rendering intent can have a subtle but meaningful impact on your prints. Don't simply leave your settings on Perceptual out of habit. Instead, preview both options, especially during soft proofing, and decide which best preserves the integrity of your image.

Ultimately, the goal is to produce a print that looks as close to your vision as possible, and understanding rendering intents is a key part of that process.

BLACK POINT COMPENSATION (BPC)

Once Rendering Intent is selected, the next key setting to consider is Black Point Compensation. This option is available in many printing applications, but not all. Depending on the software you're using, you may be able to manually toggle it on or off, or it may be automatically enabled without user control. For example:

• In Epson Print Layout and Canon Professional Print & Layout, you can choose to enable or disable BPC **(Figures 5.34 and 5.35)**.

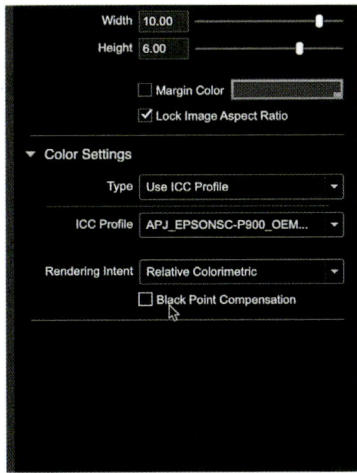

FIGURE 5.34

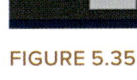

FIGURE 5.35

- In Photoshop, the option is also available **(Figure 5.36)**.
- In Lightroom Classic, however, Black Point Compensation is always on by default, with no option to turn it off.

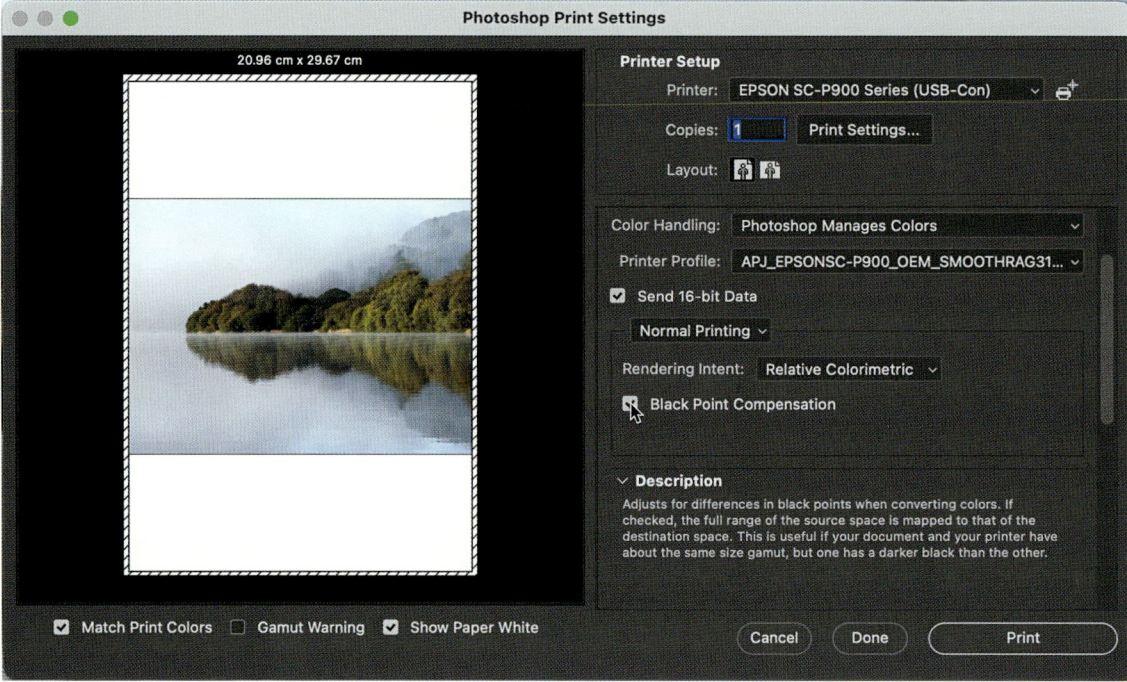

FIGURE 5.36

WHY YOU SHOULD ALMOST ALWAYS USE BLACK POINT COMPENSATION

When printing photographs, I always recommend keeping Black Point Compensation turned on. The reason is simple: Turning it off limits the tonal range your printer uses, especially in the darkest areas of your image. Think of it this way, without BPC, the printer tends to take a "lazy" approach, skipping over the deepest blacks. With BPC enabled, the printer makes full use of the available tonal range, resulting in more detail and richness in shadows.

Let's consider a specific example to illustrate this. Using an evaluation print file, you can visually inspect how tonal range is handled. Look at the bottom-left section of the chart with dark values from 0 through 24 **(Figure 5.37)**.

- With BPC enabled, the printer renders dark tones from a value of 0 all the way to 24 and beyond.

- With BPC disabled, the printer might ignore tones darker than a value of 6, losing vital shadow detail.

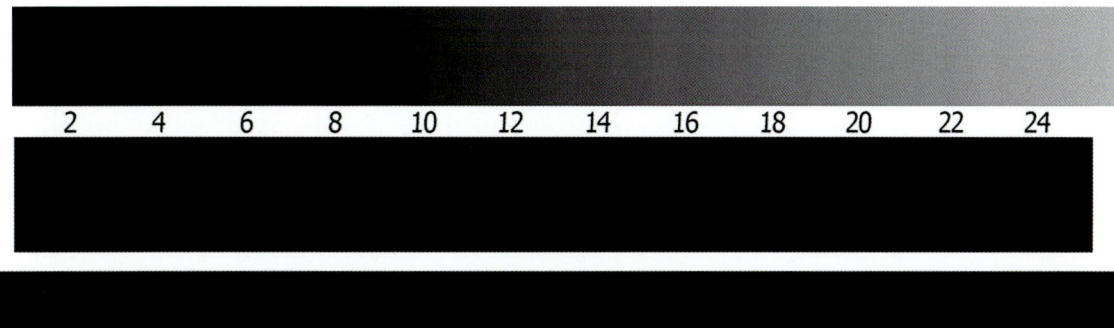

FIGURE 5.37

COMPATIBILITY WITH RENDERING INTENT

It's important to note that Black Point Compensation is only relevant when using the Relative Colorimetric Rendering Intent. If you're using Perceptual, Black Point Compensation is effectively always applied. This is a technical detail, but one worth remembering when adjusting your print settings.

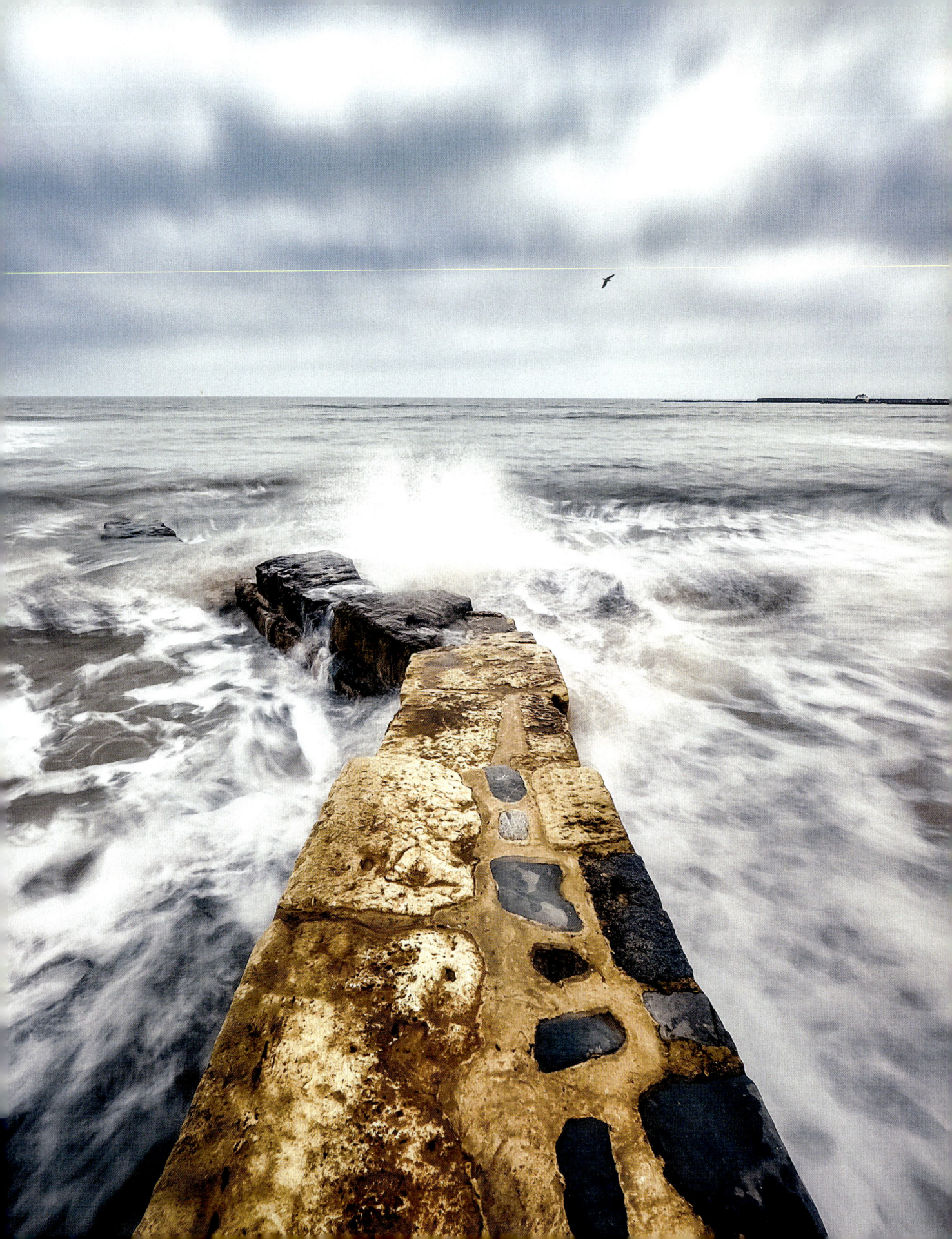

CHAPTER 6
COLOR SPACE

COMMON COLOR SPACES

Before we dive deeper into the technical side of color management with expert insights, let's first cover the three most commonly used color spaces: sRGB, Adobe RGB, and ProPhoto RGB.

This chapter is not a deep dive into color theory. I'm certainly not claiming to be a color scientist, but I've worked with these spaces in my own photography workflow for years, so this is meant to be a practical explanation to help you understand how they work and why they matter in your editing and printing process.

sRGB: THE SAFE AND FAMILIAR CHOICE

First there's **sRGB**, which is the smallest of the three common color spaces you'll come across in your editing and printing workflow **(Figure 6.1)**. It's often referred to as the **"web color space"** because it's the standard for images shared online, but that's not its only use.

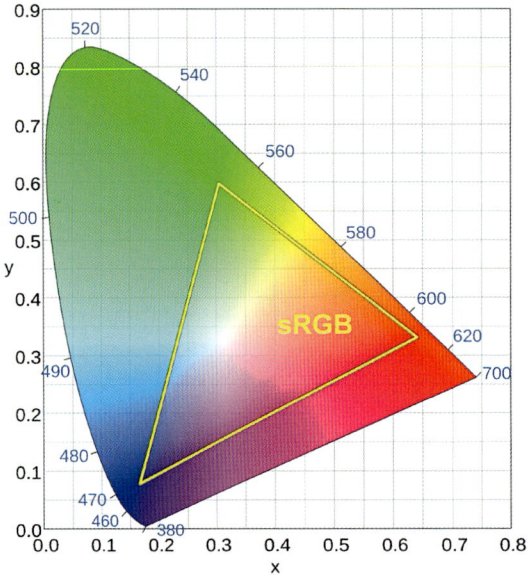

FIGURE 6.1

In fact, many professional printing labs prefer or even require images to be delivered in sRGB, with the main reason being that it's extremely consistent across different stages of image processing:

- Capture (especially when shooting in JPEG)

- Display on most monitors and screens

- Editing

- Printing

- Sharing online

Because of this consistency, sRGB is often considered a "safe" color space, especially for beginners or for photographers looking for predictable results without worrying about color mismatches.

ADOBE RGB: A BIGGER CONTAINER FOR MORE COLOR RANGE

Next we have **Adobe RGB**, which is approximately **35% larger** than sRGB **(Figure 6.2)**. This expanded size means it can represent a broader range of red, green, and blue tones, especially in the **greens**.

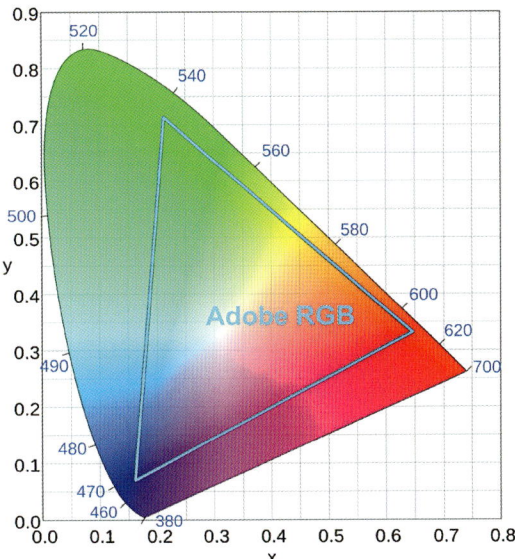

FIGURE 6.2

This makes Adobe RGB a great option for photographers who want to preserve more color data when editing and printing, particularly if you're printing your images yourself or working with a lab that accepts Adobe RGB files.

However, if any part your workflow, especially your display or printer, doesn't support Adobe RGB, you may not benefit from using it, and the image may look different when viewed on an sRGB-only device.

PROPHOTO RGB: THE LARGEST OF THEM ALL

Finally, there's **ProPhoto RGB**, the largest color space of the three; so large, in fact, that it includes what are often referred to as "imaginary colors," or colors that go beyond what the human eye can perceive **(Figure 6.3)**.

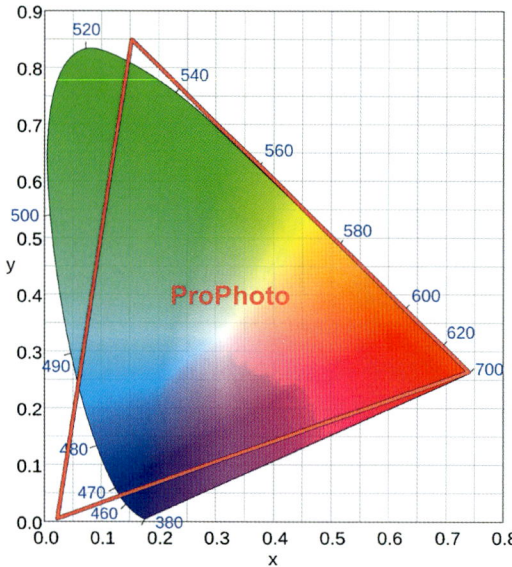

FIGURE 6.3

Because of this vast range, ProPhoto RGB gives you the most flexibility when editing images, particularly RAW files. However, there's a critical technical detail to understand:

The bigger the color space, the more risk there is of color banding, unless you're working in a higher bit depth.

A BIT ABOUT BIT DEPTH

Let's break down bit depth to understand why it matters.

An 8-bit image, regardless of whether it's in sRGB, Adobe RGB, or ProPhoto RGB, contains 16.8 million color values. Here's how that is calculated:

An 8-bit image contains:

- 256 shades of red

- 256 shades of green

- 256 shades of blue

Multiply those together:

256 × 256 × 256 = 16.8 million RGB combinations

So even though ProPhoto RGB covers a wider range of colors, it still uses the same number of color values as sRGB in 8-bit **(Figure 6.4)**.

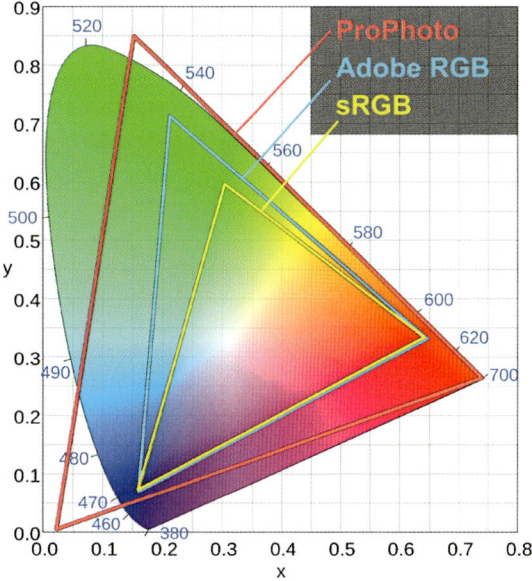

FIGURE 6.4

This means those 16.8 million colors are spread out further to cover the larger space. This "spreading" can lead to visible banding in gradients or subtle tones, especially in skies or shadows **(Figure 6.5)**.

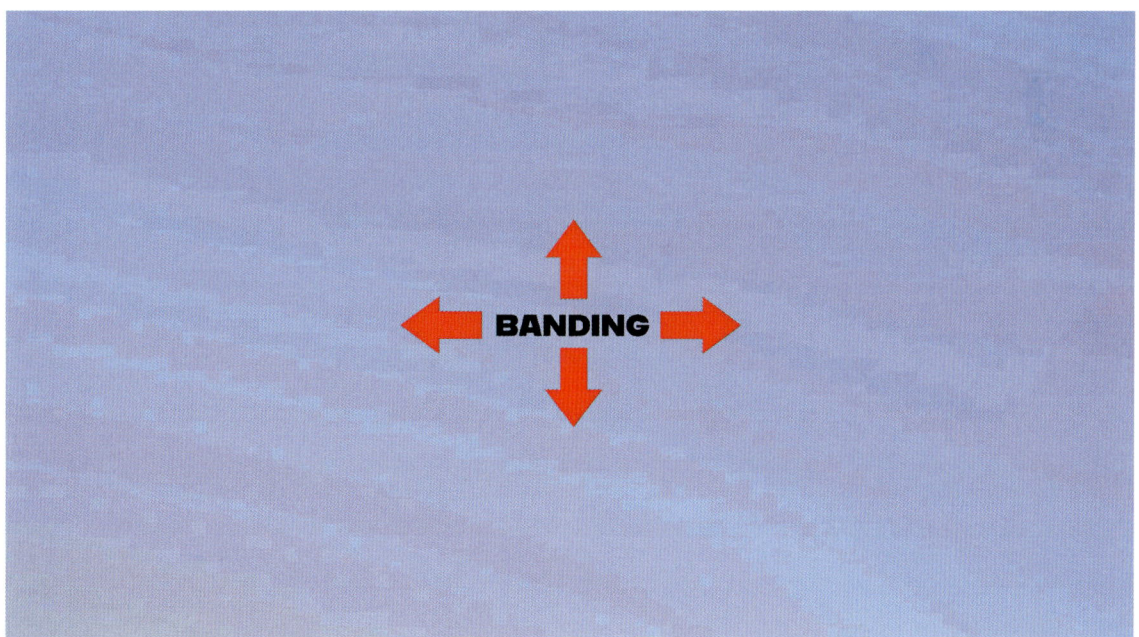

FIGURE 6.5

This is where 16-bit editing comes in. A 16-bit image contains over 281 trillion possible color values. That's enough to fill even the largest color space, like ProPhoto RGB, without gaps or banding.

THE CONTAINER ANALOGY

To simplify all this, imagine you have three containers, each one containing three colors: red, green, and blue.

- sRGB is the smallest container, and everything fits neatly inside **(Figure 6.6)**.

- Adobe RGB is a larger container. It holds the same amount of color, but it's spread out over a wider range **(Figure 6.7)**.

- ProPhoto RGB is even larger still, and to fill it, the colors must be spread even further **(Figure 6.8)**.

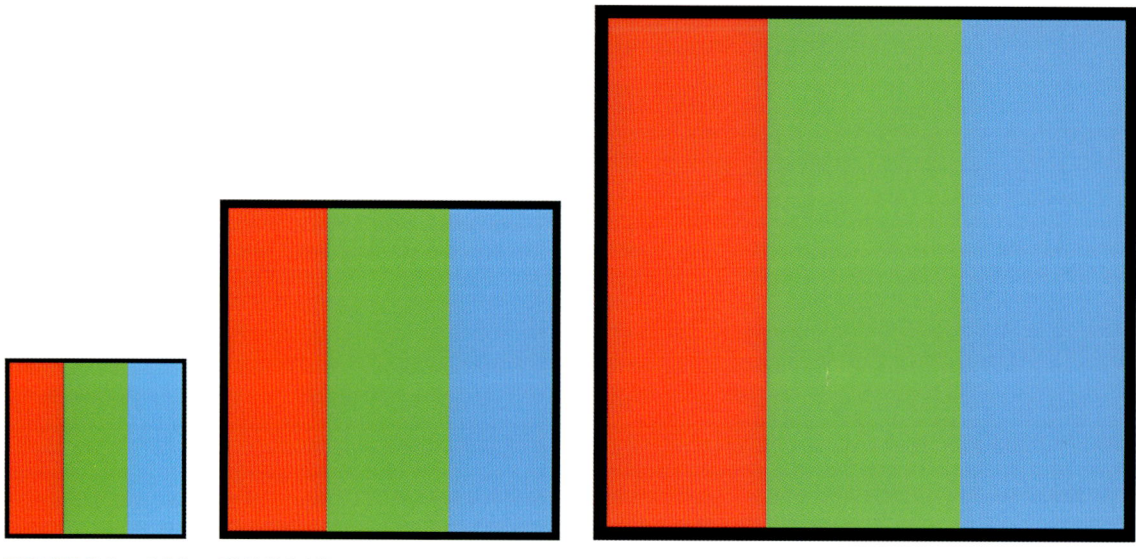

FIGURE 6.6—sRGB   FIGURE 6.7—Adobe RGB   FIGURE 6.8—ProPhoto RGB

This "spreading" of colors is what makes high bit depth essential. In large spaces like ProPhoto, more color steps are needed to keep the image smooth and free of visual artifacts.

SO WHICH COLOR SPACE SHOULD YOU USE?

There's no universal answer because each color space has its role:

- Use sRGB if you're sharing images online or sending them to labs that require it.

- Use Adobe RGB if you're printing and your devices support it.

- Use ProPhoto RGB if you're editing RAW images and want maximum flexibility, but always in 16-bit to avoid banding.

A CONVERSATION WITH A COLOR SCIENTIST DR. CHRIS BAI

So I've just explained in practical terms the differences between sRGB, Adobe RGB, and ProPhoto RGB. Now I'd like to share a conversation I had with Dr. Chris Bai **(Figure 6.9)**, a world-leading authority on color, who offered critical insights into how these color spaces actually function in practice.

> **NOTE:** *You can watch the full video interview at www.thehowtoprintbook.com.*

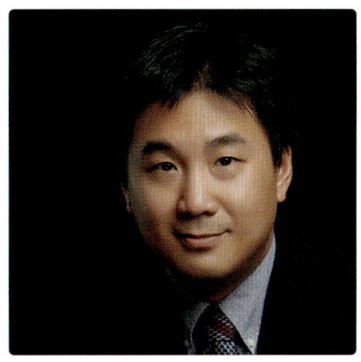

FIGURE 6.9—Dr. Chris Bai

Dr. Bai holds several prestigious roles:

- Vice Chair of the International Color Consortium (ICC)
- Chair of the ICC's Display Working Group
- Senior Color Expert and Manager of the Color Technology Lab at BenQ **(Figure 6.10)**

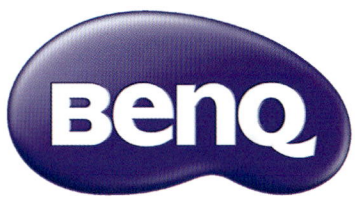

FIGURE 6.10

We sat down to discuss whether Adobe RGB or ProPhoto RGB is the better working color space for photographers, and his thoughts may challenge some common assumptions.

WHY DR. BAI DOESN'T USE PROPHOTO RGB FOR EDITING

Dr. Bai began by clarifying that while he's not claiming there's one "correct" workflow, he personally chooses not to use ProPhoto RGB in his editing process. His reason? ProPhoto RGB is a theoretical color space, meaning it's so large that it includes colors we can't even see, let alone display.

"There is no device that can actually display the ProPhoto color space, so when you're retouching an image, your only feedback is what you see on your monitor. If your monitor can't represent those colors, how can you make accurate decisions?"

Because there are no ProPhoto RGB displays, any image in that space must first be converted to the color space your screen can show. That conversion depends heavily on the quality of the algorithm used. A good one will preserve most of your image's color fidelity, but if it's poorly handled, you could end up with any or all of the following:

- Clipping (where colors are cut off and lost)
- Artifacts
- Contouring or banding in gradients

"We have no way to judge how well that conversion worked," Dr. Bai added, "because we never actually get to see the original ProPhoto colors."

THE ADOBE RGB ADVANTAGE FOR PRINTING

So if ProPhoto RGB is too large to be viewed or printed, what about Adobe RGB?

"To my knowledge, no current printers can print outside of Adobe RGB," says Dr. Bai. "There may be some experimental machines, but for practical purposes, including high-end pigment-based printers like the Canon Pro-300, Adobe RGB is the limit."

This surprised me because I remembered a discussion I'd had previously in which I'd been told that printing in ProPhoto RGB would yield better results because printers can supposedly print beyond Adobe RGB. But Dr. Bai clarified this is a myth. The real-world devices most photographers use, including professional lab printers, do not exceed Adobe RGB. He went on to explain the origins of Adobe RGB itself:

"It was created because sRGB was too small to match the color gamut of most printers. Adobe RGB was designed to include more of those printable colors, especially in the greens and cyans, and to ensure monitors could show what printers could produce. That's why it's still the recommended space for soft proofing and print workflows."

WHY SOME LABS STILL USE sRGB

Now with all of this considered, I once had a gallery exhibition displaying large-format prints, which were produced by Digitalab, a professional printing lab in the North East of England. Their file submission instructions? Send files in sRGB. But given everything I'd discussed with Dr. Chris Bai, why would this be the case?

According to Dr. Bai, "Some labs use algorithms to enhance skin tones or boost contrast. So your final print may still look great—but it's not because sRGB is better. It's because the lab has optimized the output using internal adjustments."

Before we wrapped up, Dr. Bai asked me to pass along two final technical insights that are important for anyone managing a serious image library:

1. *ProPhoto RGB is ideal for archival purposes in that its vast color space can accommodate potential future devices and standards that don't yet exist. If you're storing master files or digital negatives, keeping them in ProPhoto RGB (in 16-bit) preserves maximum flexibility for future edits or reprints.*

2. *Adobe RGB is larger than most printer color gamuts with one exception: The cyan channel in some printer profiles is more saturated than what Adobe RGB can hold. This is a rare case, but worth noting if your images rely heavily on subtle blue/green transitions.*

KEY TAKEAWAYS

- sRGB, while limited, is often used by labs due to standardization and consistency, and some make manual adjustments to improve output.

- Adobe RGB is the best practical choice for most printing workflows and soft proofing.

- ProPhoto RGB is too large to view or print directly; it should only be used for high-bit-depth editing or archiving.

- Always calibrate your monitor and understand the limitations of your devices before choosing a working color space.

MY PREFERRED COLOR SPACE PREFERENCES AND WORKFLOW

I get that this might be a lot to take in, especially if you're very new to printing, so I thought it might be helpful to talk about my color space preferences and workflow, and more importantly, why I use what I do. It's a question I get asked regularly, and the answer has evolved over time.

Currently, and for the foreseeable future, I work primarily in ProPhoto RGB and Adobe RGB color spaces because each plays a distinct role in my photographic and printing workflow. I'll explain …

THE ROLE OF LIGHTROOM IN MY WORKFLOW

Lightroom is my main software for importing and retouching raw image files, whether they come from my mirrorless camera or my iPhone. One common misconception is that Lightroom converts raw files into a color space. It doesn't. Instead, Lightroom displays your images using a color space that's based on ProPhoto RGB called Melissa RGB (Adobe's internal name). This means that while you're working inside Lightroom, you are essentially editing in ProPhoto RGB (Melissa RGB), even though you don't technically assign a color space to the file at this stage.

Why is this important? Because ProPhoto RGB (Melissa RGB) is an extremely large color space, with parts of it extending beyond what the human eye can see. Despite that, it contains an incredible amount of color information, which allows for more detailed adjustments without degrading image quality. You're less likely to introduce banding, color artifacts, or other unwanted issues during editing.

MOVING FROM LIGHTROOM TO PHOTOSHOP

In Lightroom's Preferences under the External Editing tab, I've set it up so that when I export an image to Photoshop, it's sent as a TIFF file, in ProPhoto RGB, and at 16-bit depth **(Figure 6.11)**.

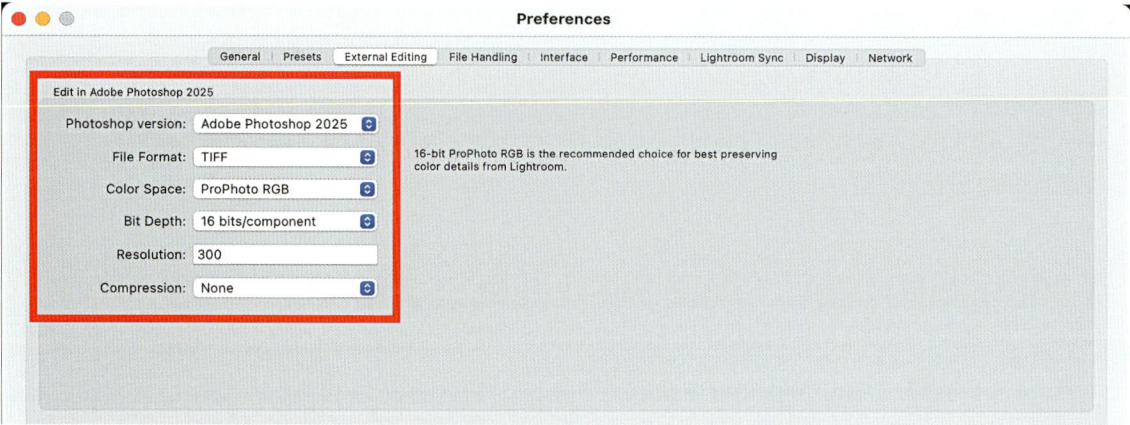

FIGURE 6.11

This setup is ideal for preserving the most color detail when moving between programs. So when I open an image in Photoshop for more advanced retouching (things I can't do in Lightroom), I ensure that Photoshop's working color space is also set to ProPhoto RGB. This consistency is crucial.

I often hear from photographers who are puzzled by why their image looks different in Photoshop than it did in Lightroom. The culprit is almost always a color space mismatch. How different the image looks can vary based on the dominant colors in the photo. But to avoid this completely, make sure your working color space in Photoshop matches Lightroom's display color space **(Figure 6.12)**.

In Photoshop, go to **Edit** > **Color Settings** > **Working Space**, and select ProPhoto RGB from the RGB menu.

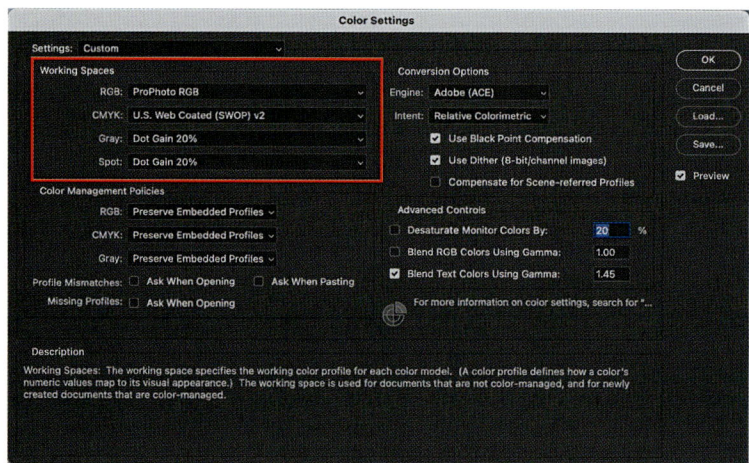

FIGURE 6.12

SWITCHING TO ADOBE RGB FOR PRINTING

While I retouch in ProPhoto RGB, my printing workflow uses Adobe RGB, and this is a deliberate switch. Later on in this book, you'll see that I resize images in Photoshop, not Lightroom. Once an image is ready for print, I export it from Lightroom into a desktop folder, and then open it in Photoshop for final tweaks. This final phase, especially if I need to apply any print sharpening, is where I set Photoshop's working color space to Adobe RGB.

Why Adobe RGB? Because this is the color space that my prints are made in, and I want to see the image exactly as it will appear on paper without any surprises due to mismatched color profiles. Make sense?

> **TIP:** *In Photoshop, if you see an **asterisk symbol** next to the image name in the tab, that indicates a **color space mismatch** between the image and Photoshop's working space.*
>
> *To avoid issues:*
>
> - *Do all retouching in **ProPhoto RGB** for maximum color flexibility.*
> - *Switch to **Adobe RGB** before sending your images to the printer.*

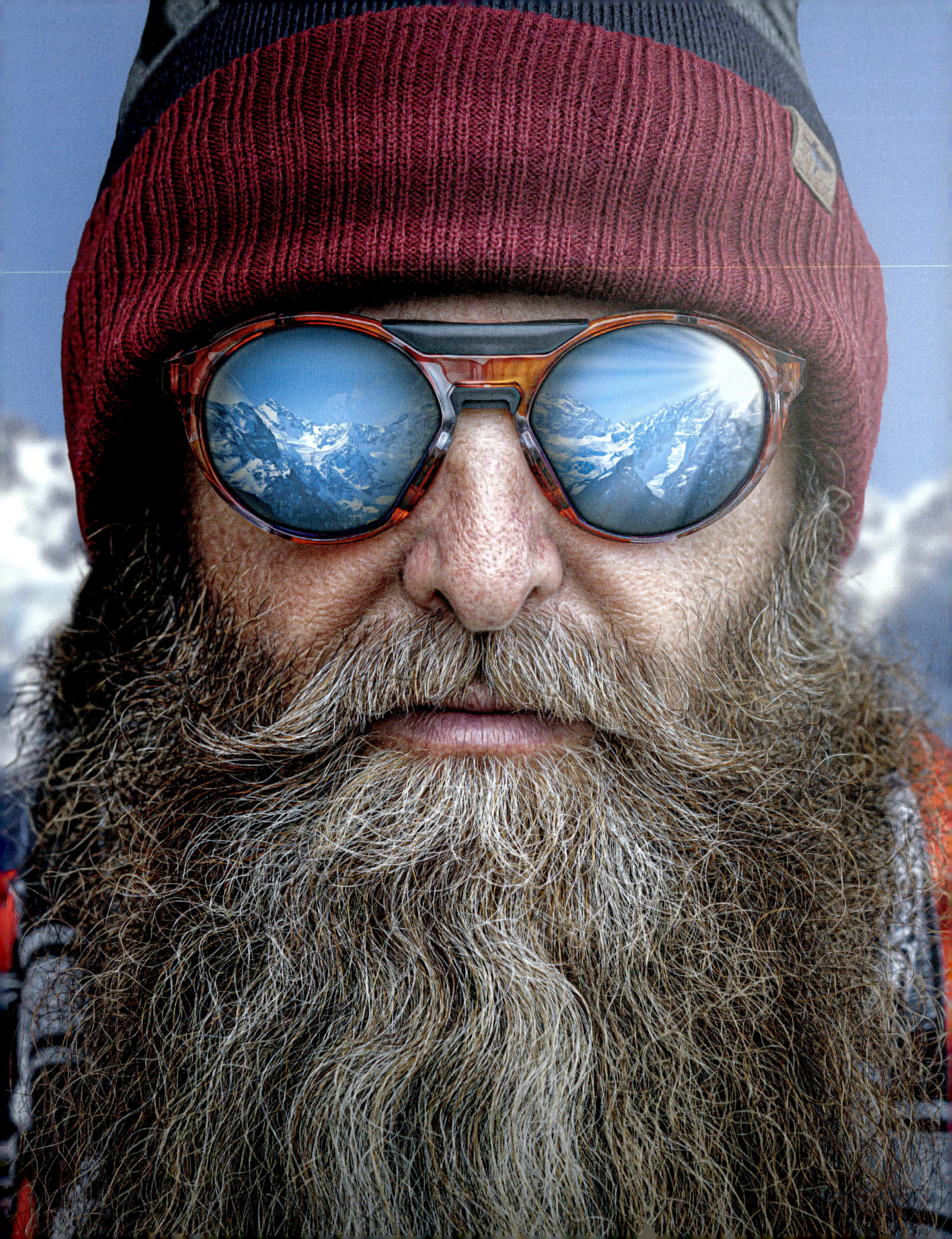

CHAPTER 7
RESOLUTION AND RESIZING

PIXELS, DOTS, AND PRINT QUALITY

When preparing images for print, understanding resolution is essential for achieving optimal quality. In digital imaging, **resolution** is measured in **pixels per inch (PPI)**; this refers to the number of pixels contained within one inch of an image on a digital display.

In contrast, **print resolution** is measured in **dots per inch (DPI)**, meaning the number of ink droplets a printer lays down in a single inch. These dots are created by the printer's nozzles and form the printed version of your image.

There are two key reasons why understanding resolution is important:

1. To achieve the highest possible print quality from your printer.
2. To correctly resize images for print, whether enlarging or reducing them.

NATIVE PRINTER RESOLUTION

All printers operate with a **native resolution**, the ideal input resolution that the printer driver expects for maximum quality without resampling.

Canon printers typically have a native resolution of **300 PPI**.

Epson printers often use **360 PPI**.

However, this doesn't mean one pixel in your image equals one dot on the paper. A single image pixel is usually made up of multiple ink dots from your printer. To visualize this, imagine a single image pixel represented on the left and the multiple ink dots required to reproduce it on paper shown on the right **(Figure 7.1)**.

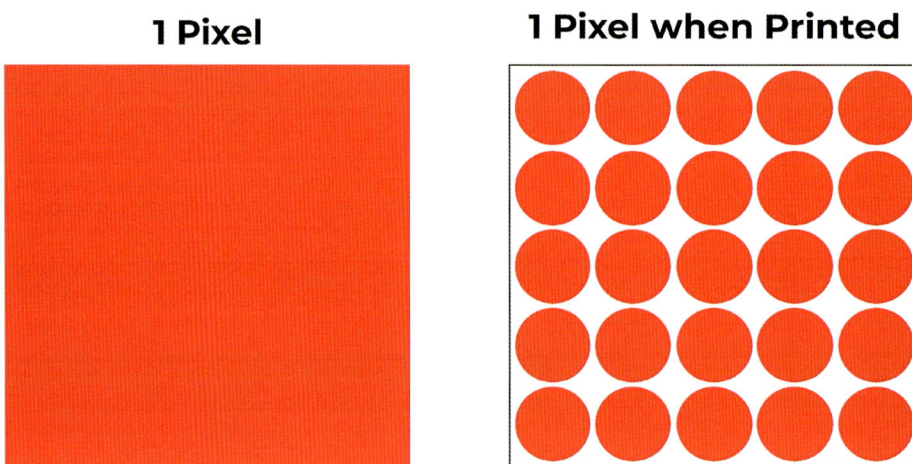

FIGURE 7.1 – Not to scale. For illustration purposes only.

MATCHING IMAGE AND PRINTER RESOLUTIONS

If the resolution of your image doesn't match your printer's native resolution, the printer driver compensates in one of two ways:

• If the image resolution is lower than the printer's native resolution, the driver adds pixels, a process known as **interpolation**.

• If the image resolution is higher, the driver discards pixels, which is also interpolation.

Although modern printer drivers are generally good at handling these adjustments, results can vary.

For full control and predictability, you may prefer to manage image resizing and resolution adjustments manually using editing software. This process is straightforward, and once you're familiar with it, you'll likely find it easy to handle.

That said, if you're satisfied with the results your printer produces using its default settings, there's no need to change your workflow.

DETERMINING MAXIMUM PRINT SIZE FROM IMAGE RESOLUTION

Before resizing an image for print, it's helpful to understand how large it can be printed in its current form (i.e., without introducing interpolation or resampling). This involves checking the image's dimensions in pixels and comparing them with the **native resolution of your printer**.

As previously mentioned, Canon printers typically use a native resolution of **300 pixels per inch (PPI)**, while Epson printers often use **360 PPI**. We can use these values to calculate the **maximum printable size** of an image.

EXAMPLE 1: PRINTING WITH CANON

Let's consider this image that I have open in Lightroom **(Figure 7.2)**.

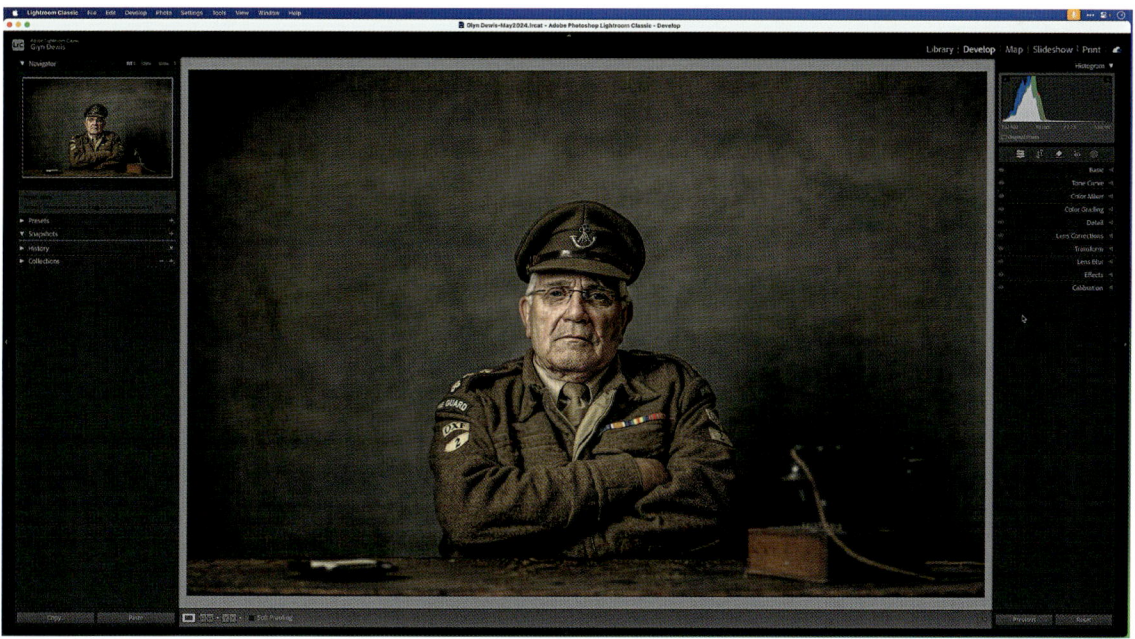

FIGURE 7.2

Pressing the letter **I** (that's a capital i) on my keyboard reveals information about the image, and we can see that the dimensions are **5712 × 3808 pixels (Figure 7.3)**.

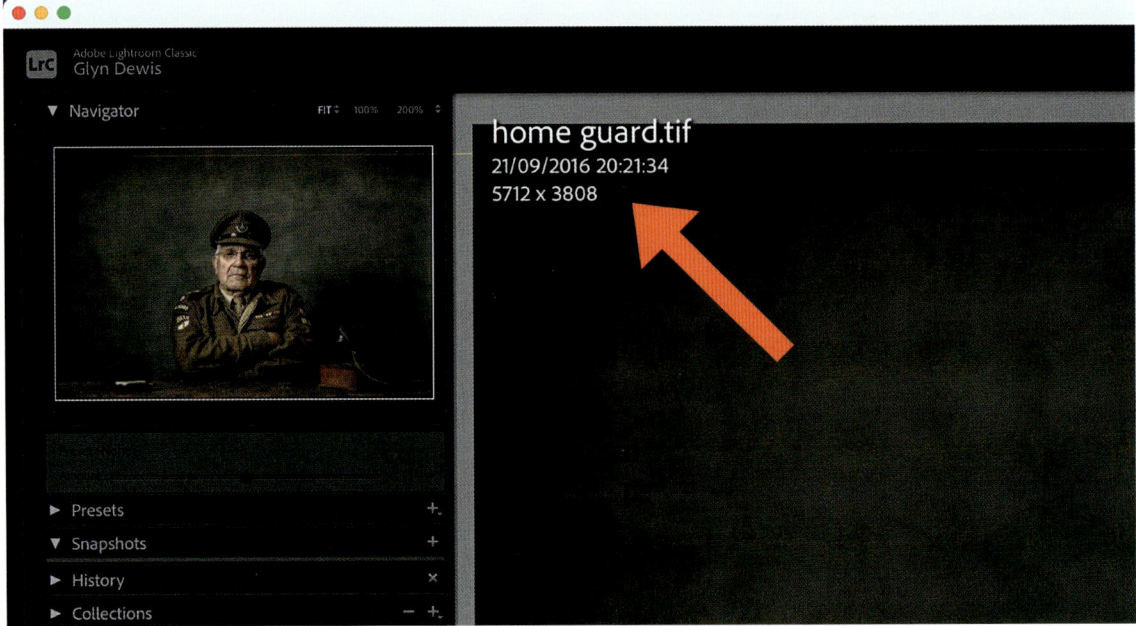

So to figure out the maximum print size I could produce on my Canon Pro-300, all I have to do is:

1. Take the **longest side** of the image: 5712 pixels.

2. Divide that number by Canon's native resolution (300 PPI).

5712 ÷ 300 = 19.04 inches

This means the image can be printed at just over **19 inches** on its longest side without needing to upscale (interpolate).

EXAMPLE 2: PRINTING WITH EPSON

If I were to print the same image on an Epson printer, such as the Epson P900, with a native print resolution of 360 PPI, this is what I would do:

1. Take the longest side of the image: 5712 pixels.

2. Divide that number by Epson's native resolution (360 PPI).

5712 ÷ 360 = 15.87 inches

In this case, the maximum print size would be just under **16 inches** on the longest side.

EXAMPLE 3: PRINTING AT A SPECIFIC SIZE

Now let's say that I would like to print the image shown in **Figure 7.4** at 16 inches on the longest side.

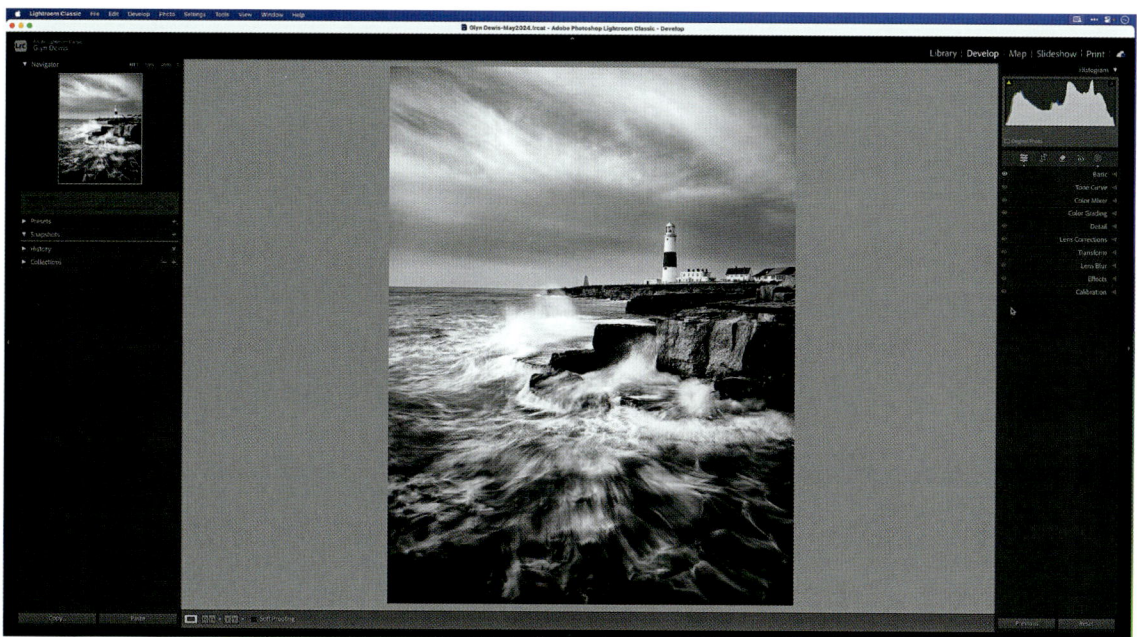

FIGURE 7.4

First, I need to find out what size it currently is, so with it open in Lightroom I press **I** on my keyboard to reveal the information and can see that the dimensions of the image are 2500 x 3350 pixels **(Figure 7.5)**. So how big will it print at its current dimensions?

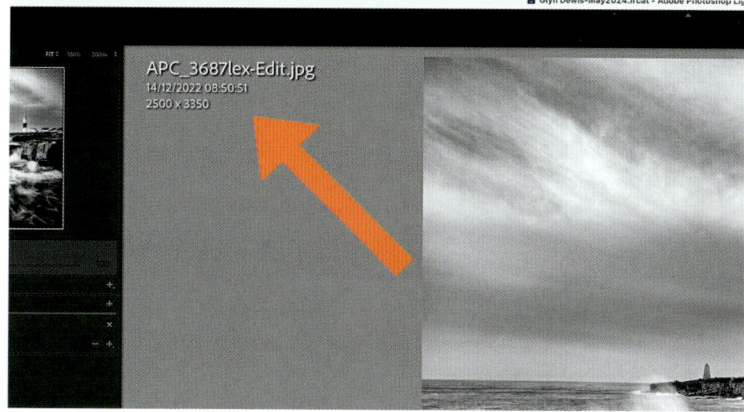

FIGURE 7.5

Canon: 3350 ÷ 300 = **11.17 inches**

Epson: 3350 ÷ 360 = **9.31 inches**

So, this image can be printed at just over **11 inches** on Canon or just over **9 inches** on Epson, before requiring any resizing. Since the image's native dimensions aren't sufficient to print at 16 inches on the longest side at either printer's native resolution, I would need to **increase the image size through interpolation**, either manually or by letting the printer driver handle it.

Understanding this relationship between image resolution and printer capabilities enables you to make informed decisions about resizing and ensures consistent, high-quality print results.

HOW IMAGE SIZE AFFECTS RESOLUTION

One fundamental concept to grasp when preparing images for print is how **reducing the size of an image increases its resolution**. This may seem counterintuitive at first, but it becomes clear when we look at an example.

Suppose you have an image that measures **10 inches by 8 inches at 300 pixels per inch (PPI)**. If you scale it down to **5 inches by 4 inches**, you are reducing the dimensions by half. However, because the same number of pixels are now spread over a smaller physical area, the resolution effectively **doubles** to **600 PPI (Figure 7.6)**.

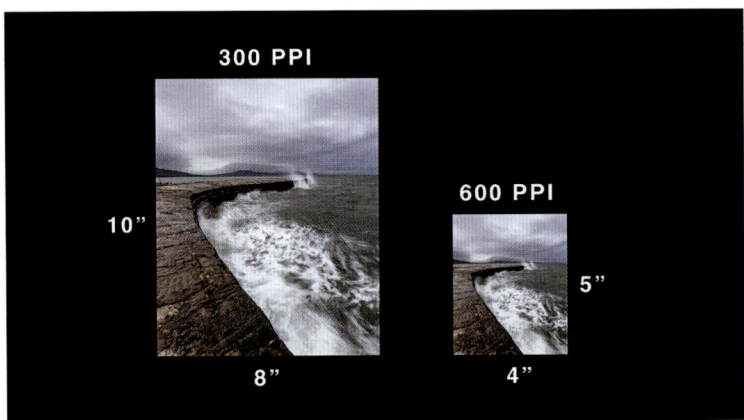

FIGURE 7.6

Let's walk through this using Photoshop:

1. Create a new document with dimensions set in inches **(Figure 7.7).**

2. Set the width to 10 inches, height to 8 inches, and resolution to 300 PPI.

3. Click **Create** to generate the new document.

Once the document is open:

1. Navigate to **Image** > **Image Size** to open the Image Size dialog box **(Figure 7.8)**.

2. Ensure the units are set to inches. You'll see the document is 10 × 8 inches at 300 PPI, which equals **3000 × 2400 pixels.**

3. Note the **chain link icon**. This indicates that the proportions are locked, meaning any change to width or height will maintain the aspect ratio. Now, if you reduce the width from **10 inches to 5 inches**, the resolution automatically increases from **300 to 600 PPI**, because the total number of pixels hasn't changed **(Figure 7.9)**.

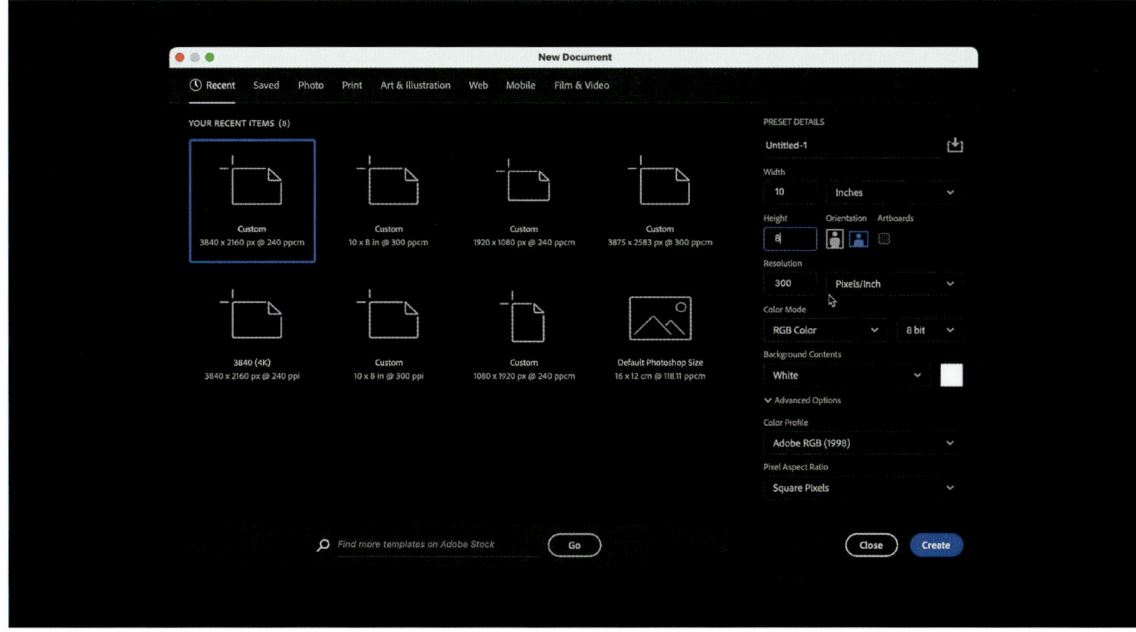

FIGURE 7.7

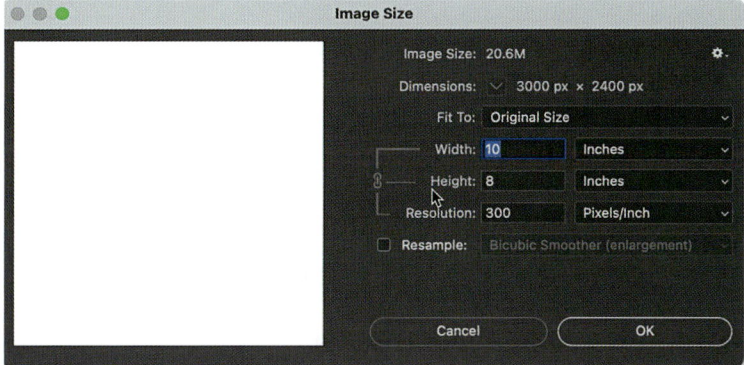

FIGURE 7.8

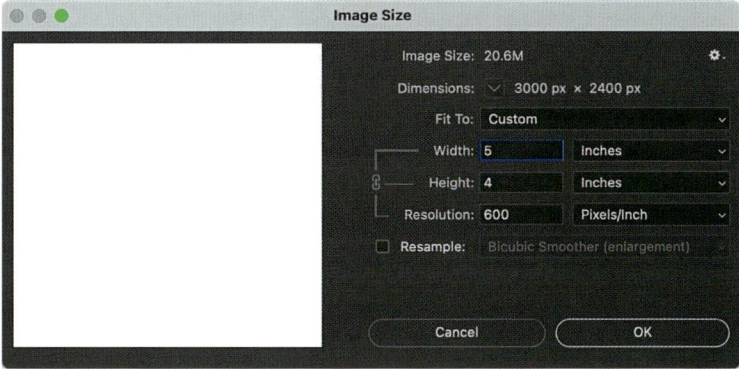

FIGURE 7.9

MAINTAINING RESOLUTION WHEN RESIZING

In many situations, such as when sending files to a professional print lab, you'll need to deliver images at specific dimensions and resolutions (commonly **300 PPI**). To do this, **resampling** is required. **Resampling** is the process of changing the number of pixels in an image, which allows you to adjust its physical size while keeping the desired resolution.

- If you're making the image **smaller** or **larger**, your **resampling.**

- When resampling, the process of removing or adding pixels is called **interpolation**.

Both functions are handled under the same **Resample** option in Photoshop's Image Size dialog. Here, you'll find algorithms for both enlarging and reducing an image, all under one unified interface **(Figure 7.10)**.

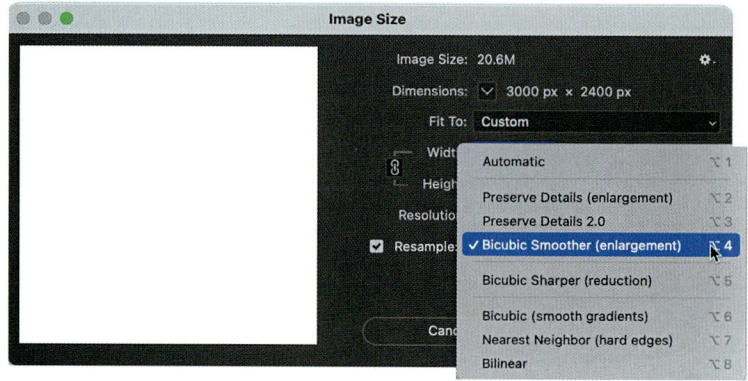

FIGURE 7.10

WHY THIS MATTERS

Understanding how resolution shifts when resizing an image, and how to control it, ensures your final output meets both your quality standards and any specific technical requirements from print labs or publishers.

Next we'll take a look at how to **resample images step-by-step,** and what methods produce the best results depending on whether you're scaling up or down.

CHOOSING THE RIGHT RESAMPLING METHOD

When reducing the size of an image while maintaining a specific resolution, such as 300 PPI, it's important to understand that Photoshop gives you control over **how pixels are discarded** during the resampling process. The method you choose can influence the final quality of the downsized image.

RESAMPLING OPTIONS IN PHOTOSHOP

Photoshop offers several resampling algorithms, each optimized for different tasks:

- **Automatic (Auto):** Photoshop chooses what it considers the best method based on the operation (upscaling or downscaling).
- **Bicubic Sharper (Reduction):** Specifically designed for reducing image size while preserving detail.
- **Bicubic Smoother (Enlargement):** Intended for upscaling.
- Others include Nearest Neighbor, Bilinear, and more.

There's debate among professionals about whether to trust the **Auto** setting or to manually select the method best suited to the task, so let's look at a practical comparison.

COMPARING AUTO VS. BICUBIC SHARPER IN PHOTOSHOP

To compare these two resampling methods, I'll use the image shown in **(Figure 7.11)**, which I have open in two separate tabs in Photoshop, and go through the following steps:

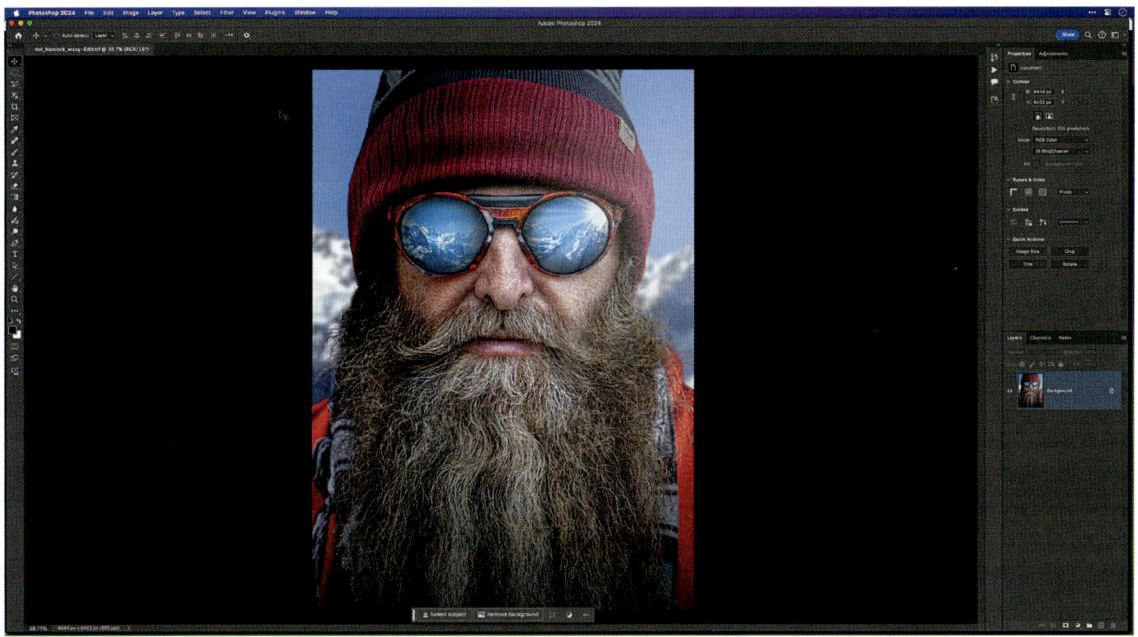

FIGURE 7.11

1. Duplicate the image by going to **Image** > **Duplicate**. Name the duplicate "Auto" and click OK.
2. Open the Image Size dialog via **Image** > **Image Size**.
3. Set the **resolution to 300 PPI**, the native resolution for my Canon Pro-300 printer.
4. Reduce the image dimensions by **50%**.
5. From the **Resample** drop-down menu, select **Automatic (Figure 7.12)**, then click OK.

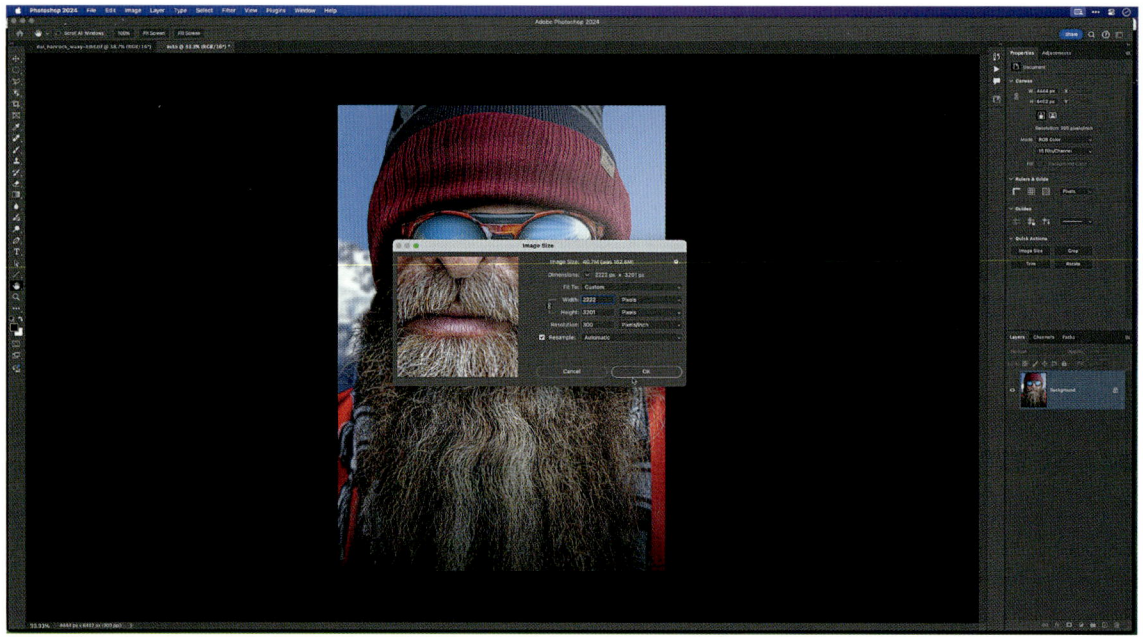

FIGURE 7.12

Next, I'll follow the same steps on the image that I have open in the other tab, except this time I'll choose **Bicubic Sharper (Reduction)** from the **Resample** menu **(Figure 7.13)**.

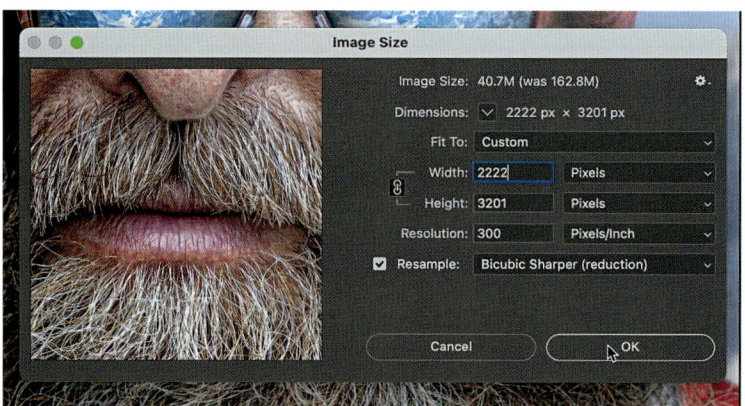

FIGURE 7.13

To compare the results side-by-side:

1. Go to **Window** > **Arrange** > **2-Up Vertical**.

2. Zoom in on one image.

3. Then go to **Window** > **Arrange** > **Match All** to synchronize the zoom and position.

Upon close inspection there's little to no visible difference between the two images **(Figure 7.14)**. So in this case, Photoshop's Auto setting performed just as well as a manual selection.

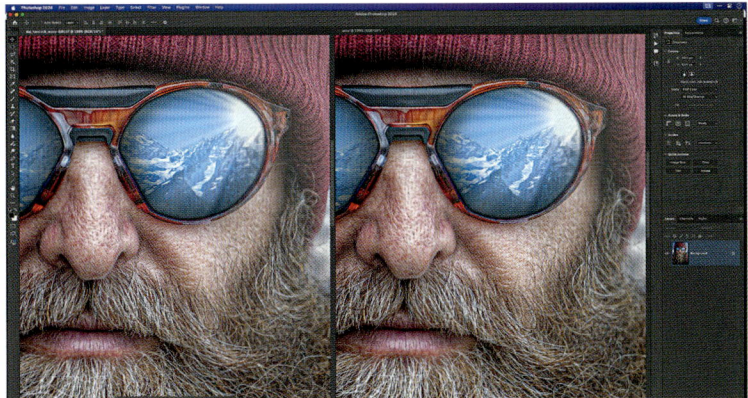

FIGURE 7.14

RESAMPLING IN LIGHTROOM

Lightroom simplifies this process even further:

1. Go to **File** > **Export**.

2. In the **Image Sizing** section, check **Resize to Fit**.

3. Select **Long Edge** from the drop-down menu and choose a specific size (e.g., 8 inches).

4. Set the **Resolution** to **300 PPI**.

5. Click **Export (Figure 7.15)**.

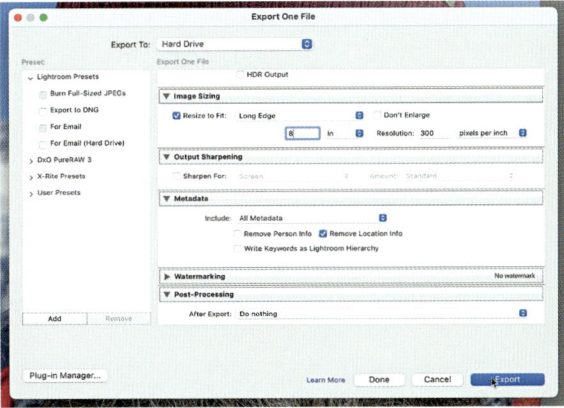

FIGURE 7.15

Unlike Photoshop, Lightroom does not provide manual control over the resampling method. Instead, it uses **Bicubic Auto**, the same Auto mode found in Photoshop. This helps streamline the process, particularly when batch exporting multiple images.

KEY TAKEAWAY

Whether you're using Photoshop or Lightroom, automatic resampling generally performs well, especially for moderate resizing. However, for maximum control and when working with critical image detail, manual resampling methods, such as Bicubic Sharper, may offer a slight edge, particularly in downscaling scenarios.

Next we'll take a look at **upscaling** images effectively and what to do when you need to print larger than your image's native resolution allows.

CROPPING IMAGES WITHOUT LOSING CONTROL OVER QUALITY

Cropping is a fundamental part of image editing, especially when refining composition. However, cropping also affects image size and resolution. When an image is cropped, fewer pixels remain, effectively reducing the file size. If no resampling is applied, the resolution increases automatically, which may not be desirable, particularly when preparing an image for print at a specific size and resolution.

CROPPING FOR PRINT IN PHOTOSHOP

Let's walk through cropping an image in Photoshop to fit a standard **10 × 8 inch frame**. We'll use the image show in **Figure 7.16** as an example.

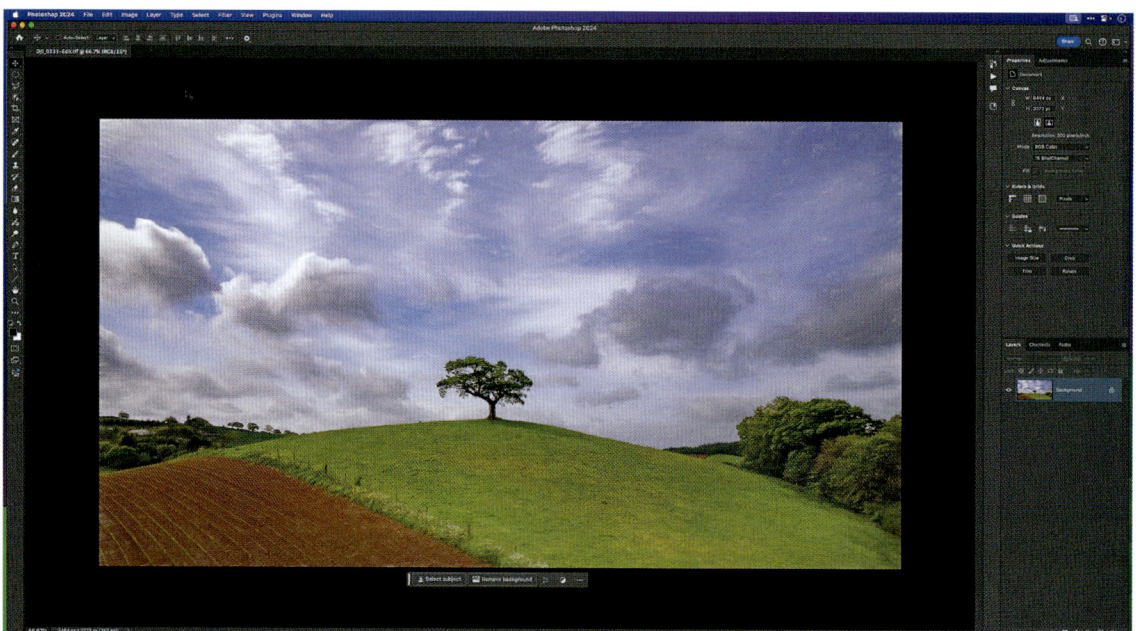

FIGURE 7.16

1. Open the image, then go to **Image** > **Image Size**.
2. Switch the unit to inches and note the dimensions.

In this example, the image is approximately 18 inches wide and 10 inches high at 300 pixels per inch (PPI) (Figure 7.17).

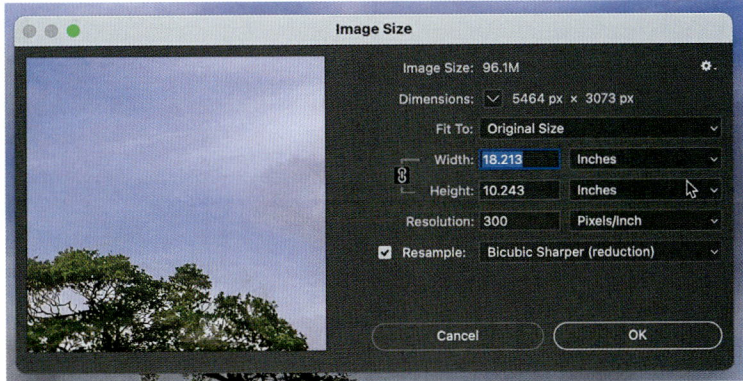

FIGURE 7.17

1. Select the **Crop Tool.**

2. Choose the preset aspect ratio of **4 : 5**, which matches an 8 × 10 frame **(Figure 7.18).**

3. Press **X** to rotate the crop if needed, then **Enter** to apply.

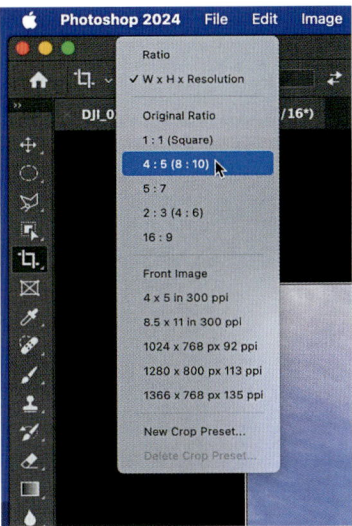

FIGURE 7.18

At this point, the image has been cropped but no resampling has occurred, so although the image is physically smaller **(Figure 7.20)**, the resolution has increased. This might not be desirable if you're targeting a specific output resolution.

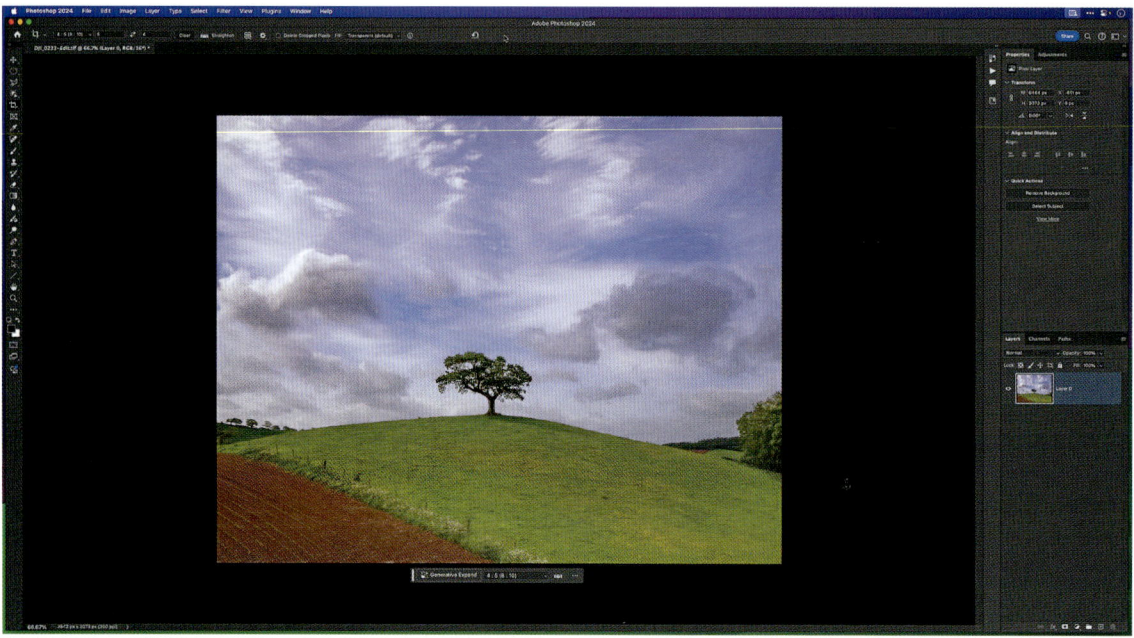

FIGURE 7.19

CROPPING WITH DEFINED DIMENSIONS AND RESOLUTION

In Photoshop, we do have the option to set the resolution while we're cropping to a specific dimension or aspect ratio:

1. With the **Crop Tool** selected, go to the options bar and choose the **W × H × Resolution** preset **(Figure 7.20)**.

2. In the options bar, enter the target dimensions; e.g., **10 in** (width) and **8 in** (height).

3. Set the resolution box to **360 PPI** (for Epson printers), making sure to choose **Pixels/Inch** as the unit.

4. Apply the crop.

Photoshop will now resample the image during the crop using its Auto method.

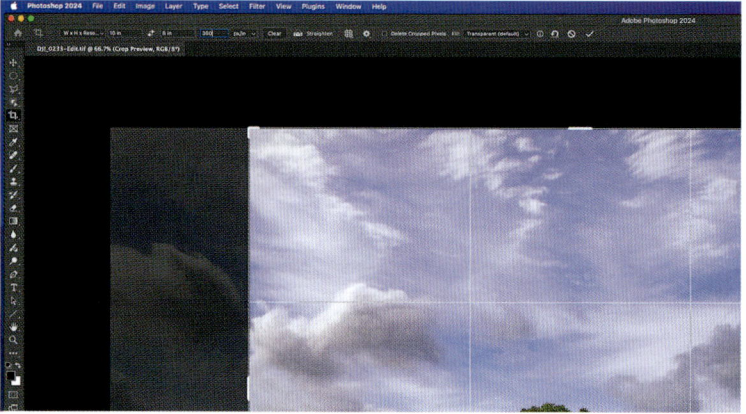

FIGURE 7.20

When checking **Image** > **Image Size**, the result will show exactly **10 × 8 inches** at **360 PPI**. No unwanted increase in resolution has occurred **(Figure 7.21)**.

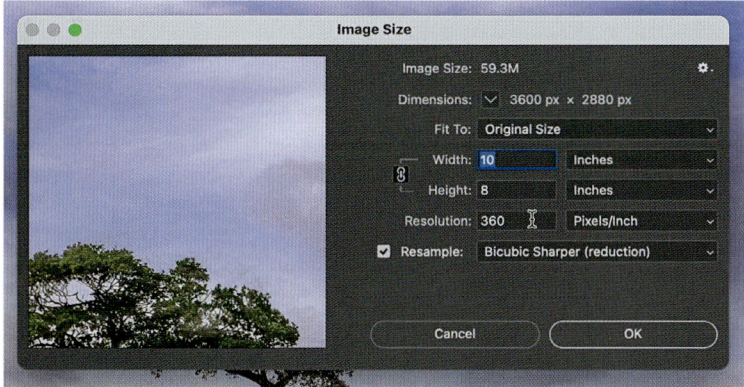

FIGURE 7.21

CROPPING FOR PRINT IN LIGHTROOM

In Lightroom, the approach is slightly different:

1. Use the **Crop Overlay Tool**, and choose **4 × 5 / 8 × 10** from the aspect ratio presets **(Figure 7.22)**.

2. Reposition the crop area as needed, then press **Enter (Figure 7.23)**.

At this stage, Lightroom does not perform any resampling; that step happens during export or print.

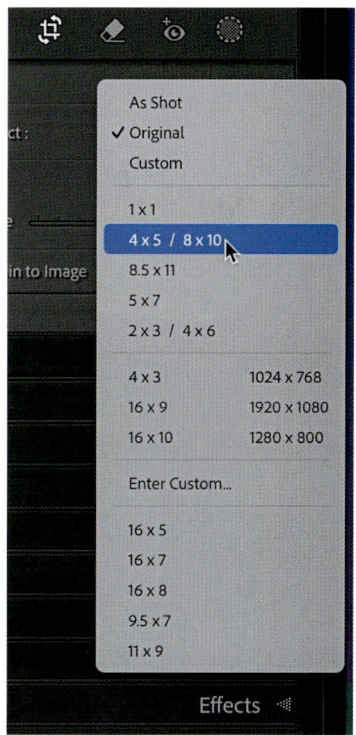

FIGURE 7.22

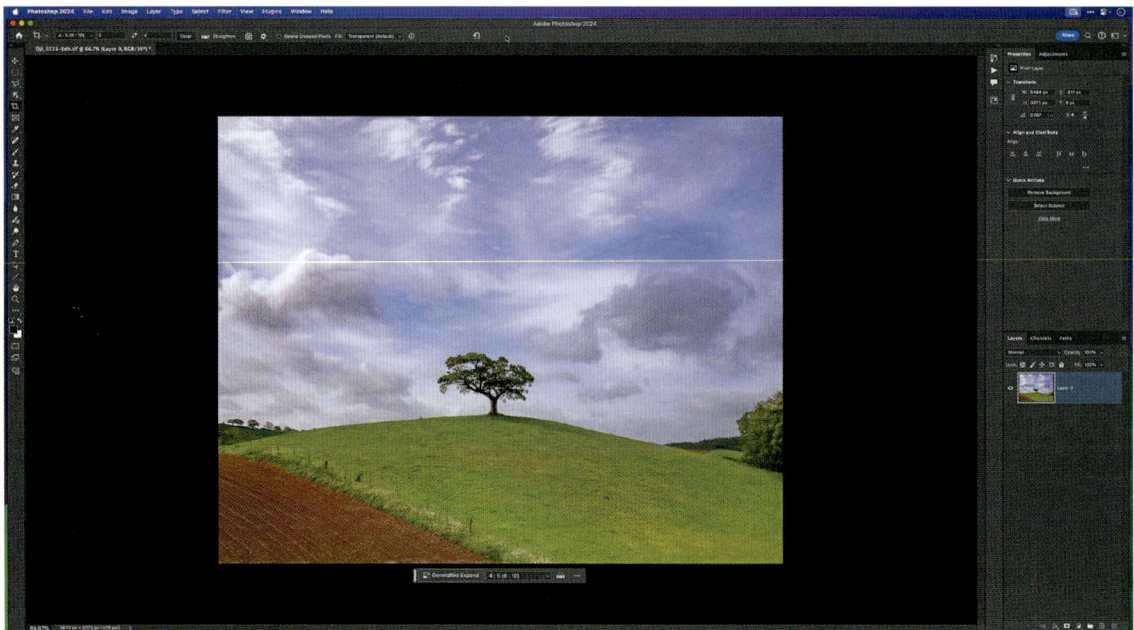

FIGURE 7.23

RESAMPLING ON EXPORT

To resize and resample the image upon export:

1. Go to **File** > **Export**.

2. In the **Image Sizing** section, enable **Resize to Fit** and select **Long Edge** from the drop-down menu **(Figure 7.24)**.

3. Enter **10 inches** as the target size.

4. Set the resolution to **360 PPI**, and click **Export**.

Lightroom will apply automatic resampling using its internal algorithm (Bicubic Auto) to ensure the exported file matches your print dimensions and resolution requirements.

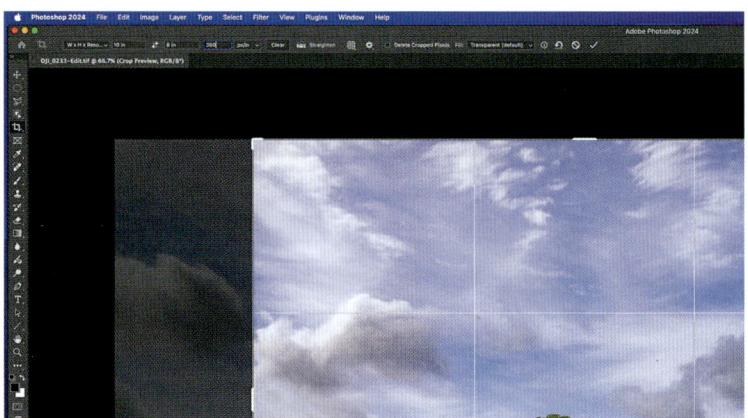

FIGURE 7.24

RESAMPLING DURING PRINTING FROM LIGHTROOM

If you're printing directly from within Lightroom Classic, the printer driver will handle the resampling at the point of print. While this can work well, it may not reflect adjustments like sharpening that you've made in Lightroom Classic. These edits could appear differently once the image is downsized, and you won't know the final result until the print is made. If it's not as you had hoped, it's an unfortunate waste of paper and ink.

This is one of the key reasons many photographers prefer to handle resampling themselves before printing. It allows you to preview exactly what the final image will look like at print resolution, ensuring that effects like sharpening, noise reduction, and detail retention behave as expected.

This level of control can help you to avoid surprises and wasted paper and ink when producing final prints.

ENLARGING IMAGES FOR PRINT

So far, I've covered reducing image size, throwing away pixels and resampling. And as we've seen, that's generally quite straightforward. But things get a bit more involved when we want to go the other way and increase the size of an image, because this means we're adding pixels, and the challenge is doing that while still keeping the image looking as sharp and clean as possible.

Thankfully, there are some very clever people out there who've created some equally clever software. Today, it's possible to enlarge images far beyond what used to be considered realistic, and do so with incredible results.

REAL-WORLD EXAMPLE: AN IPHONE IMAGE TURNED POSTER

Let me give you a real-world example. I took a photo with my iPhone, and when I opened it in Lightroom and pressed I to see its info, I saw that it measured 1,916 × 2,560 pixels. At 300 pixels per inch, that would give me just over 8 inches on the longest side, so not that big at all.

But I had that exact same image printed at a massive 72 inches wide by a professional lab called Digitalab, based in the north of England. That's nearly a 900% increase in size. And the result? Genuinely incredible. Not just good from a distance, but even up close, it held together really well **(Figure 7.25)**.

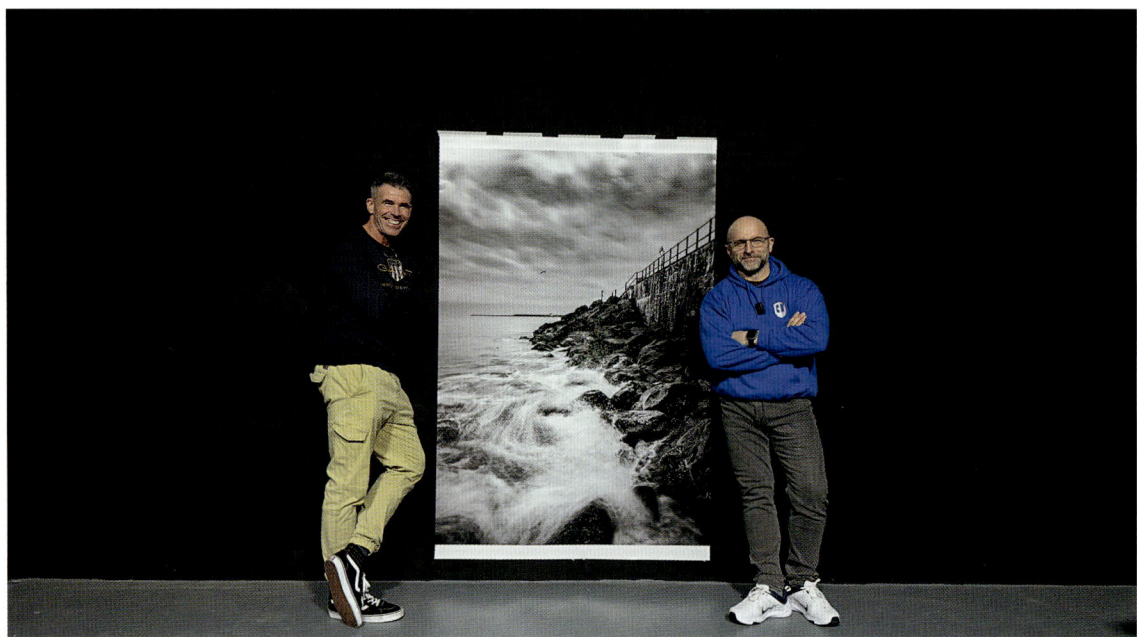

FIGURE 7.25

The software I used for that job was Topaz Gigapixel, which I'll show you a little later.

First though, let's look at the options we have in Photoshop and Lightroom (including Classic) for enlarging images.

USING PHOTOSHOP TO ENLARGE IMAGES

You'll remember from earlier that when you go to **Image** > **Image Size** in Photoshop, there's a **Resample** checkbox **(Figure 7.26)**; that's the option that tells Photoshop whether it should add or remove pixels when changing the image size.

When you're enlarging an image, you're not throwing away pixels, you're asking Photoshop to invent new ones, and this is where things get tricky.

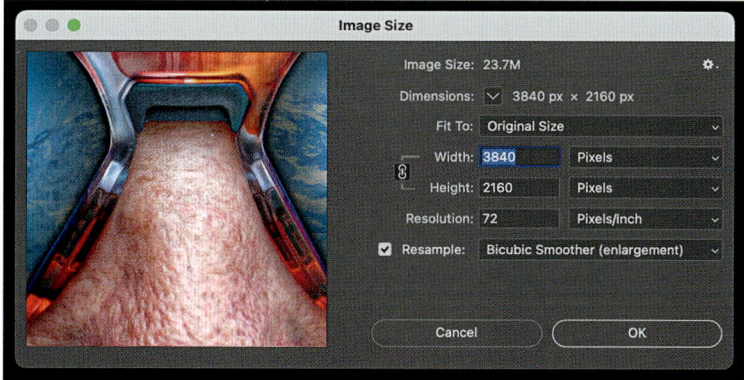

FIGURE 7.26

Generally, when you make an image bigger, it starts to look softer or less sharp. So if you are going to use Photoshop to do this kind of upscaling, I'd recommend **not** using the Auto resample setting.

Instead, try out some of the specific options like **Preserve Details (enlargement)** and see which gives the best result for your image.

> **A QUICK NOTE ON HOW IT WORKS:** *Tick the **Resample** box. When you change the dimensions (say, increase the width), the resolution number won't change until you hit **OK**. Photoshop only applies the actual resampling once you confirm your settings.*

That said, I personally don't use Photoshop for enlarging images anymore, at least not for big enlargements. It works, but it's a bit limited in how much you can scale things up before quality takes a hit. And there are much better tools available now.

SUPER RESOLUTION (IN LIGHTROOM AND CAMERA RAW)

Adobe has developed some AI-based technology called Super Resolution, and it's a huge step forward. You'll find it in Camera Raw and in both Lightroom and Lightroom Classic, and it's built to handle exactly this kind of upscaling.

USING SUPER RESOLUTION IN CAMERA RAW

You can't access Super Resolution via the Camera Raw Filter in Photoshop. Instead you have to open the image directly in Camera Raw. If you're opening a Raw image, it will automatically open in Camera Raw, but you can also use Super Resolution on other file formats such as JPG and TIFF.

To open your image in Camera Raw, use one of the following methods:

- Open Adobe Bridge and find your image, then right-click it and choose Open in Camera Raw.

- Use **File** > **Open** in Camera Raw and navigate to your image.

Once the image is open, you'll see a filmstrip at the bottom. Hover over the image thumbnail and click the three-dot icon (the ellipsis), or just right-click the thumbnail, and choose **Enhance** from the menu **(Figure 7.27)**.

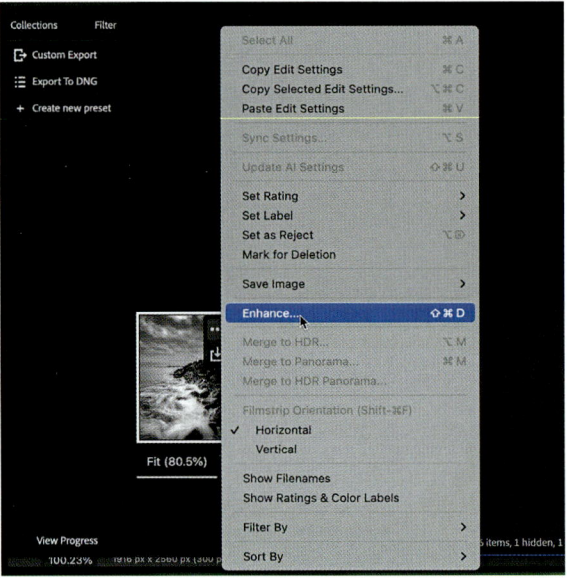

FIGURE 7.27

A box appears with the **Super Resolution** option **(Figure 7.28)**. If you hover over the little info icon, it says: "Doubles image resolution. Ideal for large displays and prints." And here's where we need to clear something up.

You might think, "But I don't want to double the resolution. I'm already at 300 pixels per inch, wouldn't that make it 600 PPI?"

Actually, no. When Adobe says it "doubles the resolution," it means it doubles the pixel dimensions, not just the PPI, and that's an important distinction.

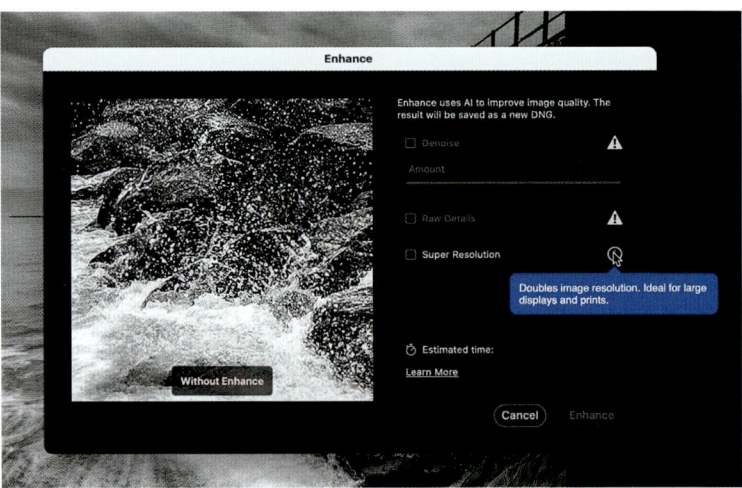

FIGURE 7.28

UNDERSTANDING WHAT "DOUBLING THE RESOLUTION" REALLY MEANS

Let's go back to basics for a moment. Earlier, I mentioned how when reducing the size of an image, the resolution increases, and vice versa.

Here's a quick recap:

Let's say you start with a document that's **10 × 8 inches** at **300 PPI**. If you scale it up to **20 × 16 inches**, the resolution is cut in half, down to **150 PPI**, because you're spreading the same number of pixels over a bigger area.

So, what Super Resolution does is enlarge the image, doubling the width and height in pixels, but it also boosts the pixel count so that your resolution (PPI) stays the same. In this example, it brings 150 PPI back up to 300 PPI after enlargement. It's not making your image 600 PPI; it's just making sure that as you make the image physically bigger, the detail and resolution are preserved. And honestly, it works really well.

USING SUPER RESOLUTION IN LIGHTROOM

If you're working in Lightroom or Lightroom Classic, it's even easier. Just go to the Photo menu and choose **Enhance (Figure 7.29)**, and then you'll get the same Super Resolution dialog box as in Camera Raw.

Now for a lot of photographers, this may be all you ever need. If doubling your image size gets you where you want to be for printing or display, then Super Resolution is a fantastic solution; it's quick, simple, and built right into your workflow.

WHEN YOU NEED MORE: TOPAZ GIGAPIXEL AI

But what if you need to go beyond doubling the size of your image? Well, that's where software like Topaz Gigapixel comes in. It's a standalone app and a Photoshop plugin, and despite being incredibly powerful, it's surprisingly easy to use.

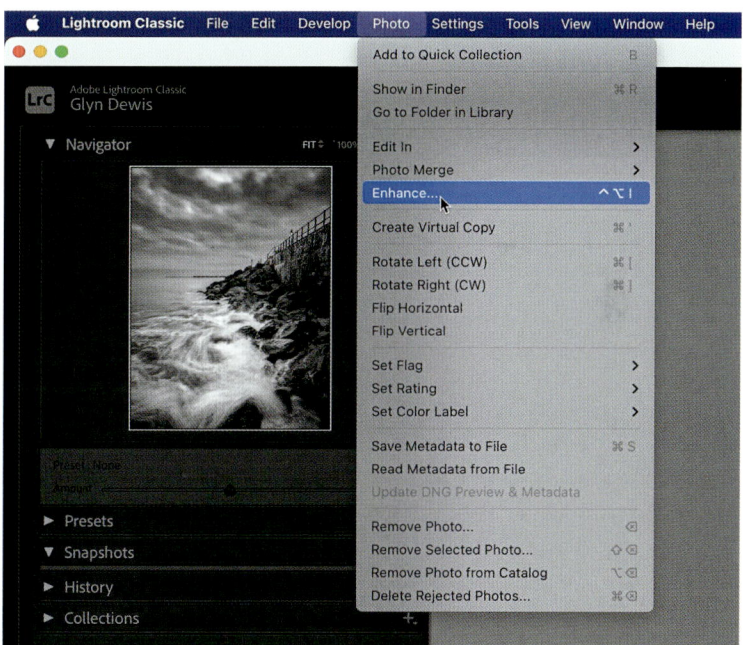

FIGURE 7.29

To launch it from Photoshop, go to **File** > **Automate** > **Topaz Gigapixel AI (Figure 7.30)**.

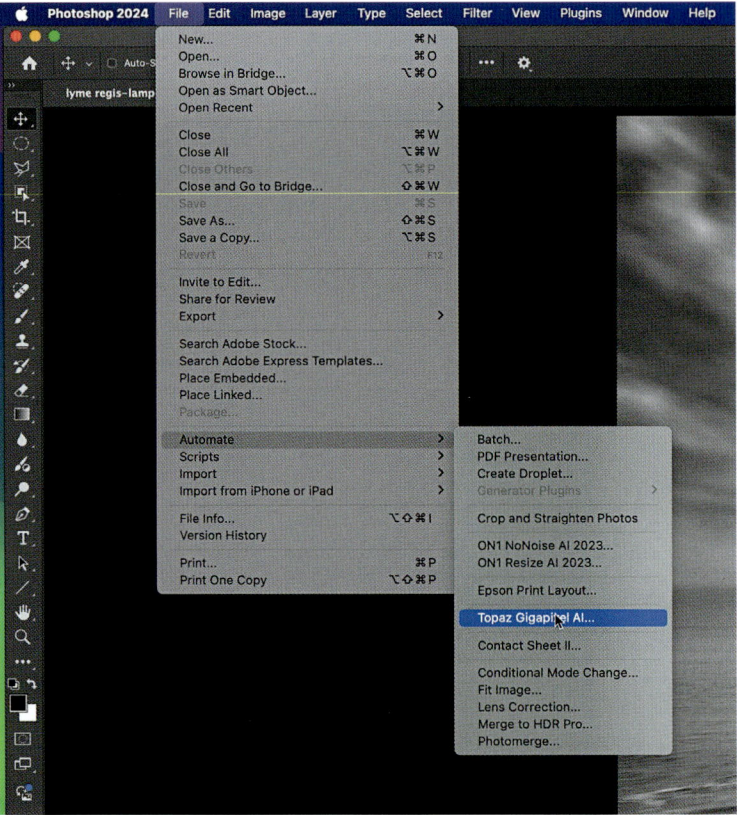

FIGURE 7.30

The image opens in the Gigapixel interface, where you then choose the scale factor (2×, 4×, 6×, etc.) and make sure the AI model is turned on **(Figure 7.31)**. You can also scale down if you want, but in this case we're focusing on enlarging.

Once the processing is done, you'll see the original and the enlarged image side-by-side. For example, here I tried a 6× increase, which is 600%, and the result was incredible. Even close up, the image held its sharpness impressively.

The image went from its original resolution of 2560 pixels to 15360 pixels on the long side, which at 300 PPI would give me a print that's just over 51 inches. That's some serious interpolation!

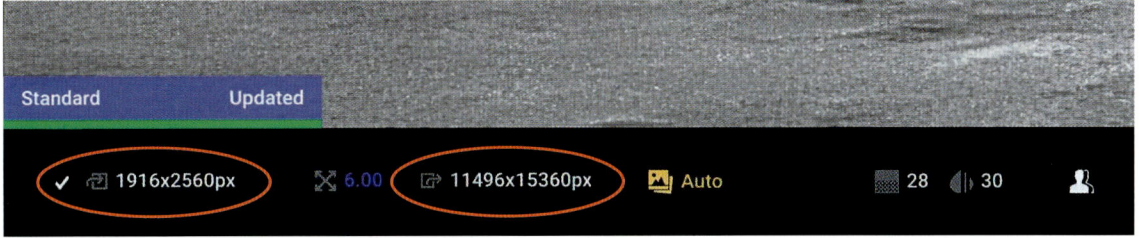

FIGURE 7.31

FINAL THOUGHTS

So, whatever the reason you need to increase the size of an image file, there's certainly plenty of options that produce incredible results:

- Photoshop is still an option, though a bit limited for big upscales.

- Adobe's Super Resolution is excellent for 2× enlargements.

- And Topaz Gigapixel AI software (and others on the market) is ideal when you need to push things even further.

The important thing is to understand what's happening under the hood so you know when and how your resolution is being affected, and how to get the best possible quality in your final print.

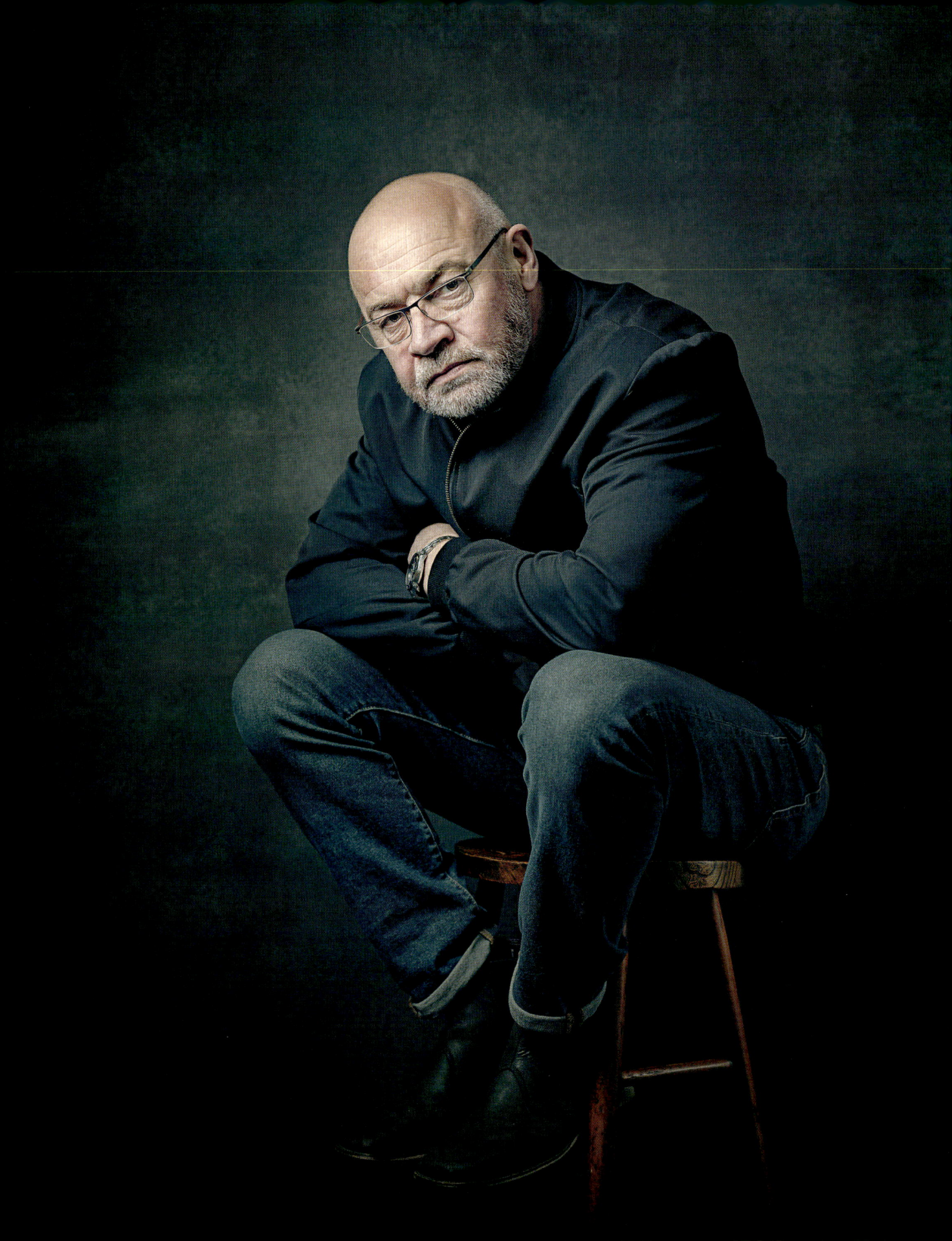

CHAPTER 8
SHARPENING

SHARPENING FOR PRINT: WHAT, WHEN, AND HOW

Some of the most common questions I get about printing, along with those about soft proofing, have to do with sharpening:

When do you sharpen? How much should you sharpen? And how exactly do you sharpen for print?

The truth is, I sharpen for print very rarely, and that's not necessarily because I don't need to, but more due to my retouching style and what I do to my images during editing. I sharpen at different stages of retouching, not just to give more definition to specific elements within a picture, but also to create certain visual effects. For example, my "2010" portrait technique is designed to make subjects appear as though they're coming out of the screen or even off the surface of the print **(Figure 8.1)**.

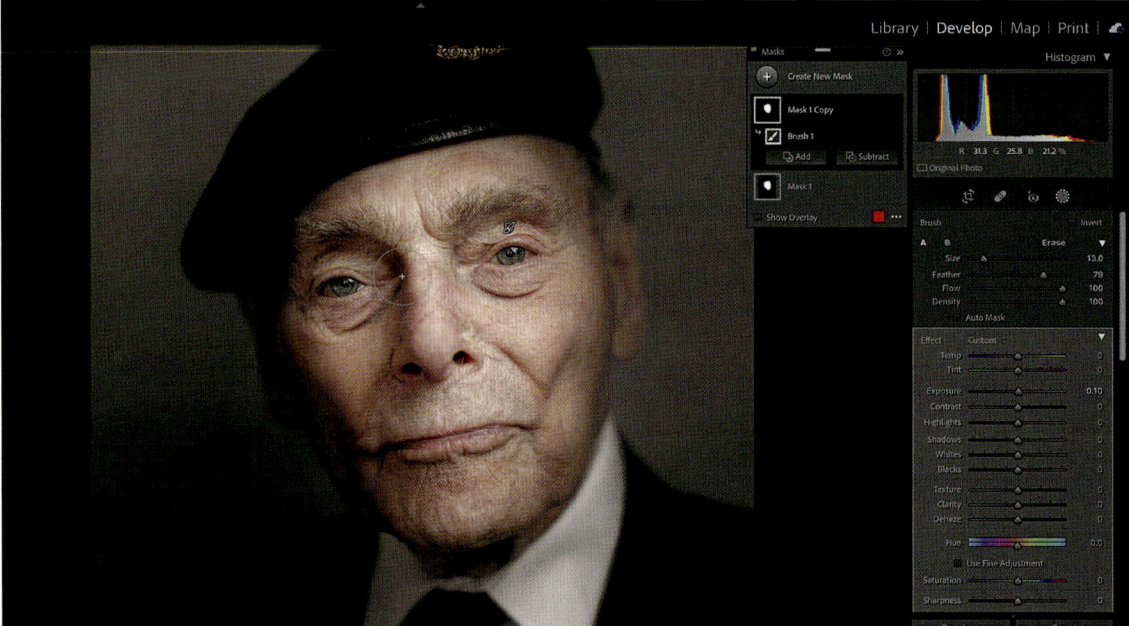

FIGURE 8.1

For images like that, I do push the sharpening a bit more. But if I were to add even a small amount more than needed, I could easily introduce halos into the image, which would absolutely show up in a final print even though printing naturally reduces contrast and sharpness to some extent, depending on the type of paper you're using.

A matte paper, which lacks a coating, will generally reduce sharpness more than a glossy coated paper because the ink on matte paper sinks deeper into the fibers.

When I do apply sharpening specifically for printing, I follow a careful workflow that I'll walk you through in this chapter.

WHAT SHARPENING ACTUALLY IS

Before we get into techniques, it's worth understanding what sharpening really is.

Spoiler Alert: Sharpening doesn't actually *sharpen* your image. Instead, it increases the *appearance* of sharpness by increasing local contrast. It does this by lightening and darkening pixels along edges in the image.

Let's take a look at a simple example in Photoshop. **Figure 8.2** shows a document with a simple shape where we have a black part and a white part. Where the two parts meet the area appears soft. That edge looks a bit fuzzy and not fully defined.

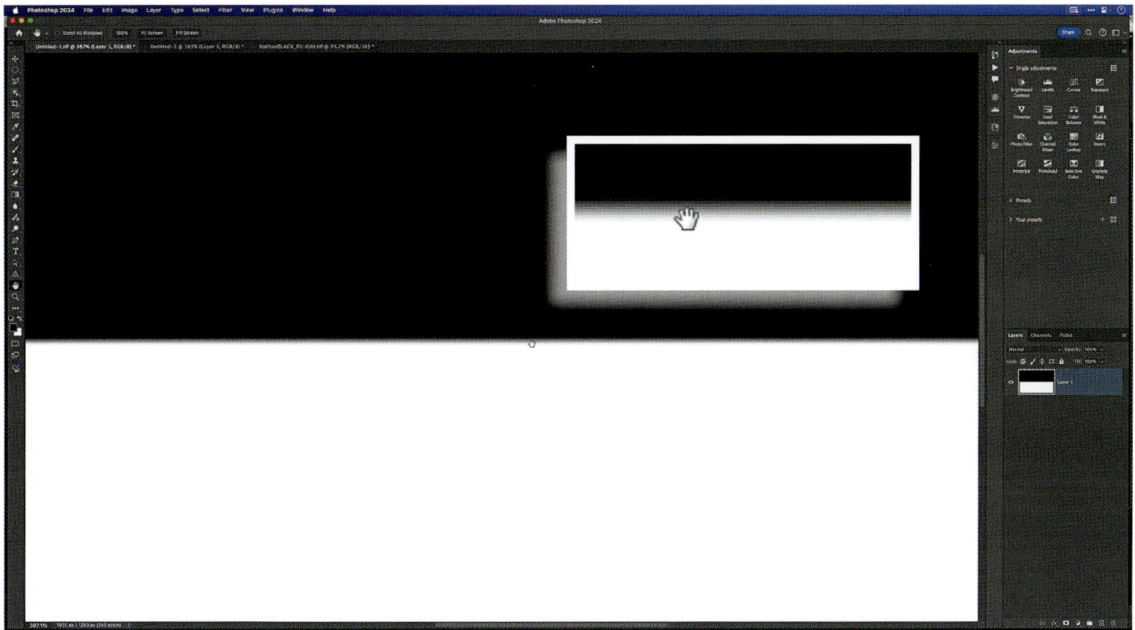

FIGURE 8.2

Now if I go to **Filter > Sharpen > Unsharp Mask** (my preferred sharpening tool for print) we'll see several controls **(Figure 8.3)**:

- **Amount:** How dark to make dark pixels and how light to make light pixels along that edge.

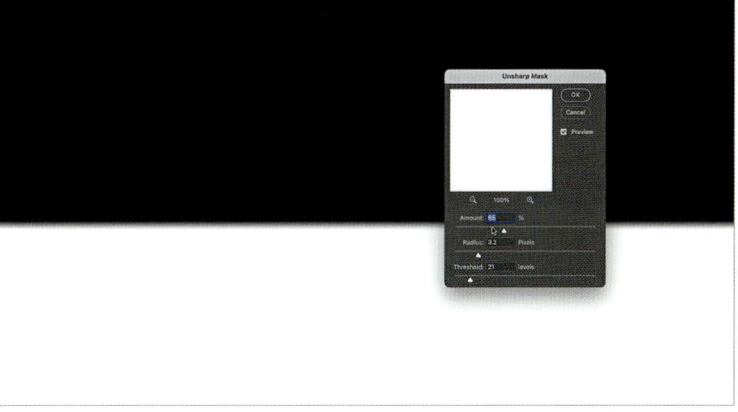

FIGURE 8.3

- **Radius:** How far out from the edge the darkening and lightening extends.

- **Threshold:** Helps reduce or control halos (over-sharpened edges).

By default, I use:

- **Amount:** 50

- **Radius:** 1

- **Threshold:** 0

This already gives a nice bump in sharpness. But let's say I increase the amount significantly and raise the Radius. Suddenly, the edge becomes much more defined **(Figure 8.4)**.

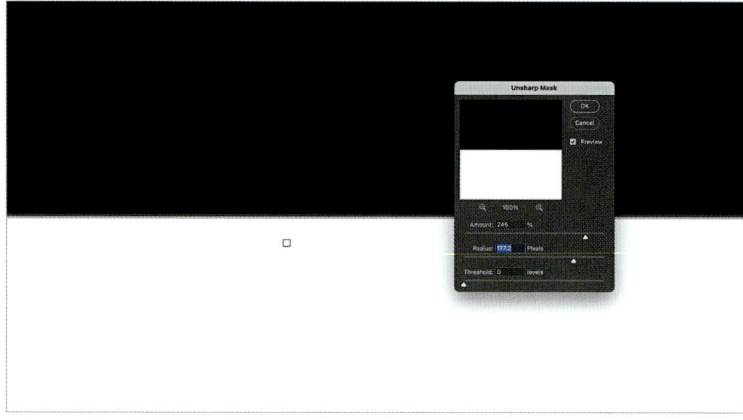

FIGURE 8.4

If I increase the Amount and Radius too much, though, we'll start seeing halos, which are unrealistic light or dark outlines around edges.

CONTROLLING HALOS

Halos are a sign that sharpening has been pushed too far. Thankfully, the Threshold setting helps manage this. Increasing the Threshold pulls back the halo effect by limiting where sharpening is applied. It's like dialing down the overall opacity of the sharpening layer.

So sharpening, in essence, is really just contrast enhancement.

REAL-WORLD EXAMPLE: A PORTRAIT OF NATHAN

Let's apply this to a real image, a portrait of my friend Nathan **(Figure 8.5)**. When zoomed in, the image already looks quite sharp. Still, I'll walk through the sharpening workflow I follow before printing:

1. **Resize First**
   This is crucial. Always resize your image to the final print dimensions before applying sharpening. If you sharpen at full size and then resize down, you'll almost certainly end up with grainy, over-sharpened results. Also, more sharpening would be needed on a larger image.

   For this portrait, I resized it from 24 inches × 24.28 inches at 300 PPI to 8 inches × 8 inches at 360 PPI (the native resolution for Epson printers), using the **Bicubic Sharper (Reduction)** resampling method **(Figure 8.6)**.

2. **Apply Sharpening Using Unsharp Mask**
   This is actually a good example to show you the halos I mentioned. If I go to **Filter > Sharpen**

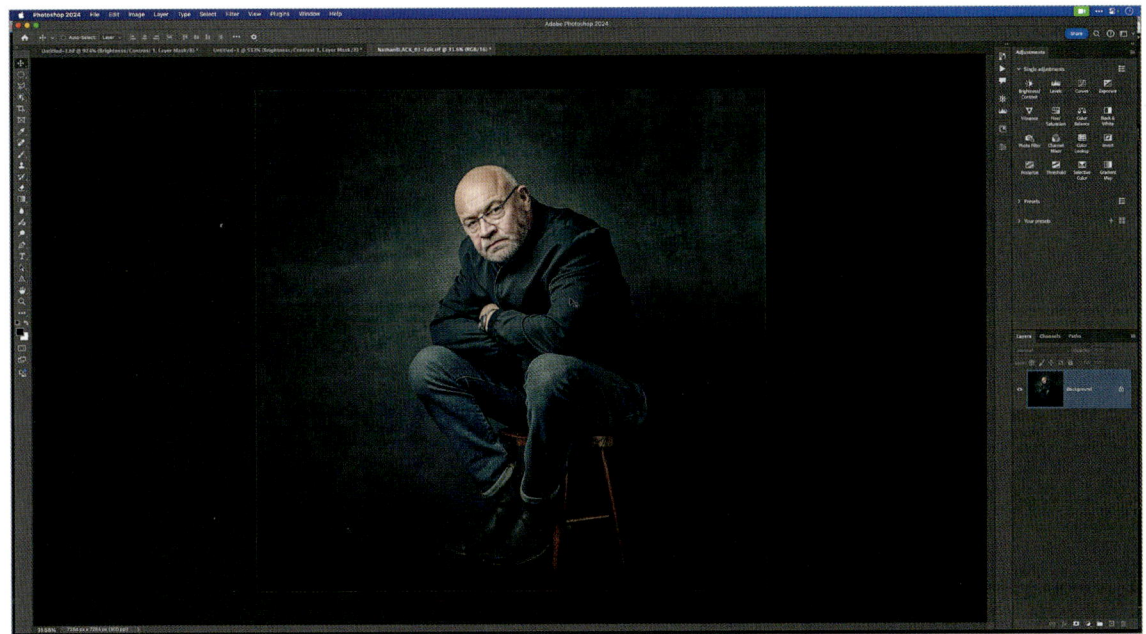

FIGURE 8.5

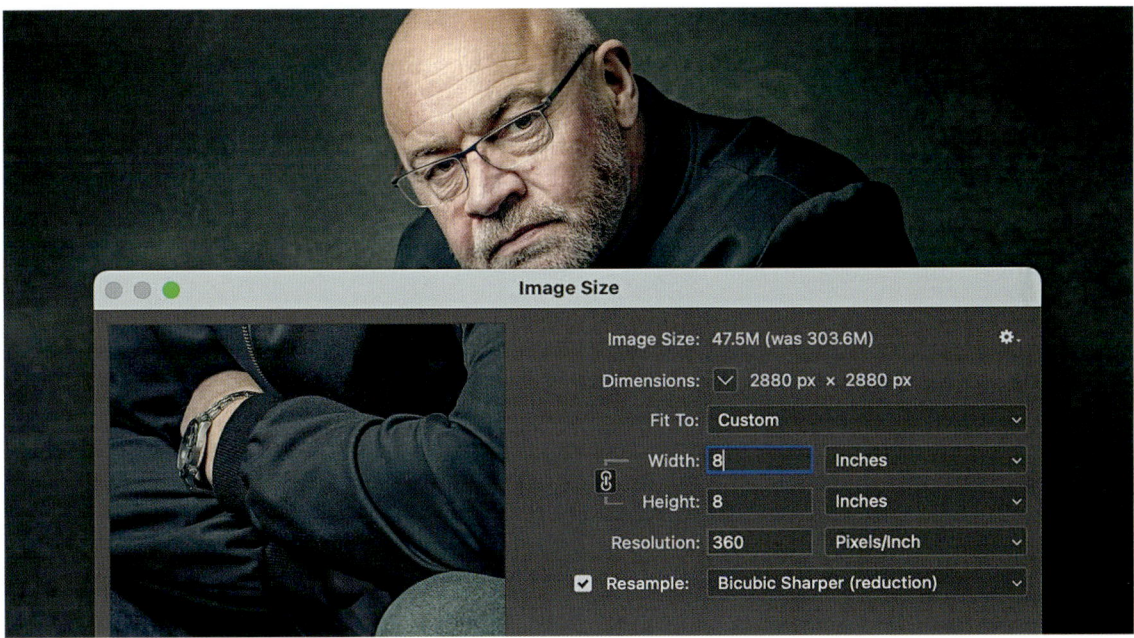

FIGURE 8.6

> **Unsharp Mask** and apply settings that are clearly too much for this image, it creates a dark halo around Nathan's head **(Figure 8.7)**.

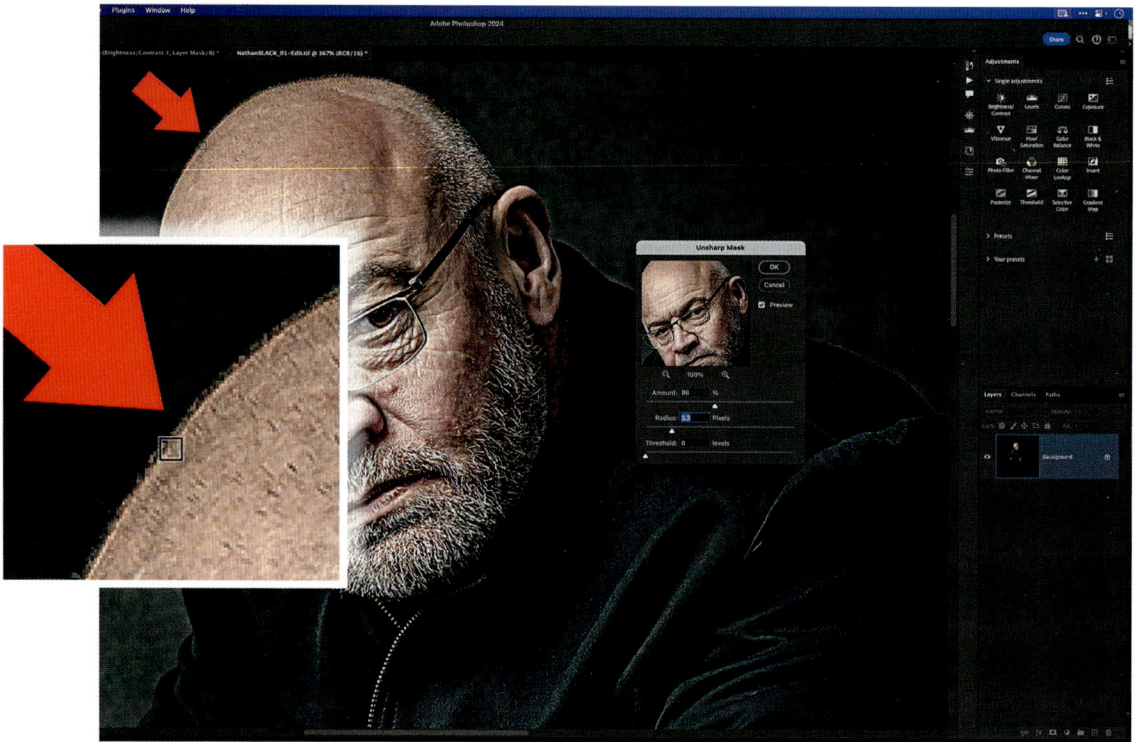

FIGURE 8.7

Now if I increase the Threshold, it pretty much removes the halo **(Figure 8.8)**.

However, these settings are way too high for this image, so I'll bring them down to:

- **Amount:** 50
- **Radius:** 1
- **Threshold:** 0

Even at these settings, there is a nice, clean boost in sharpness **(Figure 8.9)**.

I could maybe push the settings a bit more for matte paper, but I'm cautious to avoid introducing halos, especially around facial features like hairlines or beards. If you see halos on the image on screen, then they will show up in the print.

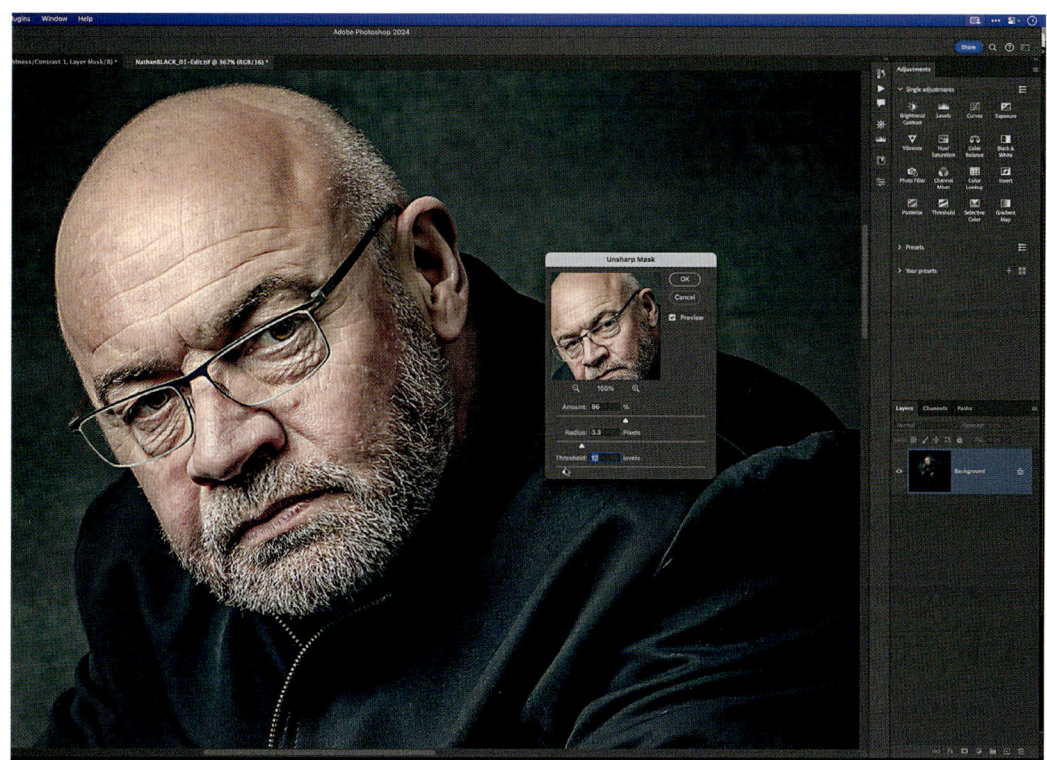

FIGURE 8.8

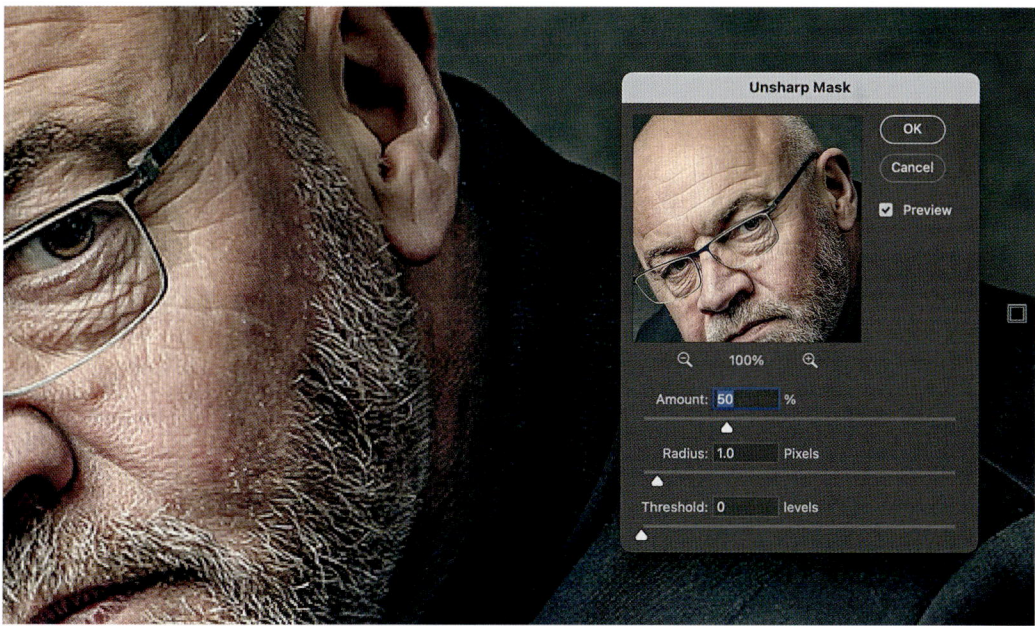

FIGURE 8.9

A NOTE ON PAPER AND PRINTER SETTINGS

Paper choice plays a big role in perceived sharpness. I often print on matte, uncoated paper, which naturally softens the look of images. I like that aesthetic; it feels painterly and subtle, which is why I often don't need to sharpen at all.

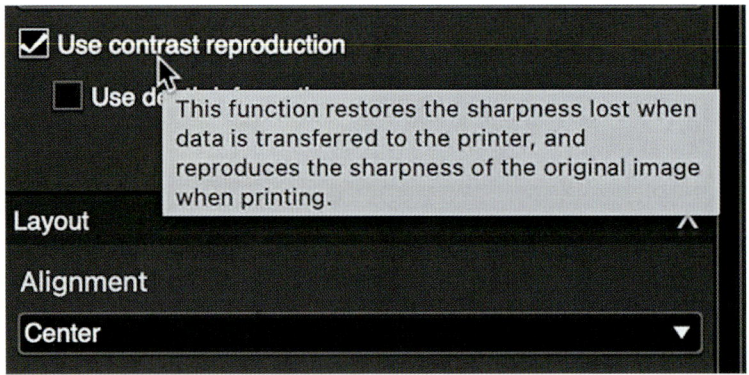

FIGURE 8.10

Also, some printing software can help. For instance, Canon's Professional Print & Layout software includes a checkbox labeled **Use Contrast Reproduction (Figure 8.10)**. Hovering over it shows:

"This function restores the sharpness lost when data is transferred to the printer, and reproduces the sharpness of the original image when printing."

I always leave that option checked. It works well and keeps prints looking crisp, even without extra sharpening. Epson software doesn't have this setting, but honestly, prints from both brands look very comparable.

WHY I RECOMMEND SHARPENING AFTER RESIZING

When should I sharpen? How much should I sharpen? And how should I sharpen?

A key point I want to emphasize is this: If you are going to sharpen an image for print ...

Always sharpen your image after resizing, and before sending it to print.

SEE BEFORE YOU PRINT

The main reason I recommend this approach is because it allows you to see the effect of the sharpening before the print is made. You can make informed decisions based on what you see, rather than relying on guesswork. This level of control simply isn't possible if you leave sharpening to happen at the print stage, and this is also one of the main reasons I choose not to print from Lightroom.

Lightroom includes a **Print Sharpening** checkbox, where you can choose between Low, Standard, or High sharpening, but selecting from these vague presets means you're essentially guessing at what the print will look like **(Figure 8.11)**. This becomes a trial-and-error process, where you only see the result after committing to ink and paper. I prefer to assess the image visually on screen before printing, knowing exactly how the sharpening looks at the final print size.

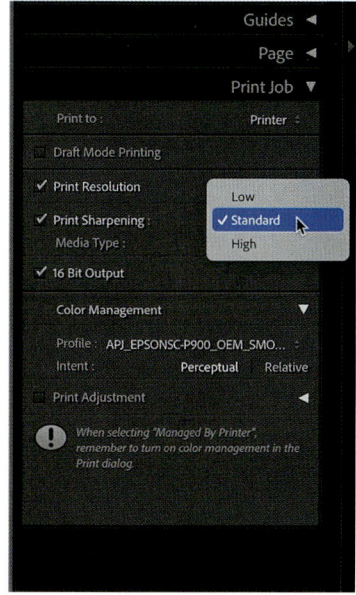

FIGURE 8.11

Using Lightroom's print sharpening also implies that you haven't resized your image beforehand. Typically, you'll have just cropped the image to a certain aspect ratio and set the output cell size. This means you don't know what sharpening will look like at the final print dimensions, and worse still, you can't tailor the sharpening to that final size.

Since sharpening needs vary based on image dimensions and output media, choosing a preset like Low or High without understanding its impact is just leaving too much to chance.

BEST PRACTICE

So, my advice is simple:

1. Resize your image to the final print dimensions.

2. Sharpen your image while viewing it at that final size.

3. Send the image to the printer.

This ensures that what you see is what you get, without relying on trial and error.

FINAL THOUGHTS ON SHARPENING WORKFLOW

There's not a massive amount to cover on sharpening for print, but because so many people ask about it, I wanted to share my approach. If you take nothing else away from this chapter, remember the most important part:

Resize First. Then sharpen. Then print.

And don't sharpen out of habit. Try printing without sharpening and see how it looks. You might find you're perfectly happy with it as is.

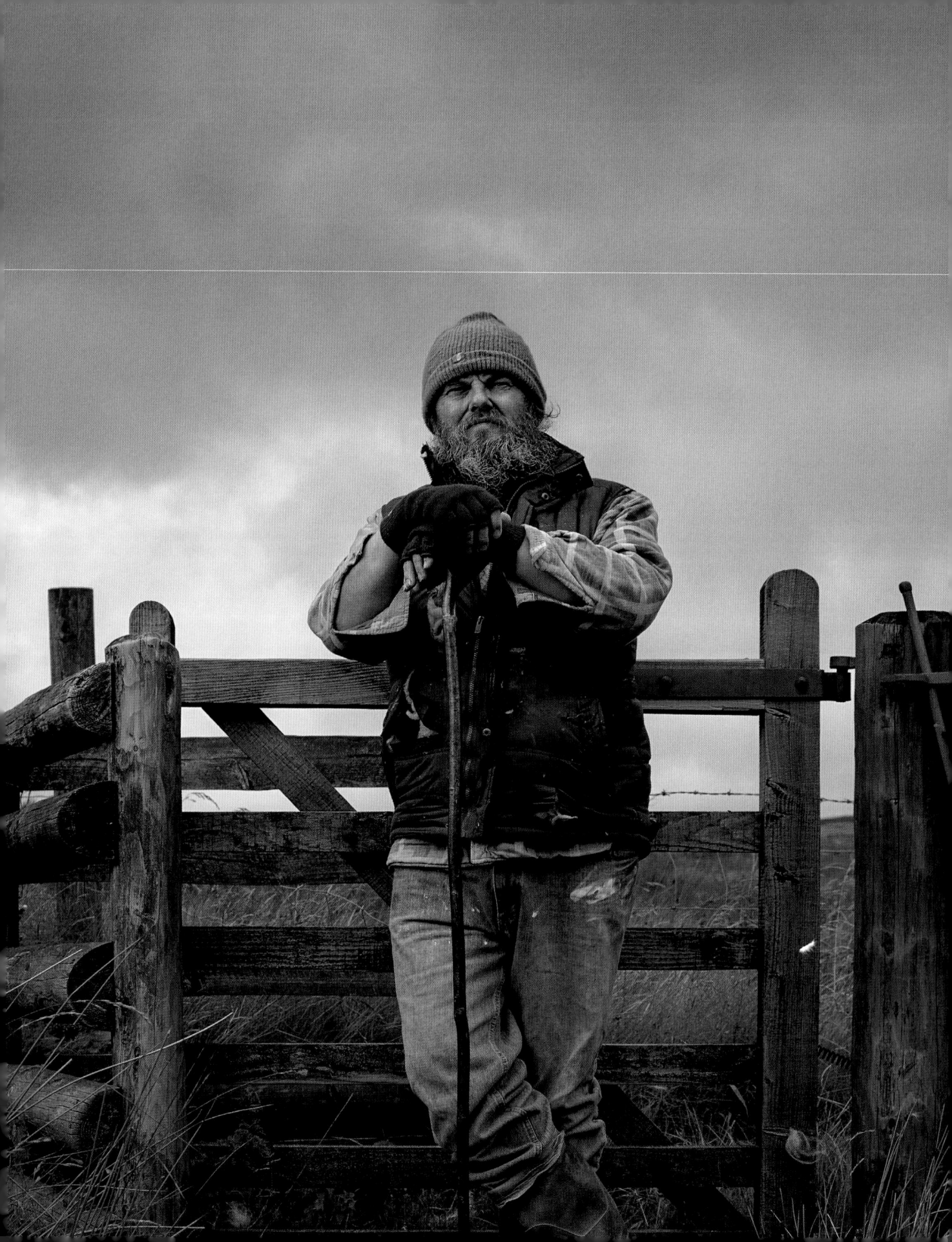

CHAPTER 9
SOFT PROOFING

In this chapter, I want to take you through a process called soft proofing. This is where we pre-view on screen how an image will appear when printed before actually committing it to paper. However, it's important to clarify that what you see during soft proofing still won't be entirely accurate. This is due to the nature of backlit displays and the fact that each type of paper has different characteristics.

SIMULATE PAPER AND INK: USEFUL OR GIMMICK?

Some software offers options to mimic the appearance of the paper. For example, in Lightroom, there's a setting called **Simulate Paper and Ink (Figure 9.1)**. Personally, I find this more of a gimmick than a helpful tool. I'll show you why I think so shortly. In fact, over the last couple of years while putting this book together, I've spoken with numerous printing professionals at high-end labs and they've consistently advised me not to rely on these simulate paper and ink options.

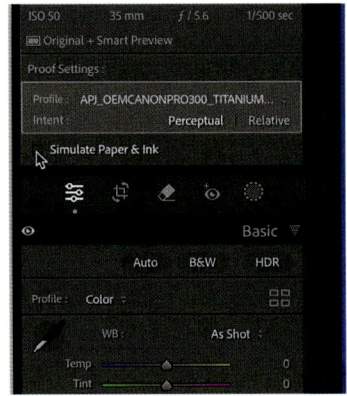

FIGURE 9.1

PRINTING AS A CREATIVE PROCESS

Let's move on to the actual process. I'll guide you through soft proofing and printing three different images. These range from:

• Straightforward: Requiring little or no adjustment

• Moderate: Needing a few tweaks

• Complex: Requiring significant adjustments and further evaluation after the first print

The goal is to demonstrate that achieving a print you're completely happy with on the first try can vary from image to image. In my view, this variability is part of the beauty of the process and is something to be embraced and enjoyed. Printing is an art form in itself. It involves making thoughtful decisions about paper choice and should not be treated as a mere final step.

We spend a great deal of time and money capturing images we're proud of, but we must remember: **The art doesn't end at the edit.**

CASE STUDY 1: SOFT PROOFING AND PRINTING A PORTRAIT

INITIAL IMAGE EVALUATION

On screen, I really like how this image looks **(Figure 9.2)**. The lighting creates a mood I love, and if I weren't planning to print it, I'd probably leave it as is. But putting on my "printing head," I need to approach it differently.

Looking at the histogram, I see that the image contains plenty of dark tones and midtones, but is lacking in highlights **(Figure 9.3)**. This lack of highlight information will become more pronounced in print because paper tends to rob an image of its contrast and sharpness, depending, of course, on the paper type.

SOFT PROOFING IN LIGHTROOM

Working in Lightroom's Develop Module, I turn on **Soft Proofing**, located in the bottom of the interface **(Figure 9.4)**. This gives the image a white surround to represent paper.

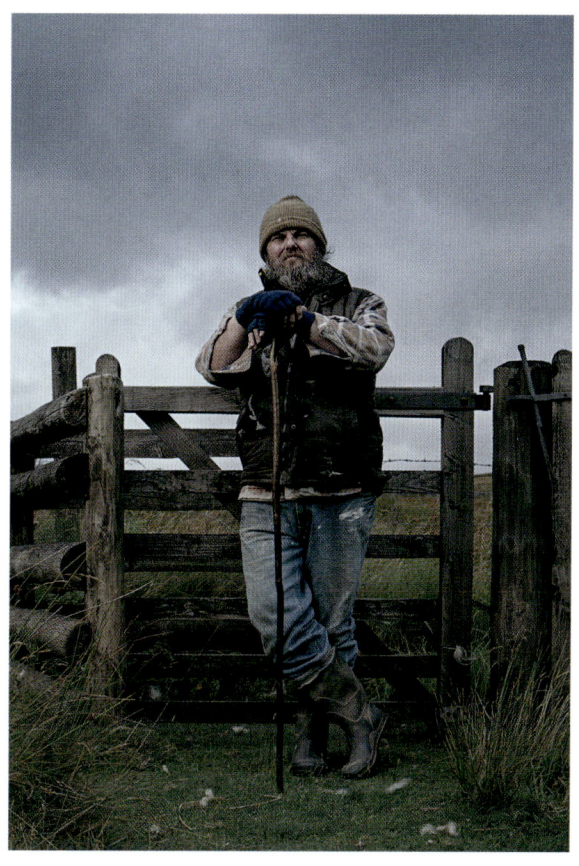

FIGURE 9.2

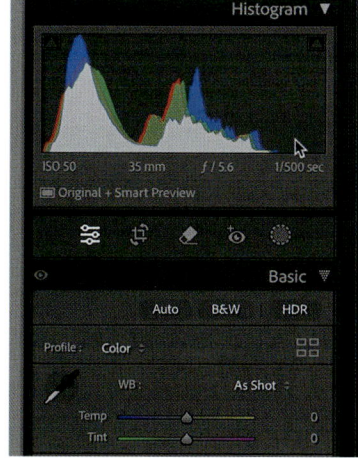

FIGURE 9.3

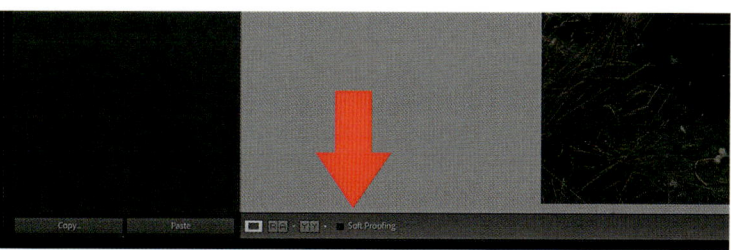

FIGURE 9.4

At the top, I click on **Create Proof Copy (Figure 9.5)**. This leaves the original image intact, and if you check the thumbnail view, you'll now see a copy of the original image **(Figure 9.6)**. The copy is the one I'll be working on.

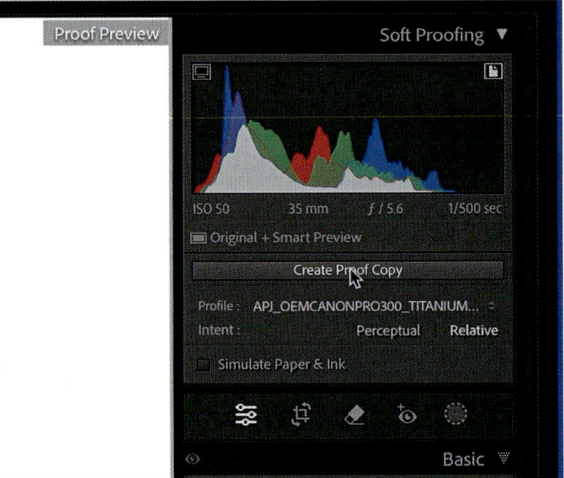

FIGURE 9.5

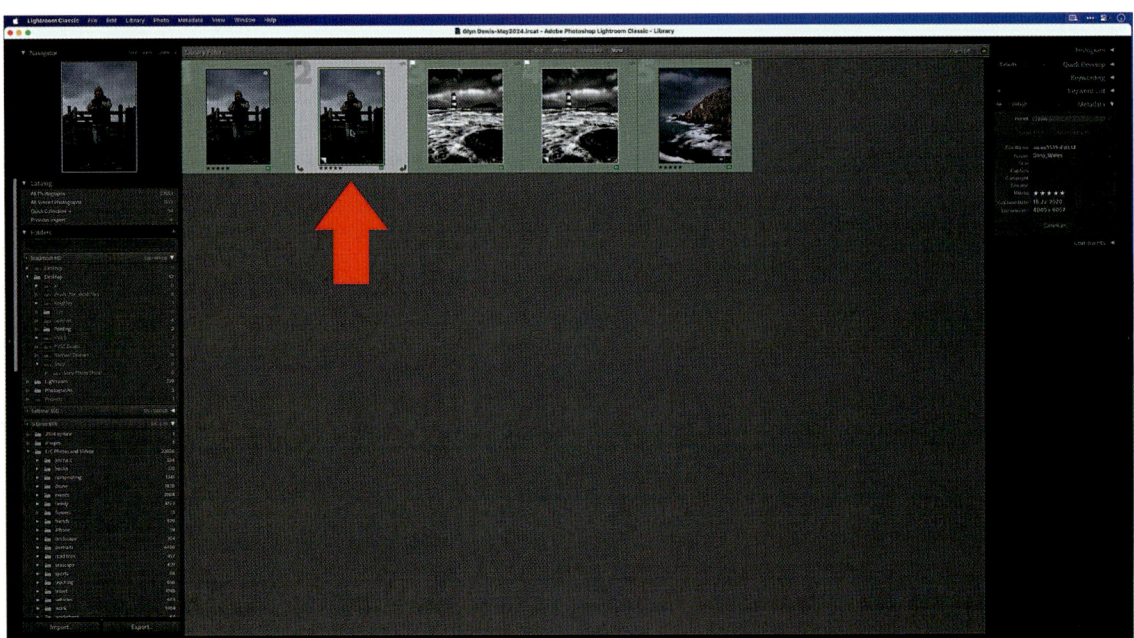

FIGURE 9.6

In the top-right corner of the histogram, there's a **Destination Gamut Warning (Figure 9.7)**. This helps identify which colors can't be accurately reproduced with the chosen printer and paper combination. (You may remember this from the earlier when printing a color image.) I'll turn it on.

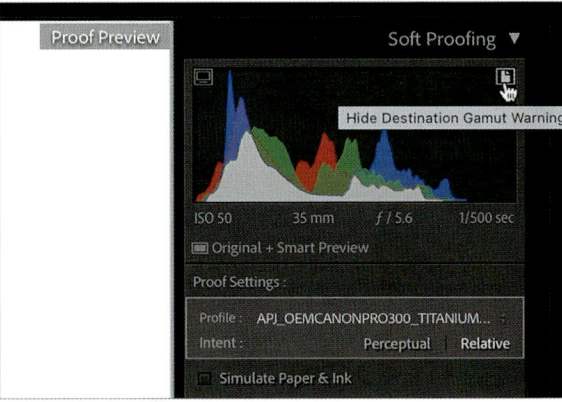

FIGURE 9.7

Next, I go to the **Profile** section and select the paper profile. For me, it's the Smooth Rag from PermaJet, and since I'll be printing on an Epson printer, I choose the appropriate profile **(Figure 9.8)**.

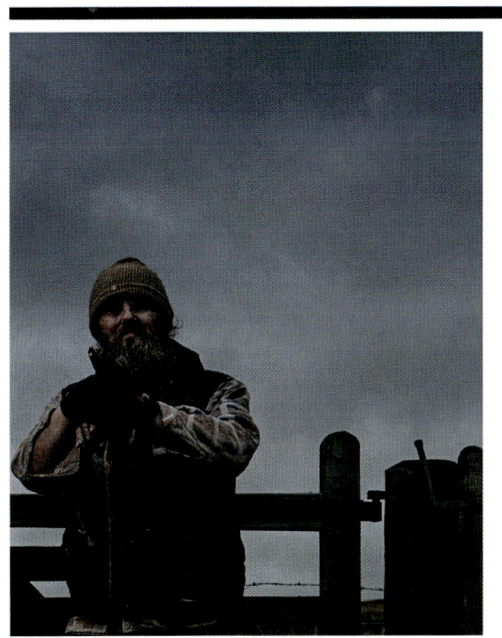
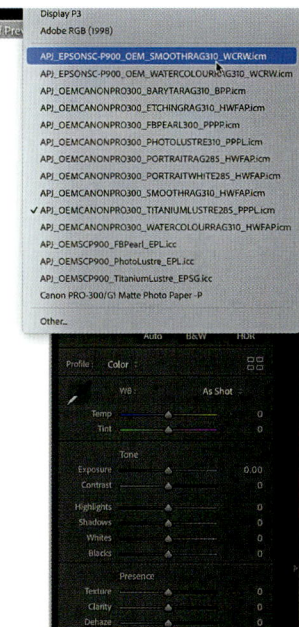

FIGURE 9.8

RENDERING INTENT

We now reach the **Rendering Intent** option: **Perceptual** or **Relative Colorimetric**. Since this image contains skin tones, I'll begin with **Relative**, but I'll revisit this choice after making some adjustments **(Figure 9.9)**.

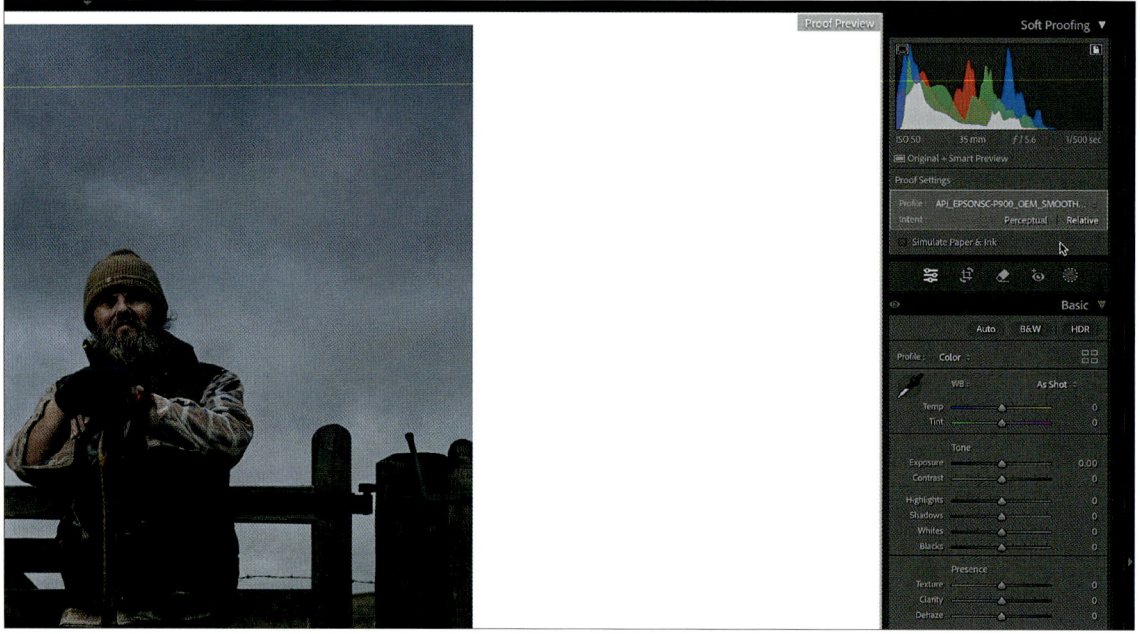

FIGURE 9.9

MAKING ADJUSTMENTS

Under the **Basic** panel:

- I drag the **Whites** slider to the right to populate the right-hand side of the histogram.

- I'll also increase the Highlights.

- To view a comparison, I press the **backslash key** (\) on my keyboard.

- After reviewing the adjustments, I reduce the **Contrast** slightly, which I feel helps improve balance in the image.

- Having made these changes, I revisit the **Rendering Intent** setting. Initially, I set this to **Relative**, but when I switch to **Perceptual**, I notice it adds something extra to the sky. I prefer it this way, so I'll stick with **Perceptual** **(Figure 9.10)**.

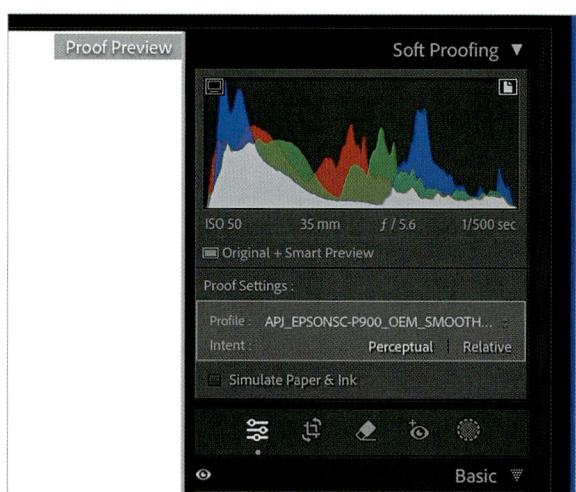

FIGURE 9.10

EXPORTING THE IMAGE

- Once satisfied, I export the image from Lightroom using the **File** > **Export** command.

I prefer printing with the printer's own software, and I like to import the file directly, rather than send it from Lightroom. This is purely a personal taste; you could simply send the image direct from Lightroom into Photoshop if you wish.

Here are the export settings I use **(Figure 9.11)**:

- **Destination:** A folder named *Printing* on my desktop

- **Filename:** *Foxy*

- **Image Format:** TIFF, no compression

- **Color Space:** Adobe RGB

- **Bit Depth:** 16-bit

- **Image Size:** 10 inches on the long edge

- **Resolution:** 360 pixels per inch (as I'm using the Epson)

Then I click **Export**.

PRINTING THE IMAGE

I then open the file in the Epson Print Layout software.

I select the correct Media Type for the Smooth Rag from PermaJet, choose the appropriate ICC profile (since it's a color image), and set the Rendering Intent to Perceptual, which is consistent with the Rendering Intent I chose when soft proofing in Lightroom **(Figure 9.12)**.

With everything set, I hit **Print**.

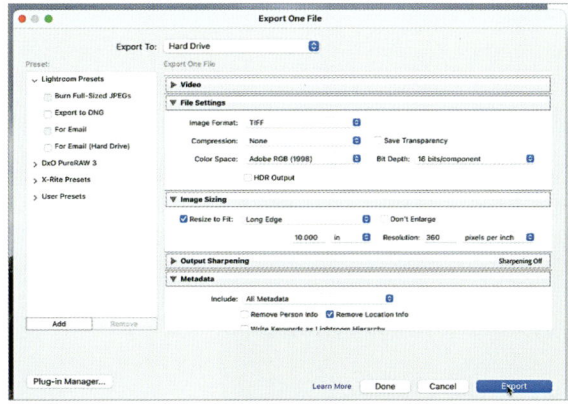

FIGURE 9.11

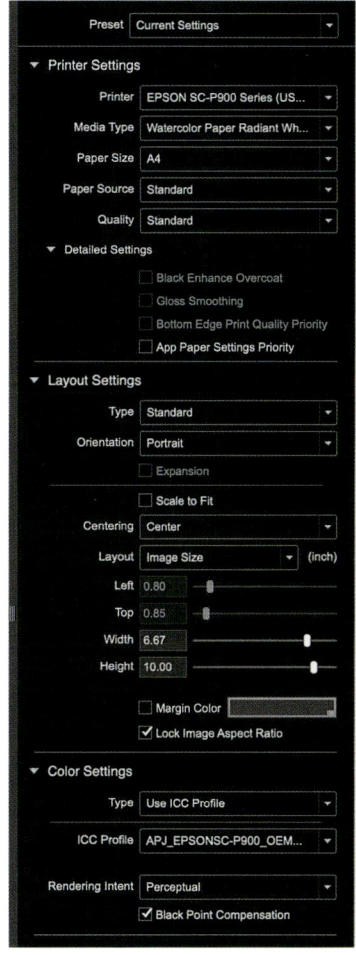

FIGURE 9.12

Figure 9.13 shows the print, which I'm really happy with. Colors look great. There's just the right amount of contrast. Plenty of detail and, yeah, it looks fantastic on matte paper.

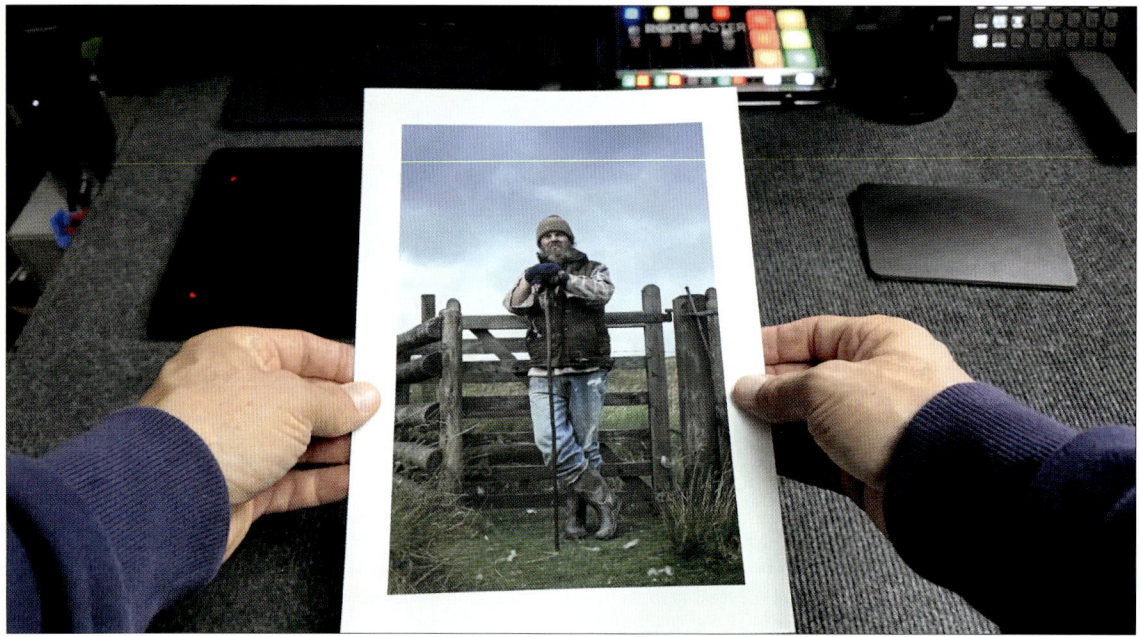

FIGURE 9.13

CASE STUDY 2: SOFT PROOFING AND PRINTING A HIGH-CONTRAST BLACK-AND-WHITE IMAGE

STARTING THE PROCESS

The next image I want to soft proof and print is **Figure 9.14**, a black-and-white image that is already quite contrasty.

So just like before, I begin by enabling Soft Proofing in Lightroom. Then, I go to the top-right corner and click **Create Proof Copy** to ensure my original image remains intact. This new copy is the version I'll be working on and printing.

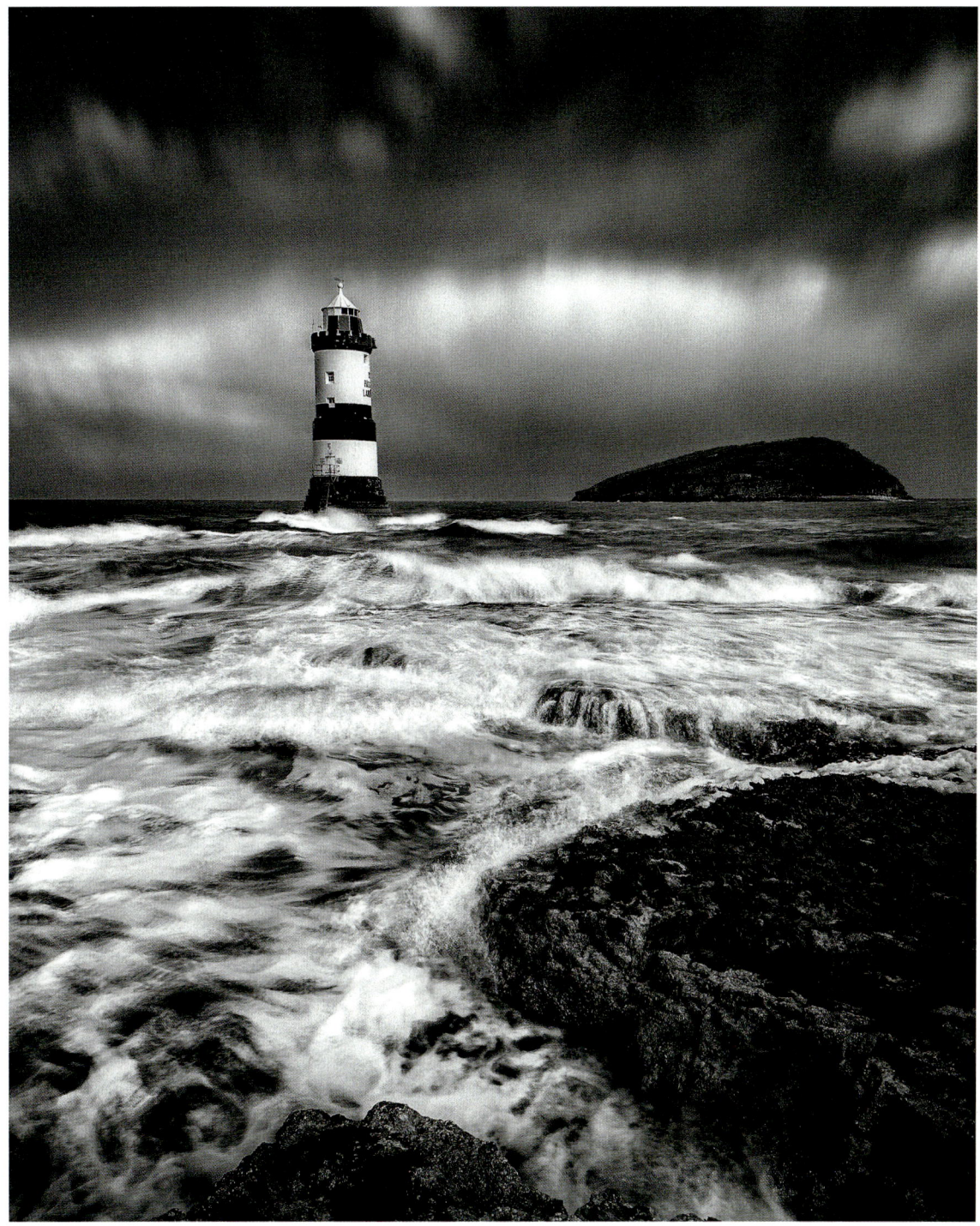

FIGURE 9.14

EVALUATING THE HISTOGRAM

Looking at the image, the histogram shows a strong push into the darks, with only minimal reach into the highlights. So before diving in and making some adjustments, I'll briefly exit Soft Proofing mode to check for potential clipping issues.

In the histogram, I'll turn on the Highlights and Shadows warnings by clicking on the icons in the upper left and right of the histogram **(Figure 9.15)**, and sure enough, a blue overlay appears in the foreground. This indicates we're losing detail in that area.

There's also some minor highlight clipping in the image, which we can see on the water surface **(Figure 9.16)**.

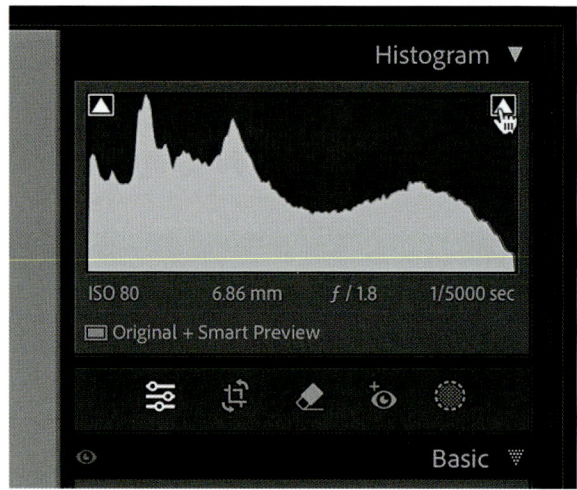

FIGURE 9.15

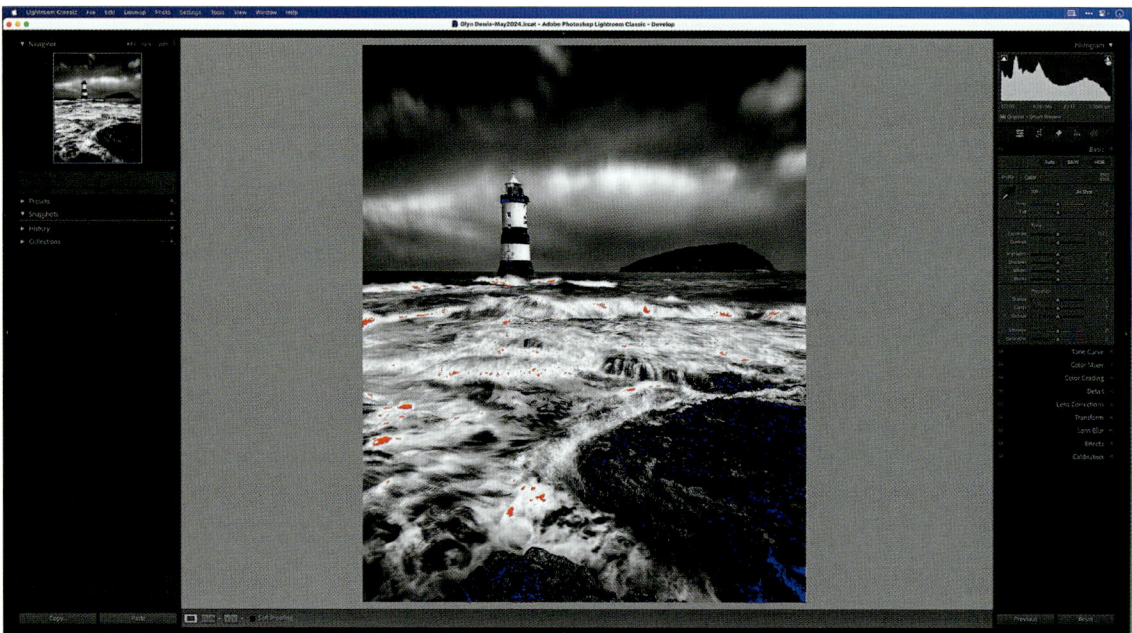

FIGURE 9.16

ADDRESSING HIGHLIGHT AND SHADOW CLIPPING

To fix the highlight clipping, I'll reduce the Highlights slider slightly, which effectively removes the red overlay from the clipped highlights, showing that now we have detail in those areas.

Next, I need to address the blue overlay in the foreground indicating lost shadow detail. To do this I could reduce the Blacks globally, but that would affect the rest of the image, so instead, I'll take a more targeted approach:

1. Open the **Masking** tools.

2. Select the **Brush** option.

3. Ensure the brush settings are:

   - **Feather:** 100%

   - **Flow and Density:** 100%

4. Brush over the foreground rock area so this is the only area to be adjusted, then reduce the Blacks.

   As I apply the adjustment, the blue overlay disappears, indicating that I've recovered detail in those deep shadows. I'll do the same for a small patch on the lighthouse as well **(Figure 9.17)**.

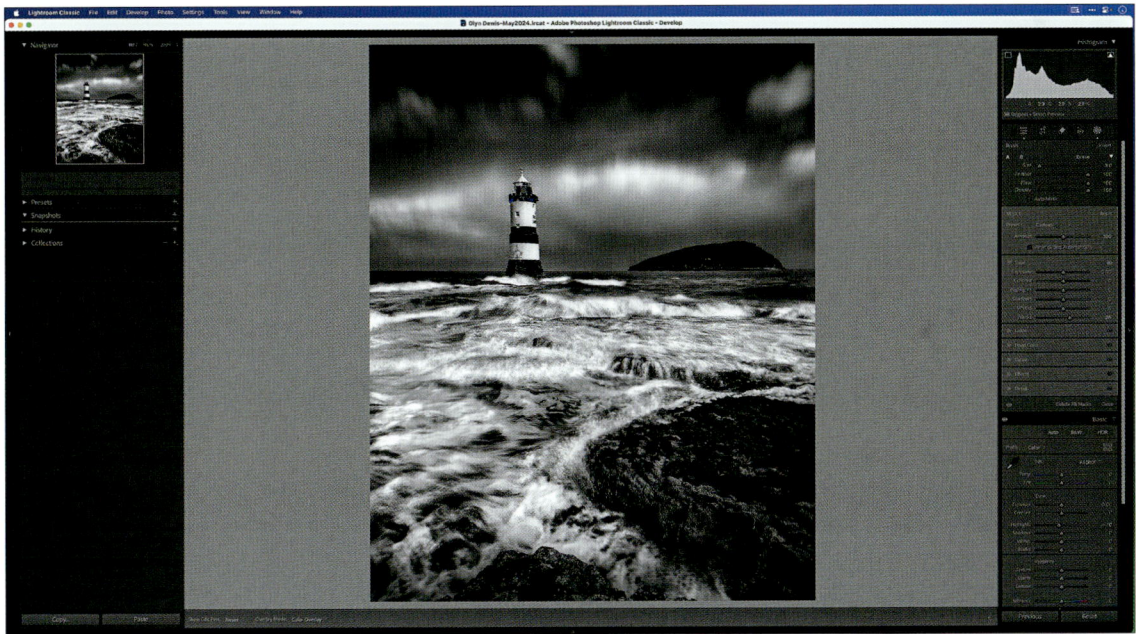

FIGURE 9.17

Zooming in, the recovered detail is impressive. I can see every bit of seaweed and texture on the rocks **(Figure 9.18)**.

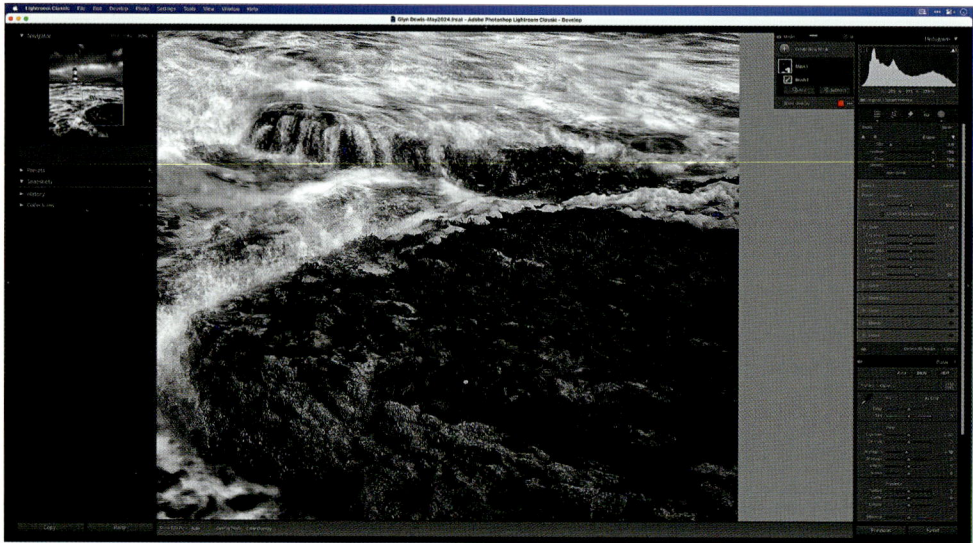

BALANCING THE SKY

Now looking at the image, I get the feeling that the area of sky at the top of the image might print too dark, so I'll make some adjustments there, too, by simply adding another mask … this time a Linear Gradient. I'll drag down from the top of the image (red overlay), and then simply reduce the Blacks in that area by dragging the Blacks slider to the right slightly **(Figure 9.19)**.

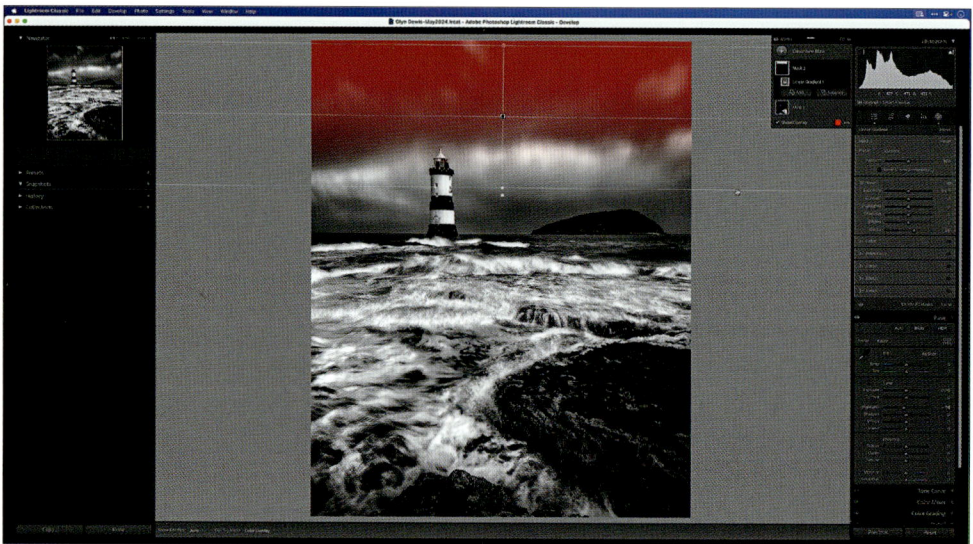

RETURNING TO SOFT PROOFING

So with the adjustments having been made, I turn on Soft Proofing and I can see that the histogram has been corrected. I re-enable the **Destination Gamut Warning** and see no clipping warnings, meaning that everything is within the printable range **(Figure 9.20)**.

Next, I change the Paper Profile to Smooth Rag, which does change the histogram ever so slightly, but it's still looking good and ready for printing **(Figure 9.21)**.

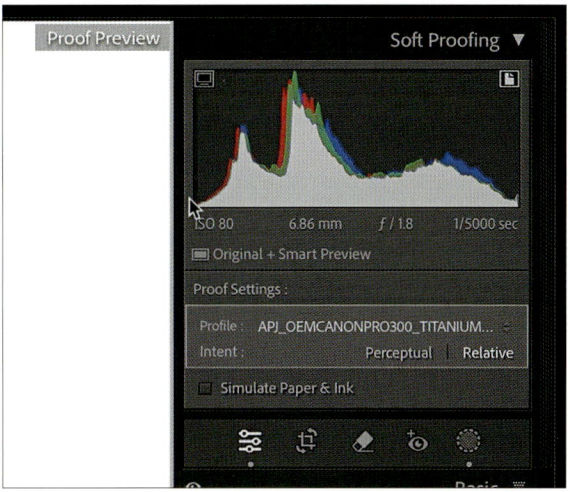

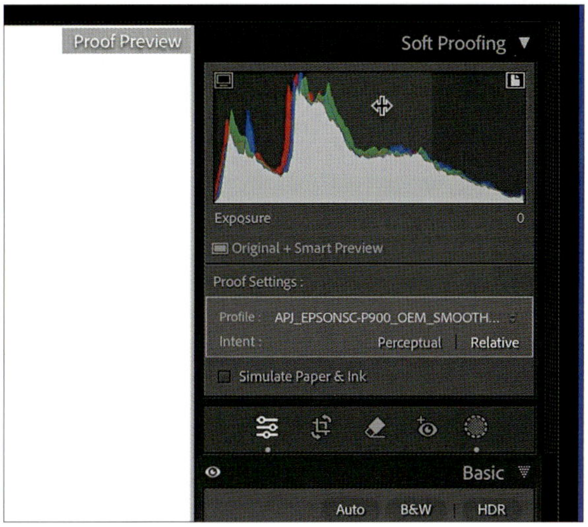

FIGURE 9.20

EXPORTING THE FILE

In Lightroom, I go to **File** > **Export** and choose the following settings:

- **Destination:** *Printing* folder on the desktop
- **Filename:** *Penmon*
- **Image Format:** TIFF
- **Color Space:** Adobe RGB
- **Bit Depth:** 16-bit
- **Image Size:** 8 inches on the long edge
- **Resolution:** 360ppi (printing to the Epson)

Once configured, I click **Export**.

FIGURE 9.21

PRINTING IN EPSON PRINT LAYOUT SOFTWARE

I open the exported file in the Epson Print Layout software, with settings similar to the previous image:

- **Media Type:** Watercolor Paper Radiant White, which corresponds to PermaJet Smooth Rag
- **Paper Size:** A4
- **Profile:** This time, I'm *not* using an ICC profile as I'm printing a black-and-white image. Instead, I select the **Advanced Black and White mode**, which allows fine-tuning of tonality.

In the Advanced Black and White Settings, I'll go with **Normal** for the **Tone**, with no added tint. With everything in place, I click **Print.**

The result is a beautiful neutral black-and-white image with no visible color tint, excellent detail in the dark shadow areas, and a pleasing level of contrast. Yeah, I'm really happy with how this one turned out **(Figure 9.22)**.

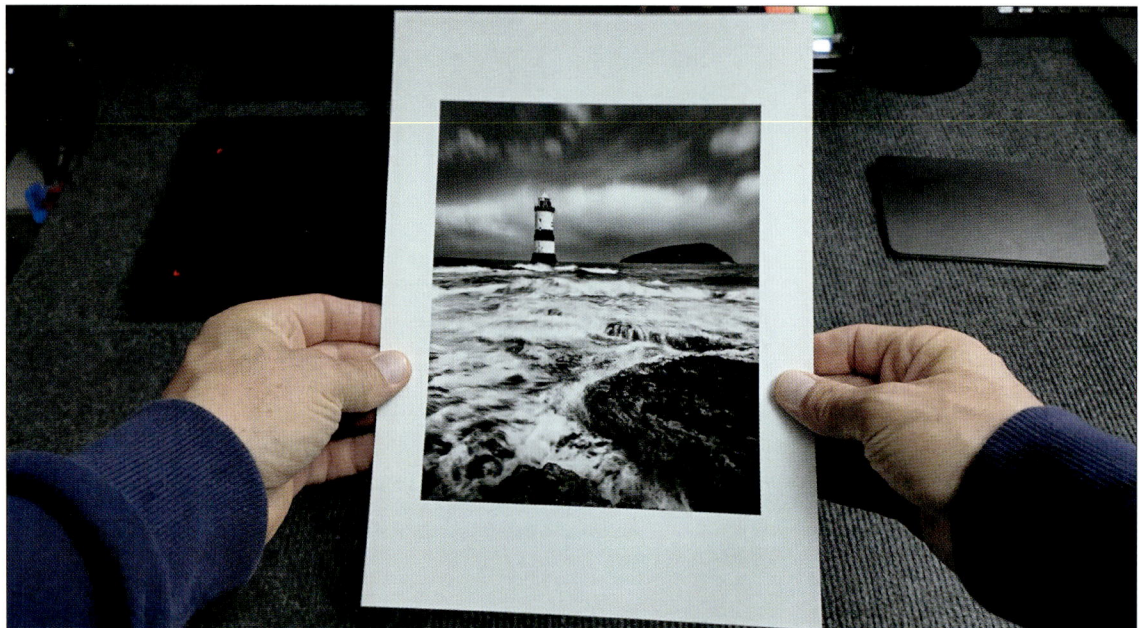

FIGURE 9.22

CASE STUDY 3: SOFT PROOFING AND PRINTING WITH PHOTOSHOP

The final image I want to soft proof and print is **Figure 9.23**, and you'll see there's a bit more involved with this one. I'll be working from Photoshop rather than Lightroom; in fact, both the soft proofing and the printing will be done within Photoshop.

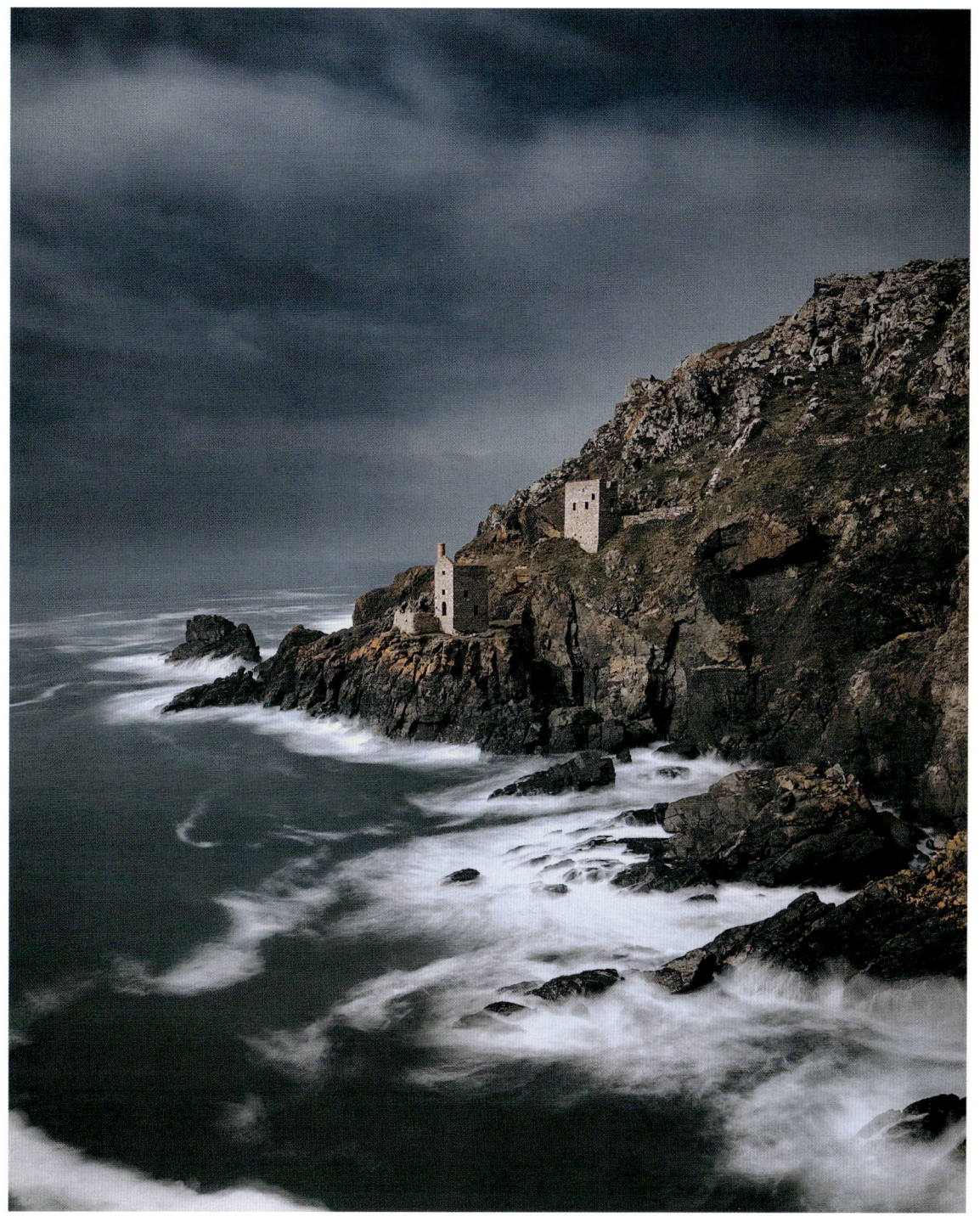

FIGURE 9.23

EVALUATING THE HISTOGRAM

With the image open in Photoshop, I begin by going to **Window** > **Histogram** to assess the image.

Now if I wasn't printing the image, I'd be more than happy with it as is. However, the histogram shows the image is weighted heavily in the midtones, with a lack of tones in both the darks and highlights **(Figure 9.24)**. So to correct this, I'll apply a Levels Adjustment Layer, but before adjusting anything, I set the blend mode to **Luminosity** to prevent any unintended shifts in color while increasing contrast. I adjust the black and white points to align with the base of the histogram and brighten the midtones slightly **(Figure 9.25)**.

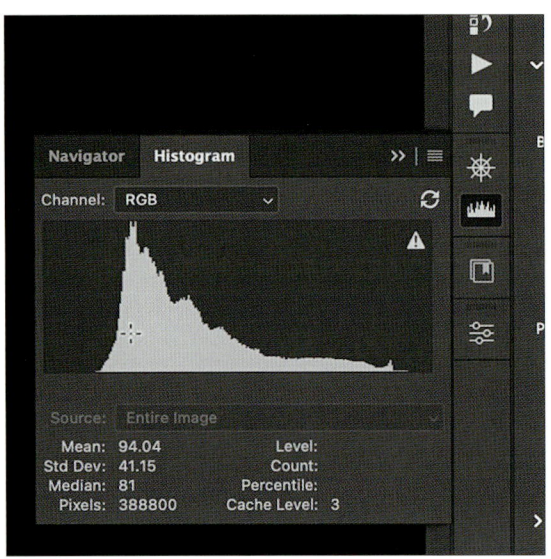

FIGURE 9.24

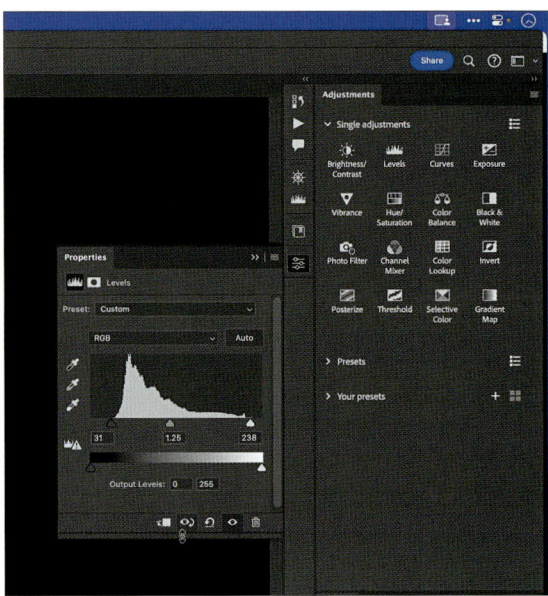

FIGURE 9.25

Toggling the adjustment layer off and on shows a significant improvement. I'm happy with the result.

SOFT PROOF SETUP IN PHOTOSHOP

To begin soft proofing, I go to **View** > **Proof Setup** > **Custom (Figure 9.26)**. In the **Customize Proof Condition** dialog, I choose the ICC profile for the paper I'll be printing on, which will again be the Smooth Rag from PermaJet. This time, I'll be printing using the Canon Pro-300, so I select the corresponding PermaJet ICC profile **(Figure 9.27)**.

Next, I experiment with the Rendering Intent, comparing Relative Colorimetric with Perceptual. I also toggle Black Point Compensation on and off when checking out Relative Colorimetric. I find that Perceptual gives the sky a touch more punch, so I'll stick with that and click **OK**.

The name of this soft-proofed image plus other details is now included in the tab for this image **(Figure 9.28)**.

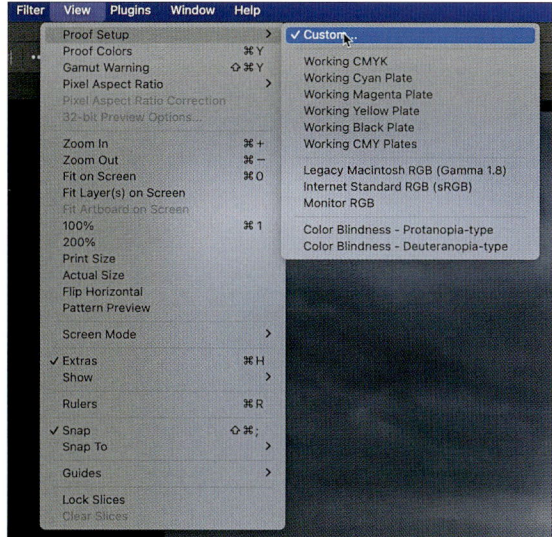

FIGURE 9.26

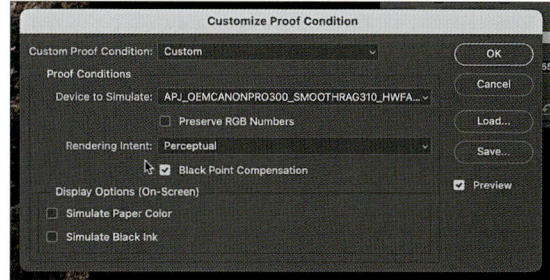

FIGURE 9.27

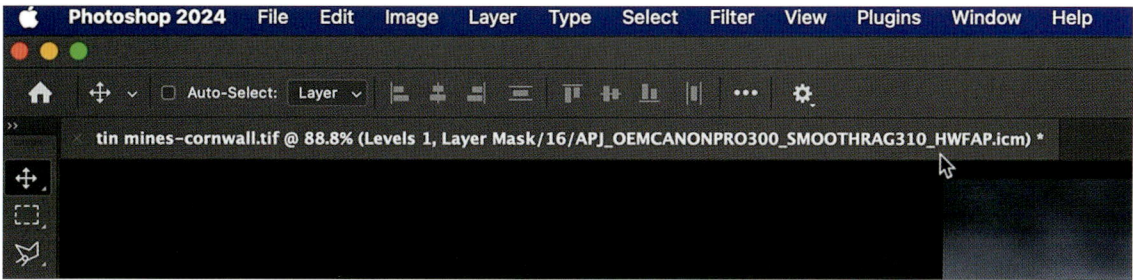

FIGURE 9.28

GAMUT WARNINGS AND IMAGE SIZE

I can check the **Destination Gamut Warning** in Photoshop by going to the **View** menu and choosing **Gamut Warning**.

If I now zoom in, no warnings are shown, meaning everything is within the printable range of this printer and paper combination.

Next, I'll check the sizing of this image by going to **Image > Image Size**:

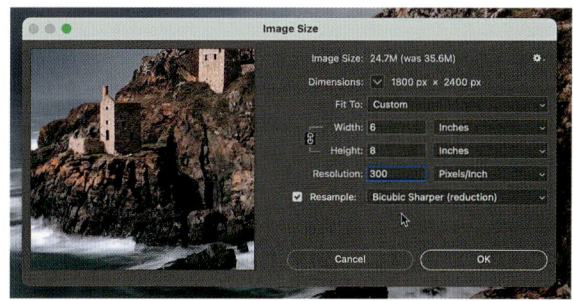

FIGURE 9.29

- **Width:** 6 inches

- **Height:** 8 inches

- **Resolution:** Changed to 300 PPI, as I'm printing this on the Canon. Since I'm reducing the size, I choose the **Bicubic Sharper (Reduction)** interpolation method **(Figure 9.29)**. The image is now properly sized and the resolution has been corrected for the Canon printer.

FIRST PRINT ATTEMPT USING ICC PROFILE

I go to **File** > **Print** and choose the following settings **(Figure 9.30)**:

- **Printer:** Canon Pro-300
- **Color Handling:** Photoshop Manages Colors
- **Printer Profile:** Smooth Rag profile for Canon
- **Rendering Intent:** Perceptual

In Print Settings, I choose:

- **Color Matching (on Mac):** Automatically disabled **(Figure 9.31)**
- **Media Type:** Canon's Heavyweight Fine Art Paper (recommended by PermaJet) **(Figure 9.32)**
- **Paper Source:** Top Feed
- **Print Quality:** Highest

With everything set, I click **OK**, **Save**, then **Print**.

EVALUATING THE FIRST PRINT

The print looks good, but it's noticeably different from the original image **(Figure 9.33)**. There's a definite color shift, even though both the working space and image are in Adobe RGB, and one possible reason for this could be that the ICC profile may be outdated or not fully compatible with the latest operating system.

Rather than make changes to the image, I decide to try a different print method.

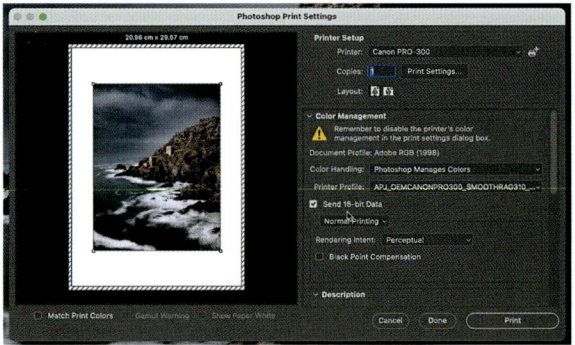

FIGURE 9.30

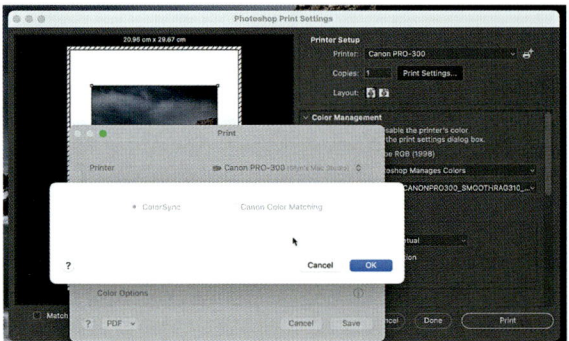

FIGURE 9.31

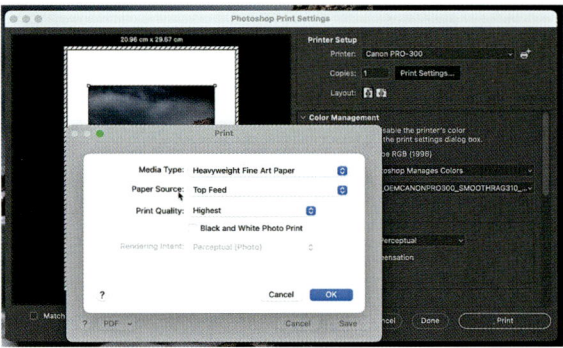

FIGURE 9.32

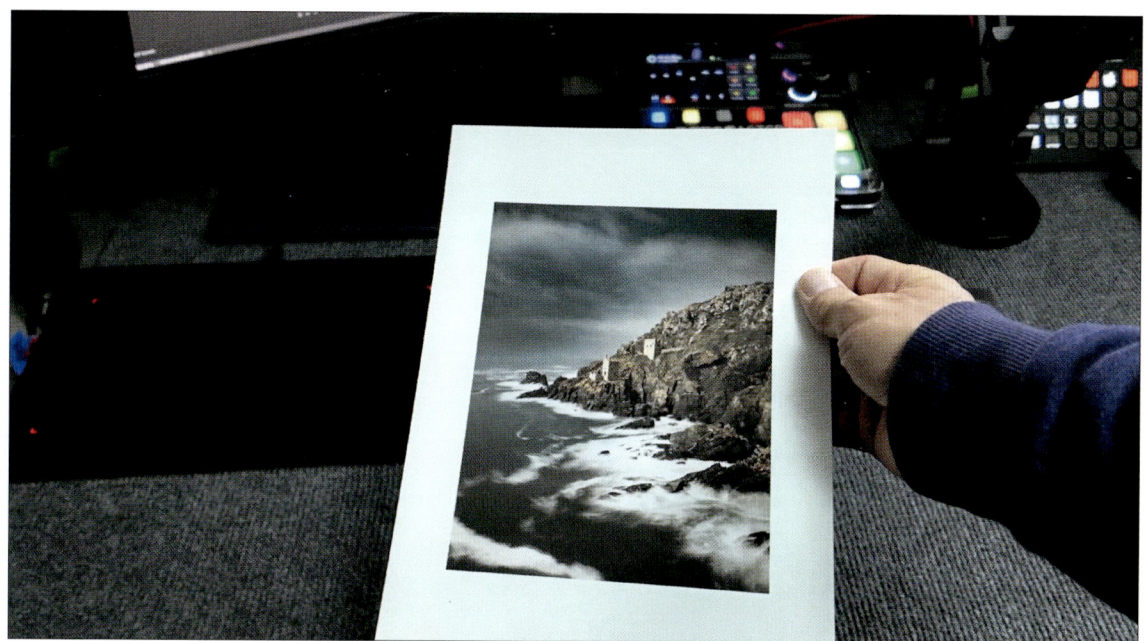

FIGURE 9.33

SECOND PRINT: PRINTER MANAGES COLORS

So now I'll print it out again from within Photoshop, making no further adjustments to the image itself.

I go to **File > Print**, but this time I make the following selection:

- **Color Handling:** Printer Manages Colors **(Figure 9.34)**

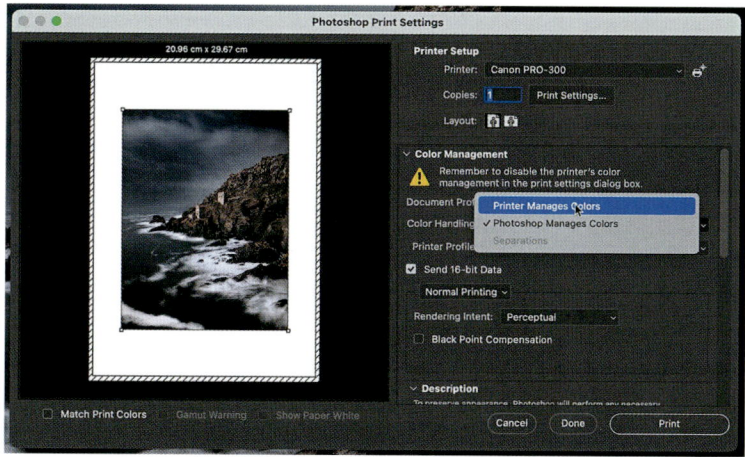

FIGURE 9.34

Modern-day printer drivers are exceptionally good, meaning they are highly accurate when it comes to the color and contrast of a printed image. All I need to do is tell the printer the appropriate Media Type for the paper I'm using so that it knows which black ink to use, how high or low to raise the printhead, how hard or soft to grab the paper, and so on.

In Print Settings, I set the following:

- **Media Type:** Heavyweight Fine Art Paper **(Figure 9.35)**
- **Color Matching:** Canon Color Matching **(Figure 9.36)**

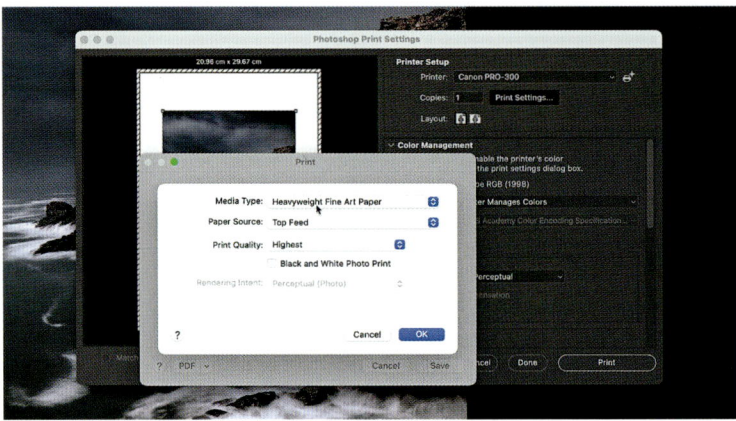

FIGURE 9.35

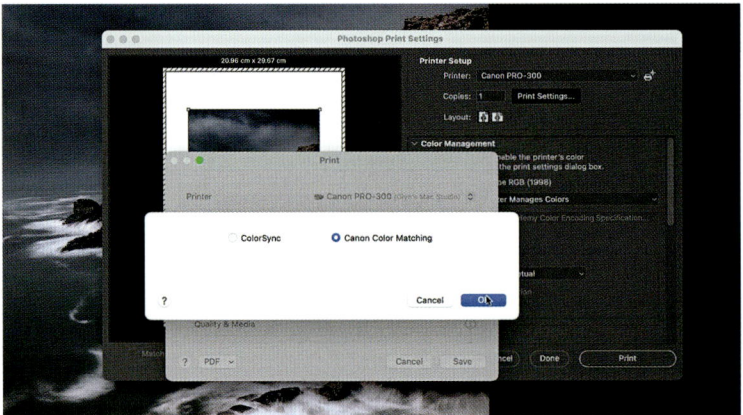

FIGURE 9.36

As for all of the other settings, I choose:

- **Paper:** A4
- **Printer:** Canon Pro-300
- **Print Quality:** Highest

I then click **Save**, then **Print**.

This second print looks much better **(Figure 9.37)**. It accurately reflects the color of the original image. However, from a personal, artistic standpoint, I find the sea and sky a little too dark, and this brings me back to a key point from earlier...

Even when the technical setup is flawless, your own artistic preference may call for adjustments, and that's not just perfectly fine and acceptable, it should be encouraged.

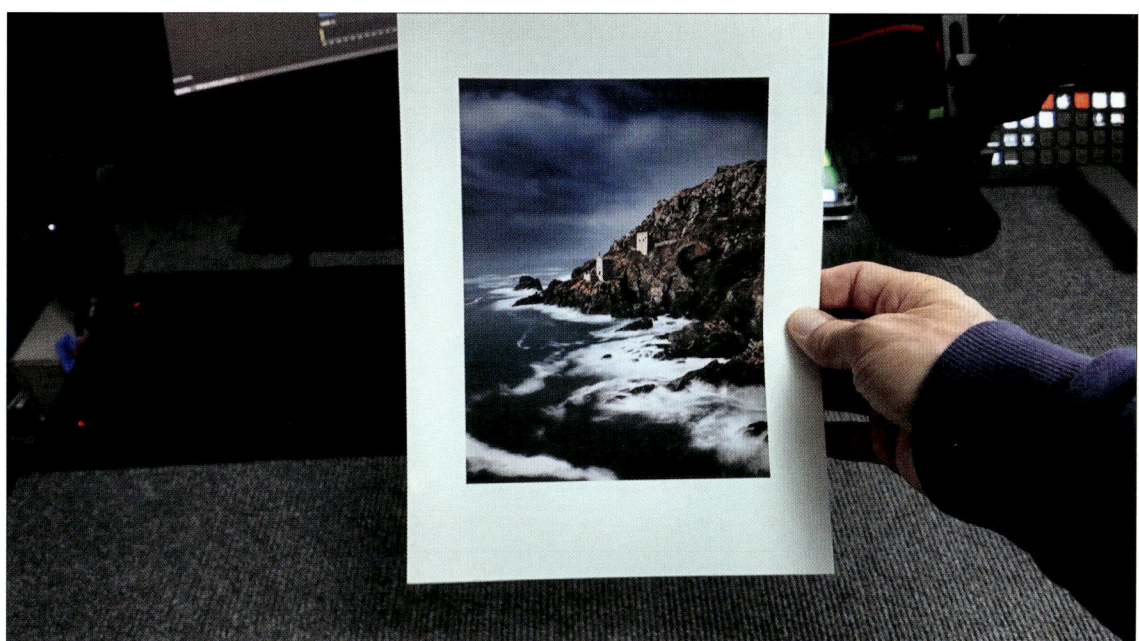

FIGURE 9.37

FINAL THOUGHTS ON SIMULATE PAPER AND INK

Now that you've seen all three images soft proofed and printed, I want to revisit the Simulate Paper and Ink function because it's important to address its role in the workflow.

When I'm in the Develop Module in Lightroom and turn on **Simulate Paper and Ink**, it's clear that what you see on screen **(Figure 9.38)** doesn't accurately represent the final print **(Figure 9.39)**. Comparing the preview to the actual printed result shows a noticeable difference.

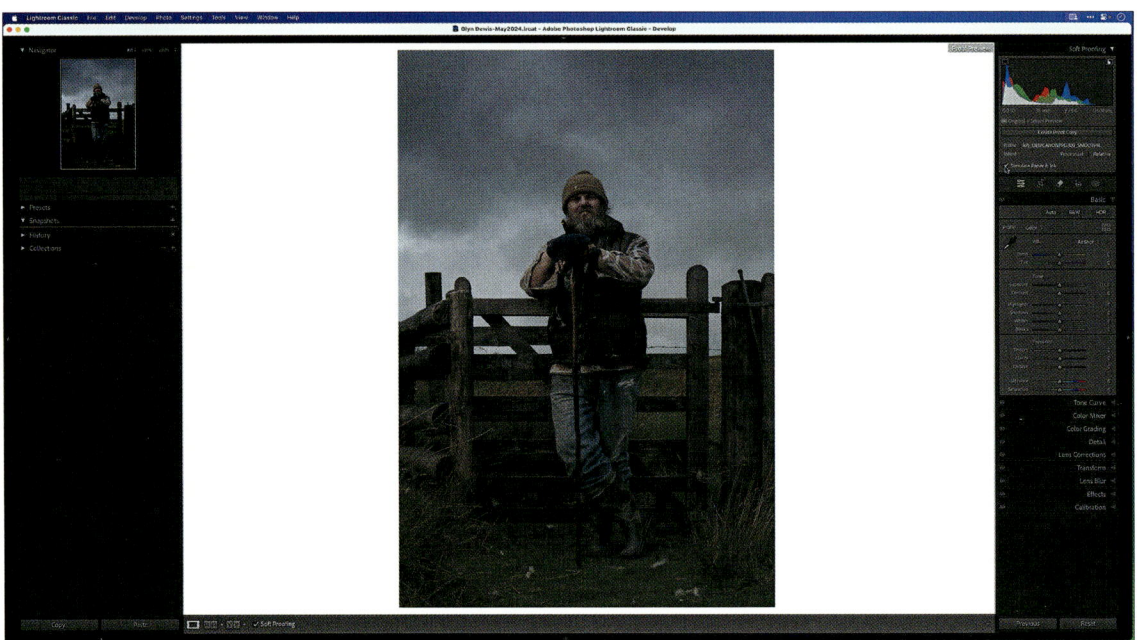

FIGURE 9.38 – Simulate Paper and Ink

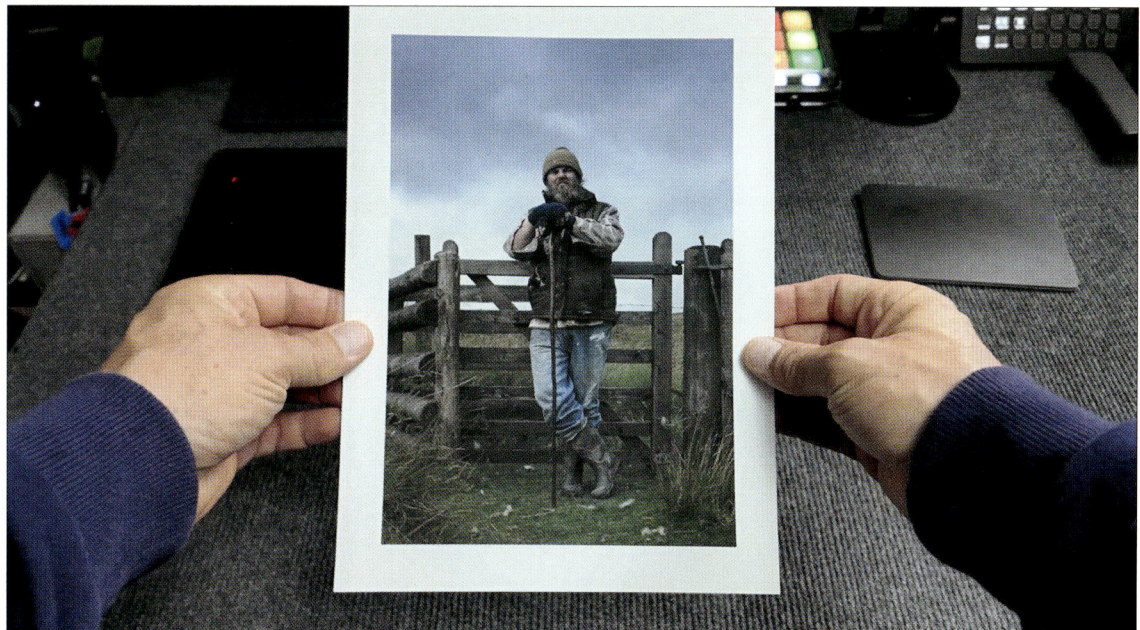

FIGURE 9.39 – Final Print

The Simulate Paper and Ink feature appears to lower both exposure and contrast in an attempt to replicate how the image might appear on paper. While it's a nice idea in theory, in practice it just doesn't work well, and in my opinion, it's an unnecessary consideration when soft proofing.

Each of the images I printed on Smooth Rag matte paper came out with plenty of contrast, brightness, and color saturation

By contrast, the images in Lightroom, when viewed with **Simulate Paper and Ink** turned on, look much duller and less compelling. Simply turning the function off produces a preview that looks much closer to the actual prints.

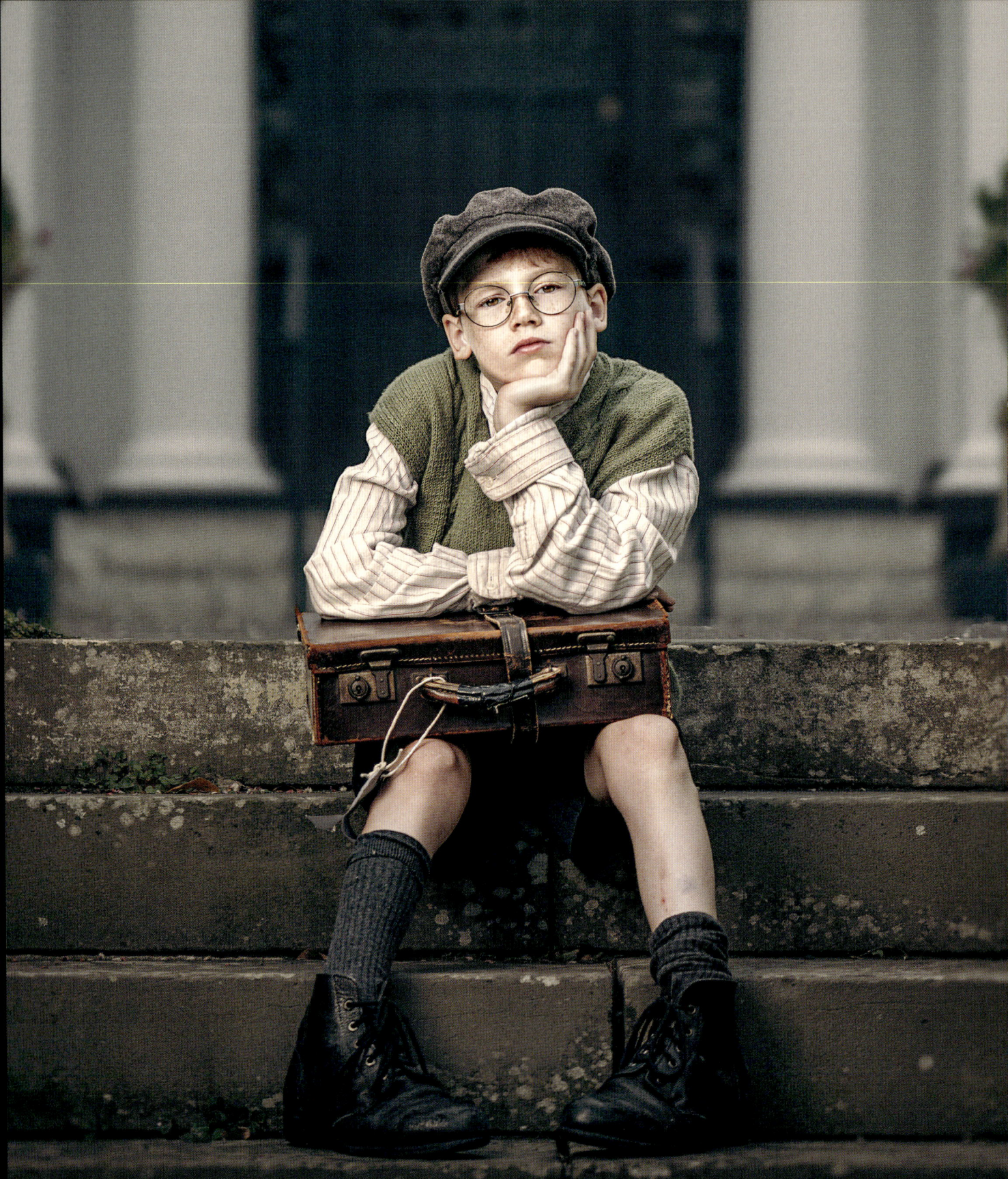

CHAPTER 10
PAPER

In this chapter we're going to be looking at all things paper related, including terminology and paper choice. This chapter is only possible because of the support provided by folks at PermaJet; in particular, Louise Hill and Colin Hulley, both of whom have vast amounts of experience in the field of printing, having worked within the industry for a number of years.

Understandably, it can be difficult in a book such as this to show how paper choice impacts an image, so to help with this you can watch the actual video interviews that were recorded when I spoke with both Louise and Colin over on the book's accompanying website at www.thehowtoprintbook.com.

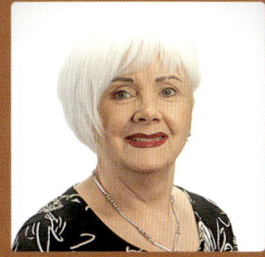

LOUISE HILL (PermaJet)

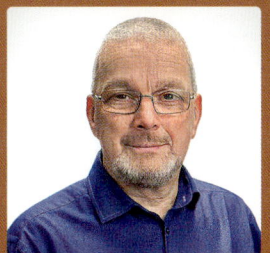

COLIN HULLEY (PermaJet)

PAPER TERMINOLOGY EXPLAINED

When selecting photographic printing papers, it's easy to gloss over the technical terms that appear on product descriptions, but these terms carry significant meaning, and understanding them can directly impact the final quality, durability, and character of your print.

So with that, here's a breakdown of some common paper terminology.

OBA-FREE

What it means:
OBA stands for **Optical Brightening Agent**. These are chemicals added to paper to make it appear brighter or whiter than it naturally is. OBA-free papers do not contain these additives.

When it's used:
Some papers include OBAs to enhance the brightness of whites (for example, PermaJet Photo Luster 310, Distinction 320, and Portrait White), which can help achieve high contrast in mono-chrome images.

Potential drawbacks:
While OBAs enhance visual brightness, they are chemically reactive, so if a print is unprotected and exposed to environmental contaminants (e.g., hairspray, nicotine, airborne chemicals), OBAs can break down over time, causing the image to yellow or discolor.

Expert advice:
To protect OBA-containing prints, always store or display them behind UV-protective glass or in archival-quality albums or sleeves.

ACID-FREE

What it means:
Acid-free paper has a **neutral pH** (typically between 6 and 7), meaning it's free of acid or excessive alkalinity.

Why it matters:
Acid-free paper ensures the **longevity** of the print. Over time, acidic materials can degrade prints, especially under storage conditions. Acid-free papers help maintain the archival quality of both the paper and the ink.

Common use:
Museums and conservationists prefer acid-free materials for storing artwork or photographs intended to last for generations.

GSM (GRAMS PER SQUARE METER)

What it means:
GSM is the **weight or thickness** of the paper, measured in grams per square meter. For example, a **310gsm** paper is heavier and sturdier than a **289gsm** paper.

Why it matters:
Heavier papers often feel more luxurious, offer greater durability, and **hold their shape better** when mounted or framed, making them ideal for exhibitions or professional sales.

ARCHIVAL

What it means:
The term "archival" refers to the expected lifespan and stability of a print; how long it will last without significant fading or degradation.

What affects it:

The type of ink is crucial. Pigmented inks (used by brands like Canon and Epson) offer superior archival stability compared to dye-based inks, which are more prone to fading.

Storage and display conditions also play a major role. Bright light, humidity, or pollutants can shorten a print's life, even on archival paper.

Best practices:
For maximum longevity:

- Use pigmented inks.

- Choose papers made from cotton rag or alpha cellulose.

- Store in a controlled environment or behind UV-protective glass.

Expected lifespan:
In optimal conditions, a properly printed archival image will outlive the photographer. In harsh conditions (like a sunlit conservatory), degradation may occur more quickly, but under good care, these prints can remain vibrant for many decades.

MATCHING PAPER TO IMAGE: A PRACTICAL CONVERSATION ON PRINT CHOICE WITH COLIN HULLEY

Paper is one of the most frequently discussed topics when it comes to printing, and understandably so. For photographers, the right paper can enhance an image dramatically. Below is a conversation that I had with Colin Hulley from PermaJet that is centered around paper choice and guided by specific image examples. While the names of papers are brand-specific, the concepts are broadly applicable to any serious printmaker.

PERSONAL TASTE AND PAPER MATCHING

Glyn

Paper is obviously a big discussion. I get asked about it a lot, and I've no doubt you get asked even more when you're traveling, teaching, and doing demonstrations at exhibitions and events.

What I did was send over three images. It wasn't to get you to tell me exactly which paper to use for each image, because I know that's impossible, as so much comes down to personal taste. But I wanted to get your thoughts on where you'd steer me within your paper range, based on the feel and character of each image.

Let's look at the first one.

IMAGE 1: MONOCHROME PRINT—MATCHING TONE AND TEXTURE

Colin

Whenever someone asks, "What paper would you recommend for this image?", my first response is always, "What printer do you have?"

For this first image, I actually printed it on Titanium Lustre. Even though you sent it over in low resolution, I just wanted to get a sense of how it would respond on paper. The silver base in Titanium Lustre works well with monochrome; it really complements the highlight and tonal range in that kind of image.

If I were looking for a fine art finish, I might go with something like Fibre Based Distinction. I worked for thirty years at Ilford, and the darkroom papers we used were traditionally cold whites with strong blacks; that's what I was used to and what influenced my preference today.

If I'd spent years working with AGFA-Gevaert (which had a much **warmer tone** due to the cadmium), I might have leaned more toward something like Gold Silk in the fine art range.

If I wanted to go with a rag paper, I'd consider Portrait White, as it offers great contrast while maintaining a classic fine art feel.

But again, not all papers are compatible with all printers. Portrait White and Fibre Based Distinction, for instance, aren't suitable for basic feed-through Epson printers. So that's why we always start by asking what printer the person is using. If their printer can't handle fine art papers, we look instead at options from the Digital Photo range.

For this image, for me, it was a no-brainer: Titanium Lustre just felt right. That said, ask five other people, and you'd get five different answers.

Glyn

Yeah, that's what's fascinating. There really are no right or wrongs, are there? It's so much about personal taste.

Colin

Exactly. At the **Print Academy** we run, and at camera club talks I used to do, I always say there needs to be a *marriage* between the image and the paper.

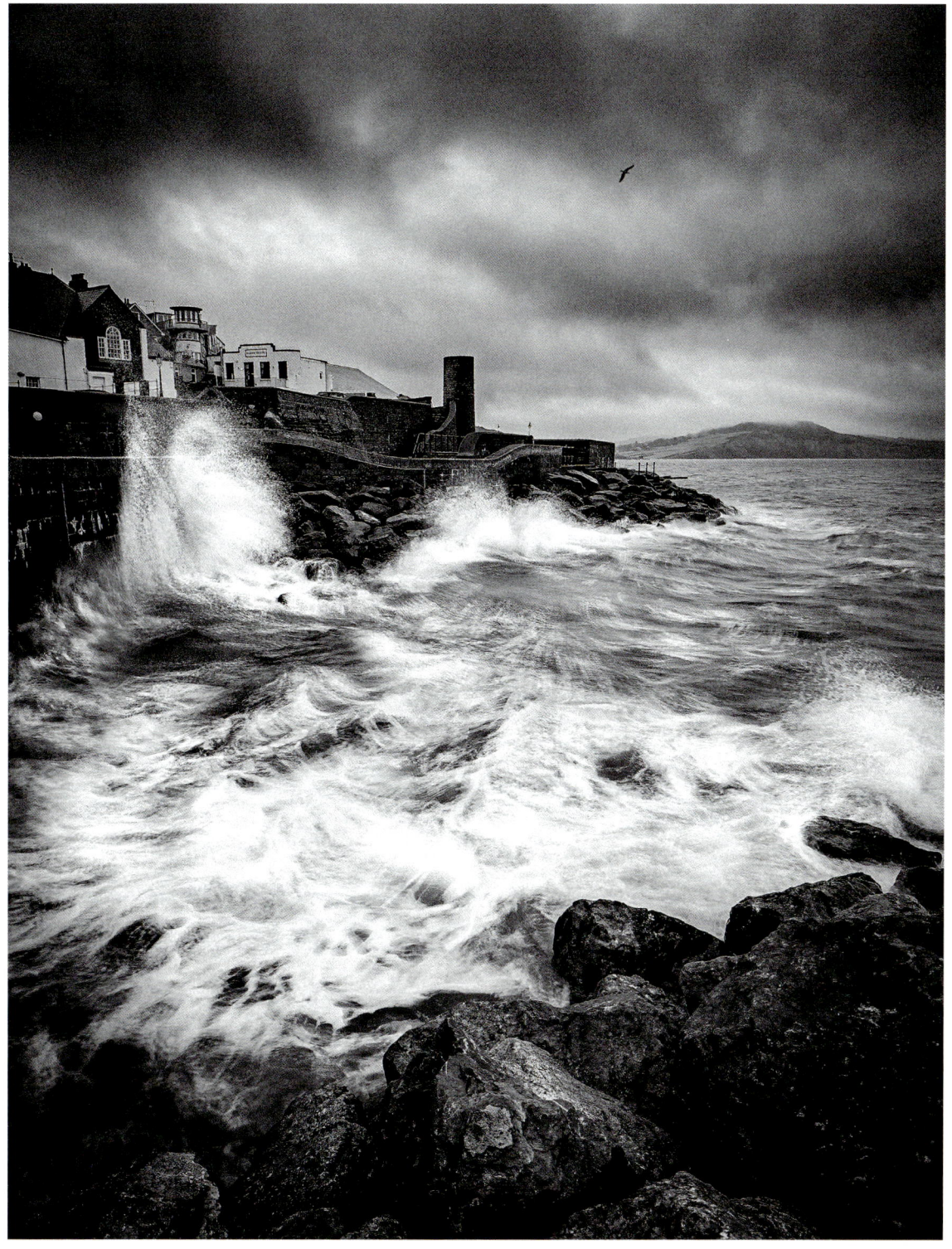

FIGURE 10.1

If the print that comes out of your printer doesn't look right, it's not necessarily the image's fault, and not necessarily the paper's fault either. Just change the paper. That's the variable.

In our courses, people often bring in a single image and we print it on three or four different papers to show how dramatically the paper affects the final outcome.

Glyn
Absolutely, the difference can be quite dramatic.

I always say: *The art doesn't end at the edit*. Choosing the right paper is part of the creative process. It has a huge impact on the final result.

Colin
It really does. And what's important is that you're printing for yourself. Not necessarily for recognition or approval from others. Whether it's to display, gift, or sell, the print needs to give **you** satisfaction. You have to be happy with it.

IMAGE 2: COLOR LANDSCAPE—AVOIDING TEXTURE INTERFERENCE

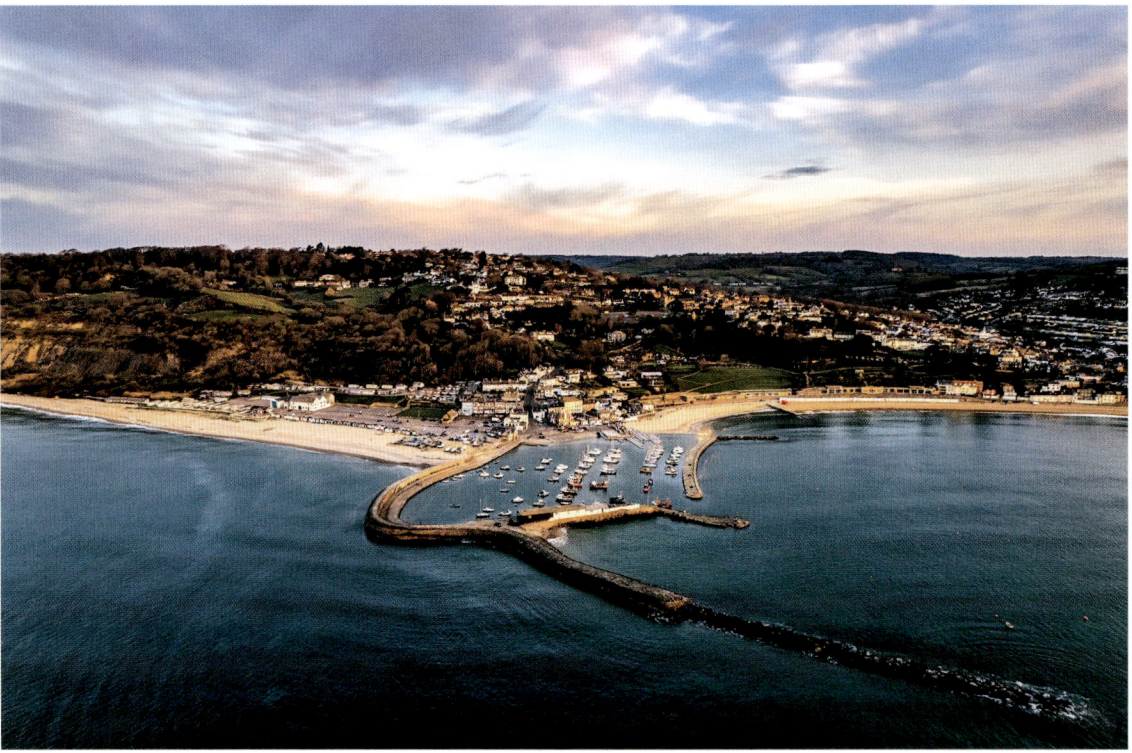

FIGURE 10.2

Glyn

Alright, so where would you steer me for this **second image?**

Colin

That one stirred a bit of discussion here. In the end, we settled on Photo Luster 310 from the Digital Photo range. The way that image appeared on screen with its mood, color, and sky detail seemed to benefit from the punchy, saturated finish that Photo Luster delivers.

We didn't feel a fine art paper was the right fit. Sometimes, the texture in fine art papers can actually interfere with the image, especially with sky detail. It can disrupt the mood or take attention away from key areas.

I considered Photo Art Silk, which is a favorite of mine; a bit of an *unsung hero*, really. It works brilliantly with images that include water, because the silk surface only reveals itself when ink is laid down. That reflective quality works beautifully with watery scenes.

But for this particular image, we thought even the texture in Photo Art Silk might detract from the sky. So we went with Photo Luster.

Glyn

Interesting. That really makes you appreciate the different considerations that go into paper selection.

IMAGE 3: PORTRAIT—MOOD AND DETAIL

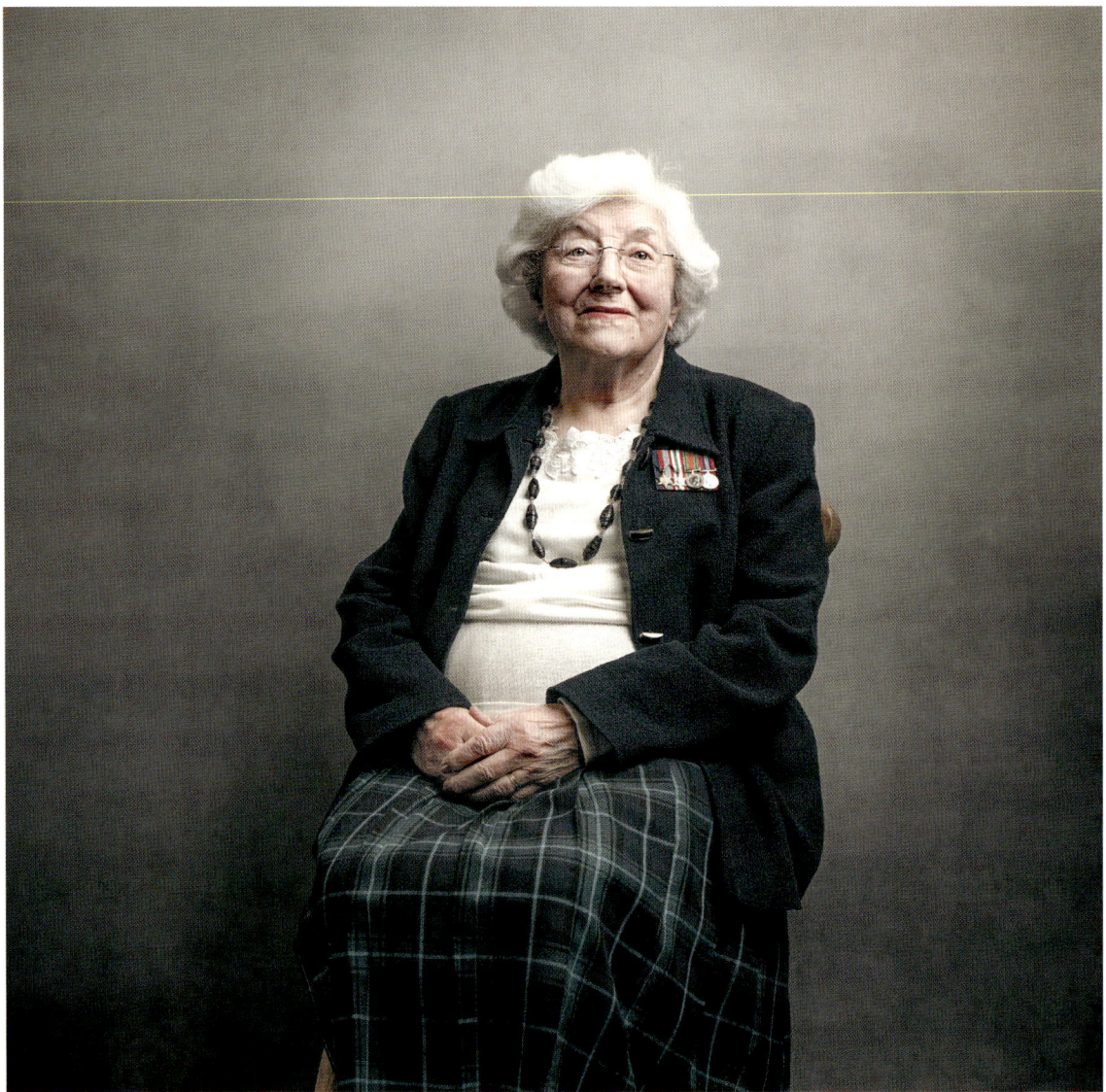

FIGURE 10.3

Colin

For this image, we chose Smooth Rag from the Heritage range. We felt the nature of the paper base, combined with the background and tone of the image, made Smooth Rag the best fit.

It's an OBA-free paper, so the whites are more neutral, which we thought worked better for the hair and jumper detail. A brighter paper base could have introduced unwanted contrast or color shift in those areas.

The tonal range and highlight detail came through really well on Smooth Rag. For us, it just matched the mood and feel of the portrait.

STORING PAPER PROPERLY

Colin

If the paper comes in a box, particularly sheet paper, always keep it in the box it came in. The reason is that reputable manufacturers, such as ourselves [PermaJet], Fotospeed, Hahnemühle, Canson, and so on, all use packaging materials that are acid-free. That ensures there's no chemical reaction from the box that might affect the paper.

If the paper is also packaged in a cellophane or plastic bag inside the box, keep it sealed in there. That reduces environmental exposure, things like humidity, dust, or air pollutants.

Also, always store your paper flat, not library style (vertically like books). Keeping it flat helps the paper remain completely even and avoids bowing, curling, or edge deformation.

The environment matters too. You want a stable room temperature. Avoid extreme environments like attics or garages that go hot and cold. A drawer, cabinet, or cupboard in your studio or office is perfect.

A COSTLY LESSON IN PAPER WARPING

Glyn

I'm really glad you mentioned keeping them flat because I remember a few years back when I used to keep my paper stored library style in a cabinet, and even though some of the boxes were unopened, when I finally did open them up, you could see the paper had **bowed slightly**. It was just enough to mess up the printer feed.

It was an expensive lesson, but one I never repeated!

WHY RETAIL STORES BREAK THE RULES

Colin

Yes, it definitely can have an effect. The bowing might seem minor, but it can interfere with the printer's ability to feed and register the paper correctly.

That said, in retail environments, papers are often stored library style just so customers can flip through them easily. But for long-term storage at home, flat is best.

WHEN AND WHY TO USE PROTECTIVE PRINT SPRAYS ON MATTE PAPERS

For photographers who regularly print on matte-based fine art papers, adding a protective coating can be a valuable final step in the printing process.

While not essential for every print or environment, protective sprays and varnishes offer benefits that can enhance both the appearance and durability of your work.

One such product is PermaSEAL from PermaJet **(Figure 10.4)**, a UV protective spray designed to provide several advantages. It helps increase the D-Max (maximum density) of a print, offering deeper blacks and richer tonal contrast. Additionally, it acts as a waterproofing agent and can add a degree of scuff resistance.

While PermaSEAL is formulated to give a subtle sheen, another option, PermaFIX **(Figure 10.5)**, is made for those who prefer to maintain a matte finish.

Both sprays are ideal for matte and fine art papers, but are not suitable for gloss or satin papers, as the chemistry doesn't bond effectively with coated surfaces.

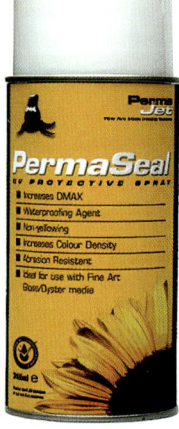

FIGURE 10.4

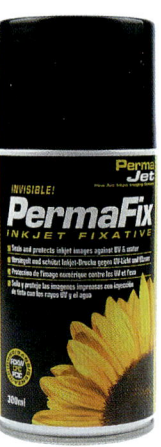

FIGURE 10.5

When choosing between PermaSEAL and PermaFIX, the type of paper and desired finish should guide the decision. For example, on papers like Smooth Rag, which is a popular OBA-free matte paper, PermaFIX is generally recommended because it preserves the natural, non-reflective appearance. However, for photographers open to a subtle sheen that enhances depth, PermaSEAL can be a good alternative.

To decide which finish is preferred, a practical approach is to test both sprays on the same image, applying each to half of the print and comparing the results. This side-by-side evaluation can be especially useful when preparing prints for display or sale, where visual presentation and surface protection are equally important.

In addition to sprays, some professionals opt for liquid varnishes like PermaPROtect, which are applied using a roller or brush. These are also designed for matte and fine art papers and provide similar archival and protective benefits. Though slightly more labor-intensive, they offer precise control over application and finish.

Ultimately, using a protective coating is a matter of both function and preference. For those printing regularly on matte media, especially for exhibitions or long-term storage, sprays like PermaFIX or PermaSEAL can add confidence in the longevity and presentation quality of the final print.

HOW PAPER CHOICE INFLUENCES THE FINAL PRINT

This is where I want to point you to this book's accompanying website, where you'll find a two-part video in which I talk with Louise Hill **(Figure 10.6)**.

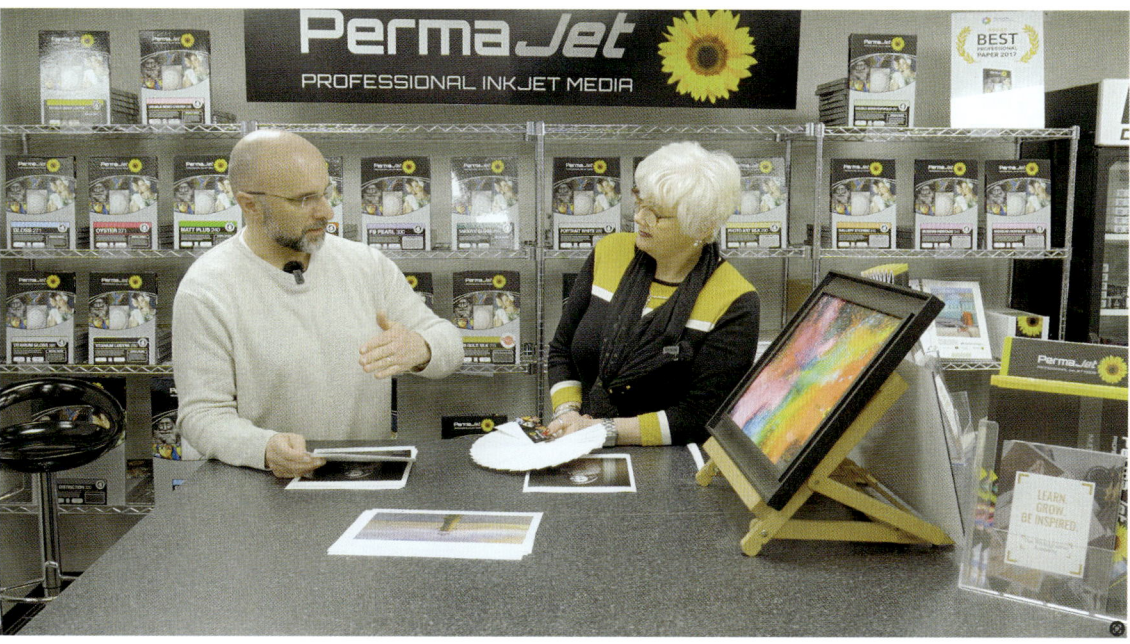

FIGURE 10.6

I originally sent two images to Louise; one black-and-white/monochrome **(Figure 10.7)** and one color **(Figure 10.8)**, which were then printed on a large selection of different papers at PermaJet to discover which paper works best, and which we prefer.

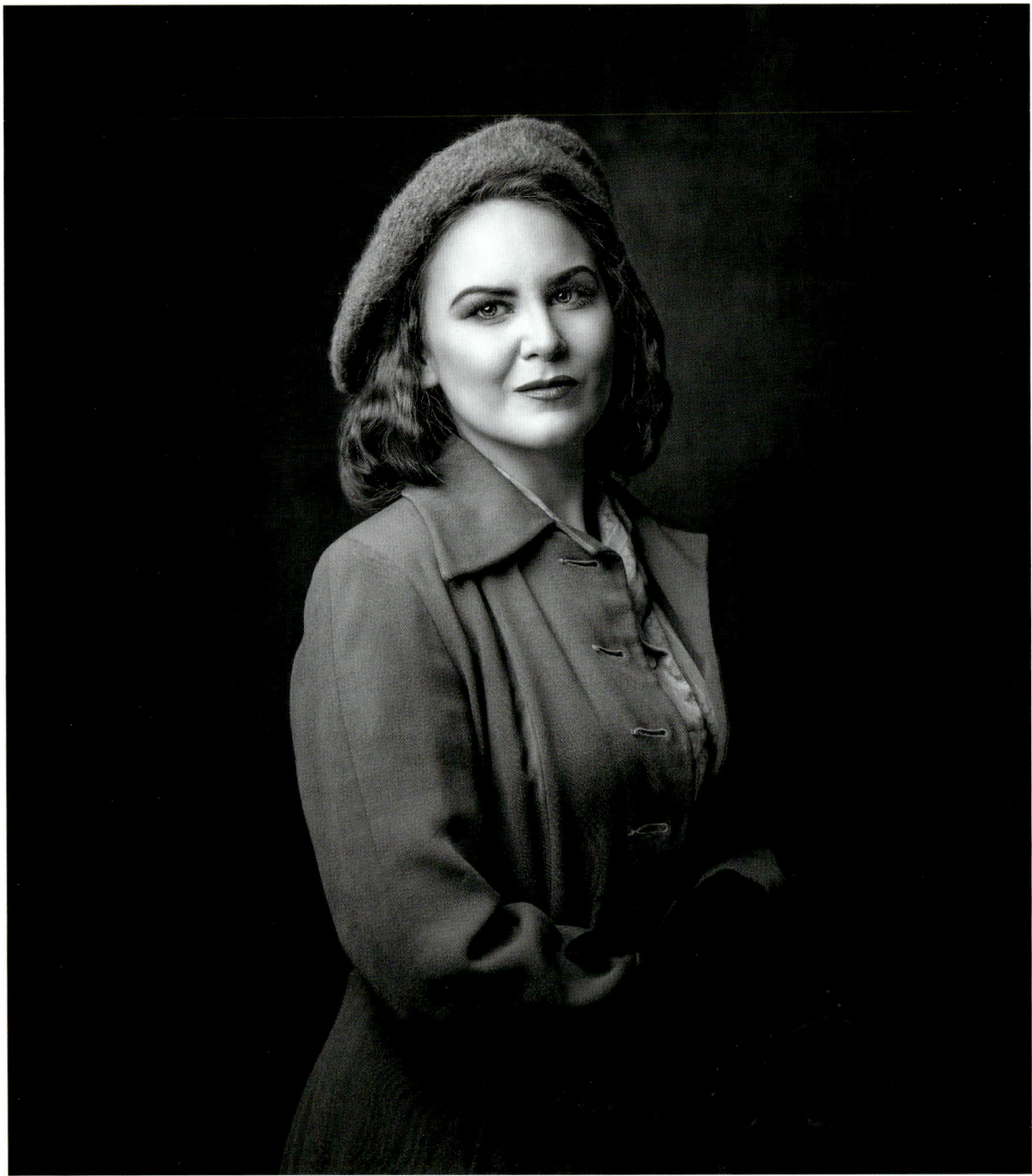

FIGURE 10.7

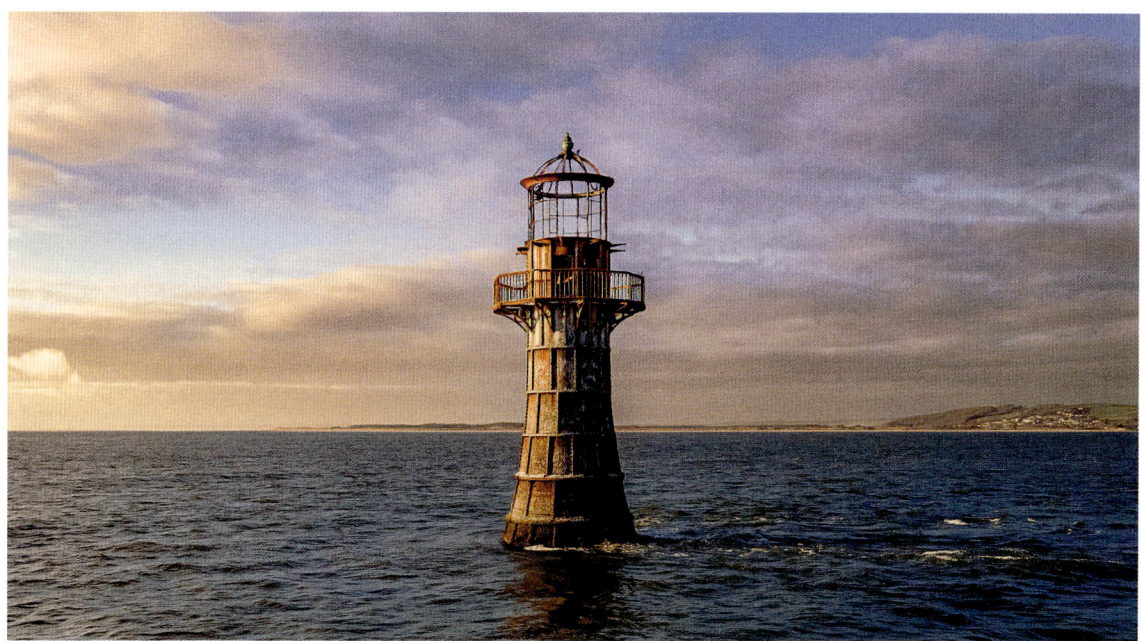

FIGURE 10.8

This is a fascinating discussion and a real eye-opener to see how the same image can look so dramatically different from paper to paper.

You can watch the videos over at: www.thehowtoprintbook.com

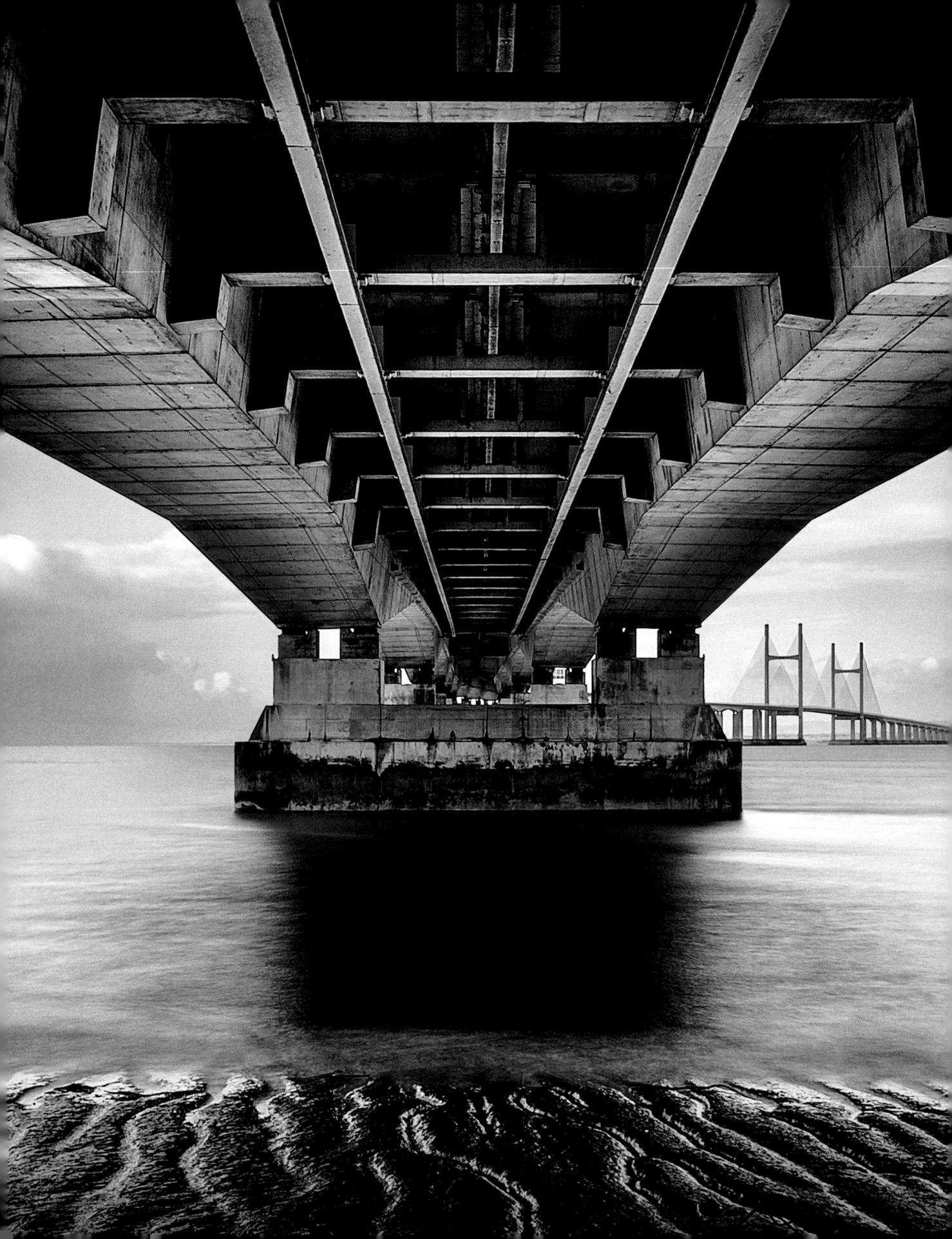

CHAPTER 11
PRINTING SOFTWARE

In this chapter, the focus shifts to printing from a range of different software applications, including Photoshop, Lightroom Classic, Epson Print Layout, Canon Professional Print & Layout, Qimage One, and ON1 Photo RAW. While each of these programs has its own interface and features, the actual printing process across them is largely identical. The steps and principles involved remain consistent, regardless of which application is being used.

What becomes evident when comparing these platforms is the power and simplicity of the printer manufacturers' own software. Applications such as Epson Print Layout and Canon Professional Print & Layout are specifically built to communicate directly and efficiently with their respective printers. One notable advantage of these manufacturer tools is the absence of certain settings, particularly those that often contribute to printing problems. A major source of such problems, beyond incorrect print settings, is excessive display brightness, which can lead to misjudging how an image will appear in print.

Ultimately, the choice of software will come down to personal preference. Each user will have their own habits and workflow comfort zones. However, based on extensive printing experience, it becomes clear that using the printer manufacturer's dedicated software tends to produce the best results. These companies have intimate knowledge of their own printers and how to optimize output quality, making their software especially well-suited for the task.

A helpful mindset is to separate software by its primary function: Retouching software should be used for editing and preparing images, while printing software should be reserved for the final output. Prepare your images in the editing software of your choice, and once they are ready, bring them into the printing software for output. This separation of tasks leads to greater consistency and better final prints.

That said, the workflow you choose is ultimately up to you. What matters most is that the method you follow includes the right steps and settings to achieve the highest-quality print possible.

PRINTING A COLOR IMAGE FROM PHOTOSHOP

To demonstrate the process of printing from Photoshop, I've chosen a portrait of a friend, titled *Foxy* (**Figure 11.1**).

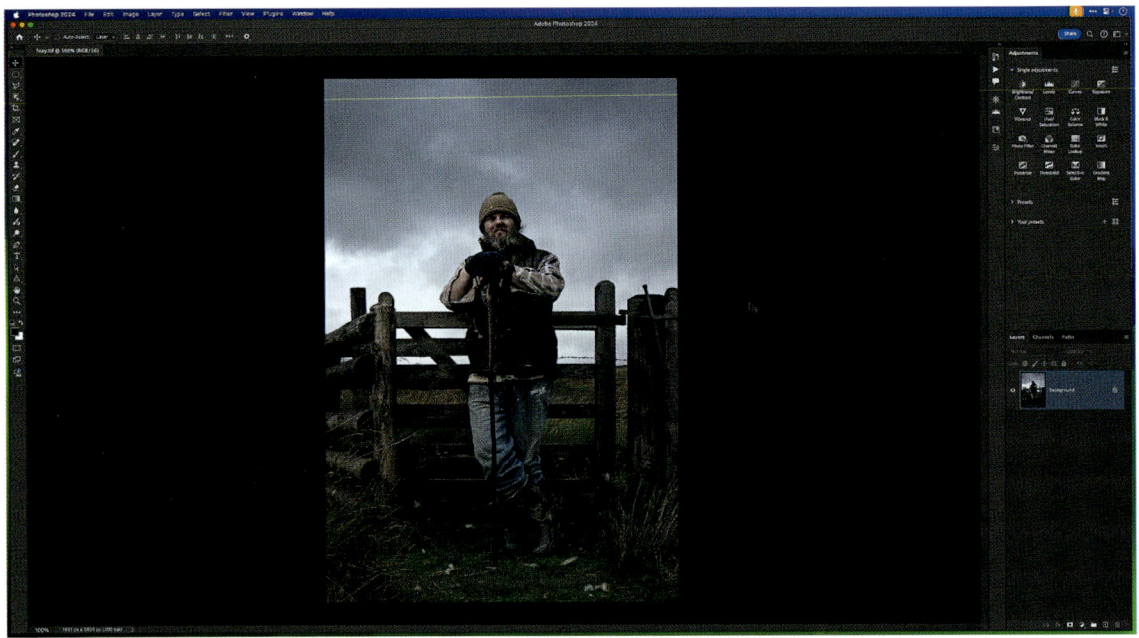

FIGURE 11.1

At this stage, all necessary adjustments have already been completed. The image has been retouched, soft proofed, resized, and, if needed, sharpened. With preparation complete, the image is now ready to print.

The printer I'm using for this demonstration is the Canon Pro-300, and the paper is Canon's own Photo Paper Pro Platinum.

Because the printer, paper, and ink is Canon-branded, an ICC profile is not required for this particular print.

PHOTOSHOP PRINT SETTINGS

The print process starts in Photoshop by navigating to **File** > **Print**, which opens the print dialog box.

At the top of this window, the printer is selected, which in this case is the Canon Pro-300. Only one copy will be printed, and the Layout is set to Portrait Orientation.

COLOR MANAGEMENT SETTINGS

Next, within the Color Management section, I need to select the setting for Color Handling. Because a Canon printer and Canon paper are being used, I'll choose **Printer Manages Colors (Figure 11.2)**. If a different, third-party paper were being used, the correct choice would be **Photoshop Manages Colors,** and an appropriate ICC profile would be selected under **Printer Profile**. However, since no ICC profile is needed in this case, I'll use **Printer Manages Colors**, and the Printer Profile field is automatically grayed out.

I'll also enable the setting for **Send 16-bit Data**, and make sure **Rendering Intent** is set to **Perceptual,** which was determined earlier during the soft proofing stage.

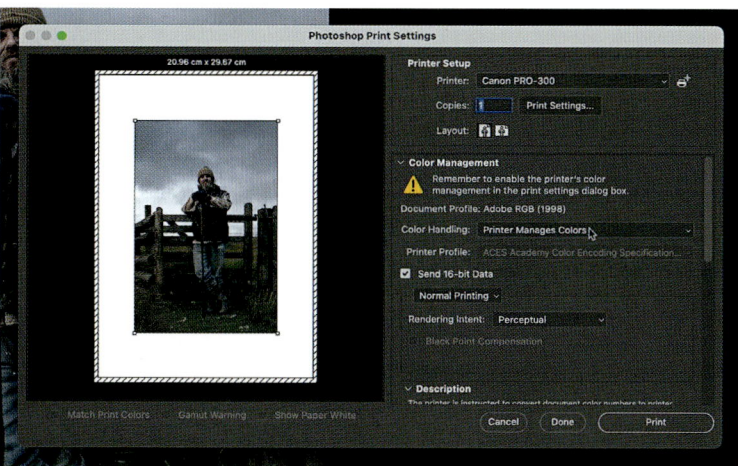

FIGURE 11.2

PRINTER DRIVER CONFIGURATION

Clicking **Print Settings** at the top of the dialog opens the printer driver dialog. Here, I confirm the number of copies, and set the paper size to **A4**.

Scrolling down to **Printer Options**, under **Color Matching**, because I'm not using an ICC Profile, Color Management is ON, so **Canon Color Matching** is selected **(Figure 11.3)**. This ensures that the printer itself is controlling the color output, which is appropriate given the use of Canon paper.

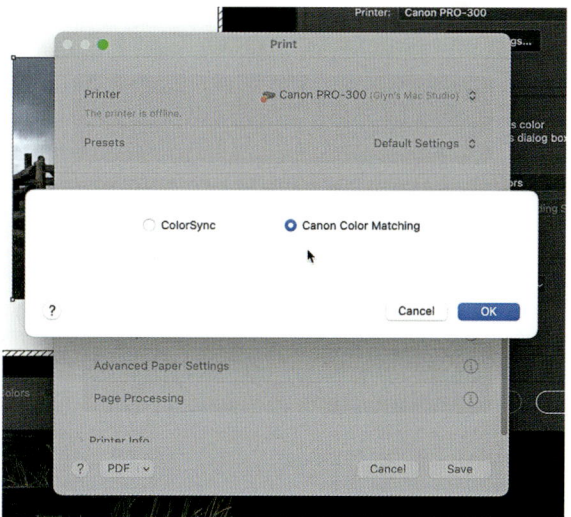

FIGURE 11.3

MEDIA AND QUALITY SETTINGS

Moving on to the **Quality and Media** section, I'll set the **Media Type** to **Canon Photo Paper Pro Platinum** to match the paper being used **(Figure 11.4)**.

No further adjustments are necessary at this point, so I confirm the settings by clicking **OK**, followed by **Save**.

FINAL OUTPUT

With all settings in place, clicking **Print** initiates the final output.

The result is a high-quality print with excellent color accuracy, sharp detail, and well-balanced brightness **(Figure 11.5)**. Everything appears just as expected, confirming the effectiveness of the workflow and settings used.

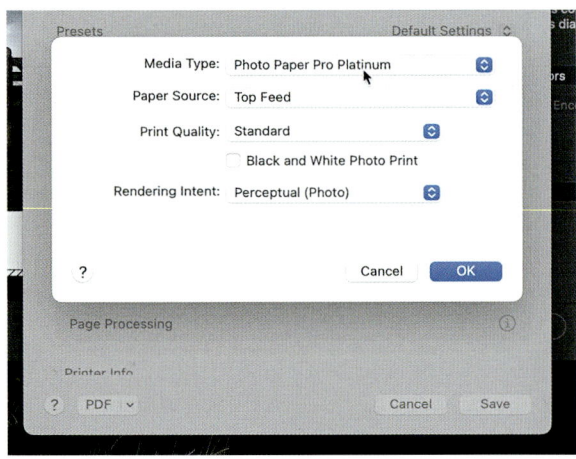

FIGURE 11.4

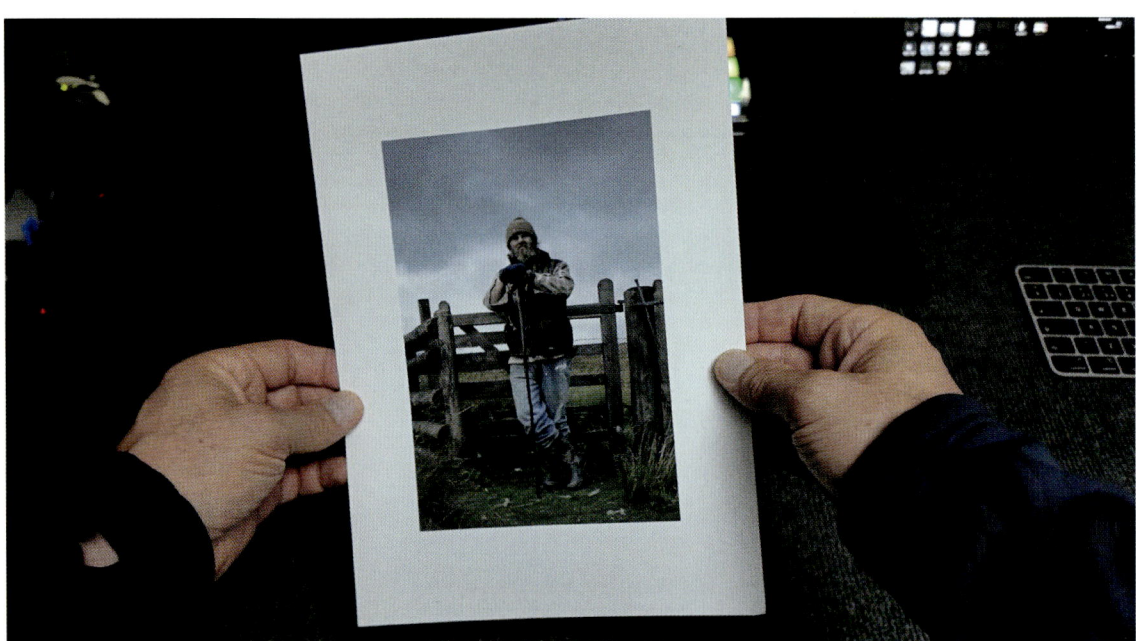

FIGURE 11.5

PRINTING A BLACK-AND-WHITE IMAGE FROM PHOTOSHOP

As with color prints, the process to print a black-and-white image **(Figure 11.6)** begins in Photoshop by navigating to **File** > **Print**.

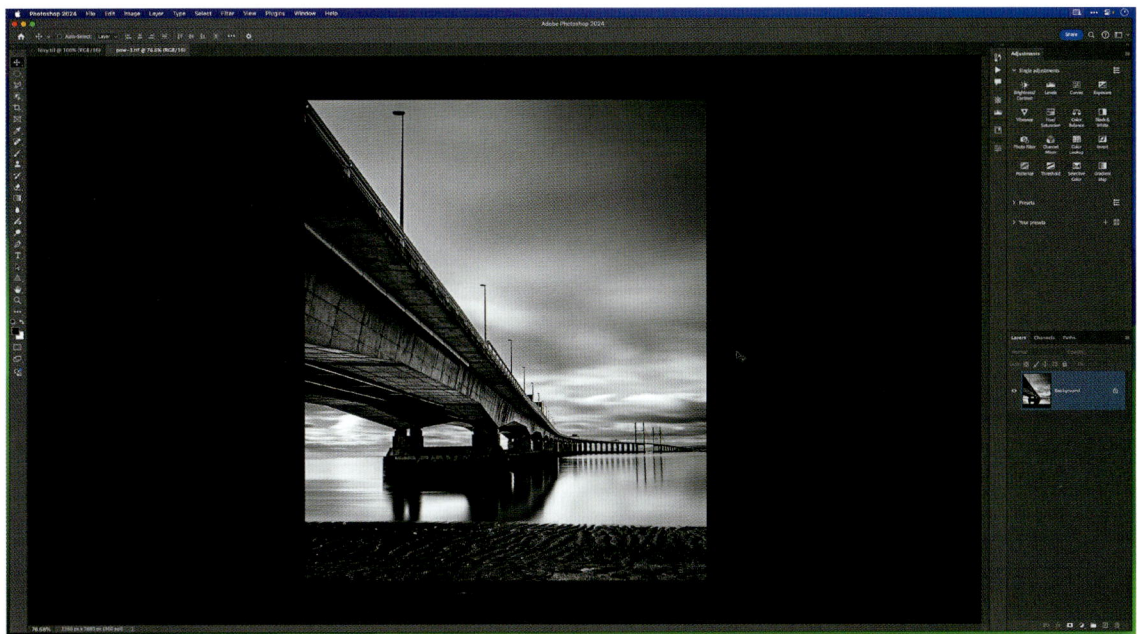

FIGURE 11.6

In the **Photoshop Print Settings** window, the **Canon Pro-300** is selected as the active printer. I am only printing **one copy**, and I've set the Layout to **Portrait Orientation**. The process remains very similar to printing in color, but with a few specific differences related to black-and-white output.

COLOR MANAGEMENT FOR MONOCHROME PRINTING

Since I'm using Canon paper with a Canon printer, there is no need to use an ICC profile. Additionally, because I'm using the Canon **Black and White Photo Print** mode, ICC profiles are not supported for this type of print. Therefore, under the **Color Management** section, **Printer Manages Colors** is selected. I'll also enable the setting for **Send 16-bit Data** to ensure optimal image quality.

PRINTER DRIVER SETTINGS

Clicking on **Print Settings** opens the printer driver window. I've set the paper size to **A4**, and it's important to scroll down to check the **Printer Options** section. Under **Color Matching**, **Canon Color Matching** should be selected. This is the correct option when ICC profiles are not in use.

MEDIA AND QUALITY SETTINGS

In the **Quality and Media** section, I'll set the **Media Type** to **Canon Photo Paper Pro Platinum**, and the Paper Source to **Top Feed**. I'll leave Print Quality at the **Standard** setting, which is typically sufficient for black-and-white prints on high-end photo paper.

To eliminate any risk of unwanted color casts, such as green or magenta tints, I enable **Black and White Photo Print (Figure 11.7)**. This ensures a true monochrome output using the printer's dedicated black-and-white processing.

Once these settings are confirmed, clicking **OK**, followed by **Save**, finalizes the setup. The print is now ready to go, and clicking **Print** sends the job to the printer.

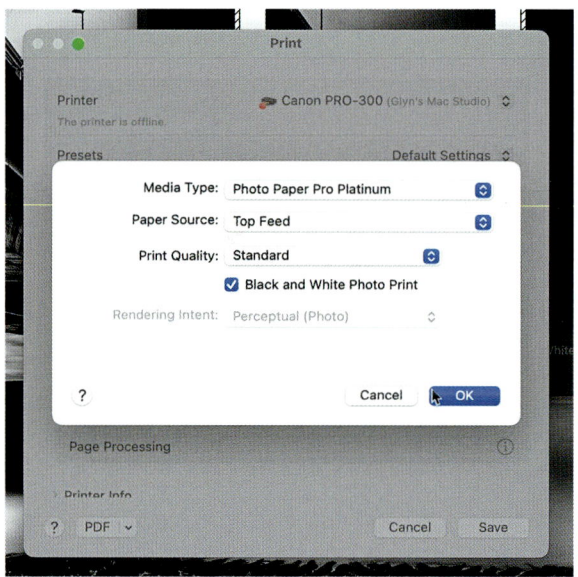

FIGURE 11.7

FINAL RESULT

The finished print looks excellent **(Figure 11.8)**. Detail and sharpness are superb, and the image shows strong contrast and balanced brightness. There are no visible color casts, and the tonal range is rich and clean. The print exceeds expectations, which is proof of how effective Canon's black-and-white printing mode can be when paired with the right paper and workflow.

PRINTING A COLOR IMAGE FROM LIGHTROOM CLASSIC

While many photographers use Lightroom Classic for their printing workflow, it has never been my preferred tool for the job. Based on my own experience, I've found Lightroom to be a bit inconsistent when it comes to print output. It can be temperamental, especially in terms of color consistency and repeatability. This is ultimately what led me to favor the dedicated software provided by printer manufacturers.

As you might expect, these companies understand their own printers better than anyone else and design their software specifically to get the most accurate, reliable, and repeatable results possible.

SETTING UP THE PRINT IN LIGHTROOM

That said, let's walk through a typical color print process using Lightroom Classic.

The image I'll be printing is a square-format photo, already retouched, soft proofed, and resized to **6 inches by 6 inches (Figure 11.9)**.

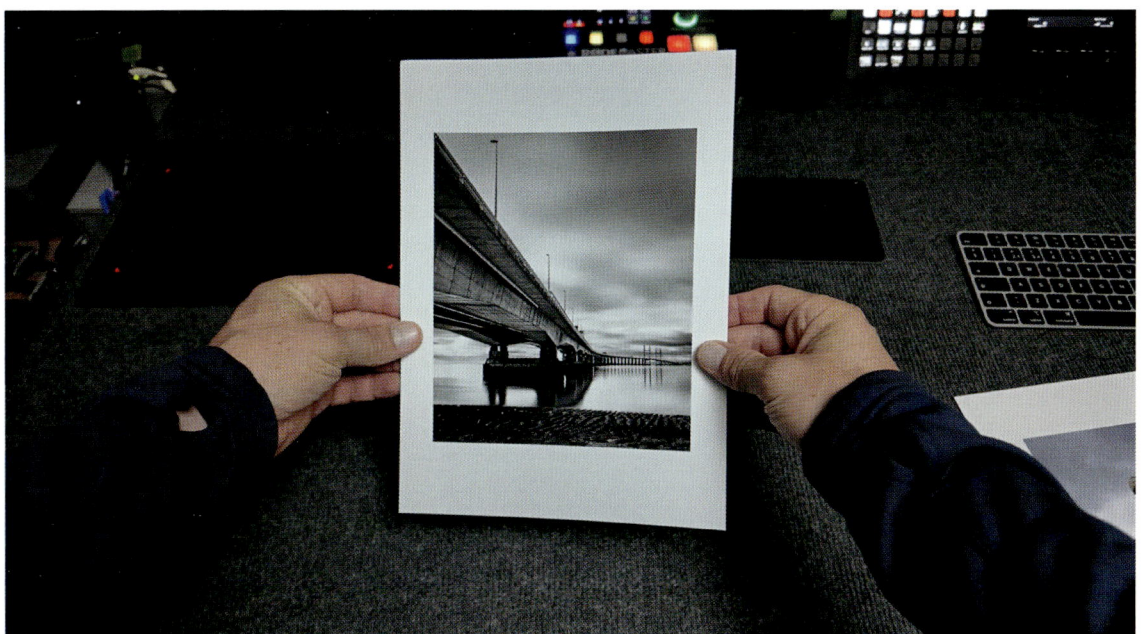

FIGURE 11.8

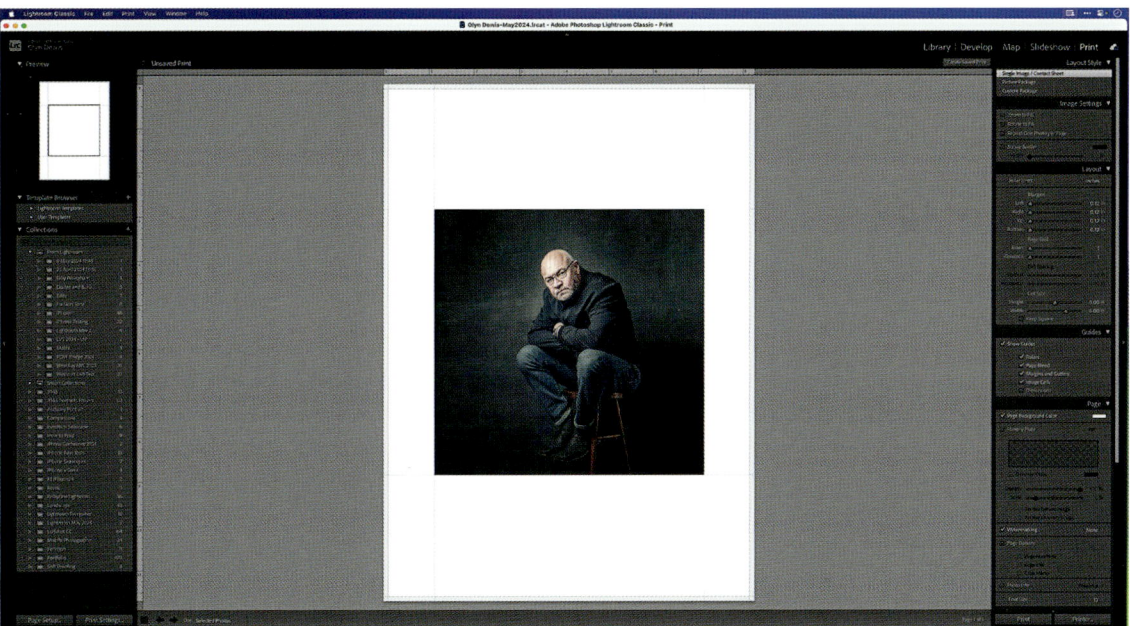

FIGURE 11.9

Once in the **Print** module, there are several layout options available, such as printing single images, contact sheets, or picture packages. For this demonstration, I'm sticking with a **single image** layout.

Lightroom offers a number of customization features, including the ability to set a page background color and add a watermark, page numbers, crop marks, and photo metadata. However, for my purposes, I'll be skipping all of that. My goal here is to produce a clean, high-quality photographic print without extra elements.

CONFIGURING THE PRINT JOB SETTINGS

Within the **Print Job** section, there is an option called **Draft Mode Printing**, which allows for quick, low-quality prints without color management or sharpening controls **(Figure 11.10)**. This mode speeds up the process but significantly reduces print fidelity—so it's not suitable here.

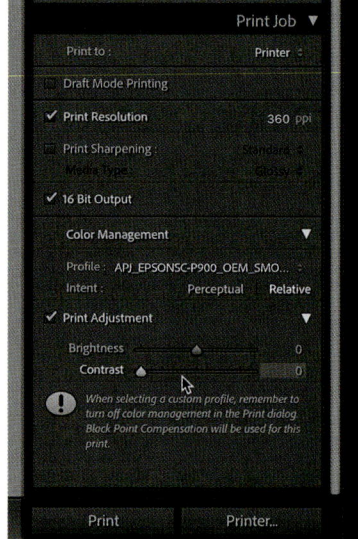

Further down, I set the **Print Resolution** to **360 pixels per inch**, which is optimal for printing with Epson printers.

I won't be applying any additional sharpening at this stage, as that has already been handled during the retouching process. I'll keep the setting at **16 Bit Output** for maximum detail.

For **Color Management**, I'll be using an **ICC profile**, so I'll select the appropriate one from the drop-down menu. The **Rendering Intent** is set to **Relative**, based on the earlier soft proofing.

Lightroom also includes a **Print Adjustment** feature with sliders for brightness and contrast, but I avoid using this entirely. It's unreliable and inconsistent, and with a properly calibrated display, it should never be necessary.

FIGURE 11.10

PRINTER DRIVER AND MEDIA SETTINGS

Before printing, I confirm that **A4** is selected in the **Page Setup**.

Then I click on **Printer** (bottom right), which opens the printer driver interface. The correct printer is already selected. Under **Printer Options**, I verify that **Color Management** is set correctly.

On a Mac system, Color Management is off by default when using an ICC profile, which is exactly what I want **(Figure 11.11)**. On a Windows machine, I would have to manually disable it.

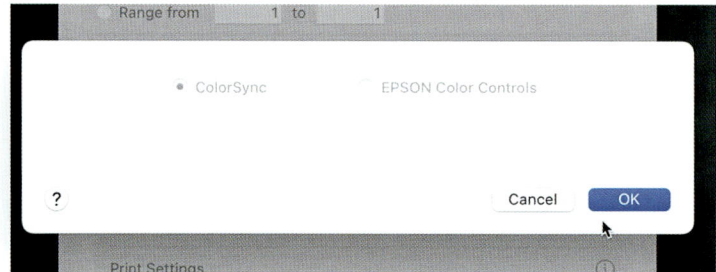

FIGURE 11.11

In the **Print Settings**, I choose the **Media Type** that best corresponds to the paper I'm using. For this print, I'm using **PermaJet Smooth Rag**, which is best matched with Epson's **Watercolor Paper Radiant White** profile in the Epson driver **(Figure 11.12)**.

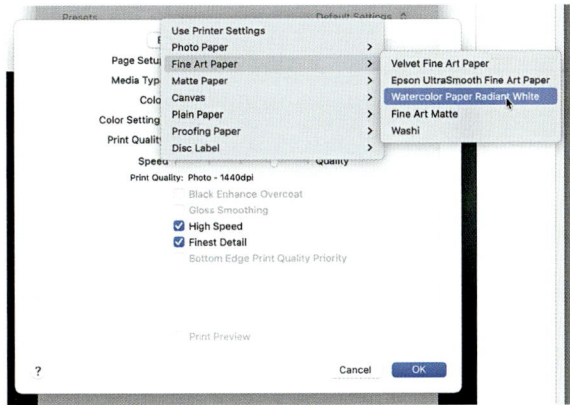

FIGURE 11.12

I'll leave **Print Quality** set at **Standard**, which defaults to **1440 DPI (Figure 11.13)**.

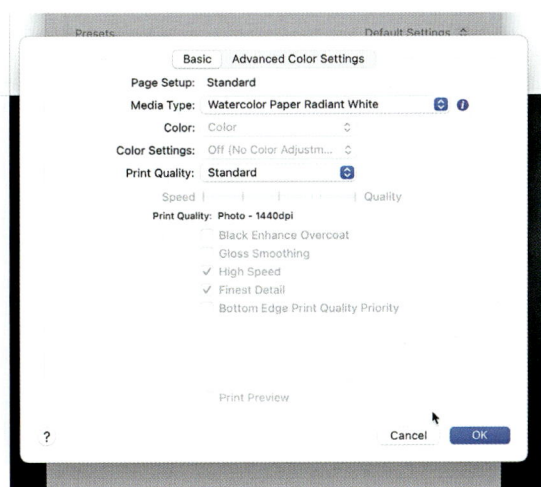

FIGURE 11.13

With everything set, I click **OK**, and then proceed to **Print**.

EVALUATING THE RESULTS

The resulting print looks good at first glance. The sharpness and detail are there, and the overall tonal balance seems fine.

However, something feels slightly off. The color balance isn't quite right **(Figure 11.14)**; specifically, some of the blue color grading that was added in the final retouch doesn't come through as clearly as expected. It's still a good print, but knowing that better results are possible leaves me a bit underwhelmed.

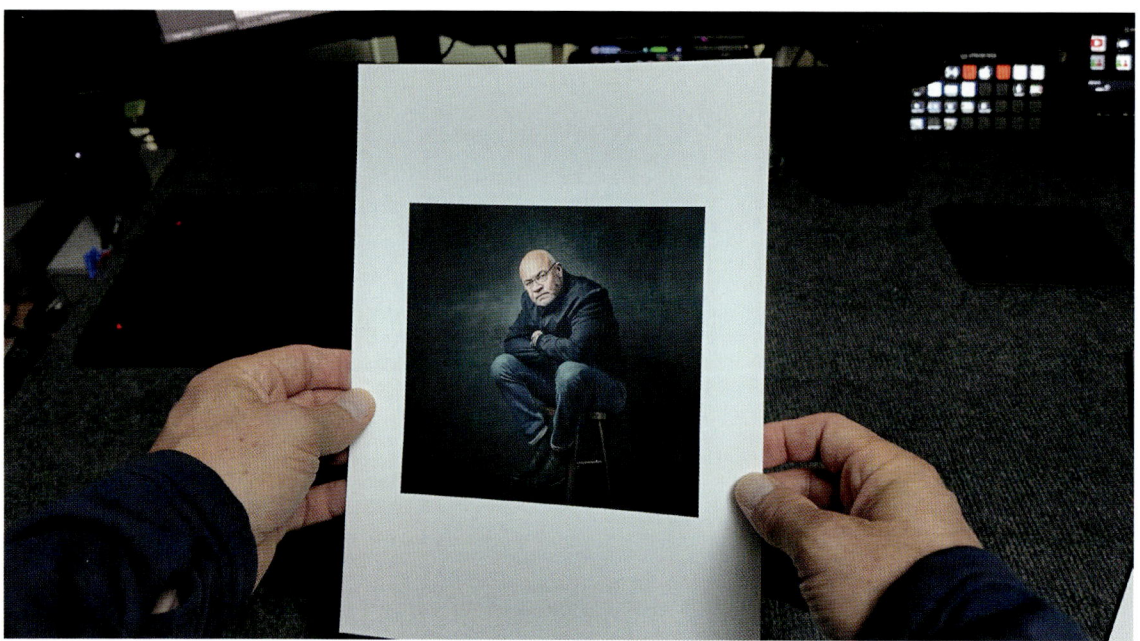

FIGURE 11.14

AN ALTERNATIVE APPROACH WITHIN LIGHTROOM

Out of curiosity, I ran another print using **Lightroom Classic**, but this time I allowed the printer to manage the colors, bypassing the ICC profile.

I used a different, but still matte, paper: **Epson Archival Matte**.

Surprisingly, this print came out looking more accurate to the original retouch. The color grading, especially in the blues, was better preserved, and there was a noticeable improvement in shadow detail **(Figure 11.15)**.

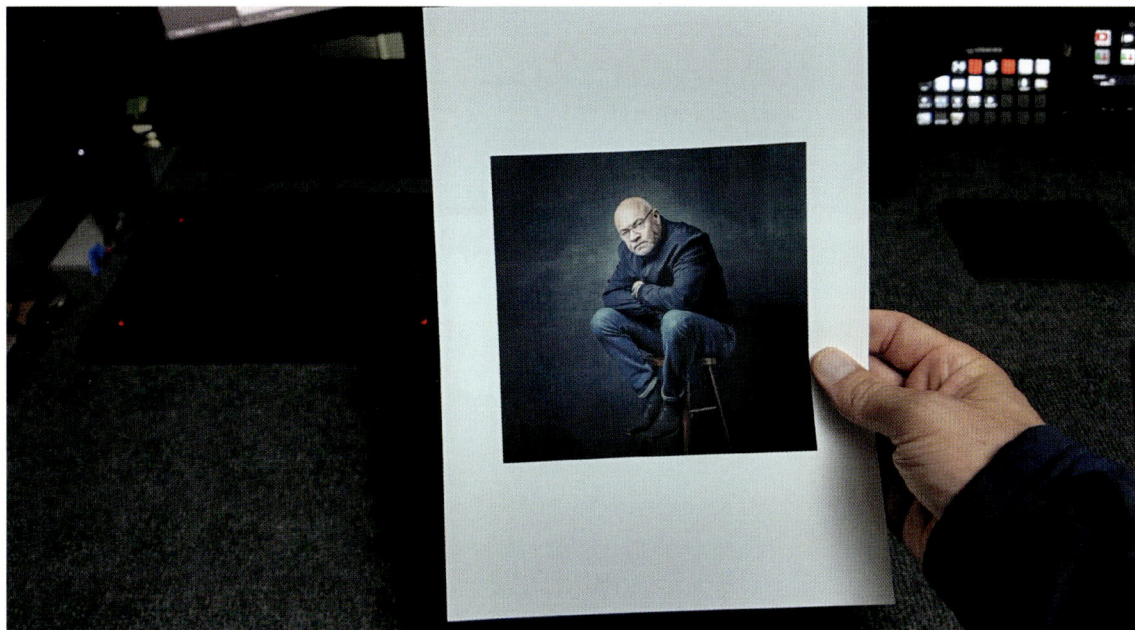

FIGURE 11.15

This underscores a key point: Sometimes, despite following all best practices, you may get better results by simply allowing the printer to handle color management, particularly when working within Lightroom Classic. It's a reminder that consistency and quality can depend not just on the software and settings, but also on the interaction between the printer, the driver, and the chosen media.

PRINTING A BLACK-AND-WHITE IMAGE FROM LIGHTROOM CLASSIC

Now let's take a look at printing a black-and-white image using Lightroom Classic.

In this case, the expectation is that the print will turn out better than the earlier color print. The key reason for this is that instead of using an ICC profile, the printer's Advanced B&W Photo mode will be used. This mode is designed specifically for monochrome printing and often delivers better tonal consistency and control.

PREPARING THE IMAGE AND SETTINGS

The image selected for this print has already been retouched, soft proofed, and resized, so it's fully prepared and ready for output **(Figure 11.16)**.

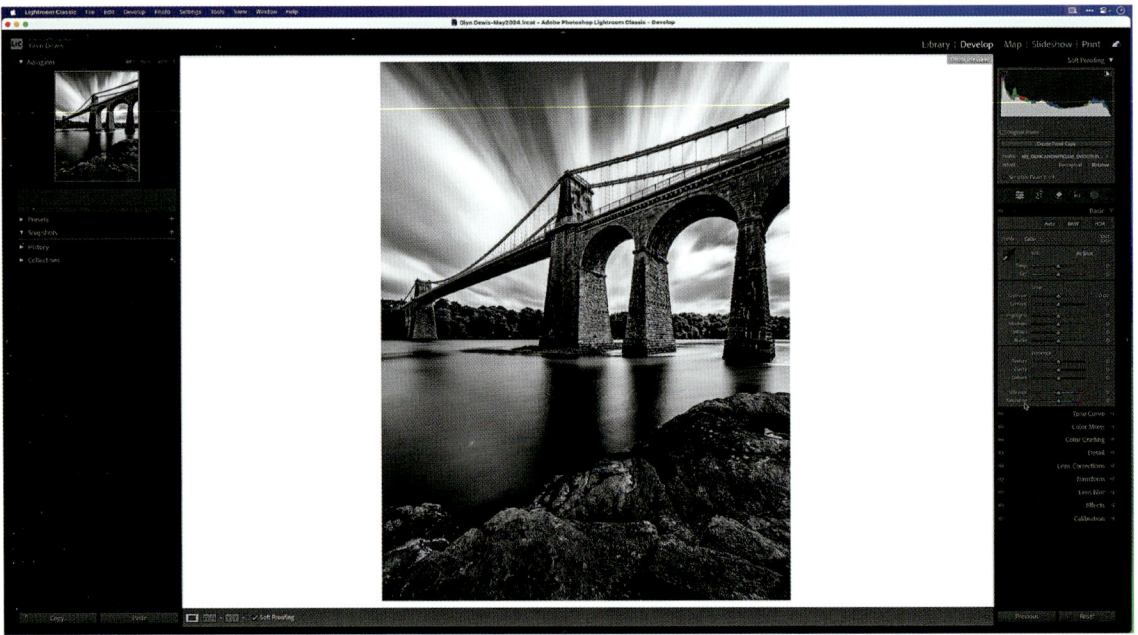

FIGURE 11.16

Since this is a black-and-white print, the only setting that needs to be changed compared to the color print workflow is in the **Color Management** section. Here, I'll switch the setting to **Managed by Printer**, which is essential when using the printer's dedicated Advanced B&W Photo mode **(Figure 11.17)**.

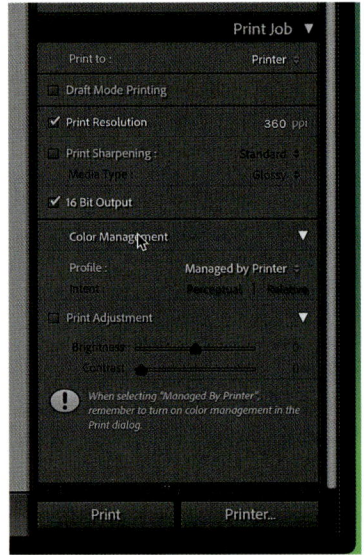

FIGURE 11.17

CONFIGURING THE PRINTER DRIVER

After adjusting the Color Management setting, the next step is to click on **Printer** to access the printer driver.

Inside the driver interface, the first task is to verify that the correct printer is selected.

From there, navigation continues to the **Printer Options** section. In **Color Matching**, since this print is being sent to an Epson printer, I'll change the setting to **Epson Color Controls (Figure 11.18)**.

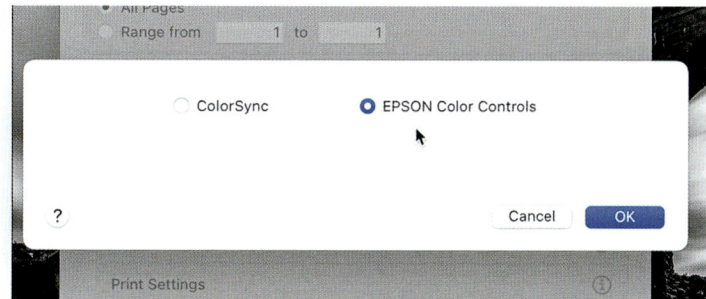

FIGURE 11.18

In the **Print Settings**, I'll confirm that the **Media Type** is set to **Epson Archival Matte Paper**, consistent with previous examples.

However, a key difference in this setup is found in the **Color** section, where I'll switch the setting to **Advanced B&W Photo** mode.

For this particular print, I'll set **Color Toning** to **Neutral**, which helps preserve a clean, balanced monochrome output. And I'll leave **Print Quality** at its default value of **1440 DPI (Figure 11.19)**.

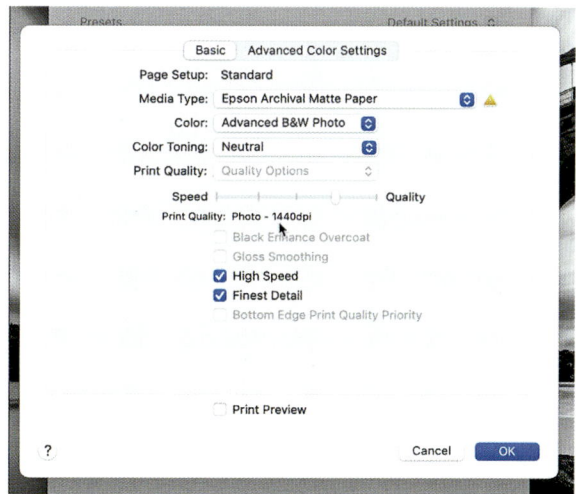

FIGURE 11.19

FINAL OUTPUT AND EVALUATION

With all settings in place, the final step is to click **OK** and then **Print**.

The resulting print is excellent **(Figure 11.20)**. The detail is exceptional, sharpness is crisp, and the overall contrast is rich and well-balanced. Every tonal transition looks natural, and there are no unwanted tints or color shifts.

This print confirms that Lightroom Classic, when paired with the printer's Advanced B&W Photo mode, can produce outstanding results, especially when ICC profiles are removed from the equation.

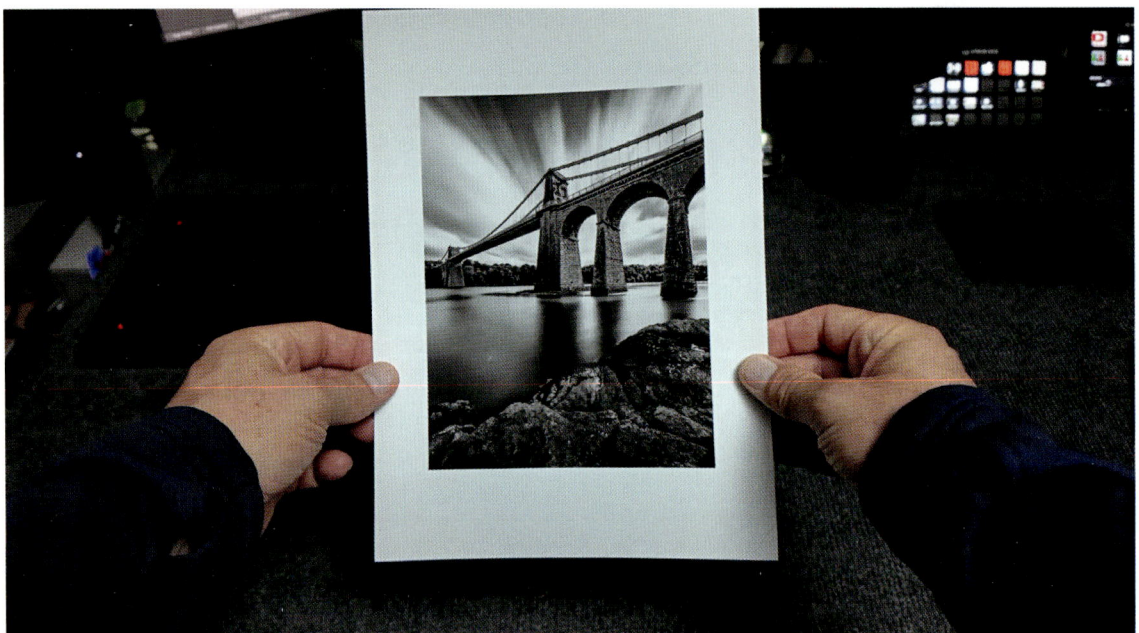

FIGURE 11.20

PRINTING A COLOR IMAGE WITH EPSON PRINT LAYOUT

The **Epson Print Layout** software offers a simple yet powerful interface for producing high-quality prints with minimal fuss.

In this example, the process begins by opening the application and navigating to **File > Open** to select the image for printing **(Figure 11.21)**. The image has already been retouched, soft proofed, and resized to print at **360 pixels per inch**, as it will be sent to the Epson P900 printer.

Upon clicking **Browse**, the image appears in the **filmstrip at the bottom** of the interface. Additional images can also be added, each placed on a new page. For the purposes of this demonstration, a second image is removed by right-clicking on it and selecting Eject, followed by closing the filmstrip to focus on the active image.

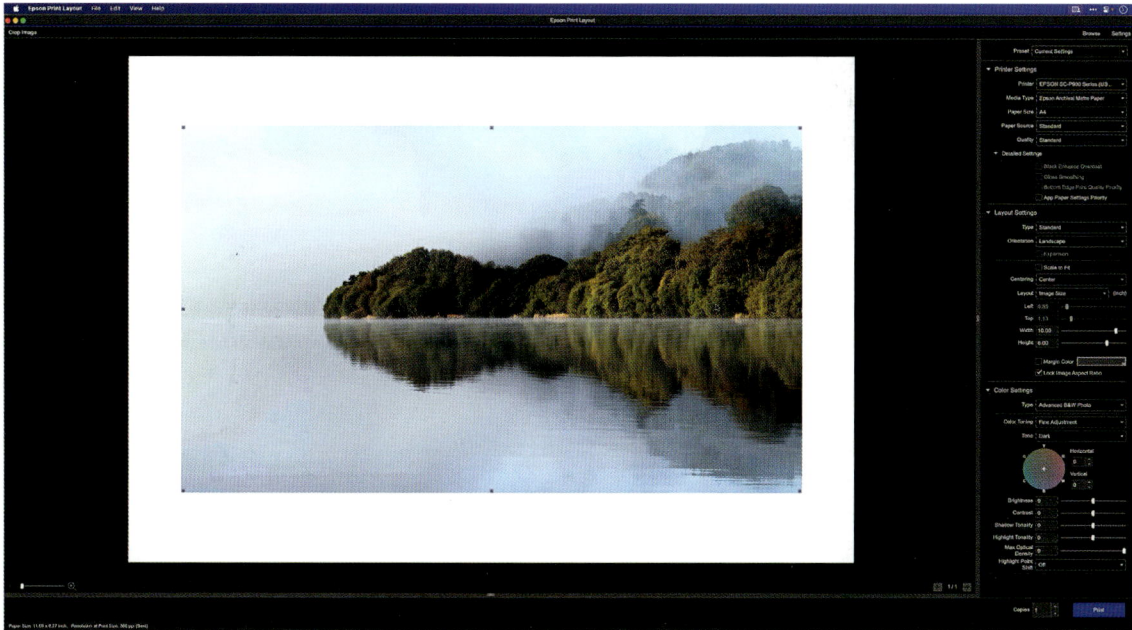

FIGURE 11.21

IMAGE SETUP AND LAYOUT OPTIONS

The image now appears centered on the page and has been imported at its original dimensions of **10 inches by 6 inches**.

At the top of the panels on the right side of the interface are options that allow for configuring the key Printer Settings **(Figure 11.22)**. First, the printer is selected—in this case, the Epson P900—followed by the **Media Type**, which is set to **Epson Archival Matte Paper**.

Because Epson paper is being used with an Epson printer, there is no need for an **ICC profile**. I'll set the **paper size** to **A4**, with the **Paper Source** as **Standard**, and I'll leave the print **Quality** at **Standard** as well.

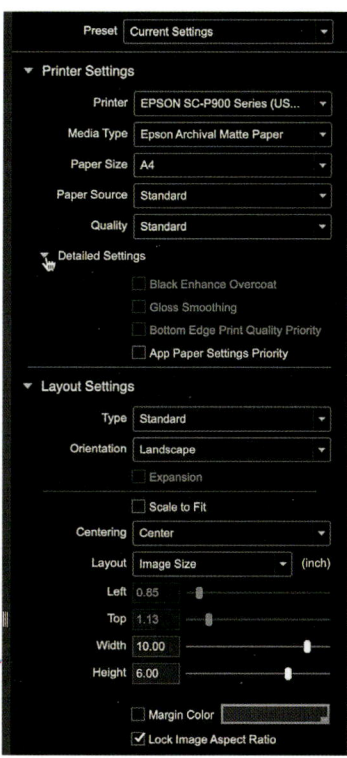

FIGURE 11.22

COLOR MANAGEMENT SETTINGS

Further down, layout and orientation settings determine how the image sits on the page. However, the most critical section is **Color Settings (Figure 11.23)**.

Under the **Type** setting, I'll change the default from **Use ICC Profile** to **Printer Manages Color**, aligning with the decision not to use a custom profile for this print.

For the **Mode**, I'll select **Adobe RGB** to maintain wide color gamut support.

That's it—no complicated steps, no additional adjustments; just a straightforward and efficient setup.

Once all settings are in place, clicking **Print** sends the image to the printer.

FINAL PRINT QUALITY

The resulting print is superb **(Figure 11.24)**. Although you're seeing this printed on a page of a book, I have to say that the physical output looks fantastic in real life. The colors are rich, detail is sharp, and the tonal balance is spot-on.

What's most impressive is the simplicity of the process—minimal steps, minimal decisions, and a maximum-quality result. It's a reminder of just how user-friendly and effective Epson's proprietary printing software can be.

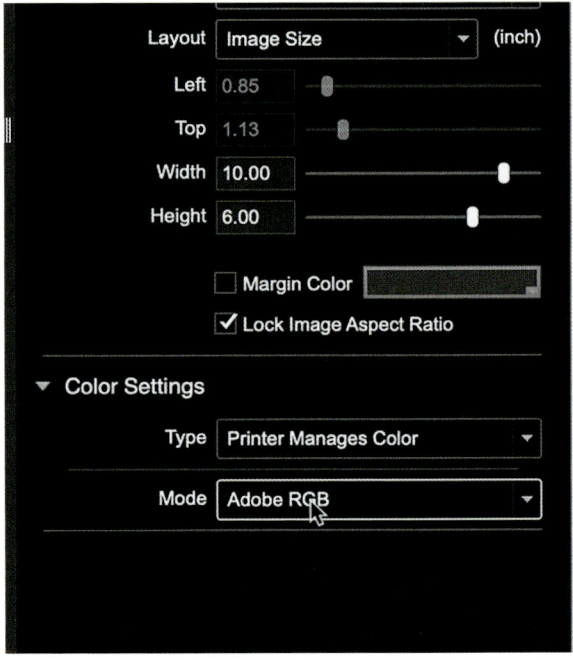

FIGURE 11.23

PRINTING A BLACK-AND-WHITE IMAGE WITH EPSON PRINT LAYOUT

Among all the printing workflows available, using **Epson Print Layout** software to create black-and-white prints is a personal favorite. The process is not only simple and efficient, but it also delivers exceptional tonal control and image quality.

The photograph chosen for this next print is a square-format image captured from underneath the Prince of Wales Bridge, looking toward Wales from the English side **(Figure 11.25)**. The image has already been retouched, soft proofed, and resized to **6 inches by 6 inches** at **360 pixels per inch**, specifically for output on an Epson printer.

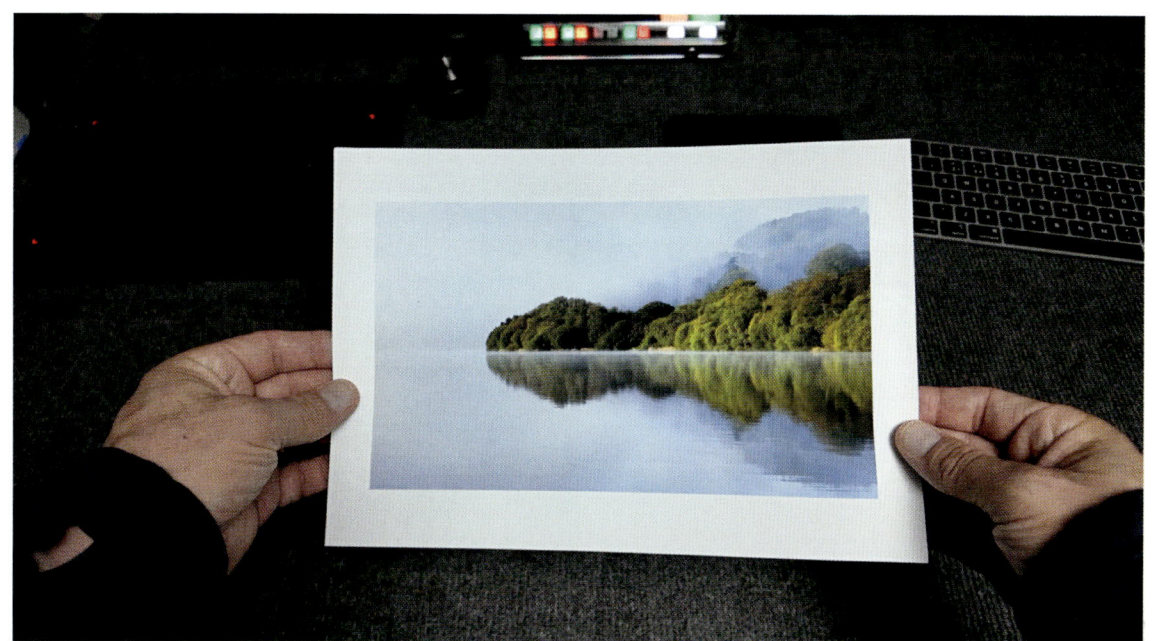

FIGURE 11.24

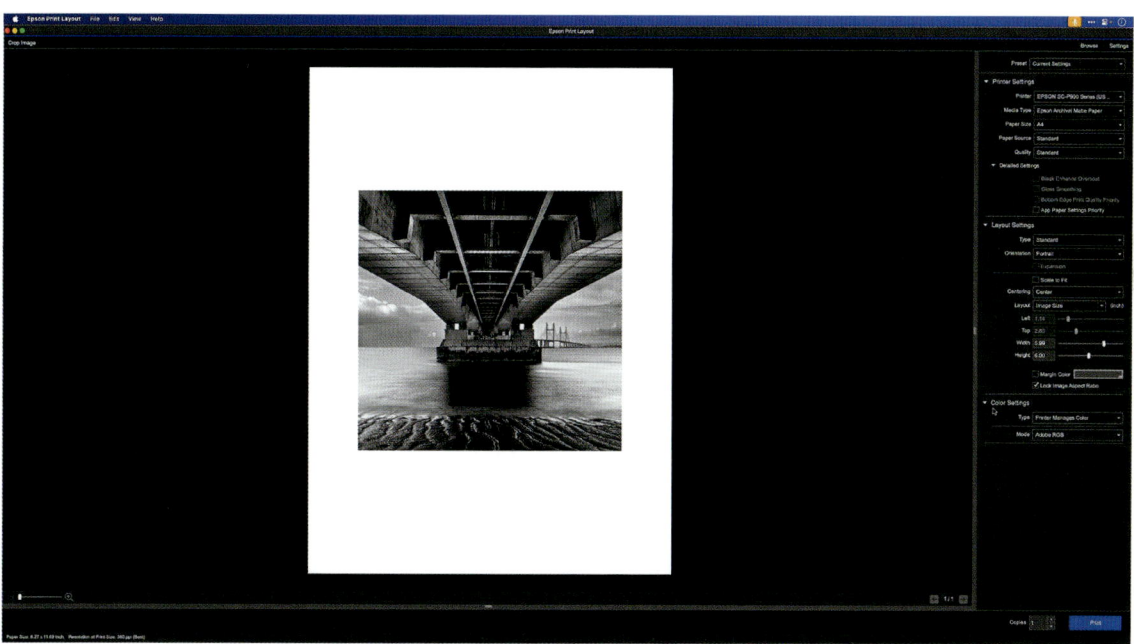

FIGURE 11.25

INITIAL SETUP AND MEDIA SELECTION

On the right side of the Epson Print Layout interface, the key settings begin with selecting the correct **Printer (Figure 11.26)**. The **Media Type** should be set to **Epson Archival Matte Paper**, consistent with previous examples.

The **Paper Size** is **A4**, the **Paper Source** is **Standard**, and the print **Quality** is left at **Standard**. These are simple but reliable defaults that provide excellent results.

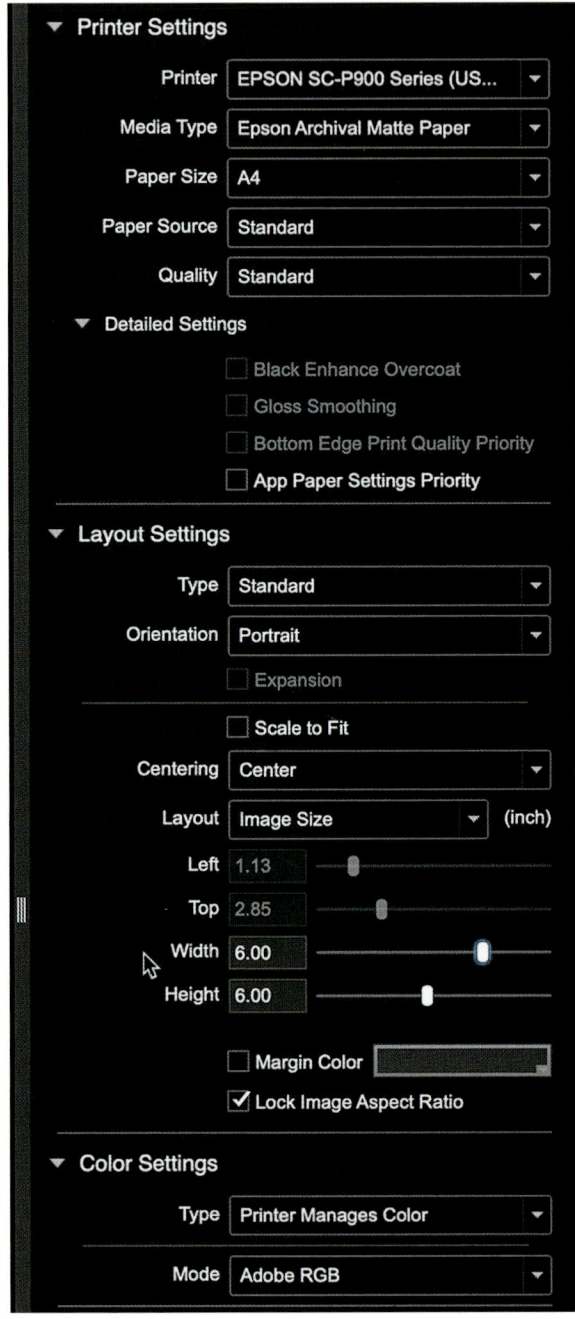

FIGURE 11.26

USING EPSON'S ADVANCED BLACK AND WHITE MODE

The real power of Epson's black-and-white workflow lies in the **Color Settings** section. Under **Type**, I'll change the setting to **Advanced B&W Photo (Figure 11.27)**. This mode offers intuitive yet powerful tools to fine-tune the final appearance of the black-and-white image.

One of the most useful features is **Color Toning**, which allows for the application of subtle tonal shifts such as cool, warm, or sepia tones. However, for this print, the aim is to produce a neutral, pure black and white output, so I'll select **Neutral**.

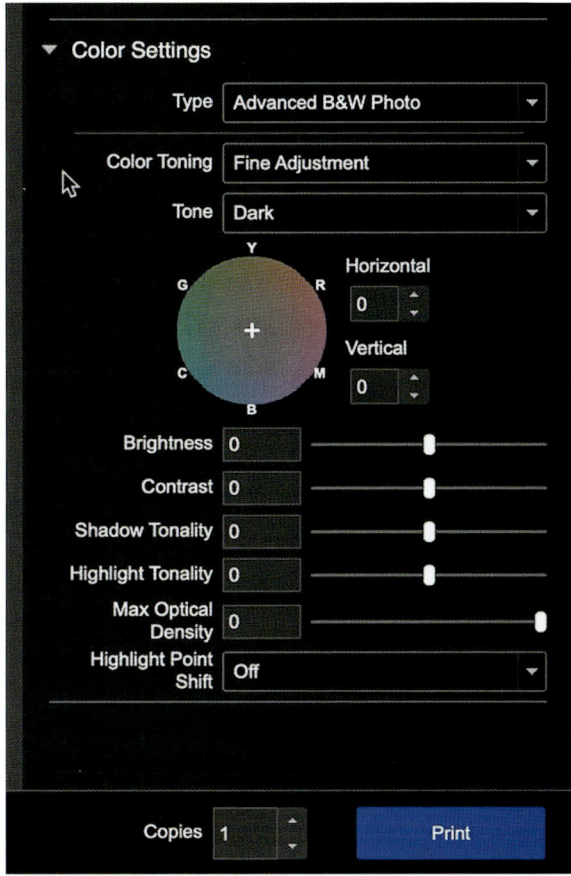

FIGURE 11.27

Another key adjustment is **Tone**, which controls the overall darkness of the print, from **Light** to **Darkest**. For this particular image, I'll choose **Dark**. The live preview confirms that this choice enhances the image's presence without losing detail. Additional fine-tuning controls are available, but in most cases, including this one, I leave them untouched.

FINAL OUTPUT AND EVALUATION

With all settings confirmed, clicking **Print** sends the image to the printer.

The result is outstanding **(Figure 11.28)**. The dark toning works beautifully, providing rich depth without overwhelming the shadows. There is excellent detail retention, strong sharpness, and impressive contrast throughout the image. Most importantly, the brightness is exactly as intended; no adjustments are needed post-print.

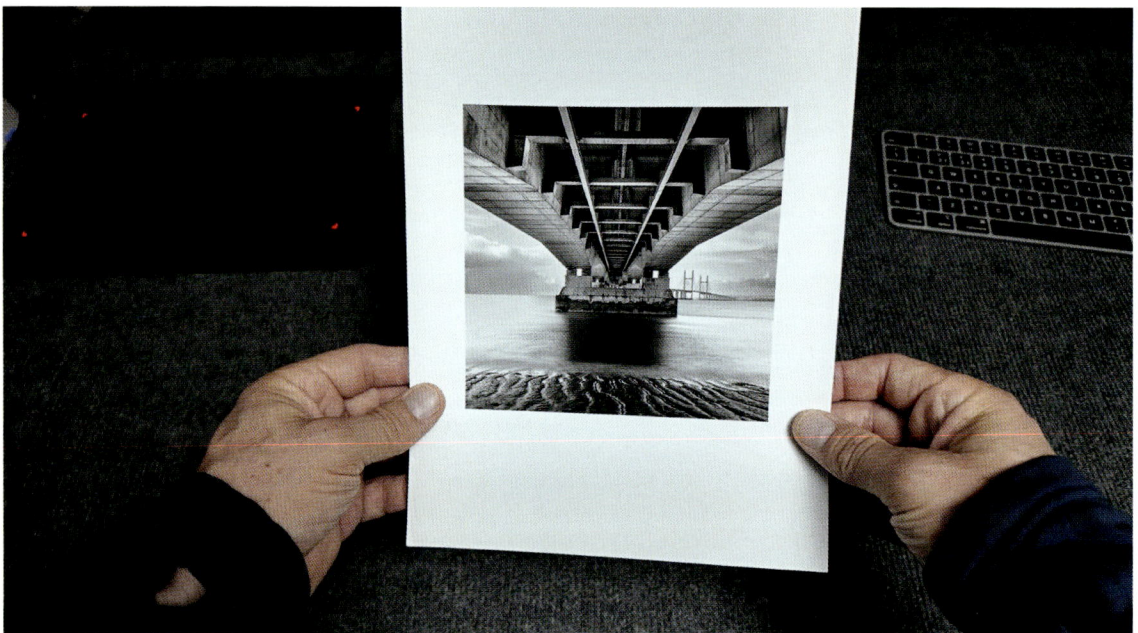

FIGURE 11.28

This example reinforces why Epson's Advanced B&W Photo mode is such a valuable tool. It offers enough control to tailor the output to your taste while remaining streamlined and intuitive.

PRINTING A COLOR IMAGE WITH CANON PROFESSIONAL PRINT & LAYOUT

In this section, we'll look at how to print using Canon's own dedicated printing software, **Canon Professional Print & Layout**, which is specifically designed for high-quality output from Canon's newer range of printers. At the time of writing, this software supports models like the **Canon Pro-200**, **Pro-300**, **Pro-100**, and the larger (and older) **Pro-1000**.

For earlier models, Canon offers alternative software such as **Canon Print Studio Pro**, which can be downloaded from the Canon website by selecting the appropriate printer model and operating system.

OPENING AND SETTING UP THE IMAGE

With **Canon Professional Print & Layout** open, the process begins by going to **File** > **Open** to load an image that has already been retouched, soft proofed, and resized. For this print, I chose an image I captured during a road trip in Wales **(Figure 11.29)**.

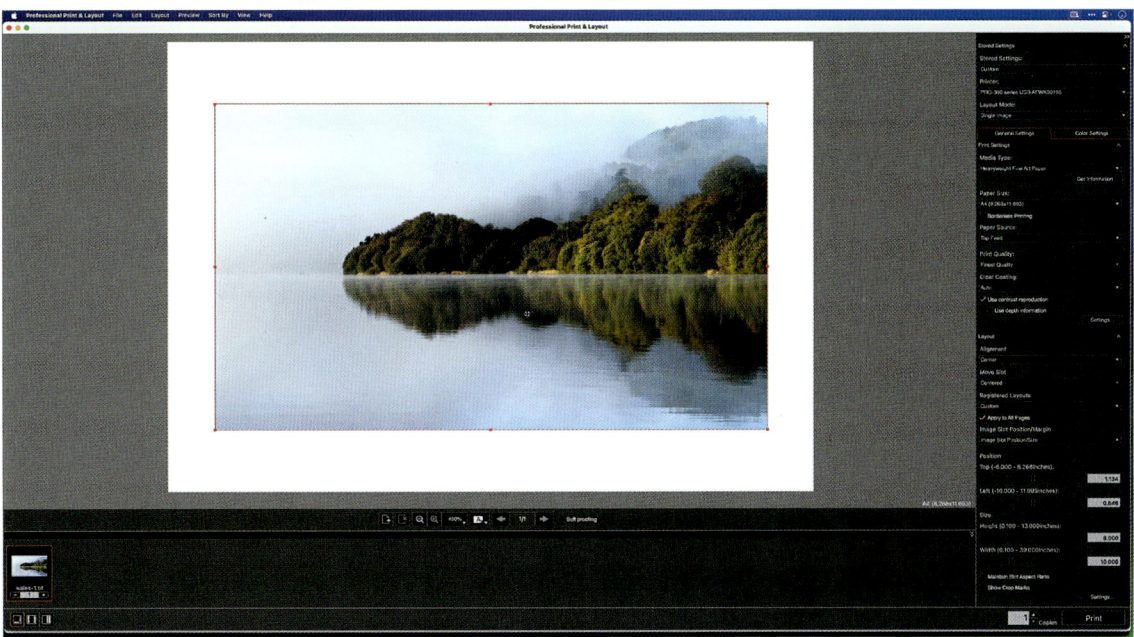

FIGURE 11.29

Once imported, the image appears in the filmstrip at the bottom of the interface. From there, it can be dragged onto the paper area, where it is centered and retains its resized dimensions of **10 inches by 6 inches** at **300 pixels per inch**, optimized for printing with Canon hardware.

PRINTER AND MEDIA CONFIGURATION

At the top-right of the interface, the **Stored Settings** menu allows users to save frequently used combinations of settings, making repeat jobs easier. For this print, the selected **Printer** is the **Canon Pro-300**, and I've set the **Layout Mode** to **Single Image**. Other layout options, such as **Multiple Images** and **Gallery Wrap**, are also available.

Under the **General Settings** tab, the **Media Type** is selected based on the paper in use, which in this case is PermaJet Smooth Rag, and the recommended Canon media type for this paper is **Heavyweight Fine Art Paper (Figure 11.30)**.

I'll set the **Paper Size** to **A4**, and the **Paper Source** to **Top Feed**.

The **Print Quality** automatically defaults to **Finest Quality**, based on the printer-paper combination.

ADVANCED PRINT FEATURES

I'll enable the **Clear Coating** option and set it to **Auto**. Canon describes this feature as a method for applying Chroma Optimizer ink to improve surface uniformity and reduce gloss variation, which is particularly beneficial when using pigment inks.

I'll also activate two additional features, **Use Contrast Reproduction** and **Use Depth Information**. The first restores sharpness potentially lost during data transfer to the printer. The second uses embedded depth information (such as from Dual Pixel RAW files) to optimize sharpness and depth in the final print.

COLOR MANAGEMENT SETTINGS

As this print is being made on non-Canon paper and contains color, an ICC profile is required. Under **Color Mode**, I'll select **Use ICC Profile** and choose the appropriate profile from the **Printer Profile** list **(Figure 11.31)**.

I'll set the **Rendering Intent** to **Perceptual**, which is ideal for maintaining visual consistency in complex tonal areas. **Use Black Point Compensation** is also checked—though it has no effect when using Perceptual, it's left enabled by default.

There are also options to include photo information, headers, or footers in the print, though I'm not using any in this case.

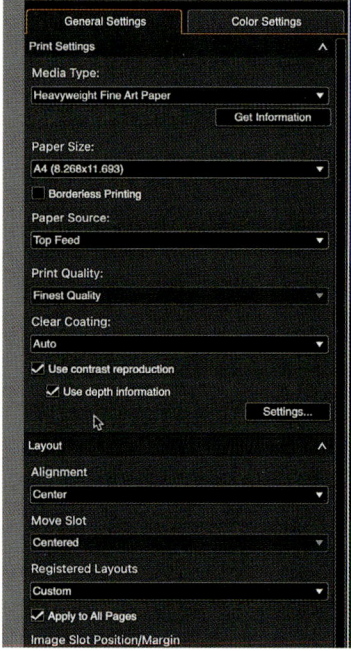

FIGURE 11.30

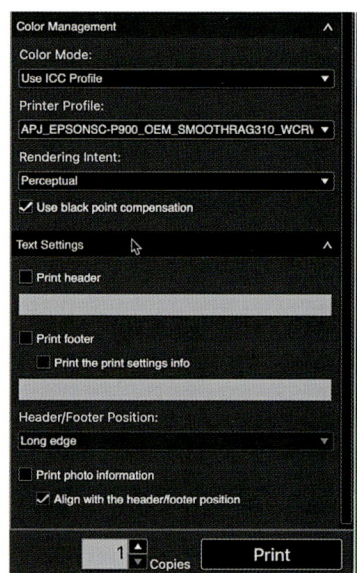

FIGURE 11.31

OPTIONAL COLOR ADJUSTMENTS AND PATTERN PRINTING

Canon Professional Print & Layout also includes a **Color Settings** tab. While not typically used, since soft proofing should already have been performed, this tab allows users to adjust image color manually.

One tool here is **Pattern Print**, which generates a grid of thumbnail previews with varying levels of cyan and magenta adjustment **(Figure 11.32)**. This is useful for visualizing how slight changes will affect the print before committing, although for color-critical workflows, soft proofing remains the more accurate and controlled approach.

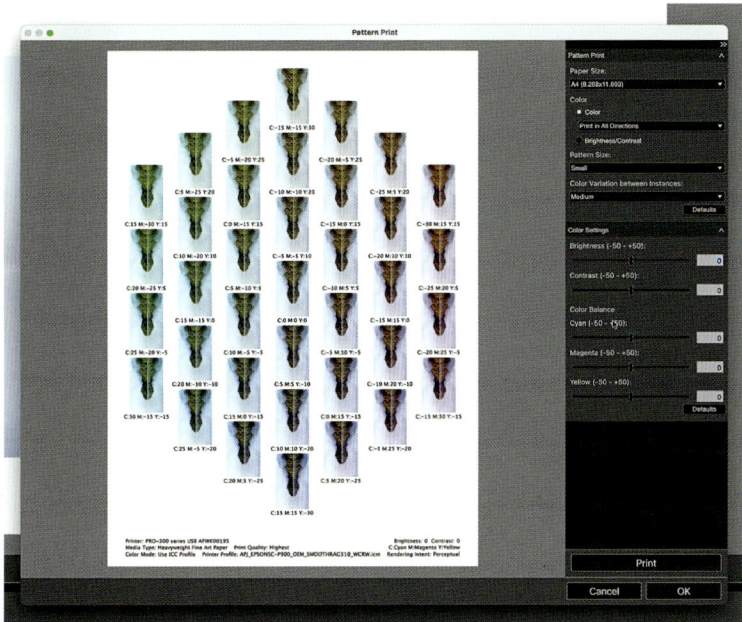

FIGURE 11.32

FINALIZING AND PRINTING

Clicking **Print** brings up a summary of the print settings for final review.

With all selections verified, I'll confirm the job by clicking **OK**.

> **NOTE:** *Although both Canon and Epson printers feature on-device menus for configuring paper settings, these are overridden by the software's settings. There is no need to manually set paper types on the printer itself when printing from Canon's dedicated software.*

OUTPUT QUALITY AND FINAL THOUGHTS

The resulting print is excellent **(Figure 11.33)**. The colors are true to the soft proofed file, the contrast and sharpness are exceptional (particularly impressive for a matte paper), and the brightness is exactly as intended.

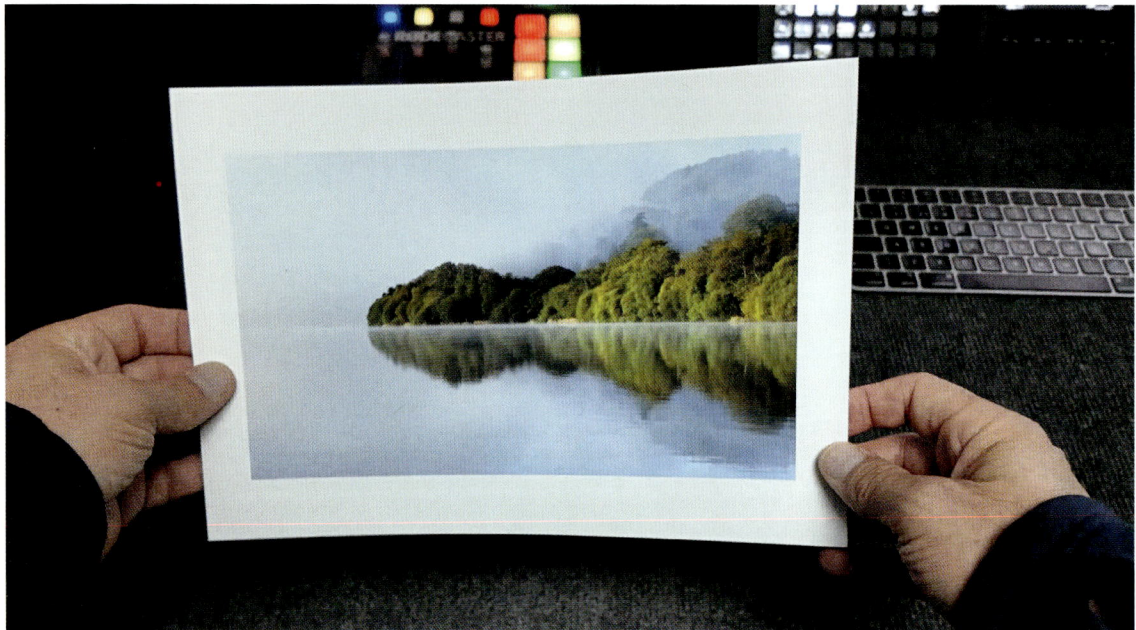

FIGURE 11.33

This highlights what makes Canon's proprietary printing software so reliable: it's a streamlined, intuitive interface that still offers deep control where needed, resulting in predictable, high-quality output every time.

PRINTING A BLACK-AND-WHITE IMAGE WITH CANON PROFESSIONAL PRINT & LAYOUT

Next I'll do a black-and-white print using **Canon Professional Print & Layout** software, paired with **PermaJet Smooth Rag** paper. This time, I won't use an ICC profile. Instead, the print relies on Canon's own **Black and White Photo** mode, a setting that orchestrates tonal precision and eliminates the possibility of color tints.

The image selected for this print has been fully prepared, retouched, soft proofed, and resized **(Figure 11.34)**.

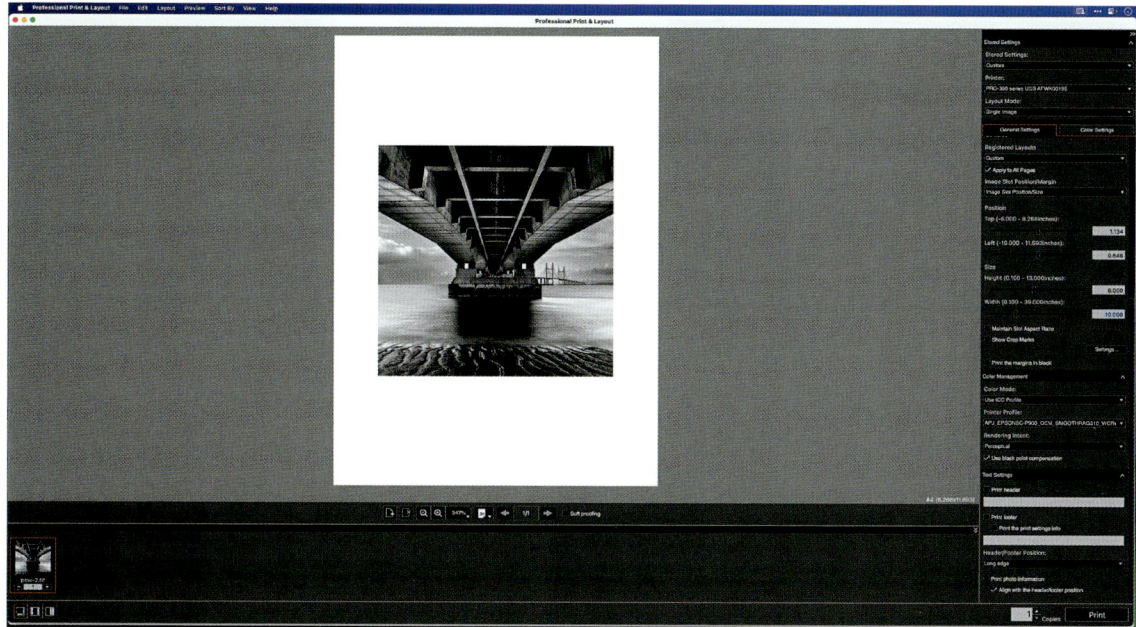

FIGURE 11.34

SETTING THE STAGE IN CANON PROFESSIONAL PRINT & LAYOUT

The settings on the right-hand panel remain largely the same as for previous prints. The printer is again the Canon Pro-300, with the **Media Type** correctly matched to the Smooth Rag paper, and the **Paper Size** set to **A4**.

Both **Use Contrast Reproduction** and **Use Depth Information** are enabled. These options help ensure the finest reproduction of sharpness and depth.

SWITCHING TO BLACK AND WHITE PHOTO MODE

In the **Color Management** section, I'll change the **Color Mode** from **Use ICC Profile** to **Black and White Photo** (Figure 11.35). The **Printer Profile**, **Rendering Intent**, and **Use Black Point Compensation** options are instantly disabled, which serves to simplify the process, and also guarantees the best possible results by avoiding the application of incorrect settings.

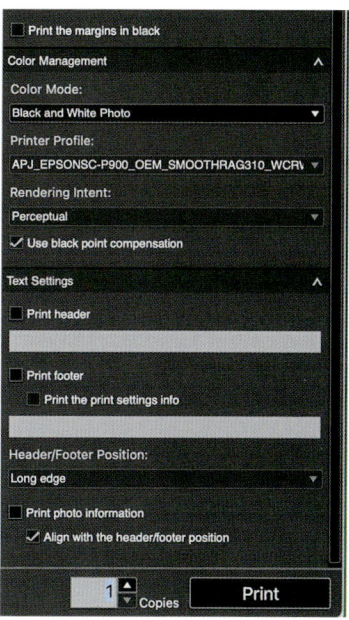

FIGURE 11.35

THE FINAL PRINT AND ITS REMARKABLE OUTCOME

With all settings confirmed, the final step is to click **Print**.

The result? Superb! Deep blacks, subtle gradients, and razor-sharp detail **(Figure 11.36)**. Contrast and brightness are perfectly balanced, and the tonal clarity feels both natural and deliberate.

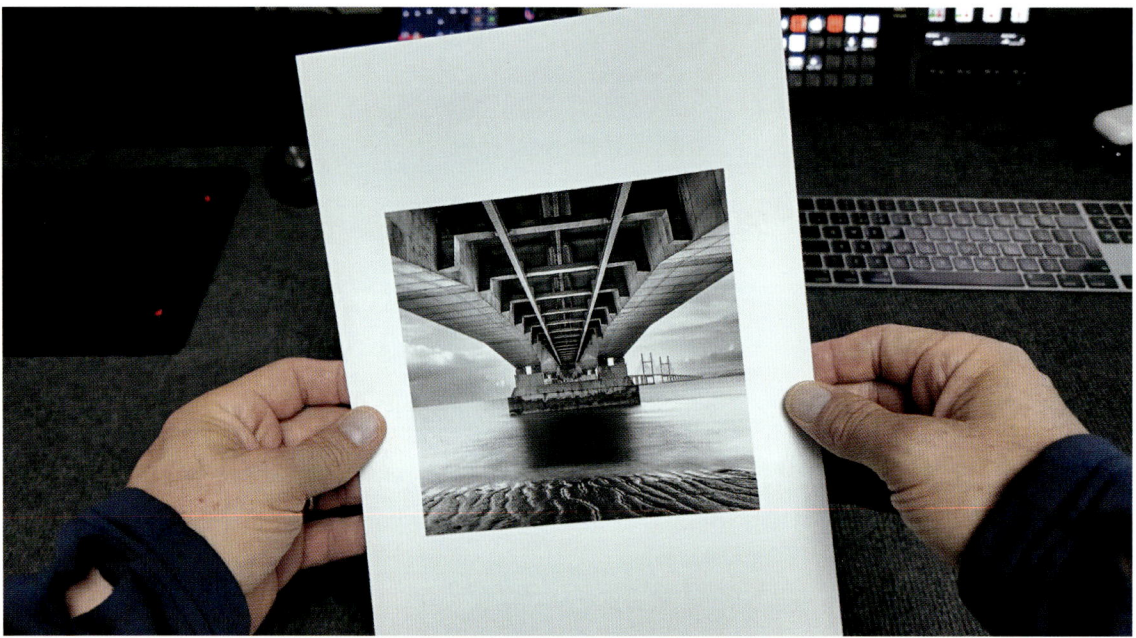

FIGURE 11.36

PRINTING WITH QIMAGE ONE: A POWERFUL, CROSS-PLATFORM SOLUTION

Now let's explore **Qimage One**, a piece of software dedicated solely to printing. One of its stand-out features is its cross-platform compatibility, making it a practical choice for both Windows and Mac users. Despite its deep functionality, the overall printing experience remains streamlined and straightforward—an ideal combination that explains its growing popularity among photographers.

Upon opening the software, the left-hand side allows users to navigate to the folders where their images are stored. For those who prefer an integrated workflow, Qimage One can also operate as a plugin, enabling images to be sent directly from Lightroom Classic or Photoshop, but in this case, I'll be using the software in standalone mode.

EXPLORING LAYOUT OPTIONS

On the right side of the interface, you'll find familiar settings: printer selection, media type, paper size, and more. Before diving into those, it's helpful to look at the layout tools available **(Figure 11.37)**. The white central area represents the page layout, set here to **A4**.

To begin, a single image is selected from the left. Once selected, the **Print Size** section appears, offering predefined sizes that can be clicked to automatically place the image on the page. If a different size is needed, simply clicking that new size adds a duplicate of the image in the new dimensions. Images are automatically arranged to optimize space, and users can manually reposition, overlap, or reorder them as desired.

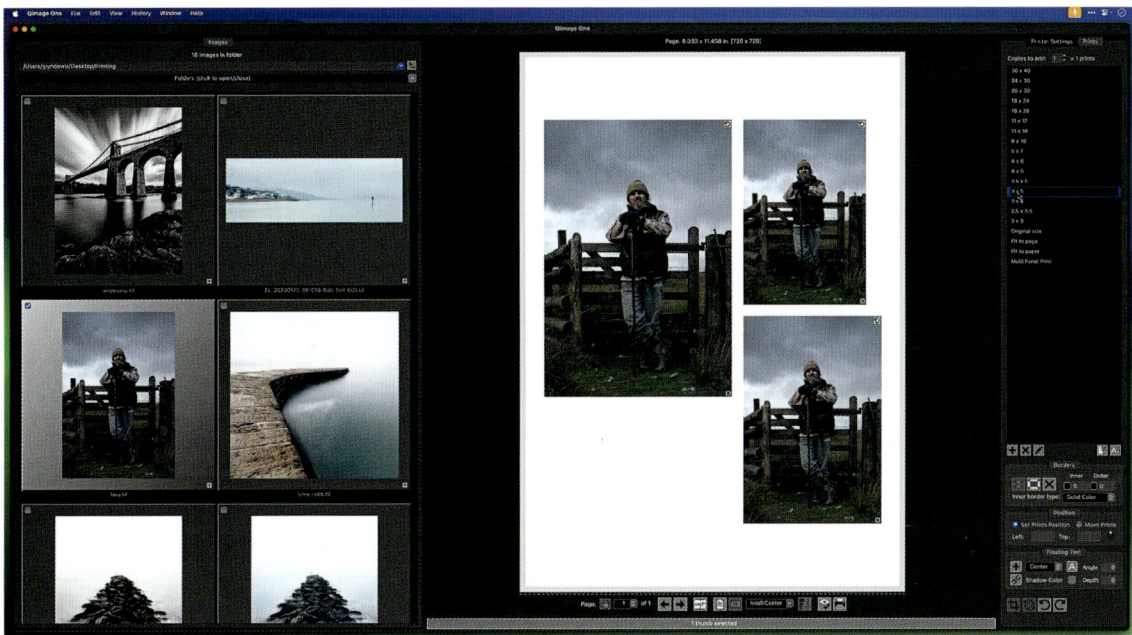

FIGURE 11.37

If a selected size doesn't fit the current page layout, the software will automatically generate a second page. To remove an image, simply click the **X** in its bottom-right corner.

This functionality extends to printing multiple images on the same page or across multiple pages by selecting additional images and applying the same method. If the required size isn't listed, custom sizes can be created by clicking on the + icon below the list of sizes, and then entering your custom size in the dialog that appears **(Figure 11.38)**.

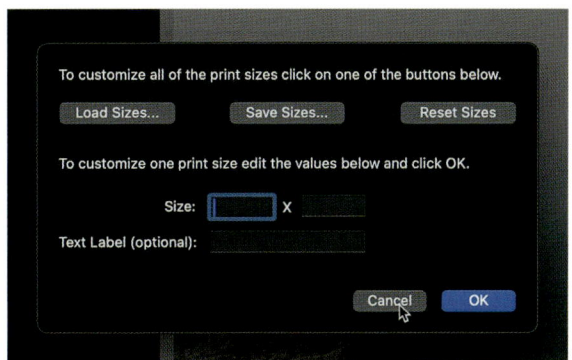

FIGURE 11.38

Qimage One also offers layout enhancements, such as adding borders and custom text. However, when it comes to image resizing, the software uses its own proprietary interpolation method to optimize for both enlargements and reductions. While it performs well, it's still recommended to resize images beforehand, so you're confident in the final composition.

PRINTING A COLOR IMAGE

To go through the process I'll print a color image of my friend Foxy that has already been resized and ready to go. Clicking **Original Size** adds it to the layout. The image can be manually repositioned, but in this case, it remains centered **(Figure 11.39)**.

Next, I'll configure the **Printer Settings** section **(Figure 11.40)**. I'll be using the **Canon Pro-300** printer and **Canon Photo Paper Pro Platinum** paper, and I'll set the **Media Type** accordingly.

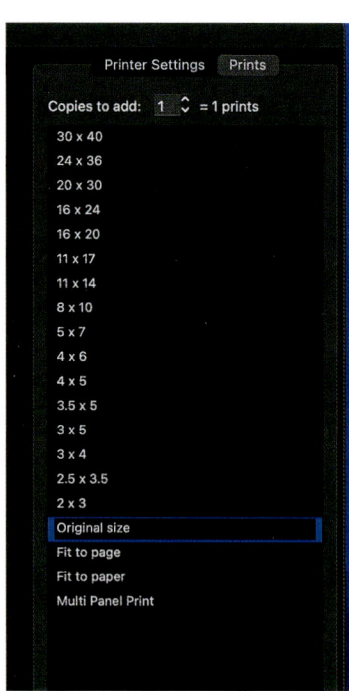

FIGURE 11.39

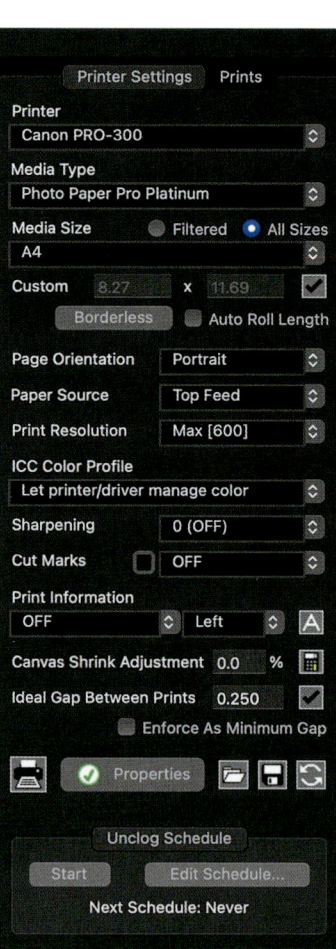

FIGURE 11.40

PRINTER AND OUTPUT CONFIGURATION

I'll set **Media Size** to **A4**, **Page Orientation** to **Portrait**, and **Paper Source** to **Top Feed**. The **Print Resolution** defaults to **600 DPI**, which I'll leave as-is, even though additional settings are available.

For **Color Management**, since I'm using Canon-branded paper with a Canon printer, I'll set ICC **Color Profile** to **Let Printer/Driver Manage Color**. If I were using a third-party paper, I'd select the appropriate **ICC profile** instead.

No sharpening is applied, as any required adjustments would have already been made in the image preparation stage. Optional settings like cut marks and **print information** can be enabled, but I'll leave them off for this print.

Next, clicking into **Properties**, under **Color Matching**, I'll select **Canon Color Matching (Figure 11.41)**. This ensures color management is handled correctly by the printer driver. On Windows, color management would need to be manually disabled if using an ICC profile.

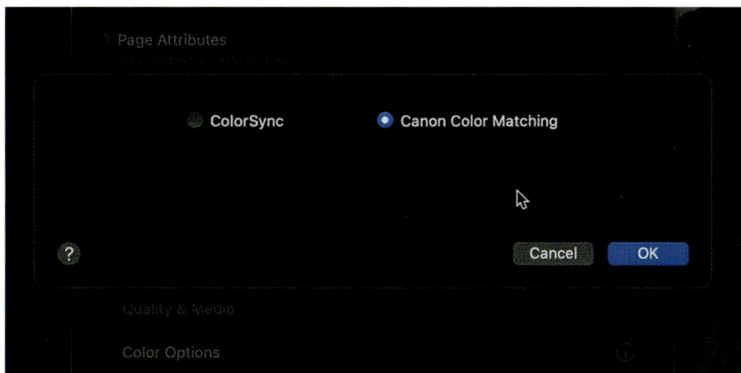

FIGURE 11.41

Under **Quality and Media**, I'll confirm the correct paper and leave all remaining settings as-is. After reviewing everything, I'll click **OK** to confirm.

FINAL PRINT AND RESULT

And that's it. Press **Print**.

The final print is then produced, and the result is exactly as expected—spot on **(Figure 11.42)**. The colors are accurate and the overall quality is excellent, reaffirming Qimage One's status as a reliable and capable printing platform.

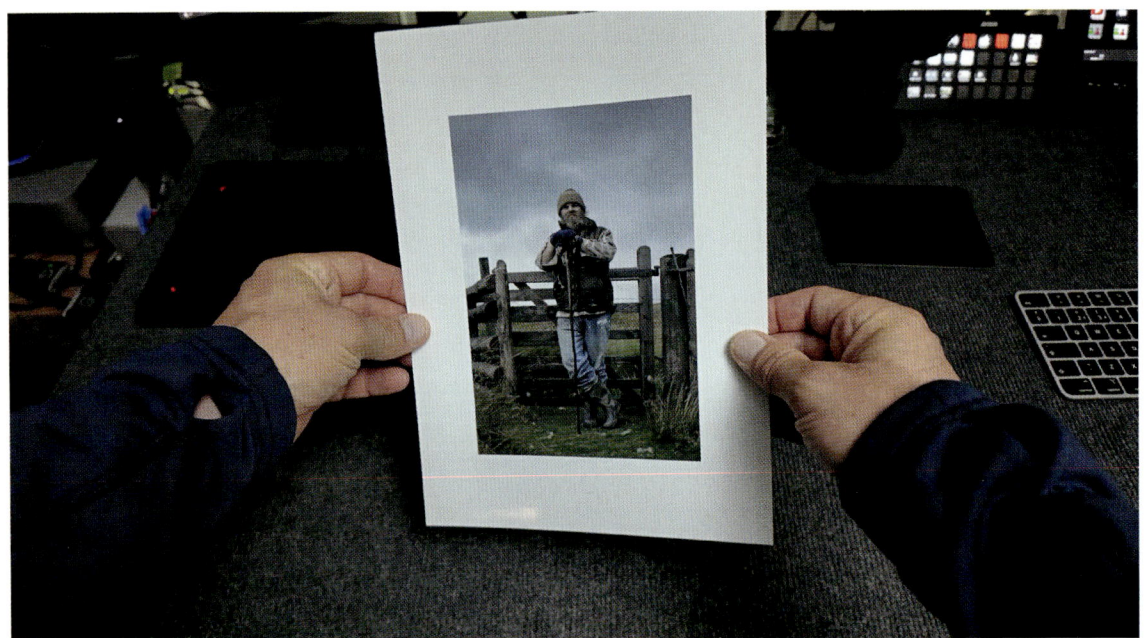

FIGURE 11.42

BLACK-AND-WHITE PRINTING WITH QIMAGE ONE

To create a black-and-white print using **Qimage One**, I'll use picture of the **Prince of Wales Bridge** that I captured with my iPhone. Once selected from the left-hand panel, I'll add the image to the layout by clicking **Original Size**, as it has already been resized in advance. The image is then automatically centered on the page **(Figure 11.43)**.

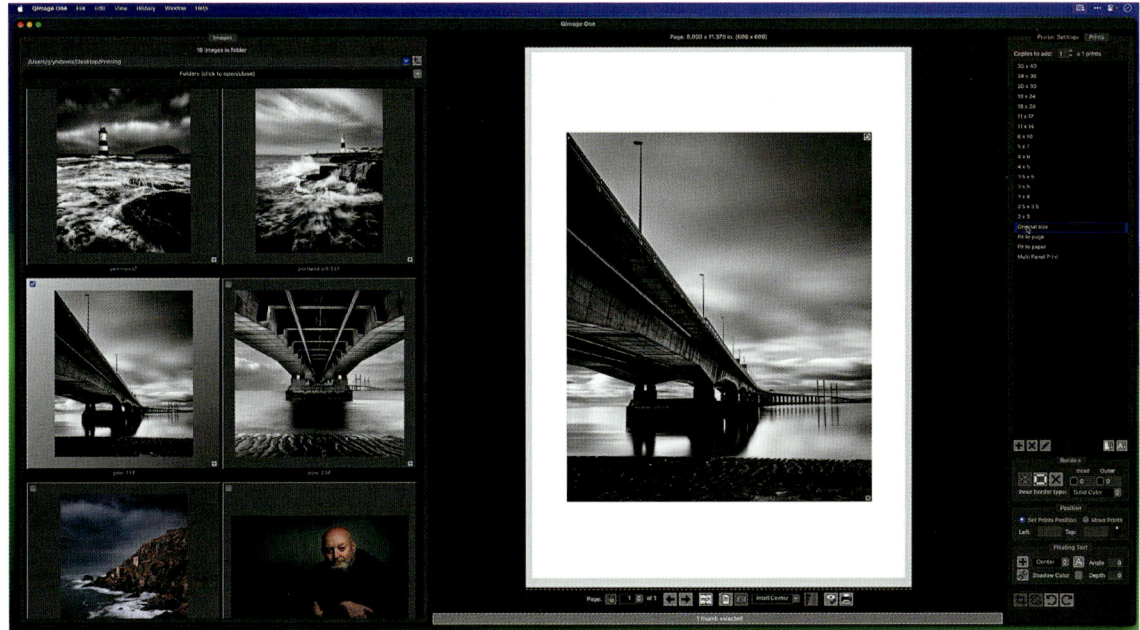

FIGURE 11.43

SETTING UP PRINT CONFIGURATION

With the image in place, the next step is to open the **Printer Settings** panel **(Figure 11.44)**. I'll select the **Canon Pro-300** printer and **Canon Photo Paper Pro Platinum** paper, sized to **A4**. I'll leave the remaining settings at their default values, which are already well-suited for high-quality output on this media.

I will give special attention to the ICC profile section. Since this is a black-and-white print, I plan to use Canon's dedicated **Black and White Photo Print** mode instead of an ICC profile. This ensures a neutral grayscale image with no risk of unwanted green or magenta tinting, which can sometimes occur when relying on color-managed ICC workflows for monochrome prints. As a result, I'll select **Let Printer/Driver Manage Color** to hand control over to the printer.

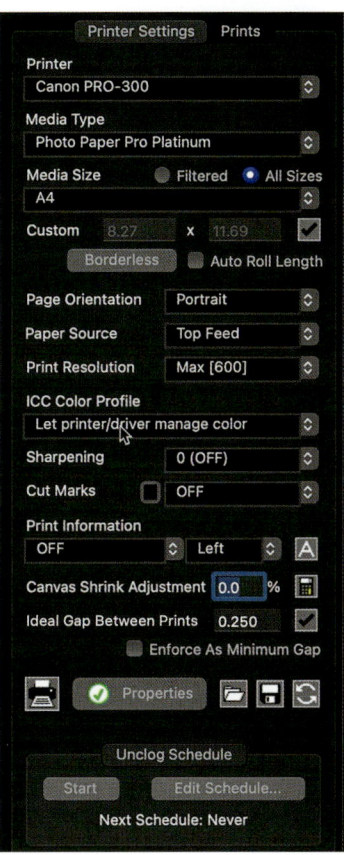

FIGURE 11.44

PRINTER DRIVER PROPERTIES

Moving into the **Properties** dialog, I'll review the **Color Matching** setting. I confirm this is set to **Canon Color Matching**, which is correct for this workflow, and click **OK**.

Next, I'll open the **Quality and Media** section to ensure the correct media type is still selected. The crucial step here is to tick the checkbox for **Black and White Photo Print**, enabling the Canon printer's built-in monochrome mode. Once confirmed, all settings are saved and the dialog is closed.

With everything properly configured, the final step is to click **Print**.

The print is produced shortly afterward, and the result looks great **(Figure 11.45)**.

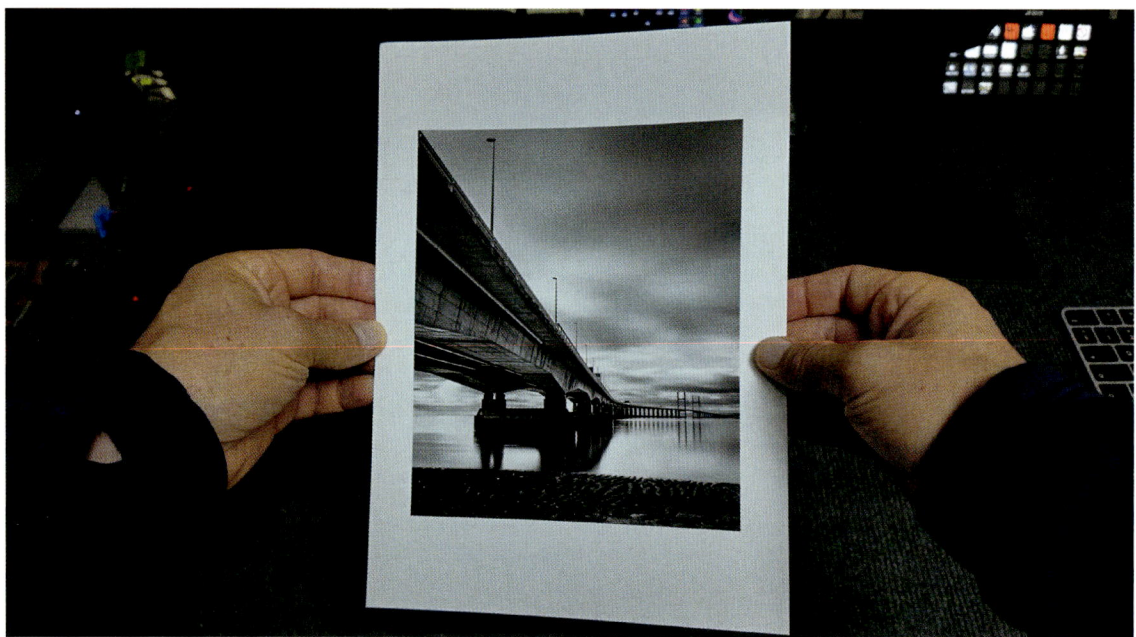

FIGURE 11.45

PRINTING WITH ON1 PHOTO RAW: A FIRST-TIME EXPERIENCE

Regardless of the software being used, printing follows a logical and repeatable process, and ON1 Photo RAW adheres to this well. What stood out to me was the clarity of the interface. Like Qimage One, and especially Canon's and Epson's native software, ON1 offers a no-fuss layout that keeps everything straightforward and accessible.

PREPARING TO PRINT A COLOR IMAGE

Inside ON1 Photo RAW, I began by selecting a color image that I had already soft proofed and resized to print with the Epson P900.

Navigating to **File** > **Print**, a dialog box opened, allowing me to choose between printing to paper or creating a PDF. I left it on **Print to Paper**.

Next, I selected the printer, the paper size, and set the print resolution to 360 pixels per inch, which is the native resolution for the Epson P900 and matches the image's resampled resolution **(Figure 11.46)**.

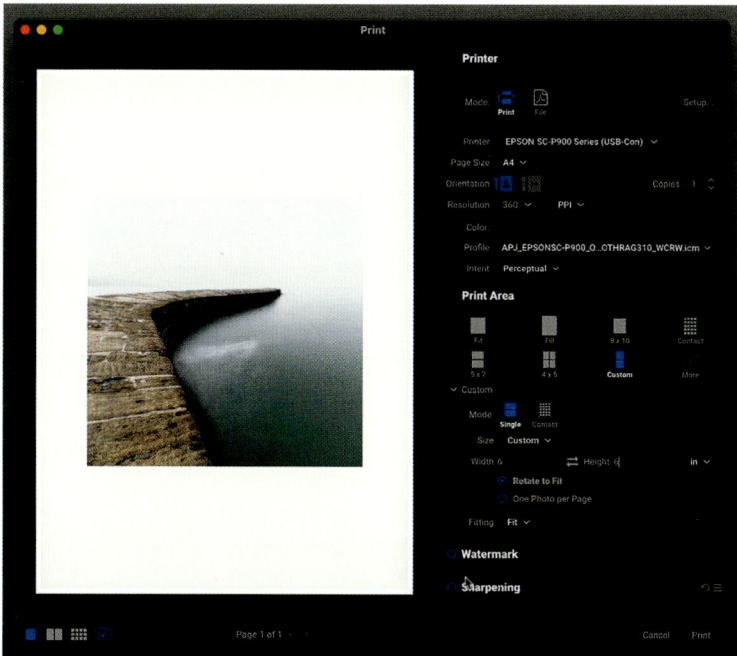

FIGURE 11.46

USING ICC PROFILES AND COLOR MANAGEMENT

Since I was printing on third-party paper (Smooth Rag from PermaJet) I opted to use an ICC profile. Under the **Color** section, I clicked **Import Color Profile**, navigated to the correct file, and imported it. ON1 stores the profile, making it available for future prints. For this job, the proper profile was already installed.

I selected **Perceptual** as the **Rendering Intent**, based on decisions made during soft proofing. The image had been resized to **6 inches by 6 inches**, so no further adjustments were needed at this stage.

OPTIONAL SETTINGS: SHARPENING AND WATERMARKS

Although ON1 offers options to add a watermark or apply print sharpening, I left both turned off. Any sharpening I do is always handled manually after resizing, not at the printing stage.

When sharpening is enabled in ON1, it applies a generic amount based on the paper type, but I prefer to avoid leaving such choices to automatic settings.

PRINTER SETUP AND FINAL ADJUSTMENTS

At the top of the interface, I clicked **Setup** to enter the printer driver settings.

In **Printer Options > Color Matching**, the color management setting was automatically **disabled** (grayed out) as expected on a Mac. On a Windows system, this would have needed to be turned off manually.

In the **Print Settings** section, I selected the appropriate **Media Type**. For PermaJet Smooth Rag, the recommendation is **Epson Watercolor Paper Radiant White**, found under the Fine Art Paper category.

The **Print Quality** defaulted to **1440 DPI**, which I left as-is. With all settings confirmed, I click **OK**, then **Save**, and then **Print**.

FINAL PRINT QUALITY

The result? Perfect **(Figure 11.47)**. The print output was exactly as expected: accurate color, clean detail, and great tonal consistency.

Despite this being my first-time using ON1 Photo RAW, it was a very simple, logical process, proving itself a strong option for those looking to integrate both editing and printing in a single platform.

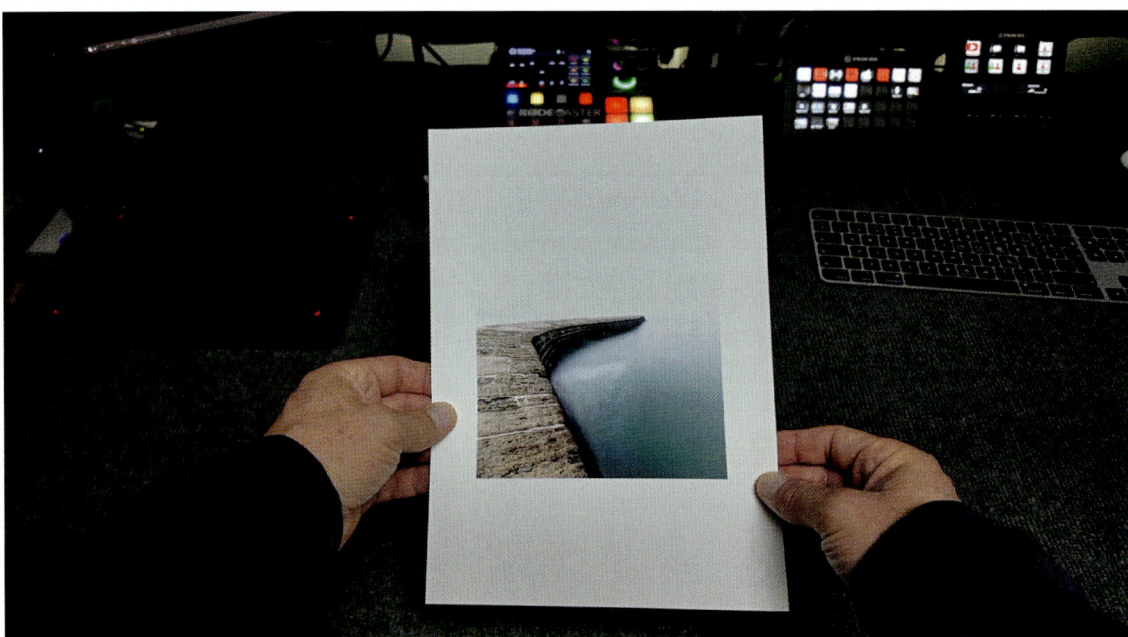

FIGURE 11.47

BLACK-AND-WHITE PRINTING WITH ON1 PHOTO RAW

Continuing with the use of ON1 Photo RAW, the next step is to print a black-and-white image. So, having located the image to be printed, double-clicking on the file opens it, and then the print process begins by navigating to **File** > **Print**.

The image dimensions are set to **6 inches by 8 inches**, so I'll confirm that within the print settings.

CONFIGURING PRINT SETTINGS

Working from the top-right of the interface, I'll set the **Mode** to **Print**, with the Epson printer selected **(Figure 11.48)**. The native resolution is specified as **360 pixels per inch**, consistent with Epson's optimal settings.

In the **Color** section, an ICC profile is not used, but instead, I'll select **Printer Managed Color** in order to use the printer's own **Black and White Photo Printing Mode**. This choice is intentional to guarantee a true monochrome output, avoiding the risk of unwanted green or magenta tints that can sometimes appear when using ICC profiles for black-and-white images.

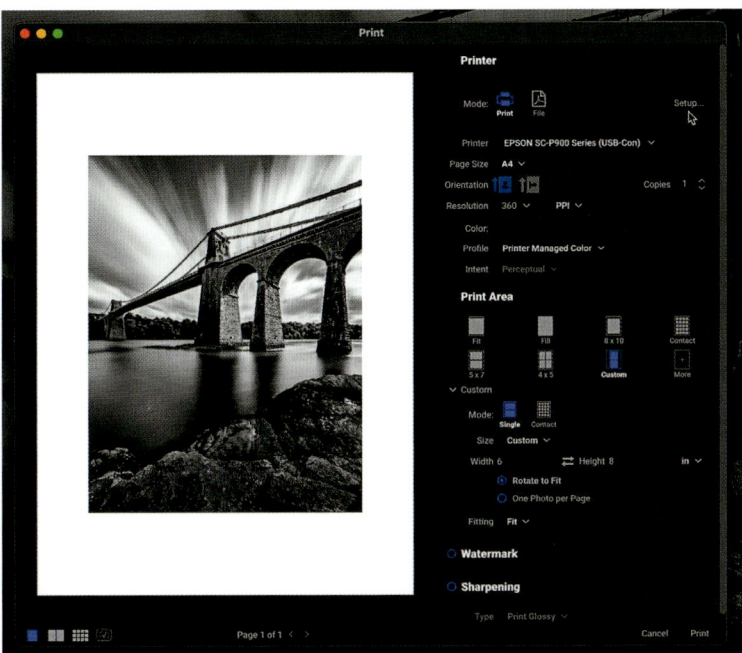

FIGURE 11.48

I'll leave additional settings, such as watermarks and print sharpening, disabled, maintaining full control over image output based on earlier retouching work.

PRINTER DRIVER AND MEDIA SETTINGS

Next, clicking **Setup** opens the printer driver interface. In the **Printer Options** menu, I'll set **Color Matching** to **Epson Color Controls**, confirming that color management is being handled by the printer.

Navigating to **Print Settings**, I'll set the **Media Type** is set to **Watercolor Paper Radiant White**, which is the recommended match for **PermaJet Smooth Rag** paper **(Figure 11.49)**. In the **Color** section of this menu, I'll change the print mode to **Advanced B&W Photo**, and set **Color Toning** to **Neutral**, preserving a clean and balanced grayscale tone.

The **Print Quality** defaults to **1440 DPI**, which is ideal. All settings are confirmed by clicking **OK**, followed by **Save**.

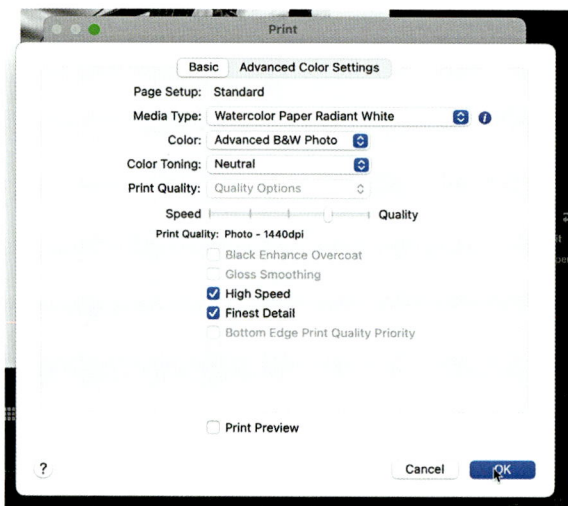

FIGURE 11.49

FINAL OUTPUT AND EVALUATION

With everything in place, the final step is to press Print, and the eventual result is excellent **(Figure 11.50)**. The print exhibits beautiful tonal range, consistent sharpness, and rich detail. The neutral tone is clean and free of any color cast, and the image looks just as intended.

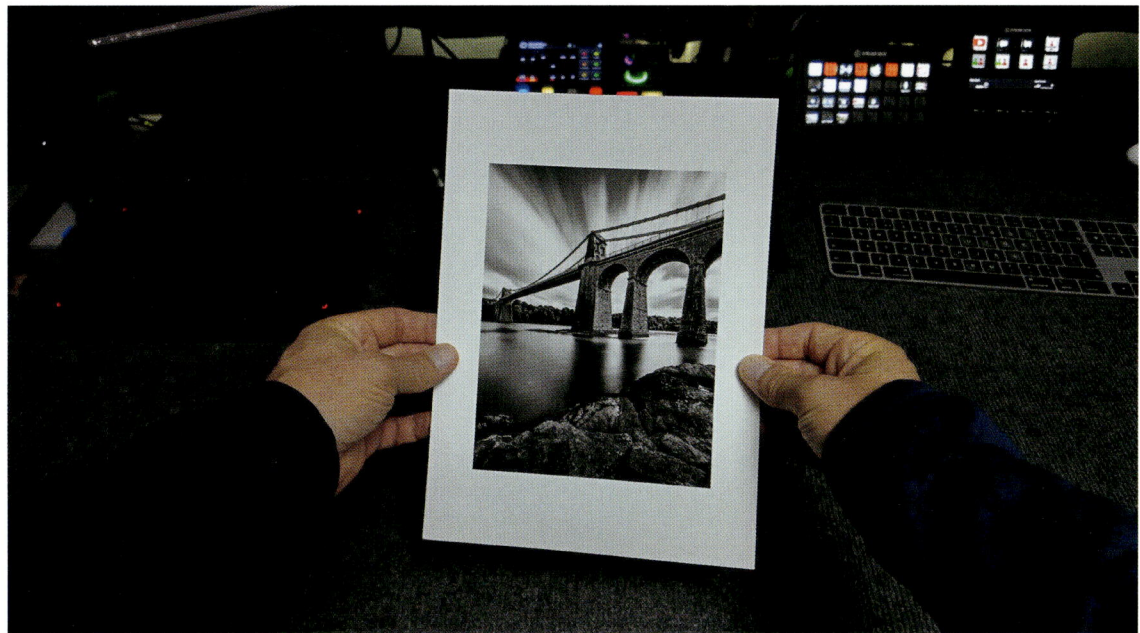

FIGURE 11.50

It's a lovely black-and-white print, demonstrating once again how even unfamiliar software like ON1 Photo RAW can deliver impressive results when the workflow is properly set.

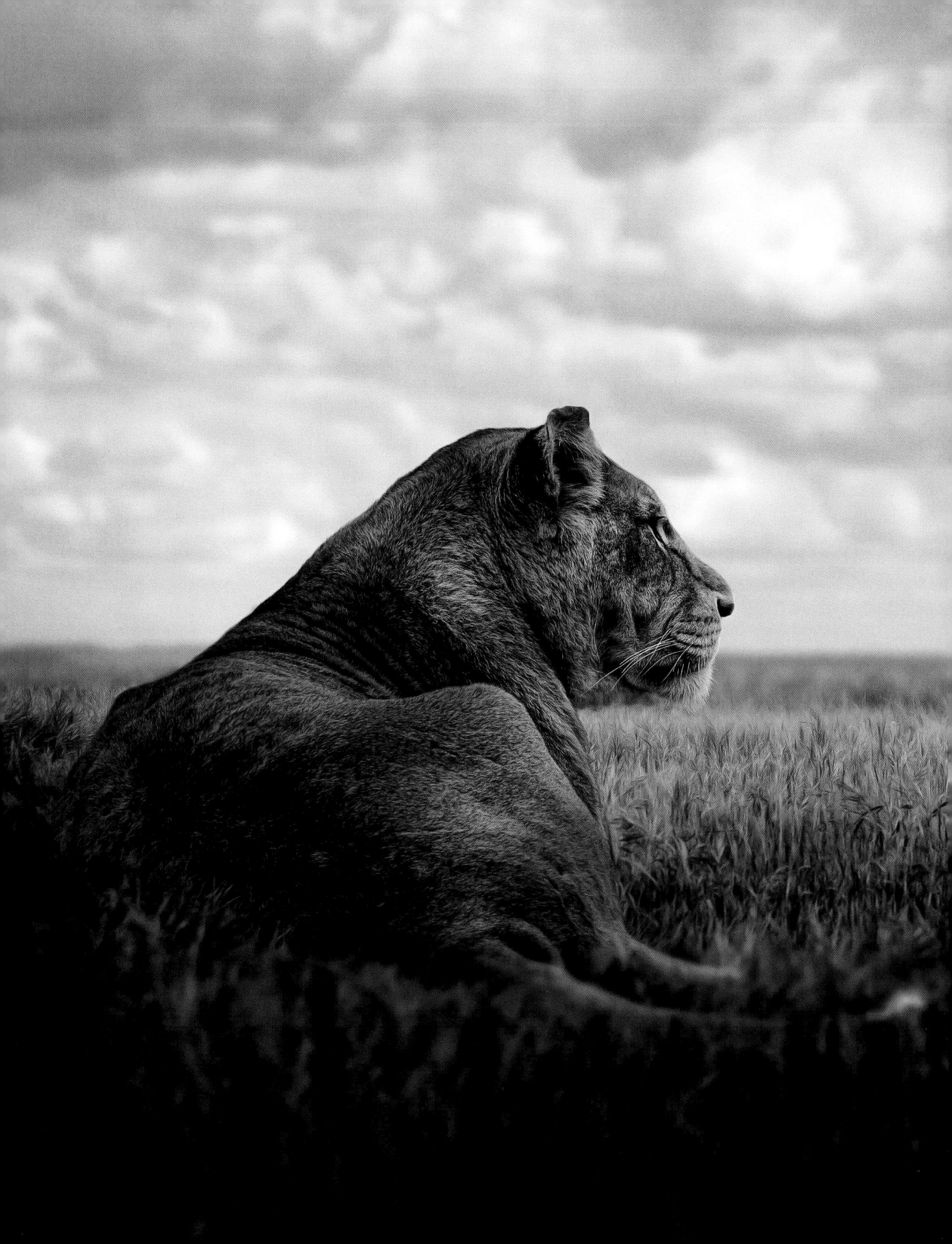

CHAPTER 12
COMPLETE PRINTING WORKFLOW

At this stage of the book we've covered a lot of information, so I thought now would be a good time to bring it all together and walk you through the complete printing workflow from start to finish, using two images as practical examples. The images I've chosen to print are these two: a black-and-white composite of a lioness that I created a few years ago **(Figure 12.1)**, and a more recent color portrait **(Figure 12.2)**.

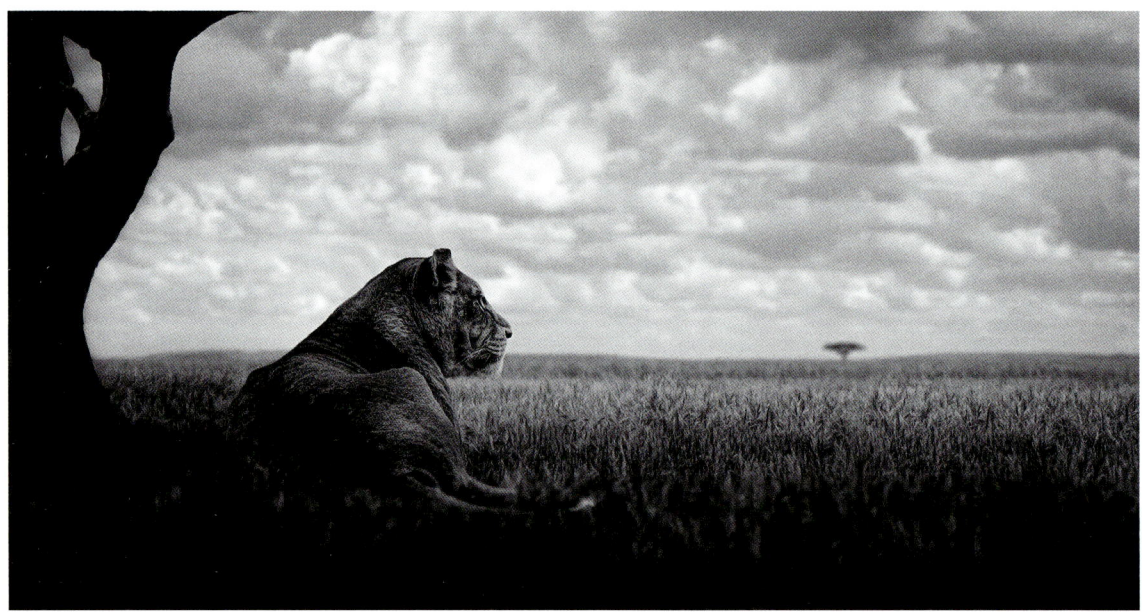

FIGURE 12.1

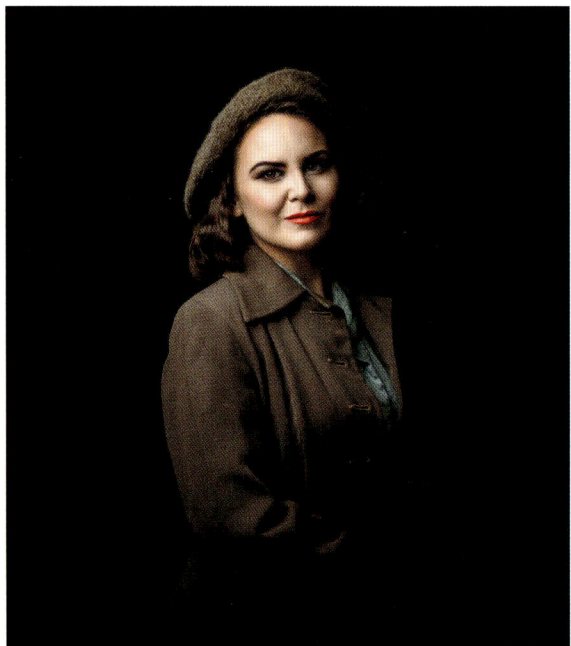

FIGURE 12.2

I've printed both images before, but one thing I've never done is print them on the particular paper I'll be using, which isn't one from PermaJet. For these prints, I'll be using paper from Hahnemühle, a very well-known and prestigious high-end paper brand. The specific paper I'm going with is their Fine Art InkJet Smooth Photo Rag, which is widely regarded as one of their most popular papers.

Because I'm going to print on this paper using both Epson and Canon printers, the first step is to download and install the relevant ICC profiles. This will allow me to soft proof and print the images accurately.

DOWNLOADING ICC PROFILES

I'll begin by visiting the Hahnemühle website, navigating to the Digital Papers section, and then accessing the ICC Profile Download Center **(Figure 12.3)**.

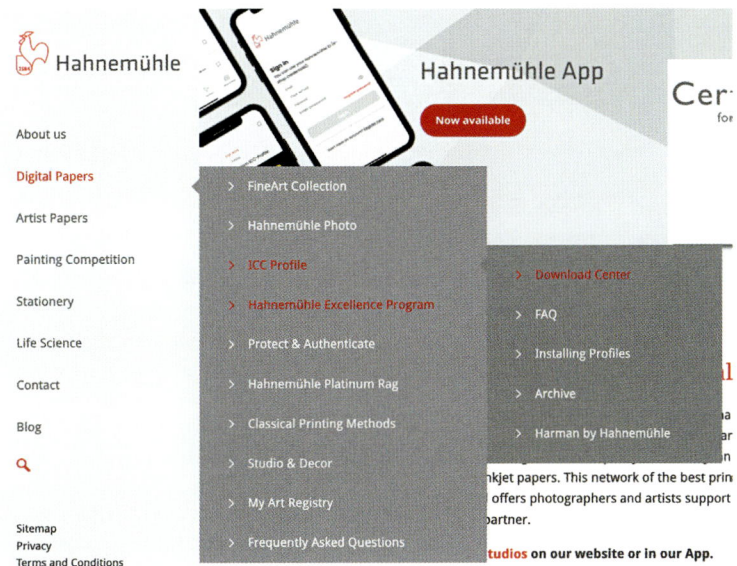

FIGURE 12.3

Starting with the Canon printer:

- I select Canon as the manufacturer.

- My printer is the Pro-300.

- I choose the paper group Matte Fine Art Smooth, and the system presents me with a list of compatible papers within that group.

I locate Photo Rag, click the ICC link to download the profile, and along with it I receive instructions on how to use the paper with the Canon printer, such as what Media Type to select during printing.

I then repeat the process for Epson:

- I select Epson as the manufacturer.

- My printer is the SureColor SC-P900.

- I again choose Matte Fine Art Smooth as the paper group.

Once the list loads, I download the ICC profile for Photo Rag, and as with the Canon version, this also comes with usage instructions tailored to Epson printers.

REVIEWING THE PAPER INSTRUCTIONS

Now that both ICC profiles are downloaded as ZIP files, I extract them.

For the Epson profile, when I open the contents and view the instructions (PDF), I see that it recommends using Epson Velvet Fine Art Paper as the Media Type.

For the Canon profile, the instructions specify Heavyweight Fine Art Paper as the recommended Media Type.

INSTALLING ICC PROFILES

Now I need to install these profiles on my Mac, which involves a few steps that are not needed with Windows; these steps are covered in detail in chapter 5 (page 88).

1. I navigate to the Go menu on my Mac, select Computer, then go into the Library folder.

2. From there, I open the ColorSync folder and then the Profiles subfolder. This folder contains all currently installed ICC profiles.

3. Next, I drag the extracted Epson profile into the folder. The system prompts me to authenticate, so I enter my password. The profile installs successfully.

I do the same for the Canon profile, dragging it over, authenticating with my password, and confirming the installation.

Once both profiles are installed in the correct directory, I close any image editing or printing software I may have open, and then reopen them. This ensures the programs can recognize and access the newly installed ICC profiles.

So now we're good to go. Let's get some prints done! I'll start with the black-and-white lioness picture and will use the Epson printer.

PREPARING THE BLACK-AND-WHITE IMAGE IN LIGHTROOM

I'll start with the image open in Lightroom Classic **(Figure 12.4)**. If I wasn't printing this out, I would leave it exactly as it is. However, when I check the histogram, it looks great on the left-hand side in the dark shadow area, but on the right-hand side, it's just not quite reaching the tonal range I'd want. So, what I'll do is slightly nudge the Whites slider so that the histogram moves closer to the far right **(Figure 12.5)**.

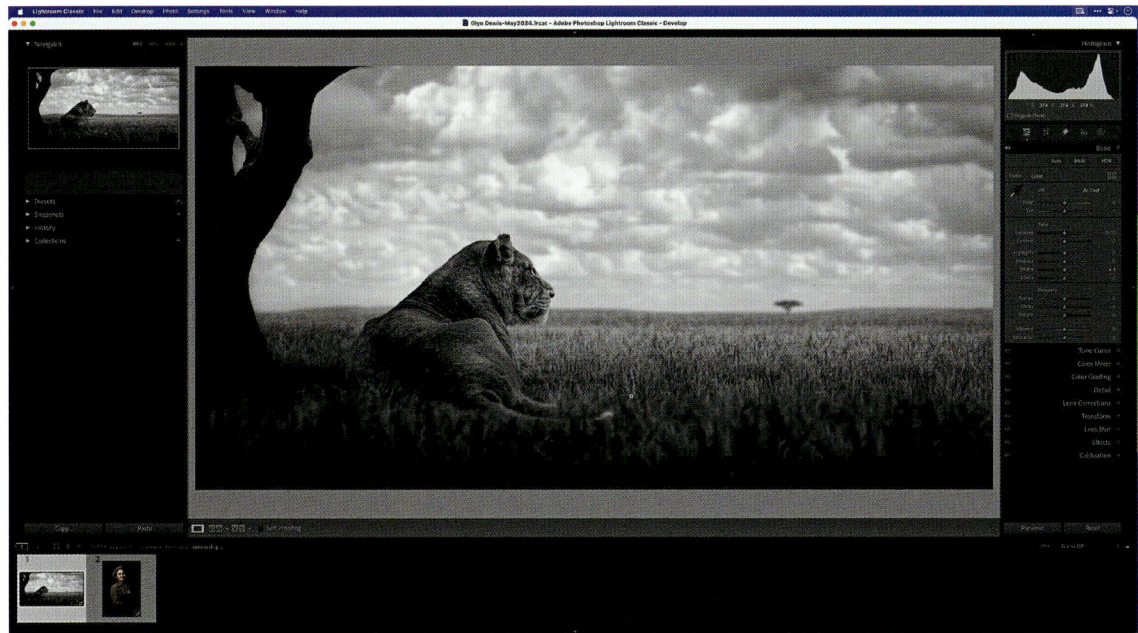

FIGURE 12.4

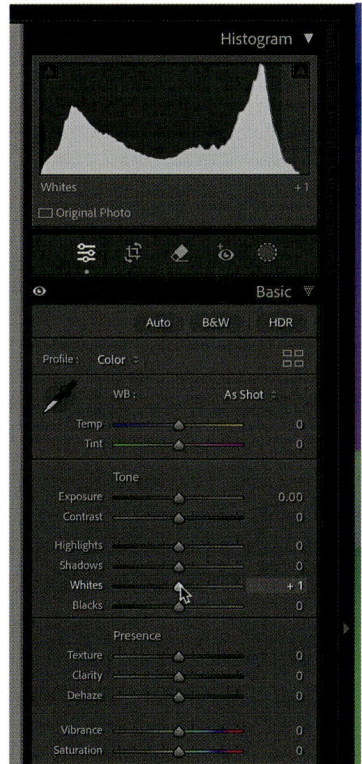

FIGURE 12.5

SOFT PROOFING SETUP

Now I'll switch to Soft Proofing to see how this will behave on the particular paper I'll be using. I'm printing this black-and-white image using an Epson printer, specifically with the Advanced B&W Photo mode in the Epson Print Layout software, but even though I'm using that mode, I always find it helpful to check the ICC profile during soft proofing to get a rough idea of how the black-and-white image will respond when printed on the selected paper.

Within Soft Proofing, I click Create Proof Copy so I'm not altering the original image, and this copy then shows up in the filmstrip at the bottom of the interface **(Figure 12.6)**. This copy is solely for printing adjustments. My original stays untouched.

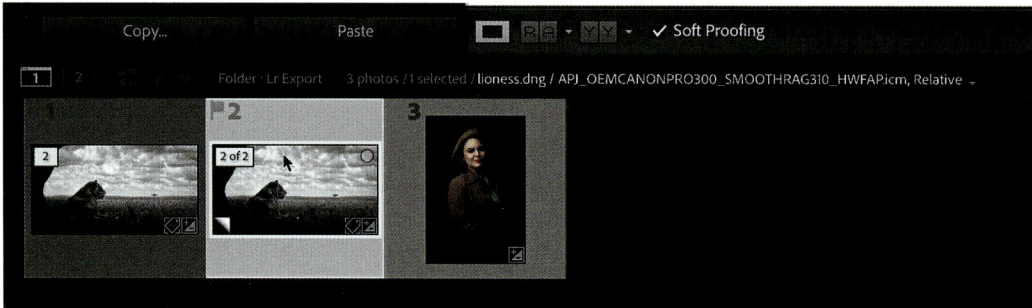

FIGURE 12.6

SELECTING THE CORRECT ICC PROFILE

Next, I select the appropriate ICC profile. It wasn't listed in the menu initially, so I clicked Other, and since I've already placed the Hahnemühle profiles into the correct folder, and then closed and reopened Lightroom, they now appear **(Figure 12.7)**. I tick both the Canon and Epson Photo Rag profiles and click OK, making sure I select the Epson one for use.

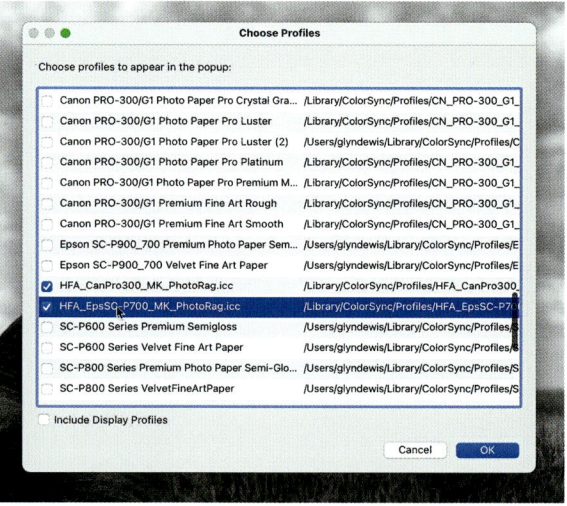

FIGURE 12.7

This gives a rough preview of how the image will look, even though I'll be using the Epson Advanced B&W mode for the actual print **(Figure 12.8)**.

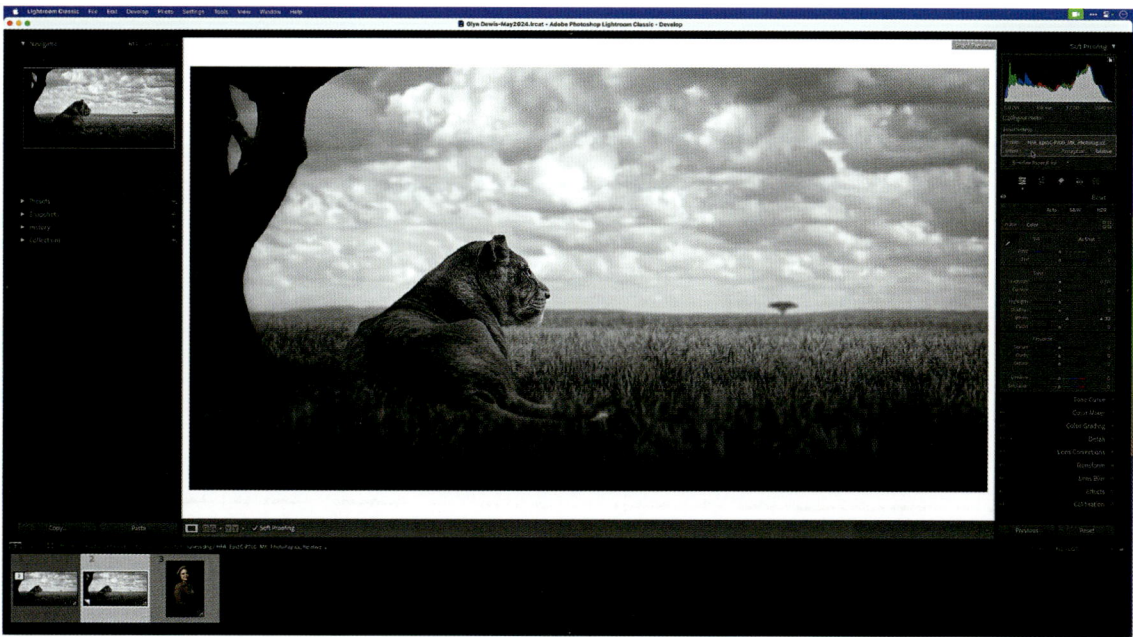

FIGURE 12.8

EVALUATING TONAL DETAIL

As I examine the preview, I notice that the dark areas of the tree on the left of the image could be problematic, and while there's no destination gamut warning and it technically should print fine, I feel I might lose some information in those dark sections. To prevent this, I increase the Shadows slightly, revealing more detail in the tree **(Figure 12.9)**. With that adjustment, the image looks much more balanced and ready for printing.

EXPORTING FOR PHOTOSHOP

At this point, I'm happy with the soft proof, so now I want to see how large I can print this image. I click to come out of the Soft Proofing mode, and then press **I** on my keyboard to bring up the information about the image **(Figure 12.10)**. I can see that it measures 7156 pixels on the longest side, so I divide 7156 by Epson's native resolution of 360 PPI, which tells me that the image as it is would print at 19.8 inches on the Epson.

Since I'll be printing on A4 paper, which is much smaller, I need to resample the image, meaning I need to downsize it. I prefer to do this manually in Photoshop rather than rely on Lightroom's automatic bicubic interpolation, which **could** subtly degrade the image.

At this stage, you could send the image directly into Photoshop from Lightroom, but my preferred workflow is to export it first into a folder. Does this make any difference? No, not at all … it's just my preferred workflow.

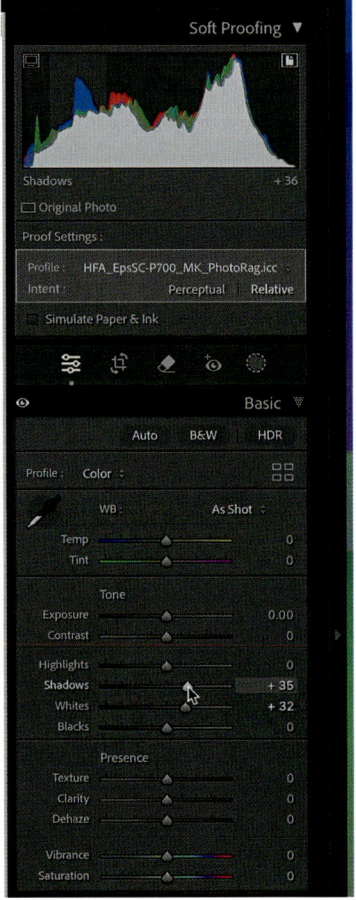

FIGURE 12.9

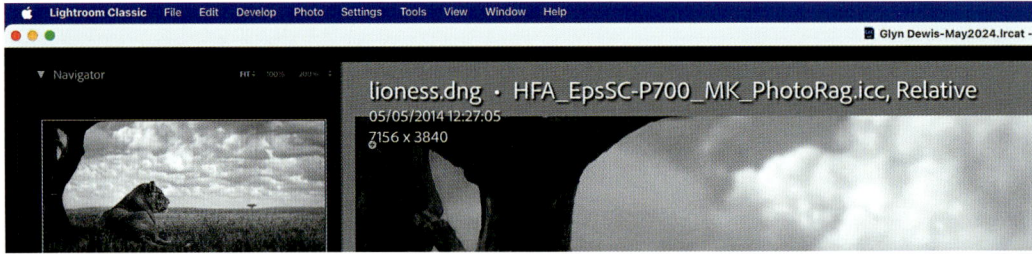

FIGURE 12.10

So, in Lightroom Classic, I go to **File** > **Export**. I choose to export the image at full size as a TIFF into a folder on my computer named "Printing" with the following settings **(Figure 12.11)**:

- **Color Space:** Adobe RGB
- **Bit Depth:** 16 bits/component
- **Resolution:** 360 PPI
- No Resizing

RESIZING IN PHOTOSHOP

Once exported, I open Photoshop and open the exported image, and then go to **Image** > **Image Size (Figure 12.12)**.

As expected, the dimensions show:

- 19.878 inches at 360 PPI

I resize the longest edge to 10 inches, and Photoshop automatically adjusts the other side to 5.366 inches.

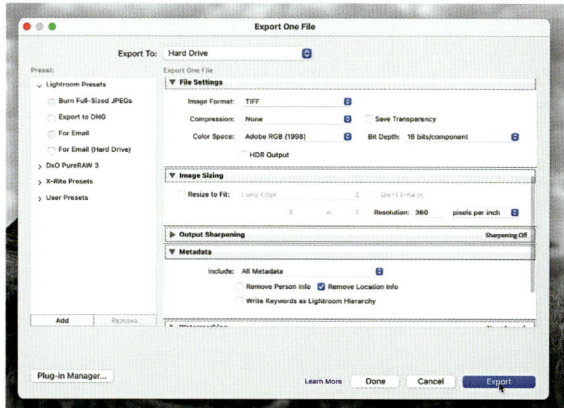

FIGURE 12.11

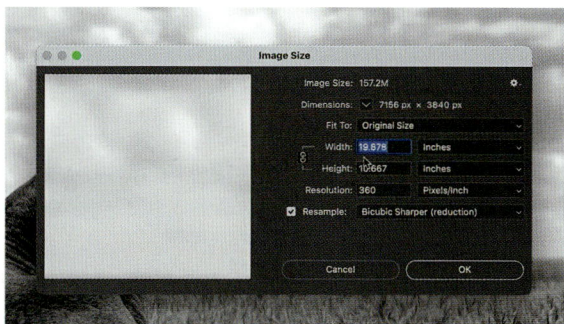

FIGURE 12.12

> **NOTE:** *I don't let standard sizes dictate my crop. I crop how the image looks best, which means custom framing is sometimes needed.*

For Resample, the Bicubic Sharper (Reduction) option is automatically applied, which is ideal for downsizing, and the resized image looks perfect: sharp, clean, and ready to go.

Next, I save the resized file by simply going to **File** > **Save**, overwriting the previous export, and prepare to open it in the Epson Print Layout software.

PRINTING WITH EPSON PRINT LAYOUT

Once the image is open in Epson's software, I'll now check the settings. From the top we have Printer Settings, and in here I choose the following **(Figure 12.13)**:

- **Printer:** Epson SC-P900
- **Media Type:** Velvet Fine Art Paper (as per Hahnemühle's instructions)
- **Paper Size:** A4
- **Paper Source:** Standard (top feed)
- **Quality:** Standard

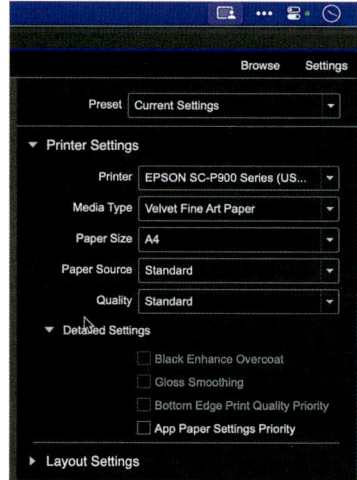

FIGURE 12.13

NOTE: *I explain why Standard is chosen for the Quality setting in the following chapter where I interviewed Dominic Gurney from Epson (page 251).*

COLOR SETTINGS

The Color Settings section is where I choose the Advanced B&W Photo mode as opposed to going with using an ICC Profile. You could, of course, use an ICC profile, but I am always so incredibly happy with black-and-white prints when using the printer's own black-and-white printing mode. This mode guarantees that I will get a true black-and-white image without any chance of tint (green or magenta), which **can** happen when printing black-and-white using an ICC Profile.

My selections for the Color Settings section are as follows:

- **Color Toning:** Neutral
- **Type:** Advanced B&W Photo mode

- **Tone:** Dark (in the preview I can see this preserves detail in the tree, which is the area I was most concerned about)

PRINTING THE FINAL IMAGE

That's it! I'm ready to print, so all I need to do now is load the paper into the printer, press Print, and let it work its magic!

EVALUATING THE FINAL PRINT

- As for the final print, yeah, I'm very happy! The tree detail came out perfectly **(Figure 12.14)**. Raising the shadows in soft proofing was clearly the right call, and the Dark Tone setting worked just right. The sharpness and contrast are fantastic, especially considering this is matte, mildly textured paper. There's no tinting; just a pure, clean black-and-white image.

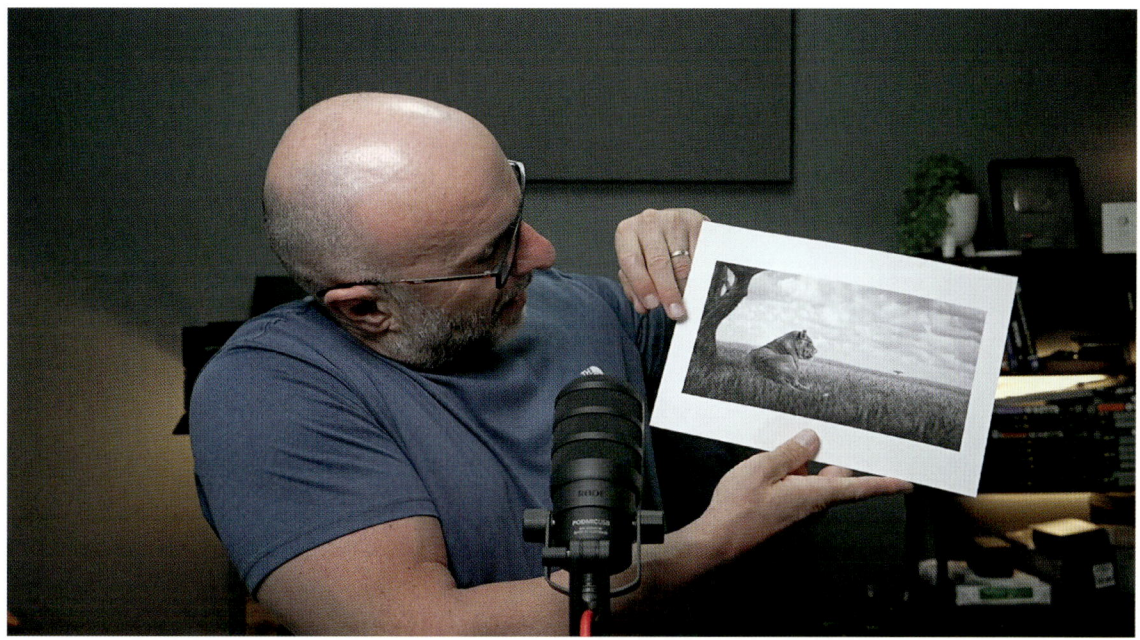

FIGURE 12.14

> **NOTE:** *Print drying time is more relevant to Canon printers, which use heat-based ink application. Epson uses cold vibration technology, so it technically doesn't require any drying time … however, when using a Matte, Uncoated Paper, leaving the print to dry for roughly thirty minutes will reveal all the true detail of the image.*

PREPARING THE COLOR PORTRAIT IN LIGHTROOM

At this point, I'm almost finished with the retouching process for the color portrait. Viewing the image in Lightroom Classic's Develop module, I notice some tonal issues in the histogram, specifically gaps in the mid-tones and highlights **(Figure 12.15)**.

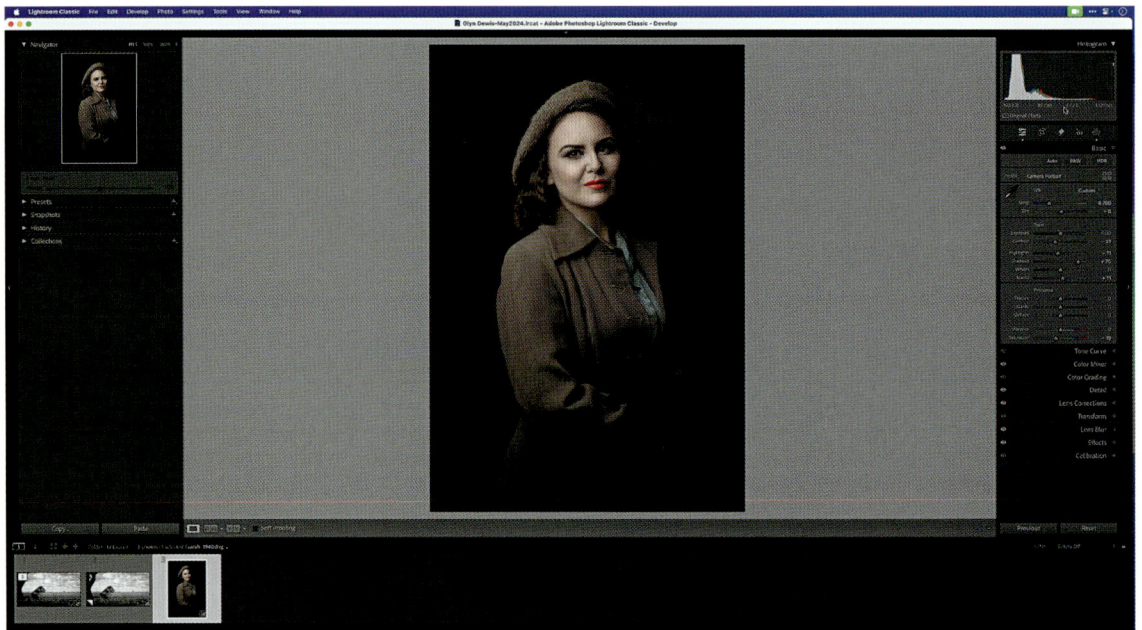

FIGURE 12.15

To correct this, I consider increasing the overall exposure, but I have to be careful. Raising the exposure will help bring out shadow detail, but it also risks overexposing the subject's skin.

BALANCING EXPOSURE WITH MASKS

I carefully raise the exposure just enough so the darker parts of the image, like the lower jacket, handbag, and gloves, show plenty of detail. But the skin now appears too bright, so I turn to Lightroom's masking tools to isolate and adjust it.

I create a new mask, choose Select People, and once Lightroom processes the image, I select both Facial Skin and Body Skin **(Figure 12.16)**. The tool mistakenly includes some areas around the wrists where it's actually just the jacket. Still, I keep Body Skin enabled to make sure the neck is included.

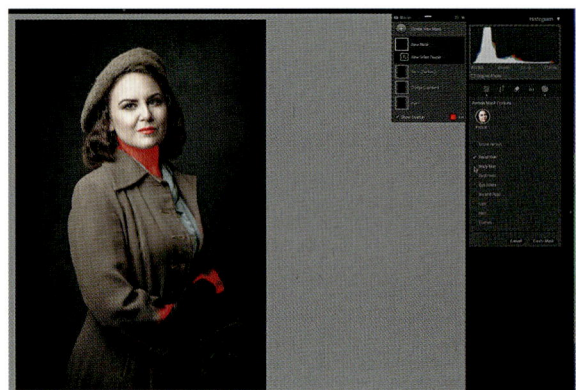

FIGURE 12.16

Next, I go into Subtract mode and use a brush to remove the selection from the jacket. With the mask now refined, I:

- Reduce the exposure of the skin to a more natural level.
- Slightly lower the saturation to balance the tones.

At this point, the image has rich shadow detail and natural-looking skin tones, exactly where I want them **(Figure 12.18)**.

PREPARING FOR PRINT WITH SOFT PROOFING

With the exposure and color now set, I move on to soft proofing for printing on Hahnemühle Photo Rag paper, this time using the Canon printer. I follow the same set of steps as before:

1. I enable Soft Proofing.

2. I create a proof copy so that any print-specific adjustments don't affect the original.

3. I select the appropriate ICC profile (the one designed for the Canon printer and Hahnemühle paper combination).

4. I turn on the Destination Gamut Warning, which shows no issues in this case **(Figure 12.19)**.

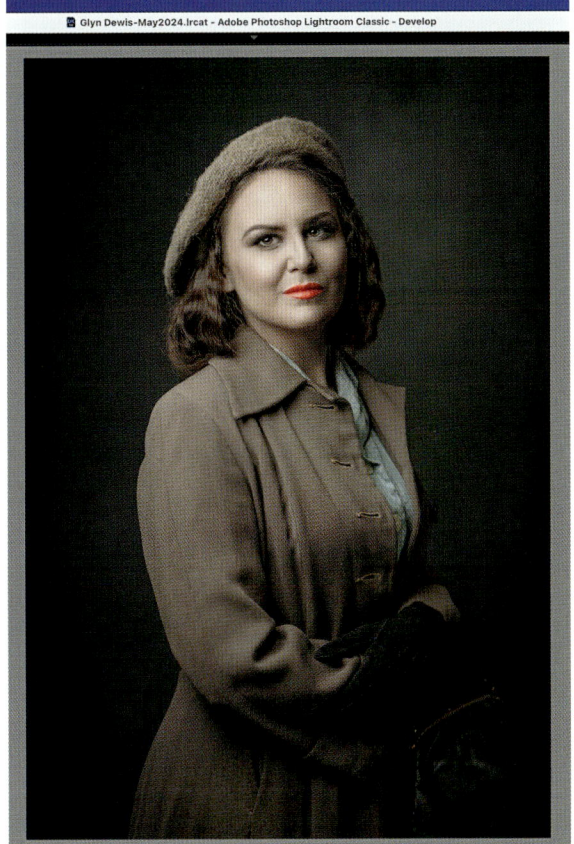

FIGURE 12.18

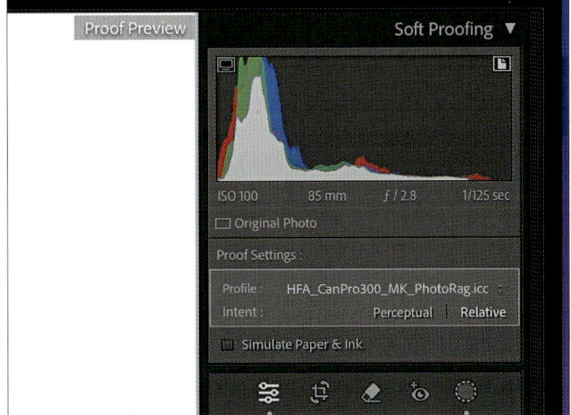

FIGURE 12.19

CHOOSING THE APPROPRIATE RENDERING INTENT

Now I need to decide on the best rendering intent to use for the image: Perceptual or Relative. When I jump between the two I can see that Perceptual slightly brightens the skin and pulls a bit more detail out of the darker areas, whereas Relative, in this case, keeps the tones closer to the original, but looks slightly flatter. I zoom in to 100% and toggle between the two **(Figure 12.20)**.

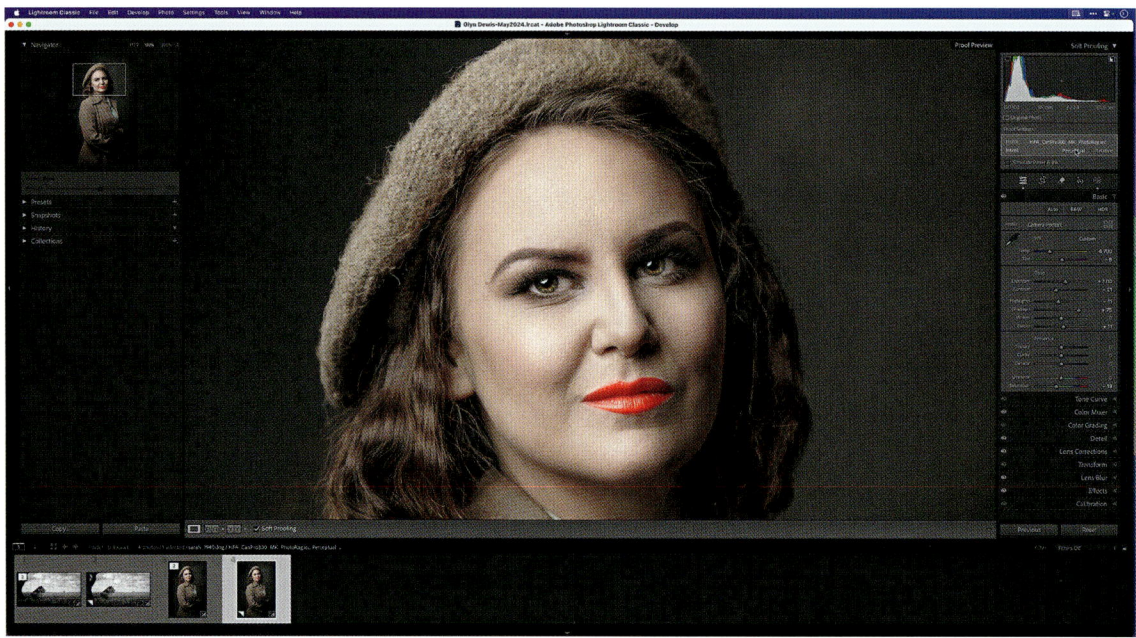

FIGURE 12.20

The Perceptual rendering looks better, as it keeps the skin tones well within the printable range and adds just a touch of brightness that feels natural. It also brings out subtle detail in the shadows. So, I go with Perceptual.

RESIZING THE IMAGE FOR A4 OUTPUT

Now that I'm happy with how the image will print, I need to look at it size. In Lightroom, I press I on my keyboard to bring up the information, and I can see that the image measures 7952 pixels on the long side. I'm going to print this on the Canon, so to find out the size it will print at if I make no changes to it, I divide 7952 by 300 (with 300 PPI being the native Canon print resolution), and this tells me that the image would print at 26.5 inches at 300 PPI. This is far larger than I need for printing at A4, so I need to resize it.

To resize the image, I follow these steps:

1. I export the image from Lightroom as a TIFF file, 16-bit, Adobe RGB, no compression, 300 PPI into the folder I have on my computer labelled "Printing" (again, you could export direct into Photoshop if you prefer) **(Figure 12.21)**.

2. I open the file in Photoshop and go to **Image** > **Image Size**.

3. I reduce the long edge from 26 inches to 10 inches, which brings the short edge to just over 6.5 inches, and I select Bicubic Sharper (Reduction) as the Resample method **(Figure 12.22)**.

Once the image is resized, I zoom in to check the image quality, which looks fantastic with plenty of detail, great texture, and a very clean look. Then I save the file, which then overrides the image that I originally exported out of Lightroom.

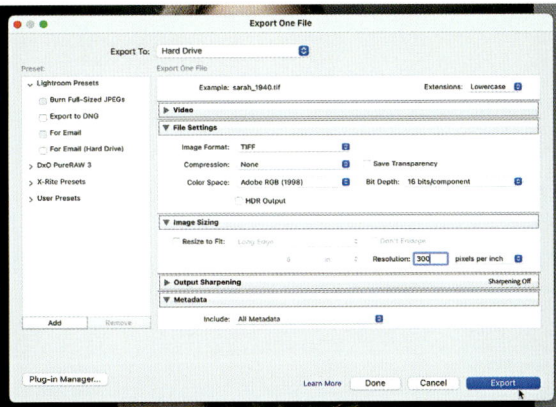

FIGURE 12.21

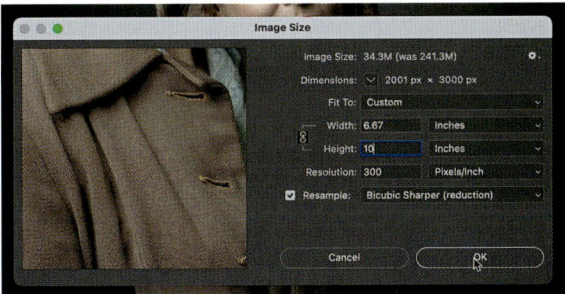

FIGURE 12.22

PRINTING WITH CANON PROFESSIONAL PRINT SOFTWARE

With the resized file ready, I open Canon's Professional Print & Layout software and start setting up the print:

1. I open the image and drag it into the main layout space.

2. I set the printer to **Canon Pro-300**.

3. I select **Heavyweight Fine Art Paper** as the **Media Type**, confirming this with information in the PDF that was included when I downloaded the ICC profile from Hahnemühle **(Figure 12.23)**.

4. I choose **A4 paper**, **Top Feed**, and the finest **Quality** setting.

5. I enable **Clear Coating** and **Use Depth Information (Figure 12.24)**.

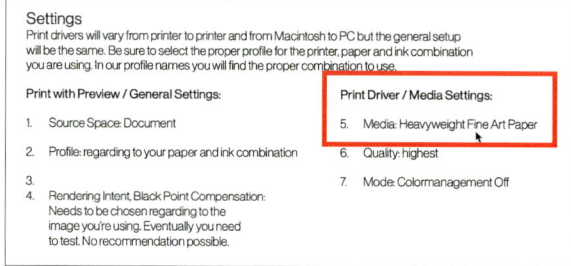

FIGURE 12.23

6. I apply the ICC profile for Hahnemühle Photo Rag (Canon Pro-300 version).

7. I select **Perceptual** as the rendering intent, and because of that, it makes no difference whether or not I tick the Black point compensation checkbox **(Figure 12.25)**.

Everything is now in place to print this image.

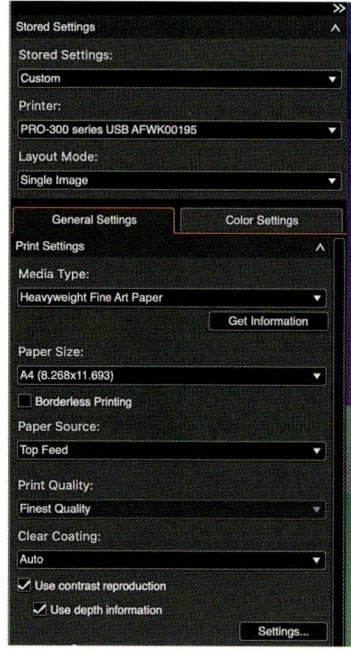

FIGURE 12.24

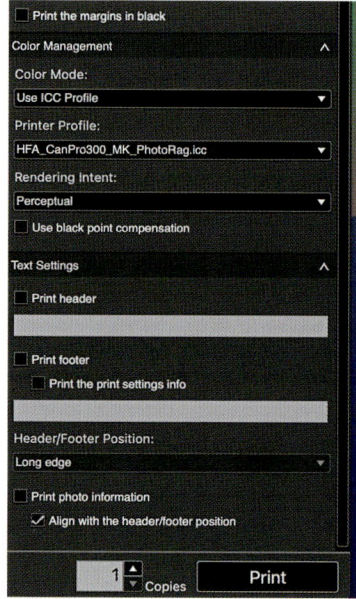

FIGURE 12.25

THE PRINT PROCESS

I carefully insert a sheet of the Hahnemühle paper, making sure the printable side is facing up, and I avoid touching the surface by pinching the edges.

When I click Print, the Canon takes a moment to respond, but then we're good to go!

> *Occasionally, the printer struggles to feed the fine art paper. This is fairly common when using non-Canon-branded paper, so I give it a gentle assist to help it grab the sheet.*

REVIEWING THE FINAL PRINT

And here's the final print **(Figure 12.26)**. Very happy indeed!

Raising the exposure slightly and then masking the skin to balance it was definitely the right thing to do. There's great detail, beautiful tone, and rich contrast. If I were to tweak anything, I might dial back the exposure on the clothing slightly, but I'm genuinely happy with the result. The paper texture is subtle but elegant, and the print feels professional and complete.

Now I'd let the print rest for about thirty minutes or so, so that the ink has time to settle and dry, and then I'll put it into a display folder.

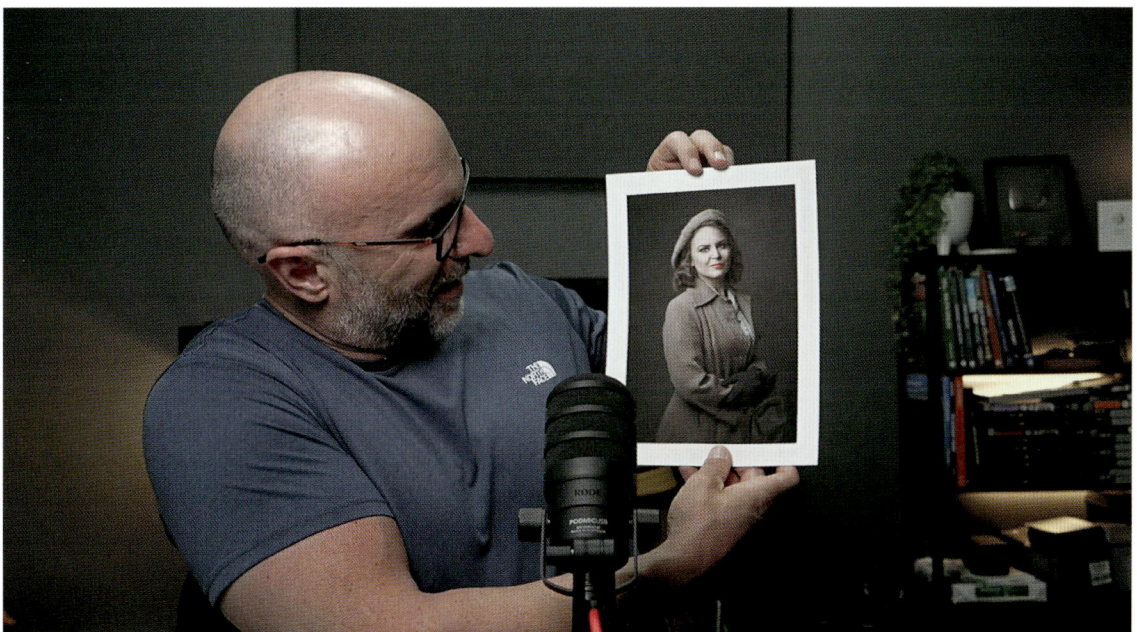

FIGURE 12.26

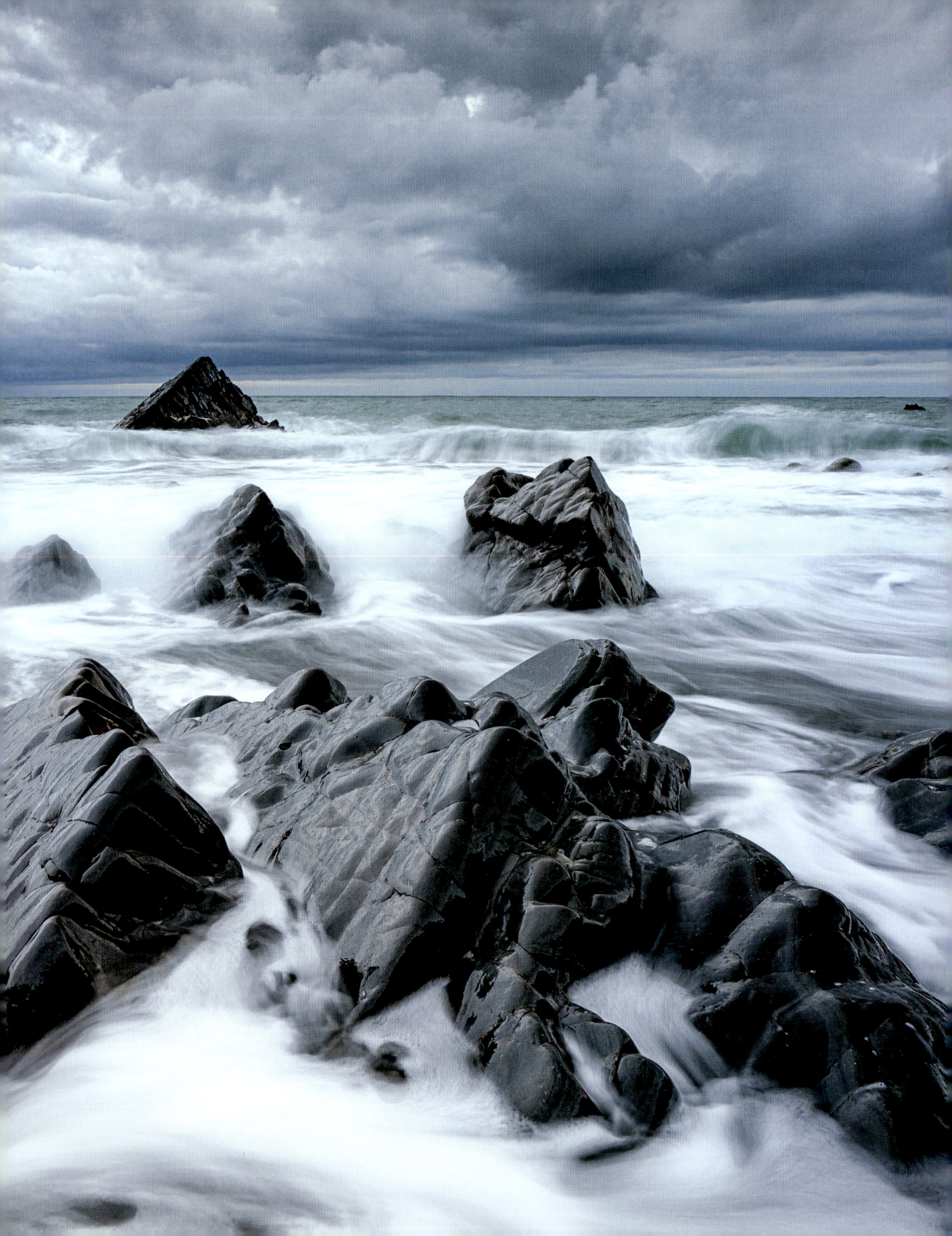

CHAPTER 13
USING A PRINTING LAB

One of the most common requests I get when teaching about printing is how to prepare image files to send them to a professional print lab. A key question that often comes up is:

Why do printing labs prefer images in the sRGB color space, rather than Adobe RGB or other wider gamuts?

To explore this topic properly, I spoke directly with Alex Ingram at **Digitalab**, the team behind all the large portraits for my 39–45 WWII Veterans Portraits Project, as well as a 72-inch print of a seascape I shot on my iPhone (shown on the opposite page). This chapter covers what I learned from that discussion, and following that, I'll take you step-by-step through the process you'll need for preparing your images before sending them to a lab for printing.

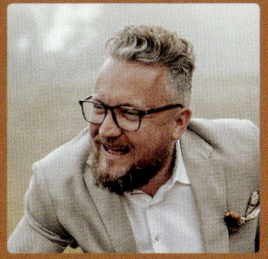

Alex Ingram, Digitalab

UNDERSTANDING COLOR SPACE: WHY LABS ASK FOR SRGB

Alex explained that the vast majority of printing at Digitalab is done using silver halide (C-type) printing, and this includes Fuji Crystal Archive paper. The printers used for this process are calibrated for the sRGB color space. Although the lab also offers giclée printing, which does support Adobe RGB for its wider gamut, Alex recommends sRGB for most work, especially if consistency is the goal.

"If you're submitting silver halide prints, album pages, or fine art work, we recommend sRGB to maintain consistency across all formats," Alex says.

IS THIS COMMON ACROSS ALL LABS?
It's About Machinery, Not Convenience

When asked whether other labs also prefer sRGB, Alex is clear: It comes down to the hardware. "It's entirely down to the machinery. We all talk to each other at trade shows, it's not a secret. Most of us use similar printers calibrated for sRGB."

This isn't about playing it safe with color spaces; it's a technical requirement for the equipment most commonly used in professional labs.

FILE FORMAT: TIFF VS. JPEG
JPEG Is Preferred for Workflow Efficiency

While many photographers print at home using TIFF files, Digitalab asks for high-quality JPEGs. Why? Simply because they process thousands of files each week. TIFFs would be too demanding on the lab's system, potentially causing crashes or delays.

"Unless you're printing larger than 60 by 40 inches, the difference between TIFF and JPEG is marginal," Alex explains.

If you do need to print larger, or for something like an exhibition, they offer an alternative upload method that accepts TIFFs.

RESOLUTION: WHAT PPI SHOULD YOU USE?
Stick to 300 PPI

At home, we often match our image resolution to the printer:

Canon printers: 300 PPI

Epson printers: 360 PPI

However, at Digitalab, they recommend 300 PPI across the board, whether it's for silver halide or giclée printing. "Both the silver halide and giclée machines perform best with images at 300 PPI," Alex confirms. This makes life easier, especially when you're looking for consistency across different paper types or print methods.

ICC PROFILES: COLOR ACCURACY MATTERS
Profiles Are Provided and Maintained

If you're printing color images and using third-party paper, ICC profiles are essential. Digitalab provides downloadable profiles for all the media they print on, whether silver halide or fine art.

Each paper has different characteristics, even down to base color, so using the right profile is crucial. If in doubt, Alex encourages customers to simply call the lab.

FINAL THOUGHTS

Printing should be the easy part. You've done the hard work capturing, editing, and refining your image. The lab should handle the rest, and with the right communication and preparation, that process becomes smooth and rewarding.

"You've taken the picture, done the retouching; printing should be enjoyable, not stressful," Alex concludes.

With labs like Digitalab, and a bit of preparation using the correct color space, file format, resolution, and ICC profiles, your images will come to life exactly as intended.

PREPARING AN IMAGE FOR PRINTING AT A LAB

Now I'll walk through the exact process I use to prepare an image file when I'm sending it to a professional print lab, which in this case, as it always is for me when I need a large volume of prints or a print larger than I can print at home, will be Digitalab.

STEP 1: CHECK THE IMAGE'S NATIVE DIMENSIONS

The image I'm working with is already open in Lightroom **(Figure 13.1)**, and I want to get this printed by Digitalab at 30 inches by 20 inches. I press **I** on the keyboard to bring up its dimensions, and I can see that the longest edge is 7588 pixels **(Figure 13.2)**.

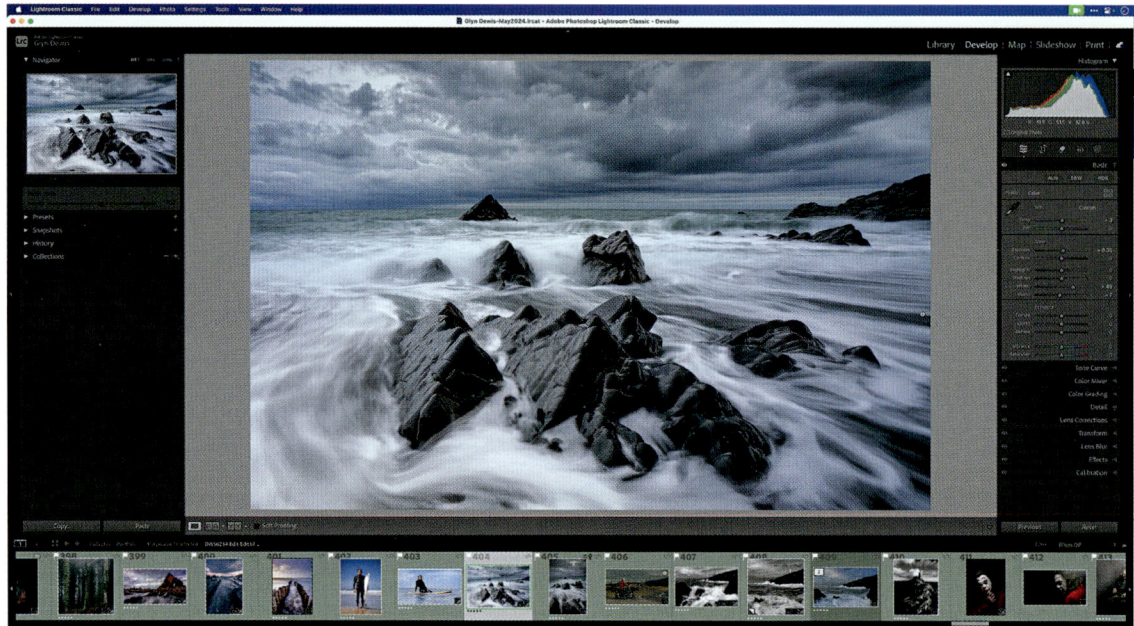

FIGURE 13.1

So how big will this print be if I use the settings that Alex mentioned are used by Digitalab? I divide 7588 by 300 (PPI), which gives me a size of 25.3 inches. That's not large enough, so I need to resample the image to reach the 30-inch requirement.

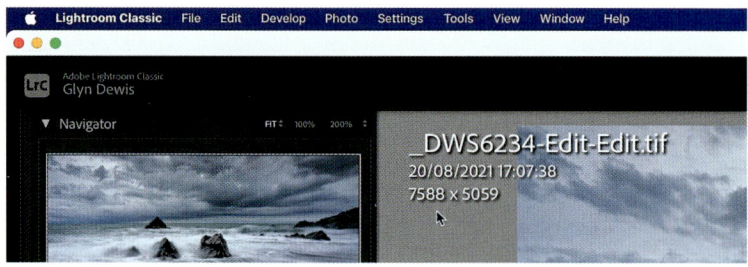

FIGURE 13.2

STEP 2: USE SUPER RESOLUTION IN LIGHTROOM

In Lightroom, I go to **Photo** > **Enhance (Figure 13.3)**, then enable **Super Resolution (Figure 13.4)**. This process doubles the file's dimensions and resolution. Lightroom shows a progress bar in the top-left while creating a new DNG file (not a duplicate, but an enhanced version with the same name plus "Enhanced" added).

Once processed, the new image appears in the filmstrip. When I press I again, I see the new image size is 15,176 pixels on the long edge, which, if I divide by the 300 (PPI), would mean a print of 50.5 inches **(Figure 13.5)**. This is now more than enough for the 30-by-20-inch print I need.

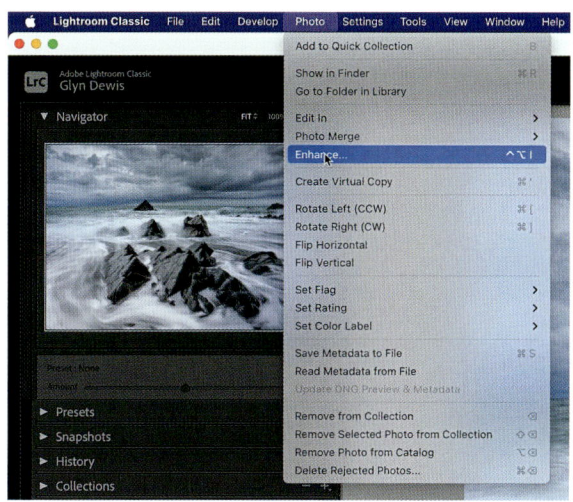

FIGURE 13.3

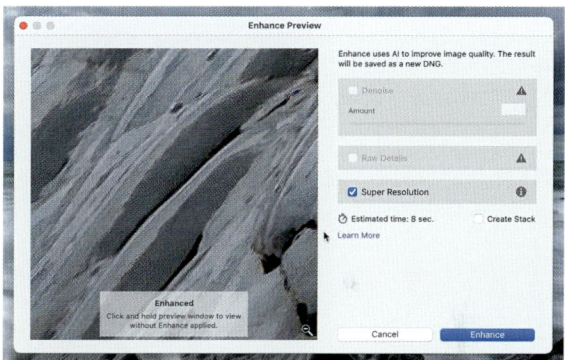

FIGURE 13.4

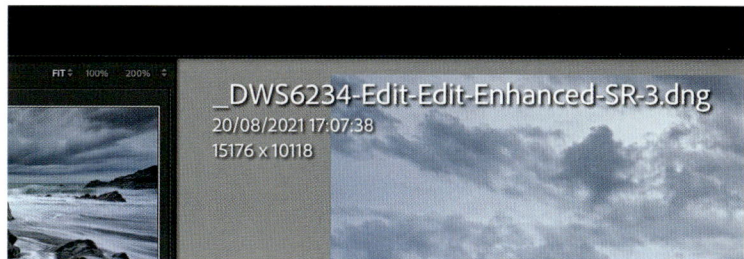

FIGURE 13.5

STEP 3: DOWNLOAD AND INSTALL THE ICC PROFILE

Before I do any resizing, I soft proof the image using Digitalab's ICC profile for the Velvet print paper on their Chromira printer.

To do this, I:

1. Go to the Digitalab website.
2. Find the ICC downloads section **(Figure 13.6)**.
3. Select and download the CHROMIRA – VELVET PRINT profile.
4. Save the ICC file.

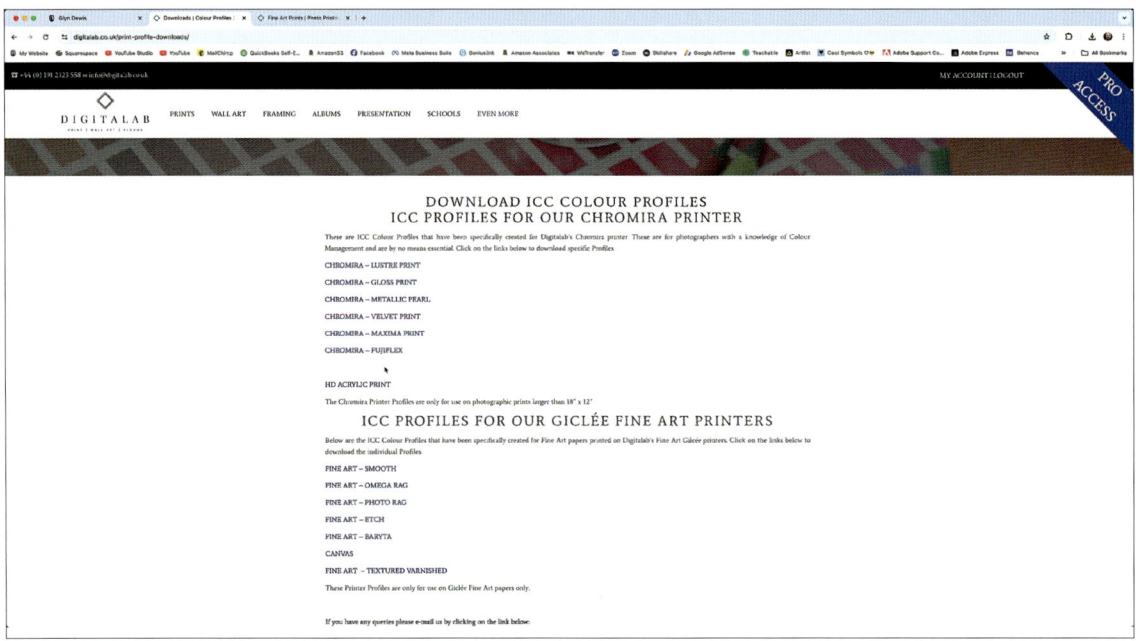

FIGURE 13.6

Next, to install the ICC profile on a Mac, I:

5. Navigate to **Go** > **Computer** > **Macintosh HD** > **Library** > **ColorSync** > **Profiles**.
6. Drag the profile into that folder.
7. Authenticate with my password.

Once installed, I restart Lightroom Classic to load the new profile.

STEP 4: SOFT PROOF IN LIGHTROOM

Now back in Lightroom, I:

1. Enable Soft Proofing.

2. Open the ICC profile drop-down.

3. Click Other to locate the new Digitalab profile.

4. Tick the checkbox beside it **(Figure 13.7)**.

5. Select it from the drop-down.

There's no visible change in the image, which is a good sign. However, when I check the histogram, I notice the highlights don't quite reach the edge, so I raise the Whites slightly to increase the overall tonal range within the image.

To avoid blowing out the entire image, I create a mask with a brush, and then brush over the few areas that are clipping to lower the white/brightness **(Figure 13.8)**. The highlights are now nicely balanced.

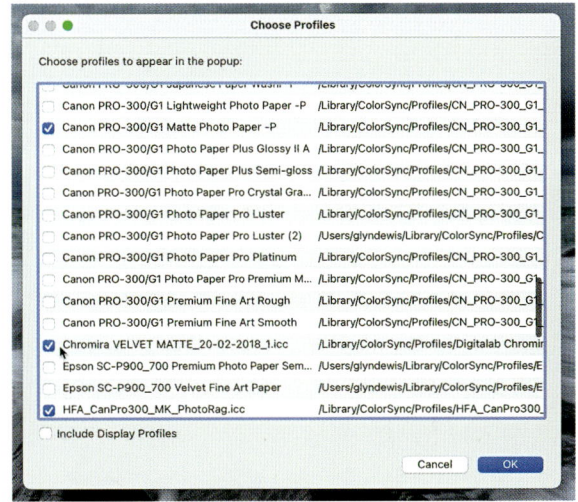

FIGURE 13.7

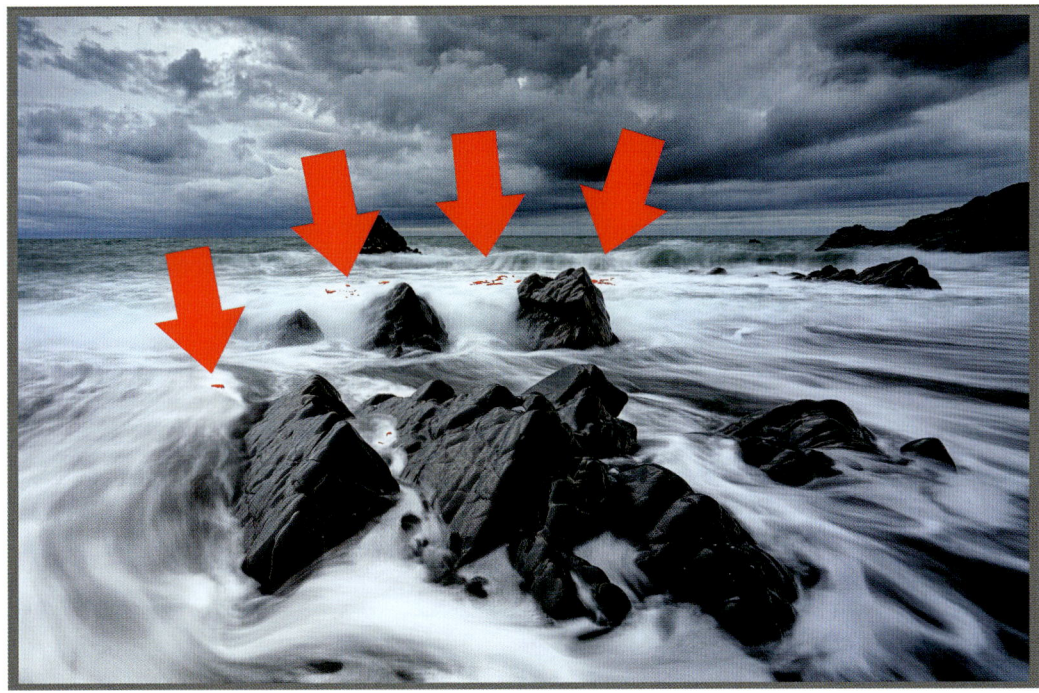

FIGURE 13.8

STEP 5: CHOOSE THE RENDERING INTENT

With the ICC profile applied, I toggle between:

- **Relative** rendering intent, which looks natural; it looks exactly as it should.

- **Perceptual** rendering intent, which seems to shift the color in an odd way, adding a magenta cast **(Figure 13.9)**.

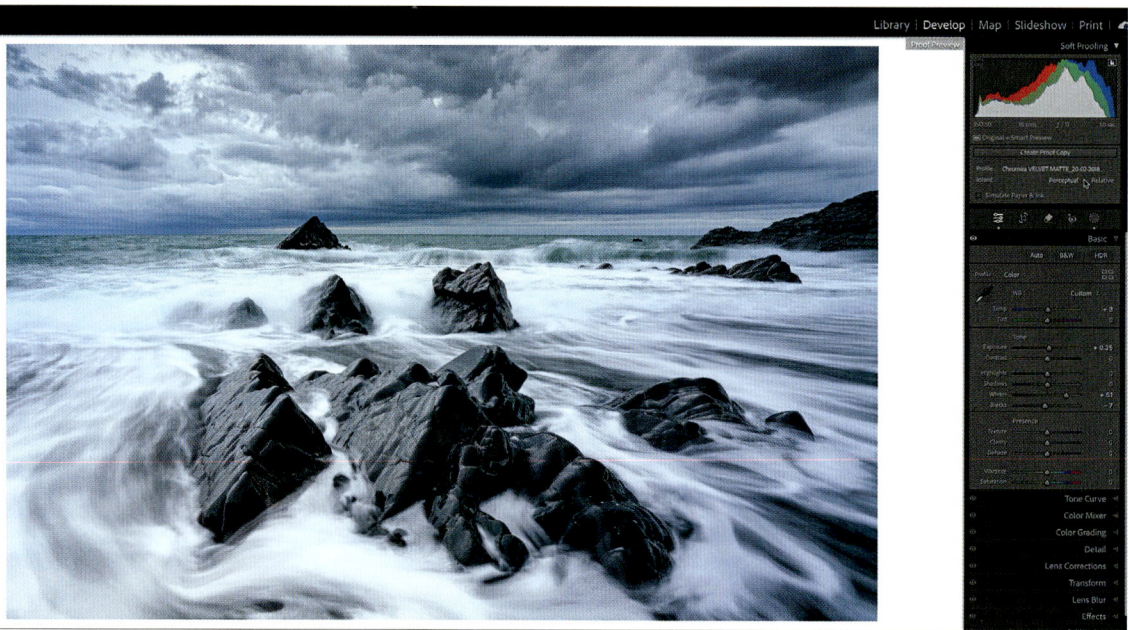

FIGURE 13.9

Relative clearly works best for this image. I then confirm that nothing is out of gamut by checking the Destination Gamut warning, and all details, including shadows and textures, look print-safe.

STEP 6: EXPORT THE IMAGE FROM LIGHTROOM

Now I export the image from Lightroom **(File > Export)** and choose the following settings **(Figure 13.10)**:

- **Destination:** "Printing" folder on my computer

- **File renamed to:** Cornwall

- **Format:** JPEG, 100% quality

- **Color space:** sRGB (as required by Digitalab)

- **Resolution:** 300 PPI

- No resizing applied yet

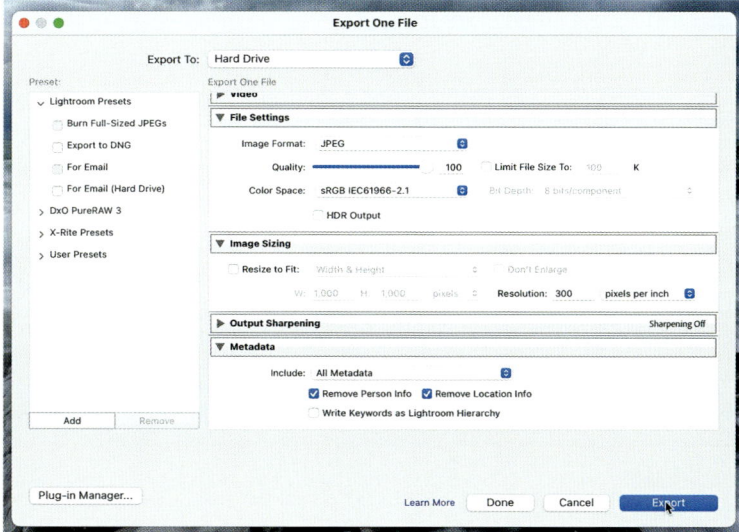

FIGURE 13.10

I click Export, and the image is now ready to open in Photoshop for final resizing.

STEP 7: RESIZE THE IMAGE IN PHOTOSHOP

I open the image in Photoshop and prepare it for print.

Using the Crop Tool, I enter **(Figure 13.11)**:

- **Width:** 30 inches

- **Height:** 20 inches

- **Resolution:** 300 PPI

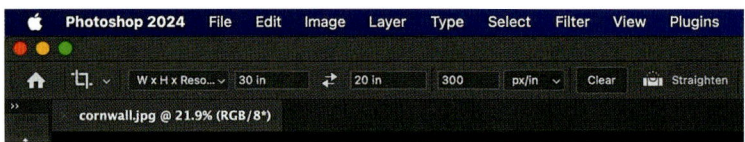

FIGURE 13.11

Photoshop shows a crop box that already matches the image exactly. This confirms the image is in the correct 2:3 aspect ratio, so no cropping is needed.

- However, if I hit Enter now, Photoshop will automatically use the Bicubic Automatic resampling method, which I don't want. Instead, I go to **Image** > **Image Size** and set Resample to Bicubic Sharper (Reduction) **(Figure 13.12)**.

I also input:

- **Width:** 30 inches

- **Height:** Updates automatically to just over 20 inches

- **Resolution:** 300 PPI

I click OK, and the image is resized manually with full control.

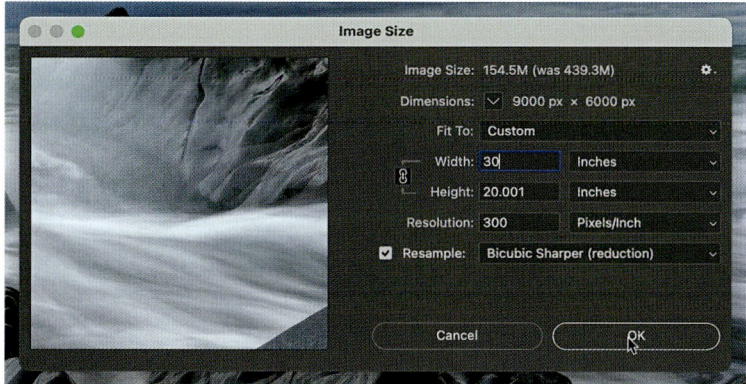

FIGURE 13.12

STEP 9: FINAL SAVE AND UPLOAD

At this point, the file is soft proofed, resized, and correctly profiled in sRGB, so it's totally ready for printing by the lab. All I need to do is to save the file and then send it over to Digitalab using their file upload system.

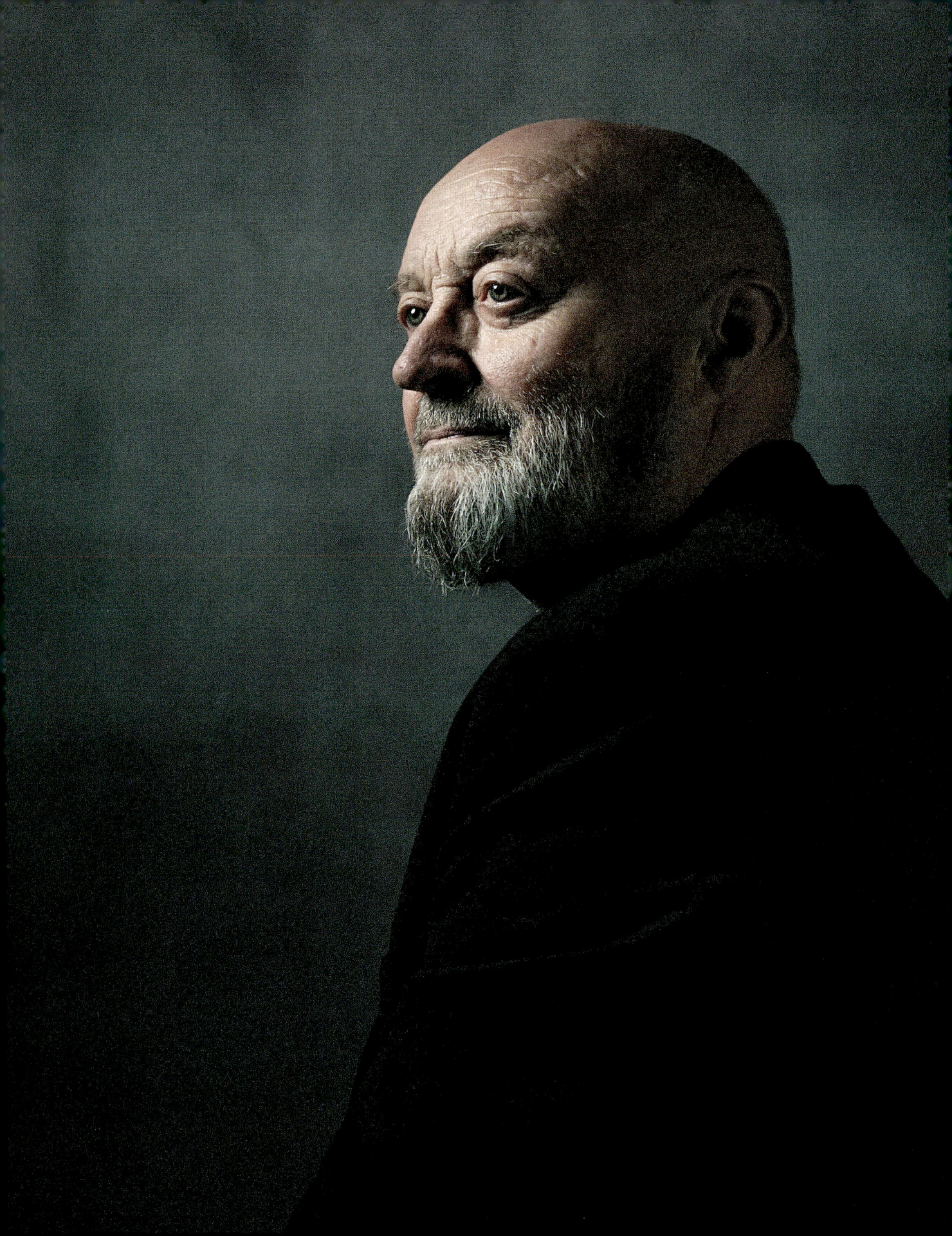

CHAPTER 14
EXTRA LEARNING

DOMINIC GURNEY, EPSON UK

In preparation for this book and my printing video course, I spoke with a number of industry professionals, one of whom was Dominic Gurney from Epson UK.

What started out as a casual conversation on Zoom quickly turned into a treasure trove of insights, so much so that I said, "Hold on, we need to get this into the book."

So to make sure that you, too, benefit from what Dominic explained to me during our chat, what follows is an overview of our conversation.

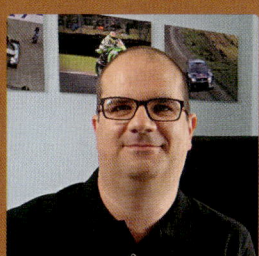

DOMINIC GURNEY, Epson UK

CHOOSING A PRINTER

UNDERSTAND YOUR PURPOSE BEFORE YOU BUY
Ask: Why Are You Printing?

Dominic explained that whenever someone approaches him at an event or trade show and asks which printer they should buy, he doesn't start with models or specs. Instead, he asks:

• What is your end goal?

• Why are you printing?

• What are you going to do with the prints?

That foundational information determines the best choice. "It could be for competitions, exhibitions, selling prints, or just personal enjoyment," he says. For example, Dominic has his own prints on the wall at home, not for show, but simply because they make him happy. That's reason enough.

MATCH PRINTER TYPE TO PRINT PURPOSE

Once the purpose is clear, Dominic helps people navigate Epson's range, and the decision depends on the intended use:

• **Personal/home use**: A basic home printer may be enough for vibrant color prints and enjoyment.

• **Professional use**: For competition or commercial sales, quality and reliability become critical.

  Things like:

  • Color accuracy

  • Gamut range

  • Longevity of print

  • Print permanence

If a print is being sold, your name is attached to it. The equipment must be able to guarantee quality that matches the value of your brand.

EPSON'S DESIGN FOCUS ON COMPACTNESS

Dominic confirms that Epson made conscious engineering decisions to shrink the physical size of their printers. "Our A2 now has the same footprint as our previous-generation A3," he says.

This design evolution was timed perfectly. The new generation of printers launched just as COVID lockdowns began, when people were working from home and space became more valuable than ever.

KEY TAKEAWAYS WHEN CHOOSING A PRINTER

- Start with the end goal: Know what you want from your prints.

- Let that purpose guide your model choice.

- Consider print permanence and quality if selling or exhibiting.

- Size matters, but compact A2 printers like the Epson P900 prove that you can go big without going bulky.

BEST PRACTICE FOR PRINTER CARE AND MAINTENANCE

Once someone invests in a high-quality photo printer, they want to make sure it stays in top condition. That's where best practices come in—everything from whether to leave it on to what kind of regular use it needs, and even whether it's worth covering it when it's not in use.

So, I ask Dominic: What does Epson recommend when it comes to printer maintenance and longevity?

SHOULD YOU LEAVE THE PRINTER ON?
The Common Myth: Leave It On to Avoid Cleaning Cycles

We often hear that leaving a printer turned on prevents it from going through those noisy cleaning cycles, the ones where you can hear the whirring and think, "There goes all my ink." But Dominic clears this up quickly.

"From Epson's perspective, that's an urban myth," he says. "It makes no difference whether you leave it on or turn it off every night."

Epson printers use an internal algorithm to track usage. They only run a cleaning cycle when necessary, not every time they're powered up. "Certainly in the last ten years, that's not been the case with Epson printers," Dominic adds.

So, if you're using an Epson printer:

- **Turn it off** if you like. There's no ink penalty.

- **Leave it on** if you prefer. It won't harm anything either way.

REGULAR USE IS KEY
Think of Your Printer Like a Machine ... Because It Is One

The real best practice, Dominic says, is to use the printer regularly. That doesn't mean daily full-bleed prints, but regular use is important.

"These are machines with moving parts, greased parts, oiled parts. Liquid runs through tubes and nozzles," he explains.

If the printer is left idle for months or even years, components can dry, seize, or clog. Regular use helps keep everything running smoothly, just like starting a classic car during winter to keep it in shape.

THE BEST LOW-INK MAINTENANCE TRICK: RUN A NOZZLE CHECK

Keep Things Flowing with a Simple Test Print

The simplest and most ink-efficient way to keep the printhead healthy is to run a nozzle check. Dominic explains this is his go-to method that only requires:

• A plain sheet of A4 copy paper

• Running a nozzle check pattern

"Each color has a block of tiny dashes and each dash represents one nozzle," he says.

For example:

• The Epson P700 has 10 color channels

• Each channel has 360 nozzles

• If any dashes are missing, it indicates a blockage from dried ink, dust, or fibers

Running a nozzle check:

• Keeps ink flowing

• Prevents blockages

• Uses less ink than a regular photo print

• Engages all colors, unlike an image print, which might not use every ink

And because it only uses a strip at the top of the paper, you can simply flip it over next month and use the same sheet again.

MAINTENANCE TIP: DON'T LEAVE PAPER IN THE PRINTER

Especially Coated Paper

Another key piece of advice: Never leave paper in the printer, especially coated or fine art paper. Why? "Coated paper builds up **static**, which attracts dust," Dominic explains. "And when that paper feeds through, the dust goes straight into the printer, onto the wheels, the internals, and even the printhead."

Since the printhead hovers just millimeters above the paper, any debris can cause:

• Smudging

• Scratches

• Clogs or nozzle damage

So:

• Don't leave paper in the printer.

• Don't store paper where dust can collect.

• Always remove unused paper after a print session.

USE A DUST COVER

Or Anything That Keeps the Dust Off

Dust is one of the biggest enemies of print quality. Dominic strongly recommends using a dust cover when the printer isn't in use. "Cat hair is another big one. We hear about that a lot," he says. "People come back saying, 'Why is there fur on my prints?' Turns out their cat's been napping on the printer."

Even if your printer has a built-in lid or tray cover, consider an extra layer of protection. A custom cover, a clean towel, or even a carrier bag works in a pinch, anything to stop dust or fibers from settling near the feed area or printhead.

SUMMARY: DOMINIC'S TOP MAINTENANCE TIPS

- Turn the printer on or off; it doesn't matter (for Epson models).

- Use your printer regularly, even if only for light prints.

- Run a nozzle check once a month using plain A4 paper.

- Don't leave paper inside the printer when it's not in use.

- Use a dust cover; even a makeshift one will help.

THE ROLE OF RESOLUTION IN PRINT QUALITY

RESAMPLING: DO IT MANUALLY IN YOUR EDITING SOFTWARE

When preparing an image for print, I talk about using the following PPI (Pixels Per Inch) for general guidance:

- 300 PPI for Canon

- 360 PPI for Epson

Rather than relying on the printer driver to scale or resample an image (and risk compromising sharpness), I prefer to resize and resample manually in my editing software.

To get Epson's view on this, I ask Dominic: What's the best practice when it comes to print resolution and resampling; should you do it manually, or leave it to the driver?

Dominic replies right away. "I let each piece of software do what it does best," he says. "So I resample and resize in Photoshop, Lightroom, or Affinity, not in the printer driver."

He explains that although you *can* resize in the Epson driver, he prefers to let the printer focus on outputting the image, not converting it. The cleaner the workflow, the better.

NATIVE RESOLUTION: WHY 360 PPI MATTERS FOR EPSON

The Difference Between PPI and DPI

Dominic confirms that Epson's native print resolution is 360 DPI, and this is where it ties into the editing process.

When you resize an image in your software, there's usually a box for PPI (pixels per inch). This is the pixel resolution of the image, not to be confused with DPI (dots per inch), which refers to how the printer physically lays ink on the page.

"With Epson printers, always set the image's PPI to 360 or 180, depending on the output size," Dominic says. That ensures your print will be sharp, optimized, and correctly matched to the printer's capabilities.

WHAT ABOUT 300 PPI?

Many photographers default to 300 PPI, either out of habit or because that's what they've always heard. "300 PPI comes from older commercial printing standards," Dominic explains. "But many photo labs are using Epson machines now, so they should be recommending 360 PPI too."

So, if you're printing with Epson, resize your images to:

- 360 PPI for maximum sharpness

- Or 180 PPI for larger prints when file size is a concern

CLARIFYING ANOTHER MYTH: 1440, 2880, AND OTHER DPI SETTINGS

Now we move into another area that often causes confusion: the print resolution settings in the Epson driver, like 720, 1440, or 2880 DPI. What do these numbers actually mean?

"They refer to the number of ink droplets per inch that the printhead lays down, but they don't necessarily equate to better image quality." In fact, choosing the highest number doesn't always mean better prints; it just tells the printer to use smaller droplets to fill the same space, not more ink or more detail.

A helpful analogy: "It's like decorating a room," Dominic explains. "You use a big roller for the walls, but a fine brush around the light switches. The printer does the same—larger droplets for broad areas, smaller ones for fine detail."

WHEN HIGHER DPI HELPS, AND WHEN IT DOESN'T

- If your image has **fine detail** (e.g., trees, leaves, textures), a higher setting like 1440 DPI can help bring out that sharpness.

- If your image has large areas of solid color, higher DPI won't really make a difference, and might just slow down the printing process and use more ink unnecessarily.

"For most of what I print, I stick with 1440 x 720 DPI," Dominic says. "It's not the highest, but it's more than enough in most cases."

DPI SETTINGS ARE ALSO CONTROLLED BY PAPER TYPE

Another interesting point: The paper you choose affects which DPI settings are even available. For example:

- Glossy or luster-coated papers allow more resolution options (e.g., standard, high quality, carbon black).

- Matte or fine art papers limit the options (usually to just standard or high quality).

Why? Because matte papers can't absorb as much ink. High DPI settings might flood the paper, causing bleeding or loss of sharpness. "The printer limits what you can do to help you get the best result," Dominic explains.

SUMMARY: KEY TAKEAWAYS ON RESIZING AND PRINT RESOLUTION

- Resize and resample manually in your editing software, not in the printer driver.

- Set image resolution to 360 PPI for Epson printers (or 180 for large prints).

- Understand the difference between PPI (image resolution) and DPI (printhead output).

- Don't assume bigger DPI numbers equals better prints; it depends on the image.

- Choose DPI settings based on the paper type; coated papers allow more flexibility.

- For most high-quality photo work, 1440 x 720 DPI is a solid default.

INK, MEDIA TYPE, AND PAPER

CHOOSING THE RIGHT BLACK INK: MATTE OR PHOTO?

In Epson printers, particularly models like the P900, we're given two black inks:

- Photo Black

- Matte Black

At first glance, it's easy to assume black is just black, but in reality, the printer needs to use the right black based on the paper type. This is something the media setting controls automatically.

When we're printing, choosing the correct media type does more than just identify the paper; it tells the printer which black ink to use, how the ink should behave, and more. To help explain this clearly, Dominic shared a brilliant analogy that really sticks with me.

THE ANALOGY: GLOSSY PAPER VS CARPET FIBERS

Coated Papers (Glossy, Lustre, Pearl, Baryta)

Coated papers have a smooth, hard surface. You can spot them by their reflective finish.

"When a droplet lands on coated paper, it stays round and crisp," Dominic says. "You get great definition, rich colors, and deep blacks." The coating prevents the ink from bleeding or spreading. That's why photo black works perfectly on these surfaces—it's designed to sit neatly on the top layer.

Matte Papers (Uncoated)

Matte or fine art papers, on the other hand, have a fibrous surface. These papers don't reflect light and have a texture that ink can soak into.

"It's like spilling wine on your carpet; it spreads," Dominic explains.

Because ink seeps into the fibers and can bleed outward, matte papers require matte black ink, which is formulated to:

• Stay closer to the surface

• Prevent spreading

• Improve sharpness

• Maintain color density

"Matte black helps retain the richness and clarity you'd otherwise lose on fibrous papers," he adds.

WHAT HAPPENS WHEN YOU USE THE WRONG MEDIA SETTING?

Dominic shares a print he made using the wrong media setting, a classic case of using the incorrect black.

"The difference is clear. The blacks look washed out, and the detail disappears," he says.

Even professionals make mistakes. That's why choosing the correct media type is essential; it controls which black ink is used and ensures proper output quality.

WHAT ELSE DOES MEDIA TYPE CONTROL?

Printhead Height, Roller Pressure, and More

When we choose a media type, the printer adjusts more than just the ink. "It controls how the printer feeds the paper, whether it uses certain rollers or changes the pressure," Dominic explains.

For fine art papers, the printer slows down in order to:

• Use fewer rollers (reducing scuffing)

• Minimize contact with the surface

• Protect textured or delicate media

"Those fibrous matte papers don't take well to rubber wheels pressing on them," Dominic notes. "So the printer uses spiked wheels or fewer rollers for gentler handling."

ADVANCED SETTING: "THICK PAPER" MODE

Sometimes, even with the right media selected, you might still notice scuff marks or faint lines on your paper. In that case, Epson printers offer a setting called Thick Paper, accessible through the printer's LCD menu. "It raises the printhead height and reduces roller pressure," says Dominic. "This prevents physical contact that could damage the paper surface."

After years in the printing industry, Dominic has developed an instinct for spotting potential issues before they happen. "With some matte papers, I just go ahead and enable the Thick Paper setting," he says. "It's not always required, but experience tells you when it might help." This kind of caution saves ink, paper, and time by avoiding preventable mistakes.

DON'T OVERLOOK PAPER STORAGE

Another common cause of printing issues? Paper curl. "Don't store your paper standing upright," Dominic warns. "It slumps in the box and can lead to warped corners."

Warped or curled paper might:

- Feed unevenly

- Cause corner smudging

- Create roller marks

- Misalign prints

Humidity and room temperature also affect paper shape, so keep an eye on how and where you store it. "If you're getting a black mark in the same spot every time, check the paper," he advises.

BONUS INSIGHT: WHAT MEDIA PROFILES ACTUALLY CONTAIN

Dominic briefly touches on something many people don't realize: ICC profiles aren't just about color. Each profile contains:

- Color data

- Mechanical data

"The mechanical data tells the printer how to behave; things like feed rate, head height, and ink limits," he explains.

If a third-party profile is missing good mechanical instructions, it's even more important to manually set options like Thick Paper to ensure high-quality output.

SUMMARY: KEY TAKEAWAYS ON BLACK INK, MEDIA TYPE, AND PAPER HANDLING

- Photo Black is used for **coated papers** (glossy, lustre, pearl).

- Matte Black is used for fibrous, uncoated papers (fine art, matte).

- Choosing the correct media type automatically:

  - Selects the right black ink

  - Adjusts printhead height

  - Modifies roller behavior

- Fine art papers need gentler handling. Use fewer rollers and Thick Paper mode when needed.

- Store paper flat and in a controlled environment to prevent curl.

- ICC profiles include both color and mechanical data, so make sure they're accurate
- If unsure, err on the side of caution; turn on Thick Paper mode and prevent problems before they start.

A QUESTION OF PRINTHEAD LONGEVITY

I was curious to learn how Epson printers actually deliver ink onto paper, and how that relates to the life of the printhead. I've heard that some printers use heat to push ink through the nozzles, and others rely on vibration. I ask Dominic to explain what Epson uses and how it affects print performance and durability.

EPSON'S PIEZO VIBRATION TECHNOLOGY

"We use vibration, not heat," Dominic explains. Epson's technology is built around something called a piezo crystal. It's a naturally forming material, and Epson even has its own lab in Japan where they grow and cut these crystals. "They slice them very thin, and when you apply electricity, they vibrate," Dominic says.

This vibration is what pumps the ink through the nozzles and onto the page. Because it's controlled by electricity, it allows for:

- Instant on/off pulsing
- Extremely precise droplet control
- Variable droplet sizes for fine detail or bold areas

This method is known as meniscus control, which refers to the precision with which the ink droplet's size and shape can be managed before it's fired onto the paper.

HEAT-BASED SYSTEMS: HOW THEY DIFFER

Other manufacturers use thermal print technology, where heat is applied to create a bubble inside the cartridge. That bubble then forces the ink out, and the process repeats with continuous heating and cooling.

"From Epson's perspective, heat-based systems are less reliable," Dominic says. He explains that Epson's non-thermal approach allows their printheads to be:

- Longer-lasting, since they're not repeatedly expanding and contracting
- More versatile, able to handle different ink types used in various industries

In fact, the same core piezo technology is used across Epson's entire printer lineup:

- Photo printers (like the P900)
- Office and home models
- Commercial signage and textile printers

This consistency ensures reliability across many different printing environments.

INK IS DRY INSTANTLY, THANKS TO THE METHOD

Because Epson doesn't use heat to fire the ink, the print doesn't come out warm or "wet."

"The ink is dry to the touch right away," Dominic says. "Technically, it's 90% dry instantly."

If you're framing behind glass, Epson still recommends waiting twenty-four hours to allow for off-gassing, but otherwise, the print is ready to hang immediately.

QUICK TIP: HOW TO FIND THE PRINTABLE SIDE OF YOUR PAPER

Loading the wrong side of the paper is a mistake many of us have made at some point. There's a quick trick I use that's worth sharing: Lightly dab your fingertip with moisture, then touch a corner of the paper. If it sticks, that's the printable side.

Simple, effective, and it can save you from wasting a good sheet of fine art paper.

SUMMARY: WHAT MAKES EPSON'S INK DELIVERY UNIQUE

- Epson uses piezo crystal technology; no heat is involved.

- Applying electricity causes the crystal to vibrate, pushing out ink precisely.

- This allows for variable droplet sizes, known as meniscus control.

- The printhead is designed to last the life of the printer.

- Prints come out dry to the touch, ideal for quick handling.

- Always check the paper's correct side before loading; a simple finger test can help.

GETTING THE FILE ONTO PAPER: WHAT SOFTWARE SHOULD YOU USE?

When it comes time to actually print an image, there are a few different software options available. Most major printer brands offer their own dedicated print software. Epson has Epson Print Layout, Canon has its equivalent, and HP has its own tools as well.

Naturally, you might expect Dominic to recommend Epson's own software, but the real reason for doing so isn't just brand loyalty; it's about practicality and consistency.

USE WHAT YOU'RE COMFORTABLE WITH, BUT WATCH FOR PITFALLS

"I always say, go with what you're most comfortable using," Dominic explains. That might mean printing directly from Photoshop, Lightroom, or other editing platforms. The key benefit there is familiarity; if you know the software well, you're less likely to make mistakes.

However, Dominic adds a cautionary note, especially for Mac users: "Printing from a Mac can be frustrating. There are so many different menus and settings. You only need to get one thing wrong and you can end up with a completely different result than you expected." These settings are usually generic, made to work across multiple brands of printers, and while that makes the software flexible, it also opens the door for confusion and missteps.

WHY USE EPSON PRINT LAYOUT?

"When it comes to outputting the file, yeah, I would recommend using the Epson software (if you have an Epson printer)," Dominic says. And the reason is simple: Epson Print Layout is built specifically for Epson printers. That means:

- Settings are clearer and brand-specific.

- The interface is designed to feel familiar (a lot like Lightroom).

- All key options (media type, layout, ICC profile) are shown on a single screen.

- There's no need to dive into complex driver menus.

"It's like the skin over the background technology. It's a cleaner, easier way of doing it," he says.

WORKFLOW ADVICE

Here's Dominic's personal workflow:

1. Edit the image in Photoshop or Lightroom.

2. Save it either directly into Epson Print Layout or onto the desktop.

3. Open it in Epson Print Layout to set print settings and output the file.

By doing it this way, you reduce the risk of altering the image unintentionally with incorrect settings in the print driver. "It just means there's less chance of you setting something that's going to change your image. Fewer mistakes, less frustration."

THE KEY: CONSISTENCY IN PRINTING

Dominic emphasizes one word: consistency. "You want your printing to be consistent. When you press print, you should know exactly what's going to come out."

That kind of confidence comes from:

- Using the same process each time

- Knowing how your images react to different papers

- Understanding your materials, like how a matte fine art paper may flatten contrast

As Dominic puts it, "You learn that when you're editing, you may need to boost contrast because you know what that matte paper does to your image." The software helps with that consistency by removing unnecessary distractions and potential mistakes.

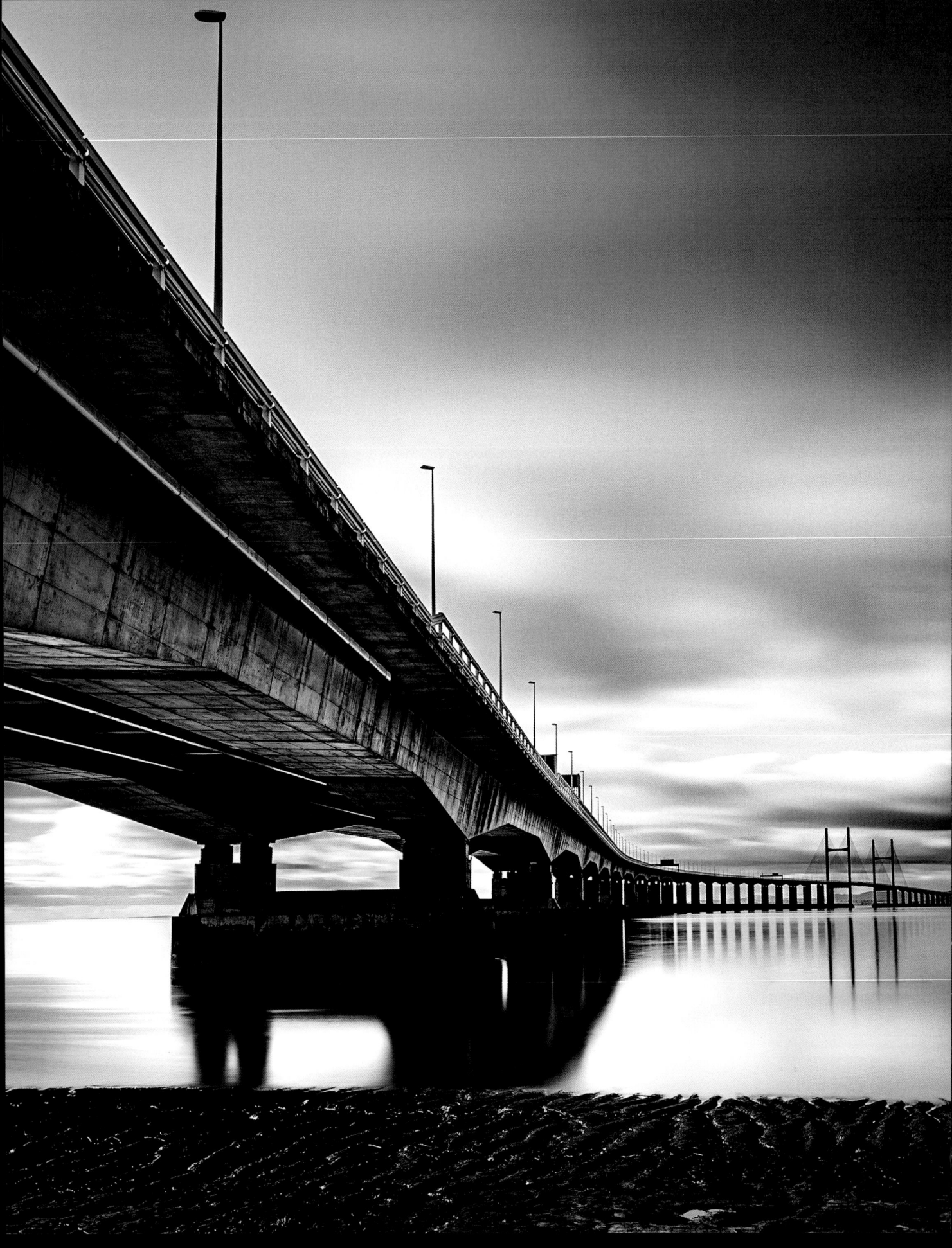

CHAPTER 15
MOUNTING & PRESENTING PRINTS

For this final chapter, I wanted to show you how you can finish your images, and by that I mean mounting them on backing board or presenting them in a more polished way.

To demonstrate this process, I visited West Street Picture Framing in Axminster, UK, which is very close to where I live. The business is owned by Trevor Williams, a professional with many years of experience in the field. In fact, Trevor was kind enough to open his store on a day they're normally closed so we could capture and share this process with you.

Trevor gives an overview of how to mount prints onto self-adhesive backing board, walking through the techniques and providing useful tips and tricks to help make your images look their best, which is especially helpful if you are part of a camera club or are planning to exhibit your work.

In addition to mounting on backing board, Trevor also demonstrates how to place your images into a beveled mount. This final step adds a professional finish and really enhances the presentation of your prints.

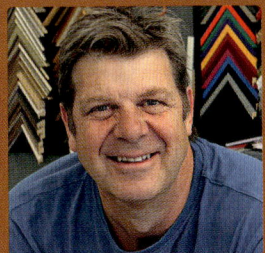

TREVOR WILLIAMS, West St. Picture Framing

MOUNTING A PRINT TO A BACKING BOARD

When preparing a print for display, one of the most effective ways to achieve a professional finish is to mount it onto a self-adhesive backing board **(Figure 15.1)**. This process ensures that the print remains flat in the frame, avoiding unwanted waves or creases.

To begin, it's important to choose the right type of sticky board. These boards are generally available in two thicknesses, and while the thinner

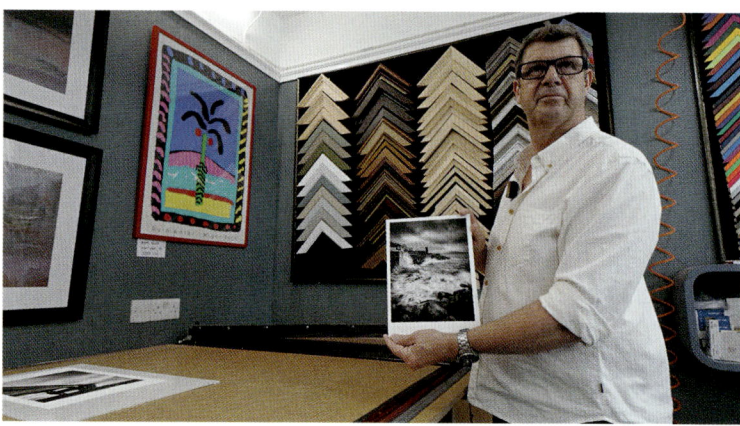

FIGURE 15.1

board is adequate, it can sometimes produce an "orange-peel effect" coming through to the print, especially with shinier photos. The thicker board, around three millimeters, is preferred for better results, even though it may be slightly more expensive.

Before applying the print to the board, always inspect the back of the photograph. Remove any labels, dust, or debris, as these can create visible bumps once the print is mounted. A simple wipe across the back can help ensure a smooth application **(Figure 15.2)**.

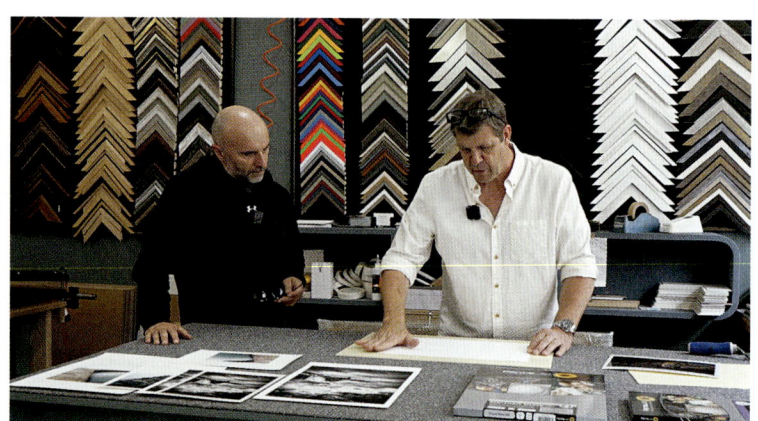

FIGURE 15.2

The board itself is referred to as a *self-adhesive* mount board, and various manufacturers produce them. Choosing a larger board and trimming it down after mounting the print often makes the process easier and reduces the chance of alignment errors.

To begin mounting, peel back a small portion of the adhesive sheet and position the print carefully **(Figure 15.3)**. The goal during this step is to eliminate air bubbles as you stick it down. While it's possible to use your hand for this, doing so increases the risk of scratching the print surface. Instead, use a clean, soft rubber roller. Clean the roller on an unused area of the sticky side of the board to remove any debris before use, then work your way down slowly, pressing the print onto the board in stages.

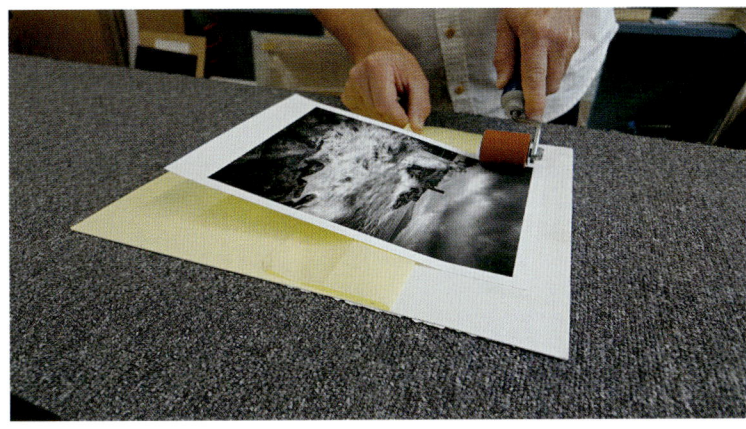

FIGURE 15.3

Once the print is fully mounted, it should lie completely flat. One way to check the adhesion is to gently bend the board and observe whether the print lifts. If it remains secure, the mount has been successful **(Figure 15.4)**.

It's recommended to do the trimming after the print is fully mounted. This approach allows you to focus solely on getting the print flat without worrying about perfect alignment beforehand.

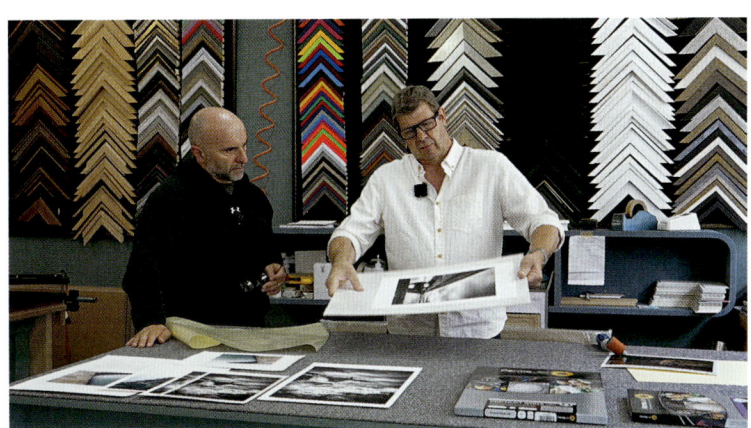

FIGURE 15.4

Using a roller poses little to no risk of damaging the print, especially if the print is on matte paper. The rolling motion applies pressure only where the roller touches, unlike rubbing, which can affect a broader area and potentially cause scratches. For those doing multiple mounts, it can be helpful to use a spare piece of mount board to press down the print as you peel off more of the adhesive sheet. Some self-adhesive boards come with a clear protective layer that simplifies this process.

If you're not planning to mount the print into a frame immediately, it's a good idea to reapply the backing sheet to protect the adhesive surface from dust **(Figure 15.5)**.

Once mounted, there's no need to let the print dry, as the adhesive bonds instantly.

Prints on thicker matte paper are particularly well-suited to this method, as their surface texture helps to avoid the orange-peel effect commonly seen with thinner or glossier paper.

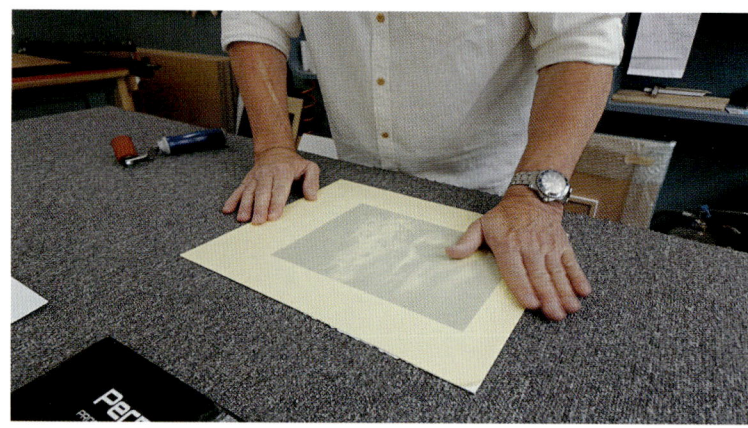

FIGURE 15.5

Additionally, matte prints are preferable when framing under glass, as they avoid the issue of double reflection.

The final step is to trim the mounted print to the desired dimensions **(Figure 15.6)**.

If you're planning to add a beveled mount, you can cut it to match the size of the backing board for a clean, finished look.

This simple process not only enhances the presentation of your images, but also prepares them for framing or exhibition.

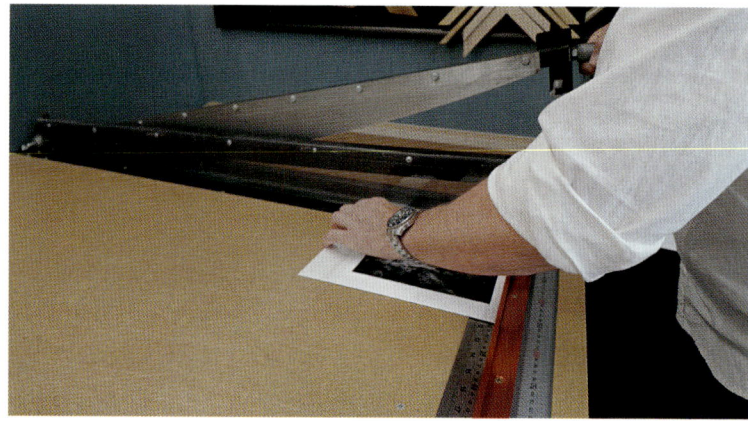

FIGURE 15.6

CONFIDENCE AND CARE IN THE MOUNTING PROCESS

Although the mounting process is relatively straightforward, it's worth revisiting some key points, particularly the importance of confidence and preparation. While it's an easy process in principle, it's crucial to approach it with the right mindset and environment.

A clean workspace is essential; any dust or debris can negatively affect the outcome. This becomes especially important when working with traditional photographic prints, as these often have more natural wave or curl to them. If a photograph has significant waviness, mounting it directly to an adhesive board may risk introducing creases. In such cases, careful judgment is needed based on the condition of the print at the time of mounting.

This concern also ties in with how prints and paper are stored before use. Although photographic papers are typically delivered in flat boxes, there's a common tendency to store them vertically or slide them into shelves in a standing position. Over time, this can introduce a warp or bend to the paper, which may complicate the mounting process. Many have experienced this issue firsthand.

A simple but effective solution is to store paper boxes flat, stacked one on top of the other. This method helps keep the paper sheets consistently flat, minimizing any distortion or curl. Maintaining flatness from storage through to mounting can help avoid issues during application and contribute to a cleaner, more professional result.

USING A BEVEL MOUNT AND CHOOSING THE RIGHT PRESENTATION

Once the print has been mounted onto a self-adhesive backing board, the next step is to add a bevel mount (**Figure 15.7**).

Bevel mounts can be purchased easily from many places such as online retailers, local framers, or art supply shops.

Before attaching the mount, it's worth addressing a common concern: the dimensions and cropping of images. Many people worry about what size

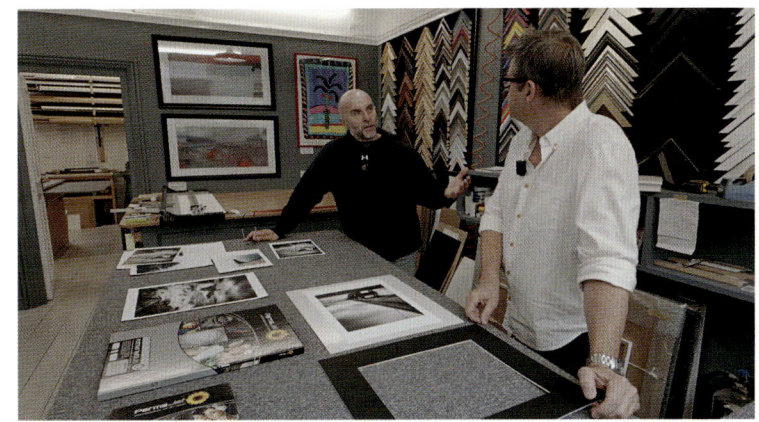

FIGURE 15.7

their images should be, especially in relation to standard frame ratios. However, the best approach is to crop the image according to what suits the composition rather than conforming to predefined formats. The image should dictate the crop, and adjustments to mounts and frames can come later.

For those wanting to work with standard frame sizes, it is possible to adapt. However, it's recommended to use a mount that is slightly larger than expected. Small mounts often look unbalanced and can diminish the impact of the image.

By choosing a larger mount, there's flexibility to adjust the aperture (the window of the mount) so that it fits the image perfectly, even if the photo is long and narrow or has an unusual shape. This can all be done while keeping the external dimensions consistent, and many framers will offer custom aperture cutting services.

Building a relationship with a local framer can be particularly valuable. Rather than ordering in bulk or from an unknown source, working with a trusted framer allows for on-demand, customized solutions. There's also more variety in color and texture when choosing mounts in person.

For example, a black mount may not be an obvious choice, but in some cases, like with monochrome images, it can dramatically improve the overall look compared to a more traditional white mount **(Figure 15.8)**.

Experimentation is key. By purchasing a single mount board, you can test different styles and colors without having to commit to large quantities or keep excess stock.

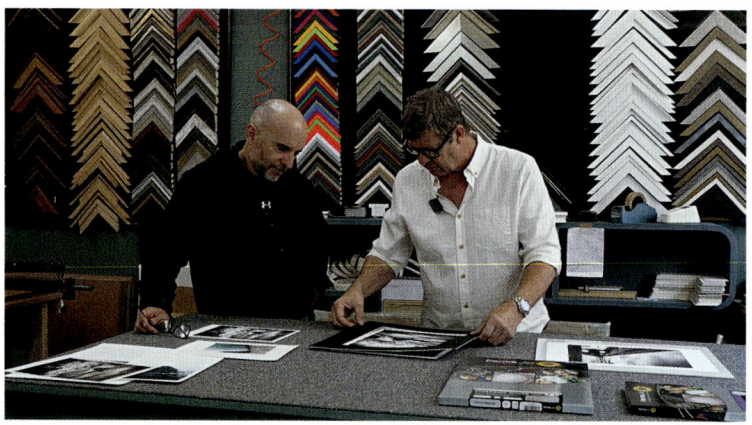

FIGURE 15.8

If you have a spare mount, you can even use it to preview how different prints might look by holding it over various corners. This allows you to assess whether the mount complements the image before finalizing your decision.

Many people are surprised by the impact a black mount can have; it can make an image pop in a way they hadn't considered before.

Leaving a white border around the image also has aesthetic and practical advantages. It offers space to sign or number the print if desired, and adds a subtle framing effect that's especially striking when paired with a darker mount **(Figure 15.9)**.

With a slightly oversized sticky board, any excess can be trimmed off later to create a clean edge.

Once the mount is placed on top of the print and secured to the backing board, the assembly becomes very stable. The print won't shift on the board, and the mount won't move either. While it's technically possible to remove the mount later, it won't come off without intent; it's securely in place.

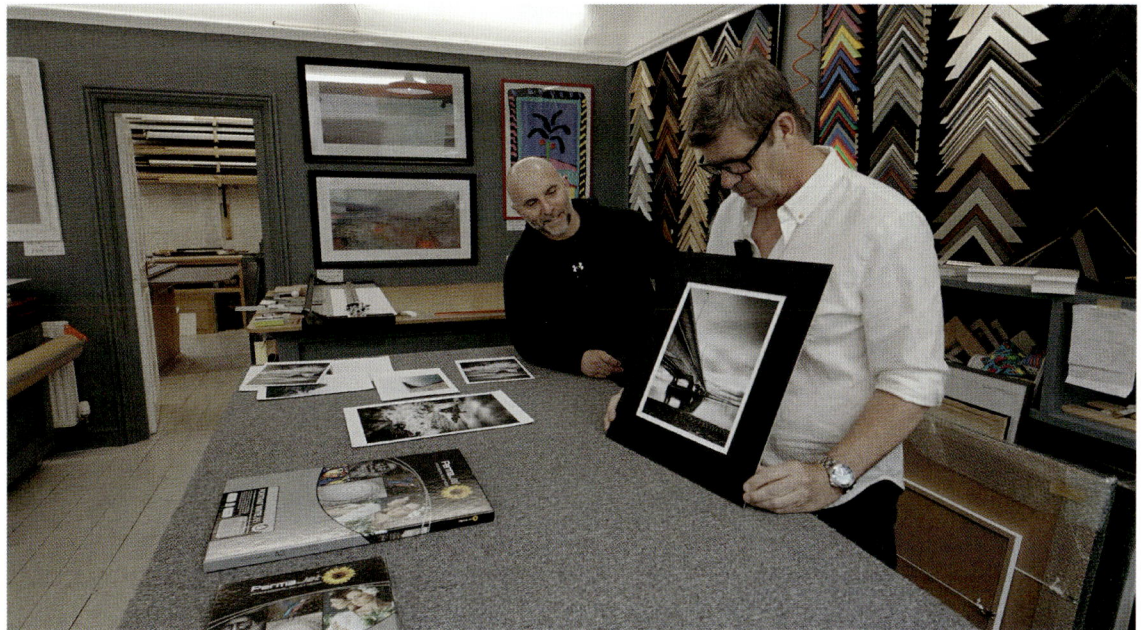

FIGURE 15.9

There are differing opinions on how prints should be mounted, especially regarding archival practices. Some people advise attaching the print with tape on only three sides, allowing the paper to expand and contract naturally in response to humidity. However, this can backfire. When the print is restricted on multiple sides, any expansion can lead to warping or creasing.

A better method, if you're not adhering the print permanently, is to tape it only at the top. This way, the print is free to move slightly within the mount and adapt to environmental conditions.

That said, for repeatable media such as photographs, mounting directly to a self-adhesive board is often the most reliable and practical approach. It prevents future movement and ensures a flat, clean presentation.

However, for one-of-a-kind artworks, sticking them down is not advised. In those cases, mounting without adhesive preserves the long-term value of the piece.

COMMON FRAMING CHALLENGES AND BEST PRACTICES

One of the most commonly raised issues, especially by professional framers, involves people printing their images right to the edge of the paper. This creates a problem when framing because a few millimeters often need to be trimmed in order to secure the print behind a mount. If the image has been printed edge-to-edge, important details or signatures can get unintentionally cropped. This becomes even more problematic if the printed area includes faded borders or key elements near the edges.

To avoid this, it's recommended that anyone printing their own work uses slightly larger paper than the final print size. For example, if printing an image that's approximately 14 inches wide, it's better to use A3+ or even A2 paper. This allows for breathing space around the image and ensures a cleaner, more adaptable finish when mounting and framing. The small sacrifice in paper waste results in a significantly more professional outcome.

PAPER CHOICE BEHIND GLASS

Matte paper is generally preferred for prints that will be framed behind glass. While glossy paper can sometimes offer more vibrancy or detail, particularly in high-color images like those of vintage cars or metallic surfaces, it tends to suffer from double reflections when placed under glass. These reflections can distract from the image and make it difficult to view comfortably.

Although it's technically possible to frame glossy prints without glass, this isn't advised; over time, dust will accumulate, and any attempt to clean the print risks scratching the surface. In general, any paper-based artwork should be framed behind glass for preservation.

GLASS CHOICES

When it comes to glass choices, there are several options available, with quality often correlating with cost.

A popular mid-range option is Art Glass, which offers low reflection and includes approximately 70% UV protection. This is particularly useful for preserving prints, even though most modern photo papers are already fairly UV-resistant.

A premium option is Museum Glass, which goes a step further by removing the iron content from the glass. This results in a "water white" appearance with no green tint. When viewed from the edge, this glass appears pure white. Though expensive, it delivers outstanding clarity and dramatically reduces glare. The visual difference on display is immediate; the viewer doesn't have to shift position to eliminate reflections, they can simply enjoy the image as intended.

FRAMING SIZES

Another area of frequent confusion concerns image and frame sizes.

Some people crop their photos to standard aspect ratios to fit premade frames. However, a more artistically satisfying approach is to crop based on the composition itself rather than trying to match standard dimensions. A print doesn't have to conform to a 3:2 or 4:3 ratio; it can be any shape that best suits the image.

Custom mounts and frames can be created to fit the final print, regardless of its dimensions. This approach preserves the photographer's vision and avoids compromising the image just to fit off-the-shelf products.

GET TO KNOW YOUR LOCAL FRAMER

Working with a local framer is invaluable when dealing with bespoke sizes.

While it's possible to buy mounts in bulk or from various suppliers, standardized options rarely fit unique crops perfectly. A good relationship with a framer means being able to order exactly what's needed, when it's needed, without settling for less-than-ideal compromises **(Figure 15.10)**.

Ultimately, the goal is to maintain creative freedom and let the image dictate the format, not the other way around.

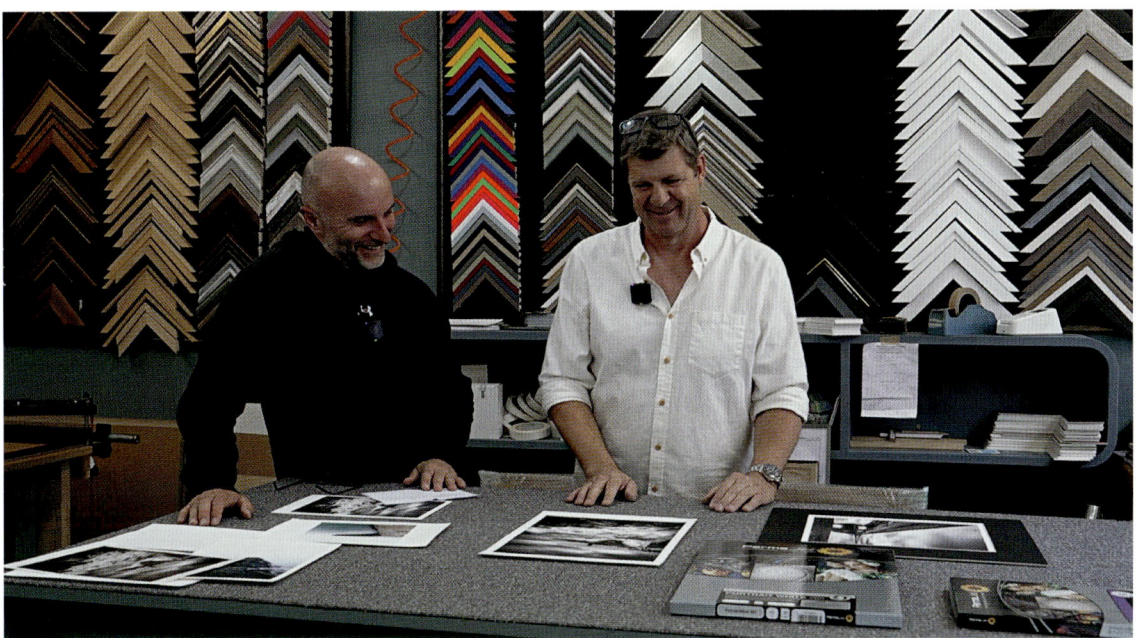

FIGURE 15.10

INDEX

A

acid-free paper, 166
Adobe Camera Raw
    enlarging images, 125–127
AirPrint, Apple, 4–6, 83
archival paper, 167

B

Bai, Dr. Chris, 1, 101–102
banding, 99
BenQ, 9
    calibration software, 20–30
    discount, 11
    hotkey puck, 30
bit depth, 98–100
black point compensation, 66,
    91–93
black point, calibration, 25
black-and-white image,
    printing, 57–67
    black point compensation,
      66
    Canon software, 202–204
    color settings, 65–66
    Epson software, 194–198
    layout settings, 64
    Lightroom, 189–194,
      220–227
    media type, 59–62
    ON1 Photo RAW, 213–215
    paper size, 63
    paper source, 63
    Photoshop, 183–184
    printer settings, 59–64
    Qimage One, 208–210
    Quality setting, 64
    rendering intent, 66
    toning controls, 65–66
    workflow, 220–227

C

calibration, display, 17–37
    BenQ software, 19–30
    Calibrite Profiler software,
      31–35
    custom target, 22–26
    Delta E, 28
    device setup, 20
    frequency, 37
    general use, settings for, 29
    hardware, 18
    photography, settings for,
      24–25
    pre-calibration, 19
    presets, 30
    results, 28
    running, 27
    software, 20
    software-calibrated display,
      37
    store settings, 30
    target, 22–26
Calibrite, 18, 20
Calibrite Profiler calibration
    software, 31–35
candelas, 24, 37
Canon
    color management, 53
    evaluation print, 40–43
    max print size, 109
    printing an image, 47–50
    Professional Print & Layout
      software, 198–204
    resolution, native, 108
color image, printing, 69–93
    black point compensation,
      91–93
    Canon software, 198–202
    ICC profiles, 71–76, 78–88
    Lightroom, 74–76, 184–188
    ON1 Photo RAW, 210–212

    paper, 70
    Photoshop, 180–182
    printer settings, 70
    Qimage One, 204–208
    rendering intent, 89–91
    third-party paper, 76–80
    workflow, 228–233
color management, turning off,
    52–55
color settings, printer, 65–66
color space, 95–105
    Adobe RGB, 97
    bit depth, 98–100
    calibration, 25
    lab, printing, 236
    preferences, 103–105
    ProPhoto RGB, 98
    sRGB, 96
    workflow, 103–105
cropping, 118–123
    Lightroom, 121–123
    Photoshop, 118–121

D

dark prints, 17–18
Delta E, calibration, 28
displays, 8–15
    Adobe RGB coverage, 8
    calibration, 17–37
    connecting, 11–15
    DisplayPort connecting, 13
    hardware calibration, 9
    HDMI connection, 11–12
    hoods, 9
    Mac and, 14
    reflection, 9
    RGB range, 12
    size, 9
    software-calibrated, 37
    sRGB coverage, 8
    USB-C connection, 13

DPI, 107, 252
  high settings, 252
dry down differential, 5
drying line, 5

E

enlarging images, 123–129
Epson
  Advanced B&W mode, 197
  color management, 54
  evaluation print, 40, 43–45
  max print size, 110
  Piezo vibration technology,
    256
  Print Layout software, 153,
    194–198
  resolution, native, 108, 252
evaluation print, 40–46
  Canon, printing on, 42–43
  Epson, printing on, 43–45
  Mac, 42–43
  opening file, 41
  Windows, 43–45

F

file format, 236
framing, 267–269

G

gamma, calibration, 25
gamut warnings, 90
GSM (paper), 167
Gurney, Dominic, 247–258

H

halos, controlling, 134
Hill, Louise, 165, 175–177
Hulley, Colin, 1, 165, 167–173

I

ICC profile, 71–76
  custom, 73, 80–87
  downloading, 78, 219–220
  generic, 72, 78–79
  installing, 88, 220
  lab, printing, 237, 240
  Lightroom, using in, 74–76
  PermaJet, 80–83
  software, 84
  tools, 84
image size
  print size and, 109–111
  resolution and, 112–118
Ingram, Alex, 235–237
ink
  black, 253
  OEM, 6–8, 73
  pigment vs. dye-based, 3
  third-party, 6–8
interpolation, 108

L

lab, printing, 235–245
  color space, 236
  dimensions, 238
  export image, 242
  file format, 236
  ICC profiles, 237, 240
  rendering intent, 242
  resize image, 244
  resolution, 236, 239
  soft proofing, 241
  upload, 245
layout settings, 64
Lightroom
  black and white, printing,
    189–194, 220–227
  color image, printing,
    184–188
  color space, 103
  cropping in, 121–123
  enlarging images, 125–127
exporting to Photoshop,
    224–225
  gamut warnings, 90
  ICC profile, printing with,
    74–76
  soft proofing, 143
luminance, calibration, 24, 37

M

Mac users, printing tips, 4–6
media type, 59–62, 254
mounting prints, 261–269
  backing board, 262–264
  bevel mount, 265
  framing, 267–269

O

OBA-free paper, 166
OEM ink, 6–8, 73
ON1 Photo RAW, 210–215

P

Palette Master Ultimate (BenQ),
    20–30
paper, 165–177
  acid-free, 166
  archival, 167
  glossy, 253
  GSM, 167
  matching to print, 168–173
  matte, 254
  monochrome prints, 168
  OBA-free, 166
  printable side, 257
  protective spray, 174
  sharpening and, 138
  storing, 173, 255
  texture, 168
  third-party, 76–80
  tone and, 168
  UV protection, 174
  warping, 173

perceptual rendering intent, 89
PermaFIX, 174
PermaJet, 1
    ICC profiles, 80–83
PermaSEAL, 174
Photoshop
    black-and-white image,
printing, 183–184
    color image, printing,
180–182
    color space and, 104
    cropping in, 118–121
    enlarging images, 124–125
    exporting to, 224–225
    resizing in, 225
    soft proofing in, 154–161
PPI, 107, 252
print size, determining, 109–111
printer
    A2 or A3, 3
    AirPrint and, 4–6, 83
    choosing, 2, 248–249
    color vs. b&w, 2
    connection, 5
    cost, 2, 3
    dye-based inks, 3
    Mac users, 4–6, 83
    maintenance, 249–251
    pigment inks, 3
    printhead longevity,
        256–257
printhead, 256–257
printing lab, see lab, printing
printing software, see software,
    printing
protective spray on paper, 174

Q

Qimage One, 204–210
quality, print, 64

R

relative rendering intent, 89
rendering intent, 66, 89–91
    lab, printing, 242
resampling, 108, 251
resizing
    cropping, 118–123
    enlarging, 123–129
    lab printing, 244
    Photoshop, in, 225
    resolution and, 114–118
    sharpening after, 138–139
resolution
    cropping and, 118–123
    doubling, 127
    DPI vs. PPI, 107
    enlarging images, 123–129
    high settings, 252
    image size and, 112–118
    interpolation, 108
    lab, printing, 236, 239
    print quality and, 251–253
    print size and, 109–110
    printer, native, 108
    resampling, 108
    resizing and, 114–118

S

sharpening, 131–139
    halos, 134
    paper and, 138
    printer settings, 138
    resizing before,
        138–139
Simulate Paper and Ink
    (Lightroom), 141, 162–163
size, print
    cropping, 118–123
    determining, 109–111
    enlarging, 123–129
soft proofing, 141–163
    black-and-white image,
        148–154

color image, 143–147
    lab printing, 241
    Lightroom, in, 143
    Photoshop, in, 154–161
    Simulate Paper and Ink, 141,
        162–163
software, calibration, 20
software, printing, 179–215
    Canon Print Studio Pro, 198
    Canon Professional Print &
        Layout, 198–204
    Epson Print Layout, 194–198
    Lightroom, 184–194
    ON1 Photo RAW, 210–215
    Photoshop, 180–184
    Qimage One, 204–210
    Super Resolution, Adobe,
        125

T

test prints, see evaluation print
toning controls, 65–66
Topaz Gigapixel AI, 127–128

U

UV protective spray, 174

W

white point, calibration, 24
Williams, Trevor, 261–269
workflow
    black-and-white image,
220–227
    color image, 228–233

X

X-Rite i1, 18